W9-BNE-058

JOSH

JOSH

MY UP AND DOWN, IN AND OUT LIFE

by
JOSHUA LOGAN

DELACORTE PRESS / NEW YORK

Copyright © 1976 by Joshua L. Logan
All rights reserved. No part of this book may be reproduced in any form or by any means without the prior written permission of the Publisher, excepting brief quotes used in connection with reviews written specifically for inclusion in a magazine or newspaper.

Manufactured in the United States of America

Excerpt from lyrics of THEY WERE ALL OUT OF STEP BUT JIM by Irving Berlin on page 4: Copyright © 1918 Irving Berlin. Copyright © renewed. Reprinted by permission of Irving Berlin Music Corporation, and Chappell & Co., Ltd doing business as Irving Berlin (England) Music.

Excerpts from lyrics of ANYTHING YOU CAN DO by Irving Berlin on page 184: Copyright © 1946 Irving Berlin. Copyright © renewed. Reprinted by permission of Irving Berlin Music Corporation, and Chappell & Co., Ltd doing business as Irving Berlin (England) Music.

Excerpt from lyrics of YOU CAN'T GET A MAN WITH A GUN by Irving Berlin on page 185: Copyright © 1946 Irving Berlin. Copyright © renewed. Reprinted by permission of Irving Berlin Music Corporation, and Chappell & Co., Ltd doing business as Irving Berlin (England) Music.

Lines from "Stopping by Woods on a Snowy Evening" from THE POETRY OF ROBERT FROST edited by Edward Connery Lathem on page 142: Copyright 1923, © 1969 by Holt, Rinehart and Winston. Copyright 1951 by Robert Frost. Reprinted by permission of Holt, Rinehart and Winston, Publishers.

Excerpt from PICNIC by William Inge on page 284: Copyright © 1953, 1955 by William Inge. Used by permission of Random House, Inc.

Lyrics from AT THE ROXY MUSIC HALL on page 104: Lyrics: Lorenz Hart; Music: Richard Rodgers. Copyright © 1938; renewed 1965 Robbins Music Corporation. Reprinted by permission.

Lyrics from I'M IN LOVE WITH A WONDERFUL GUY on pages 223, 235, and 239: Copyright © 1949 by Richard Rodgers and Oscar Hammerstein II. Williamson Music, Inc., owner of publication and allied rights for all countries of the Western Hemisphere and Japan. International Copyright Secured. All Rights Reserved.

Lyrics from WISH YOU WERE HERE on page 270: Copyright © 1952 by Harold Rome. Chappell & Co. Inc., owner of publication and allied rights. International Copyright Secured. All Rights Reserved.

FOR
NEDDA

I've searched for Beauty since I was a child,
Made fervent notes on what it was and why.
Were mountains beautiful? The sea? The sky?
Are flowers better in the yard or wild?
But soon just "pretty" things seemed flat or mild.
I found no zest to Beauty. By and by
When Beauty's graph showed neither low nor high
I stopped research. My notes—my dreams—were filed.
Until the day you sailed in through that door—
All pulsing temperament, with flashing eyes
And matchless beauty but with, oh, much more.
Through fiery years you've proved, to my surprise,
That Beauty is not Truth as Keats has said—
It's "living life completely 'til you're dead."

J. L. L.

Many Good Samaritans helped me along the way. First was my friend and neighbor, Bennett Cerf, who hounded me to write it for twenty years before his death. Then there was John Dodds, across the street, who took up the cry and even went so far as to sit through my dictation of the endless first draft, laughing at unfunny lines to keep me going. Valiant Bob Cornfield helped me cut that mass in half. Once, when it almost stumbled, Ellis Amburn picked up the pieces and with Ross Claiborne put it back on its feet. Jeanne Bernkopf edited the final and I hope readable version. Lee Tuft and Jane-Grey Dudley typed the first drafts. Joseph Curtis was not only, as always, a sounding board, but he typed all other drafts, and frequently.

Thank you, all of you.

CHAPTER

1

My life and breath is the theatre. I seem to visualize all existence in theatrical terms. Will dawn go up on time? Will the day be climactic? The night have suspense? The rest of the world (politics, religion, even some sports) is to my taste flat, stale or deadly boring. My life story itself may seem staged, contrived, even melodramatic—because it was. I was written by a madly irresponsible playwright.

When I was two, my mother fed me beauty instead of cod-liver oil. Beauty cured everything. "Just think of flowers, lacy leaves, horses' manes, or being happy—and you will be." Being *un*happy was forbidden. Should I fall on the floor, bump my head and burst out crying, she became diversionary. "Think how poor Mister Floor feels! Apologize to Mister Floor." Blubbering with self-pity, I would bend down to the planks and say, "Ex-cuse me, M-M-Mister Floor."

How did the son of a lumber-and-creosote man and the grandson of a cotton planter land on Broadway or in Hollywood?

Two dramatic events happened early. One (good), I was born on the paved side of State Line Avenue in Texarkana, Texas—just across the street from the perpetually muddy Texarkana, Arkansas side, and two (bad), my father died of pneumonia when I was nearly three, way off in a Chicago hospital, or so they kept on telling me. That was shortly after we had moved to Mansfield, Louisiana, and my baby sister, Mary Lee, had been born. Without Daddy we had to move again—Mother, Mary Lee, Amy Lane, our old Negro nurse, and I—over on Polk Street to the white gingerbread, wisteria-covered house of Granddaddy and Grandmother Nabors, Mother's parents. Years later, I wrote a play for Helen Hayes called *The Wisteria Trees,* transplanting Chekhov's *The Cherry Orchard* to that house on Polk Street—with its cascading bloom, heavy perfume, black shadow and buzzing bumblebees.

Mansfield's only mass entertainments were Sunday church and Wednesday night prayer meeting—till the town converted its funeral parlor into a tacky little movie theatre called, what else?—the Palace.

Movies! D. W. Griffith! *Judith of Bethulia!* Mother, who taught Sunday school, felt that seeing it might decorate our minds. But in our whole family of Bible readers, nobody knew the story: it wasn't in the Bible but in the Apocrypha.

The piano was banging away as we entered. Mother sat between us. On the screen, Judith, inside a tent, combed her long hair and let everybody get a peek at her breasts. A black-bearded man swaggered into the tent. He was Holofernes, the enemy general.

Judith sneakily pulled a small bottle from her bosom and spiked his wine. The general slurped it down and passed out. My little sister and I applauded. Judith's eyes gleamed as she produced a curved sword and held it poised over his muscular neck.

Mother pushed our faces behind the seats in front, saying, "Duck yo' heads and think o' fields of yellah daisies!"

I couldn't ask questions about my dead father without people coughing or changing the subject.

"Quiet," they would say, "here comes Josh Junior." They always acted so funny and secrety that I finally stopped asking questions about my daddy. How could I know it was going to take forty years and almost that many shows on Broadway for me to learn some gruesome and tragic facts about his death, and see him clearly then for the first time in my life?

Tiny Mary Lee, who grew more beautiful every day, was soon Granddaddy's pet, so I was often left with Mother, who hated the roughness of the Southwest and even found most nursery rhymes too violent. Instead, she switched me to Shakespeare songs. My grandfather and uncles would wince when I declaimed:

> Hark! hark! the lark at heaven's gate sings,
> And Phoebus 'gins arise . . .

One uncle said, "No wonder the boys call him sissy."

"Next time they do," said Granddaddy, "you beat 'em up—and I'll give you five dollars."

It was a safe offer. I couldn't beat up a flea.

When we were old enough, Granddaddy built us a little house, just big enough for us to enter. It had a front "gallery" for our chairs, wallpaper inside and a real electric light. Mother christened it "Jolly Den." It was a place to play in, hide in, and handy later for light brushes with sex.

Mother also assigned us a costume trunk in the plunder room. Now, at five, with Shakespeare's jingles as my theme, I decided to dramatize Phoebus, the rising sun. I dressed little cousin Eleanor and Mary Lee in yellow crepe paper skirts and wrapped myself as Phoebus in an orange bedspread. The girls were to be sunbeams, dancing while Phoebus climbed the "sky": a giant pecan tree nearby. Phoebus climbed majestically, shouting to the uninspired sunbeams to dance faster and faster, which they did until they collapsed on the grass.

"Get up and dance, you shiftless sunbeams," I commanded. In my rage, I stepped on air and found myself plummeting through flimsy branches, grasping at twigs, till my arms accidentally hooked over two lower branches which stopped me. I got no sympathy from my sunbeams; they were angry with me for making *them* dance too fast. Actresses, I discovered early, have something called temperament.

Mary Lee not only had great beauty but a lithe, coordinated body. She was a born athlete while I considered myself both too fat and too awkward to compete with her for Granddaddy's attention.

But I was determined to try. He loved spicy food and so to impress him I forced myself to down Louisiana pork sausage (though it made my eyes tear), smelly salt mackerel, repulsive chitterlings, reeking Limburger cheese, the hottest of chili, gumbo filé (powdered sassafras leaf)

—and with everything extra squirts of Tabasco sauce. He even convinced me to put it in my milk "to bring out the taste."

I won Granddaddy temporarily. He pronounced me a champion trencherman. Mary Lee was furious, as Tabasco made her hiccup.

Our kindergarten was part of a college that had the embarrassing name of Mansfield Female College: we were "guinea pigs" experimented on by young Methodist females studying to be teachers. We lived so near the school that I awoke each morning to arpeggios, scales and the sound of young girls vocalizing.

Each morning our teacher would read a story aloud and each afternoon we'd act it out. At recess I'd run through our back yard and demand a costume from my mother.

"Mother, I need a dog suit. It's easy. Just drive down to the store and buy some dog cloth."

And she did. I was a stunning success as a dog, then later as an elf, a Dutch boy, a prince and even a jam pot. The rest of the class were jealous of my costumes, but I never minded. Success has always buoyed me beyond crass criticism.

The beginning of the First World War reached us via phonograph records. Granddaddy bought a new one by Irving Berlin which told of an Irish mother watching her darlin' Jimmy boy in a military parade:

> There was Jimmy, just as stiff as starch,
> Like his father on the seventeenth of March;
> And tell me, tell me, did you notice
> They were all out of step but Jim?

I laughed loud at the joke in the last line, and little Mary Lee laughed even louder. But she was laughing because she thought the lady was cussing: "They were all out of step! *by Jim.*"

I pointed out her error in a most condescending way, and she lost her temper.

"Ask the grown-ups," she said. "They'll tell you I'm right!"

I marched her out on the gallery and we both sang the song. Then my little angel sister in her sweetest voice said, "It's not 'But Jim'; Granddaddy, it's 'By Jim.' You know it is—you know it is!"

"Of course it is, darlin'. *'By* Jim!'"

I started to protest, but all the others howled with laughter and agreed with her.

I walked away, stricken by the ugliness of injustice. I was miserable for days.

When I was eight, Granddaddy and Mother drove me to Shreveport to see my first professional play, *Everywoman,* "a modern morality play." When I stepped into the lobby of the Sanger Theatre, I was jolted by love at first sight: those blazing fan-shaped arrangements of naked light bulbs on the ceiling. Ever since, I have been drawn like a moth to anything outlined by light bulbs: mirrors, doors, facades, bridges, ferris wheels—anything.

But there was more love to come that night. The theatre grew dark and the footlights lit up that red velvet curtain with all that gold fringe. I began to applaud.

"Not yet," said Granddaddy. "Wait."

The huge curtain went up on spooky darkness. A green spotlight picked out a hooded, faceless figure who spoke in a rich voice mixed with an evil cackle:

"I'm Nobody—cackle, cackle."

I liked him at once—his sheer delight in being mean! And boy! did I love that green light. "Nobody" snooped around the stage, telling of Everywoman and her three handmaidens, Beauty, Youth and Modesty. Cackle, cackle. Snoop, snoop.

Everywoman was an overripe glory, waist drawn so tight that her breasts and her bottom bulged. She moved in front of a tall pier-glass mirror and the *mirror spoke* to her, or rather a white-wigged man *inside* the mirror spoke, telling her how nice she was. *He* was *Flattery.*

On the drive back I stood behind the front seat, acting. "I'm Nobody!" I said, "cackle, cackle," until Mother suggested I try being Flattery for a while. I did, but it wasn't as much fun as being mean. "I'm Nobody," I cackled again, all the way home.

I've never enjoyed the so-called manly art of fighting, though I've been forced into it many times in my life. I even won the school's light heavyweight boxing championship when I was seventeen. I've sometimes felt like belting an actor in the middle of a rehearsal, but never did because I am not a born fighter. That's why it's amazing that for my first fight I subconsciously chose a spectacular background and a large crowd.

One summer, Mother, Mary Lee, Amy Lane and I went to Biloxi,

Mississippi, on the Gulf of Mexico. We stayed in a cottage at a grandish hotel called The White House. Mother dressed us up the very first day for coffee with music in the ballroom. I was stuffed into last year's white linen suit and a wide starched collar with a tatting border, a floppy black silk bow tie, and, of course, short pants and white socks held up at midcalf by rubber bands.

Amy led us into the vast room just as a plump lady in glasses started a violin solo. Amy got us to a horsehair settee.

A mean-looking older boy in knickerbockers and long black stockings came in, holding onto his nurse's hand. As he passed me, he sneered, "You sock-wearing sissy." I glanced at Mary Lee. She had heard it, so there was no way out. I stood up on the settee, aimed my overstuffed body and dived at him. He fell under my weight and we slid on the polished floor almost to the center of the room.

Ladies screamed, the violin played louder and Amy shouted, but I could hear my little sister yelling:

"Beat him up good, Josh! Remember that five dollars!"

We rolled over until he pinned my arms to my side. I bit hard into his neck. He let out a bloodcurdling scream and released my arms. I straddled him, my bite holding fast.

Some men pulled us apart. The boy writhed on the floor. Amy dragged me from the room, Mary Lee skipping behind us, crowing, "He gave up, Josh. If you want my opinion, you sure won that five dollars! That's my opinion!"

There was nothing for Mother to do but let us go down the coast to Granddaddy's hotel and collect the promised reward.

"Good boy, Josh," said the old man. "You sure earned this." He handed me a crisp five-dollar bill. I had never touched one before.

By the next summer our country had entered the war. In our classroom, hidden behind our textbooks, we boys drew pictures of airplanes in dogfights. Our house began to fill with secret hordes of sugar, flour and crates of oranges. Granddaddy was patriotic, but he loved food.

The next spring, Grandmother fell ill. We realized how bad it was when we saw men carrying out the old oak furniture from her room and moving in beautiful ivory-colored, carved pieces instead. Granddaddy had always promised her a new bedroom set, and now it seemed he had to hurry.

Just before Grandmother died, Mother organized us into making a clover ring and crowning her Queen of the May. We thought it was silly, but it was nice to see Grandmother smile. It was a little pained smile, and her last.

For years, Mother had been studying ways to get us "away": living with her father in a small town held no promise for her children.

When we went to Biloxi that war summer, Mother visited an Army training camp in nearby Hattiesburg. She went to see a man she had met years before when he taught at Culver Military Academy in Indiana: he was Captain Noble then, and had two children, much older than we, and a sickly wife.

She returned from Hattiesburg with a fine-looking visitor, Colonel Howard Noble, widower. Weeks later, after formally asking our permission, the colonel took Mother to New Orleans where they married, while we returned to Mansfield. Colonel Noble then was shipped off with his regiment to France.

Granddaddy was so hotted up by Mother's marriage that he ran off with a young woman, Evelyn Gant. In a flash we had a new grandmother and father.

As a colonel's son, I was now an authority on the war. The other boys brought their dogfight drawings to me for approval. Just having a father, and a tough military one at that, gave me the buoyant feeling that my soft boyhood was over.

CHAPTER

After Father returned from France, he took us to his concrete-block house on Lake Maxinkuckee in Culver, Indiana, and soon showed us he could be razor-sharp, rough and sarcastic.

He criticized my walk: "Don't swing your ass like a girl." Prompt attendance at meals was enforced. We had to eat everything our German immigrant cook put before us. I got rid of the horrible cauliflower by scooping the hot creamy lumps surreptitiously into the napkin in my lap.

He had one saving grace: he was just as rough with Mother. "Stop talking, Sue, you've made your point!" And she would stop, though Mary Lee and I dared not look at each other, and Lois, our stepsister, kept a noncommittal face.

Our neighbors were faculty families and their children, "faculty brats." I was sure they would call me a sissy, but they didn't; they accepted me as a boy, and friend.

Exploring the campus with them one day, we reached the huge riding hall where I exclaimed:

"Less go up in thuh tow-wuh."

They howled. "The what?"

"The tow-wuh. T-O-W-E-R."

"You mean the tow*errrr*."

In that second I denied the South and became a Hoosier. I put Rs in every word possible. "Mother-r-r" and "Father-r-r" complained at the rasping sound, but I knew what I was up to. The change in pronunciation meant acceptance by my peers.

Public school was a two-mile bicycle trip to the town of Culver. For the first time I had lots of male friends my own age. I literally threw myself into sports, which were also new to me. Here I was, a big, awkward Southern boy who had never learned to pitch or catch a baseball, but my new friends helped save my face by complimenting me on my bulk.

"Our football team could sure use a guy your size!" It seems there was a plethora of wiry quarterbacks, but at ages ten and eleven, very few beefy guards or tackles.

I learned to skate with wobbly ankles and play at ice hockey. When the lake froze thick enough, Father drove us out on it, in the car, and we cut a hole a foot deep in the ice and fished.

The first summers Mary Lee and I spent with Granddaddy and Evelyn back in Mansfield. For me, at twelve, adolescence was beginning, and I was terribly proud of the changes in my body, but I was terrified that someone in Mansfield might bring up my former childish softness. To fend that off, I affected a deep voice and held my shoulders so they would appear at their widest.

At the end of our trip we visited Aunt Irma and Uncle Ben and Eleanor in Shreveport. They gave us a swim-and-breakfast farewell party at the country club.

I was at the head of the table next to my "date," a thirteen-year-old blonde whom I had asked because she looked more like sixteen, having palpable breasts. I pointedly ignored my childish sister who sat at the far end—growing furious:

"D'jall know Josh wrote a poem that won a prize in *Little Folks Magazine?*"

I turned to my date and smiled.

"That was way back when I was a *little folk*. Six or seven, I think."

"You were *eight!*" screamed Mary Lee. "It was real cute, everybody. It went like this:

> 'The flowers had a party;
> In fact, it was a ball.' "

"Okay, Mary Lee. You've had your laugh."

> " 'They danced in couples gaily
> All up and down the hall.' "

I didn't dare look at my date's face as Mary Lee continued.
I yelled, "If you don't shut up, I'll kill you!"

> "Mr. Poppy took Miss Rose."

My date was shaking with laughter. I lost all control. I climbed onto the table and marched through grits and sausage.

My hands grabbed her throat. The tablecloth caught my foot, china crashed to the floor and food flew everywhere. We were pulled apart to face horror-stricken Aunt Irma and Uncle Ben.

"What kind of a Southern gentleman is he?"

The degree of my rage had frightened even me. I became the pariah of upper Louisiana and East Texas. Aunt Irma was frigidly sweet and Uncle Ben suddenly unavailable. Eleanor took to her room. Mary Lee walked past me, addressing her remark to the air: "Just wait till Father gets you for this! I'm going to tell him before I even kiss him."

The train trip back north was endless. Mother and Father were waiting at the door. Mary Lee cut through the hugs and kisses with her lurid tale of my attack. I pushed past them into the dining room and sat rigid with fear. Mother took her sniffling daughter upstairs and Father went into the kitchen.

I was not going to be called a coward as well as a killer, so I went in to face him. Father was sitting drinking his usual cold leftover coffee. "Josh, I've watched her get the best of you for a long time, and you, to please your mother, let her get away with it. Well, the big fat worm finally turned. Congratulations!"

He may have been wrong according to all the rules of conduct, courtesy, even perhaps of criminal law, but to me, at that moment, he became the greatest person in the world.

We spent hours together after that. He had been an engineer and topographer, and he opened up his drawing instruments and taught me how to use T squares and compasses, how to letter and sketch cartoons in pencil and then go over them again in India ink. He infected me with the fascination of working precisely with my hands. Perhaps this was his greatest gift to me, one that years later was to help me find a way to go on living while I was wanting to be dead.

His other lifelong gift was his active interest in my physical development. He pointed out how mature I was at twelve: at my full height and ideal weight. I was a strong swimmer but he arranged tennis, golf and boxing lessons. I became a health nut. I sent for Charles Atlas' *Are You a 97-Pound Weakling?* muscle-building course. I worked for hours on Dynamic Tension: pulling violently on an imaginary rope with simulated strain. I grew tough and disgustingly healthy. To match my new tough muscles I talked tough, except before my parents. Mary Lee was only moderately impressed with my cussing. Oh, well, she would be off to boarding school soon, far away in Tennessee.

I had always known I was going to the academy. As a faculty child, my tuition would be free, and since I could live at home my room would be, too. That is, unless the new baby Mother was expecting would need it.

My Culver routine began at five-thirty. In my room at home I dressed before daybreak, shined shoes, puttees and brass, stumbled down dark stairs to the cellar where I shook out the night cinders of the furnace and added fresh black coal. Then I jogged several hundred yards to the shadowy street in front of Main Barracks where Company G had reveille at six-ten, and then on to the day's rugged routine.

One morning it was still black as pitch when I came back from reveille to get my books. As I entered the dark house, my knee hit a chair. I tried to walk around it and I hit another. I angrily groped for the light switch. Six chairs were blocking my progress with a sign done in Father's best lettering: "Josh," it said, "it's Marshall Hays." A little brother. I was delighted. Now maybe they'd stop nagging me about my grades.

Culver's greatest splendor was the uniform. For parade, shakos, white crossed belts; for retreat, riding breeches, puttees, gray wool blouses with tight-fitting black braid collars and visored caps. We were spectacular, yet undistinguishable one from the other. The only chance to stand out was to become a commissioned officer. That brought long capes with velvet collars, oversized chevrons and gleaming cordovan boots with silver spurs. On occasion, red woolen sashes with huge tassels, over which were clasped elaborate buckled black leather belts with shoulder straps, supporting swords in silver scabbards with gold encrustations.

Never did I want anything as much as I wanted to wear that uniform. But it would take effort. I decided to move to the barracks. Preoccupied with little Marshall, my parents had no objections.

The monklike life in the barracks was a blessing. There was freedom in being restricted. Having a roommate was also a discovery. Cleaning corners, making beds, shining brass were almost enjoyable when shared.

But the day I got to know Charles Mather, Professor of Dramatics at Culver—the day I entered his class—I felt my life swerve and suddenly steady itself.

Mather wasn't like a teacher—he was a confidant I could trust with my most embarrassingly personal doubts. He gave me the strength to face myself and then even to try and like myself.

Company athletics were compulsory. Because I'd had boxing lessons I was urged to represent my company in that competition, but it soon became my personal hell. It wasn't the pain so much: I was too scared to feel pain. When the bell sounded, I stepped to the center of the ring and two minutes of blind oblivion. We bumped, flailed and hugged. Ding! the bell. Then to the corner, gasping for a wet sponge while I listened to my coach fuzzily. And then Ding! and off to another two minutes of pulpy blankness. The fight was over and somehow the referee was raising my glove triumphantly in the air. I was the scaredest but the strongest—I couldn't lose. But winning only meant to me that I wasn't eliminated. I would have to fight again and again. Only failure would have been success.

I got through three years and became cadet lieutenant for my fourth year. Now I could wear the shiny chevrons, the boots, those ringing spurs. Now I could look as splendid as I felt.

With Father's instruction, I had been drawing cartoons each week for the student newspaper, *Vedette*. I had played two important parts in Mather's plays. The next fall I was sure to make the varsity football team. All this glory, and I just over fifteen years old.

I was a sexual illiterate at fifteen but wouldn't admit it. I had invented a carnal repertoire from tales of older cadets. I expounded on physical techniques, always stressing the importance of complete nudity. Since I had manufactured a Charles Atlas body and seemed mature, I defied disbelief.

Then came the yearly *Vedette* trip to visit the *Chicago Tribune*. Through outside photographers we had learned that the great place for girls in Chicago was the Kitchenette Apartments. On the train we debated whether to go there first or later.

To cover my inner panic, I assumed an aggressive attitude.

"What the hell's the point of waiting?" I said. "Let's move, men!"

"Boy, is that guy hot," I heard someone say with admiration.

The maid who opened the door led us into a room where five or six bored women waited.

"What's this?" asked one. "A policemen's ball?"

"Don't be funny, Duchess," said I. "We're West Point officers and we haven't got much time to bat the breeze." I could feel relief from the others—the old campaigner had taken over.

After pairing everyone off, I was left with the one real dog. She studied me for a moment and said, "Let's go, Fancy Pants." Following her upstairs was stimulating. Fancy pants—maybe. Hot pants—definitely!

The room was faded. She sat down on the bed and pulled her single garment, a slip, halfway up, exposing sallow flesh.

"Unbutton your fly and let's get it over with."

"No, siree," I said. "I want this to be full out. You know, bare ass."

"You're gonna take off all that crap? We'll be here a week."

"I'm a military man, ma'am. It's a matter of a minute."

She proceeded to pull that slip over her head.

In my haste to unhook the stiff collar, several hooks got caught. She looked pained. Off came my sword, my shoulder belt, and I began unwinding the red wool sash. She groaned. The extra pressure in my trousers was causing me great discomfort. I got my spurs and my sweaty boots off and started to unlace my riding breeches. Dropping my trousers and my boxer shorts, I stood, overripe and ever ready.

She lay back. I climbed up, settled down on top of her, and immediately felt myself exploding. It was finished and I hadn't even started.

"That'll be ten dollars," she said.

Culver was almost over and college was in the air. We applied for the college boards. Mother wanted the University of Virginia—"nice Southern boys go there"—but I wanted Princeton. I had read about the Princeton Triangle Club show which toured the country during Christmas vacation. Students appeared in it, wrote the book, composed the music—everything. I had to be in that club.

That summer I had to attend ROTC camp. I chose the one at Platts-
burg, New York, so when camp was over I could visit New York City
and see my first Broadway play, *What Price Glory?* with the great
gnarled Louis Wolheim playing Captain Flagg.

After that one night in New York I wrote my family, "This is my
town."

I moved in with an understanding aunt, Anita, who had rented an
apartment for the summer. I had sixty-five dollars to last me my whole
stay. Sleeping on her daybed, scrounging in her icebox and spending
fifteen cents daily for a Nedick's hot dog and orange drink, I was able
to afford a fifty-cent second-balcony seat, all summer, every night. I saw
Will Rogers, W. C. Fields, Ray Dooley and Fanny Brice in *The Ziegfeld Follies,* and what I still think was the best revue ever, *George
White's Scandals,* with Willie and Eugene Howard, and Harry Rich-
man singing "Oh, Boy, I'm Lucky" and "The Birth of the Blues";
Walter Huston in Eugene O'Neill's *Desire Under the Elms; White
Cargo* with the native girl Tondeleyo gyrating her honey-colored
torso; and an imitation of it called *Aloma of the South Seas.* Sex
thrived in the theatre, I was happy to discover.

My Uncle Bill, who lived in the suburbs, took me to lunch at Sardi's
with his insurance client, the distinguished publisher and stage
producer, Horace Liveright, who made our table the center of attention. A thin young Englishman approached our table. He had acted
that season in a Liveright production of his own play, *The Vortex.* He
wanted Liveright to publish his current London success, *Hay Fever,* in
the magazine *Vanity Fair.* Mr. Liveright thought it was a good idea,
and introduced us to Noel Coward.

Back at Culver, for my senior year, I spent months praying for Princeton—but no word. I had almost given up hope when I learned I was
accepted.

Commencement week with its honors was approaching, and I knew
Mother prayed I would get some kind of recognition. But I also knew
there was no chance of that. Two other faculty sons were destined to
be Best All-Around Athlete and Valedictorian. I had gotten the lead in
the senior play, George Kelly's comedy, *The Show-Off,* but that was
not like an honor before the class.

The solemn exercises commenced, and after the most important
prizes were awarded, the headmaster announced that a new prize had
been donated by an alumnus. It was an engraved gold watch for "excel-

lence and leadership in the cultural activities of Culver Military Academy." An award, he proclaimed, "that of all those given today, I would have wanted to win myself. I have the honor of presenting it to Cadet Joshua Lockwood Logan."

I would have preferred "highest marks" or "best all-around athlete." A cultural prize sounded like something Mother invented, but as I rose the applause was tremendous and drowned my misgivings.

In September 1927, Tommy Crenshaw, a Culver classmate, who was to be my roommate at Princeton, and I, were dumped on the stone steps of Holder Hall by Tom's parents. As we sat there, I said to myself, "This is a truly historic moment in my life. I must remember every detail of entering these fabled halls, to tell my children."

Tom jolted me out of my fancy dreams. "Let's get drunk," he said, with a nervous smile.

CHAPTER

3

Since we weren't from a fancy Eastern prep school, Tom and I chose an expensive dormitory suite, hoping to make an impression. Our large dormer-windowed living room sported an oversized, acid-green velvet couch with huge mahogany ends, which the Crenshaws had been relieved to dump on us.

Our convenient location made our room a gathering place, and soon we fell into the freshman routine—all-night bridge and bull sessions with a 4:00 A.M. trip to Nassau Street for a snack before turning in. And a quick sleep it was, for classes began at 8:30. I soon mastered the trick of napping upright during lectures, my cheek resting in my open palm which was propped up by my elbow. Our crowd favored the good life and had contempt for the grinds.

Since Prohibition prevailed, at five in the afternoon hundreds of undergraduates crossed quadrangles with little brown paper bags filled with ice and mixes. Outside the ground-floor windows, bootleggers delivered expensive bad whiskey and cheap worse gin.

My greatest hindrance to being accepted was the damnable Midwestern accent I had worked so hard to master. Gone were my Southern tones which might suggest faded grandeur to this snobbish society. But my mind rebelled at re-creating Mansfield. So I must sandpaper those Rs and force my nasality back to the throat. Then I must develop an air of bland indifference.

There was much talk of the exclusive eating clubs we might be asked to join during sophomore year. Many came to Princeton for the clubs alone. Up and down McCosh Walk pranced that special breed of student—nose in the air, torso bent forward, rear end protruding—wearing white saddle shoes, gray flannel trousers and a tight-fitting tweed jacket. This said clearly that the wearer was bucking ("whoring") for Ivy, the most distinguished club of them all. To demonstrate my disapproval of this, I took to wearing loud-striped shirts, black shoes and dark suits and ties. I felt it gave me a superior-to-it-all look, and if it meant no club would take me, then so be it.

The nonsocial Triangle Club was to me the sole excuse for the existence of Princeton, but it was forbidden to freshmen. I had a year's wait before I could even try out. I had vaguely heard of the Theatre Intime, the campus dramatic organization, but I paid no attention to it as I felt my bridge-playing gang would shun me. Then one morning I noticed an announcement in the *Daily Princetonian* that the Theatre Intime was going to present a comedy called *Open Collars,* written by an undergraduate.

Many years later a doctor told me I had "an innate sense of self-direction." It must have been my "self-direction" that headed me for Murray-Dodge Hall that night.

A group of us sat around until two important-looking students came in. The first to introduce himself was the play's director, Bretaigne Windust, a junior.

Windy . . . Windy . . . Windy. How could I know that I would finally grow to like you? And that Broadway would let you direct *Life with Father, Arsenic and Old Lace, Finian's Rainbow,* the Lunts in *Idiot's Delight,* and lots of others? Could anyone seem as pretentious as you were that night?

The other student was Erik Barnouw, the author. He was also to portray the protagonist, a serious undergraduate. Windust would play the brazen aesthete who wore his collar open.

This evening they were casting. They needed someone to play Barnouw's roommate, a regular Joe, a bit stupid—in short, a typical Princetonian. Eventually chosen was a shortish sophomore with funny open-door ears and a wicked smile: Myron McCormick.

Still open was the role of Reggie, the jovial friend. To each applicant, Windust would say, "Can't you laugh a little louder?"

When it came my turn, I roared. Windust said, "Excuse me, old boy. Could you laugh a little bit *less?*" But that laugh got me the part.

During rehearsals, I noticed a senior hanging around. He was Charles Arnt, Jr., who next year was to be *president* of the Triangle Club. I nearly fainted. It was like a glimpse of royalty.

Barnouw, whose Dutch father was a professor at Columbia, told me that he wanted to write next year's Triangle show and was trying to hook Arnt, also of Dutch heritage, by setting his version in the Netherlands. Ignoring the fact that I didn't know exactly where the Netherlands was, I told Barnouw it was an inspired plan, original, picturesque, in short, a show I'd want to see. Barnouw was so thrilled by my enthusiasm he asked me to be his coauthor.

My heart flew out the window, around Nassau Hall, then settled back in its rightful place. I spoke as quietly as I could manage. "Well, if you really want me to, Erik."

Under the title *Zuyder Zee*, we presented an outline to Arnt. I did some spectacular talking and wouldn't stop until he agreed. Barnouw, delighted with my aggressiveness, which counteracted his shyness, went into a huddle with Windust, who then approached me.

"Since you'll probably be working with Erik this summer, why not come up to Cape Cod? We're starting a company called The University Players made up of students from Harvard, Smith, Yale, Radcliffe, Vassar and Princeton. You could work props or something and maybe even play a few small parts. And in your spare time you could write next year's show with Erik."

I was staggered. My dream was coming true even before I could dream it!

I walked to classes in a daze. One day I even forgot to wear my freshman skullcap. It is a wonder I got through that first year at all.

On most weekends I took the little comic train from Princeton to Princeton Junction where it met the New York-bound trains. I packed as much theatregoing as I could into two days and kept writing home for more money.

Father was now retired and living in Shreveport with Mother and five-year-old Marshall. He had bought a beautiful piece of property called Woodhull where they built and where Mother planted shrubs and trees in honor of important events. A magnolia was christened, Josh's Nineteenth Birthday, a crepe myrtle, Open Collars, and an evergreen, Theatre Magazine, after our cast picture appeared in same. When Mary Lee was accepted at Wells College, a red bud was named, A Wise Decision by Wells.

The idea of the University Players had been born months before at a party given by Mr. and Mrs. Norman Hapgood for Vladimir Nemirovich-Danchenko, cofounder with Stanislavsky of the Moscow Art Theatre. When Bretaigne Windust, "Windy," president of the Intime, met Charles Crane Leatherbee, president of the Harvard Dramatic Society, they decided to form a new "Moscow Art" type company of college students and base it on Cape Cod in the Elizabeth Theatre, Falmouth, near Woods Hole, where Charles's family summered. His grandfather, Charles Crane, also lived close by. Heir to a plumbing fortune, Charles Crane was both a philanthropist and diplomat. He had been appointed ambassador to China by Wilson. He financed artesian wells in the North African desert, helped support Roberts College in Turkey, and sponsored the removal of Moslem whitewash from superb Byzantine mosaics in Santa Sophia, Constantinople.

The Elizabeth, on Falmouth's main street, was the town's movie theatre. Charlie planned to borrow it on Monday and Tuesday evenings when movie business was poor.

The knowledge that this company would produce some of the greatest talents in the American theatre would not have surprised Charlie and Windy at all. They knew what they were after. They started immediately to recruit a company from their college theatres. I came in, as they say, on a pass.

Although Windy and Charlie were directors of the company, all twenty-five of us felt it was ours. Benign anarchy might describe it, with everyone fighting for his own ideas. The only rules were: be on time for rehearsals and don't antagonize the locals.

At first, Charles Leatherbee struck me as overbred and overrefined. But I soon learned that his delicacy of mien covered a steely, obstinate will. His parents were divorced. He lived in a luxuriously renovated barn known as "the Camp" in a woodsy area near Whitecrest, his mother's handsome clapboard house.

Charles's mother, due to another remarriage, was now Frances Anita Crane Leatherbee Masaryk. Her husband, Jan Masaryk, was Czechoslovakian ambassador to the Court of St. James, and the son of the first president of Czechoslovakia. Many years later, as foreign minister, Jan Masaryk would meet a tragic end during the Nazi take-over of his country.

But now, that first summer, he was just Jan, a winning man with a crazy accent and pudgy face who was about my size and allowed me to borrow his formal clothes to use in plays. His great party feat was to line up eight armchairs on the Whitecrest lawn, then, starting his run from a thirty-foot distance, leap over them all and land on his feet. He never missed! A few minutes later he'd be at the piano playing a Beethoven sonata beautifully.

We saw him every Wednesday afternoon when the company was invited to Whitecrest for luncheon, our one decent meal.

Miss Frances, in her flowing gowns, was a New England Athena. Her home was as exquisite as she was. It was the first time I had noticed decorative detail—our homes had always been haphazard-Southern —and through her I developed a gnawing and insatiable hunger for graceful surroundings.

Charlie's camp, fifty yards away, was paneled in knotty pine with fabrics in tones of orange. The log fire and the wrought-iron Italian chandeliers made the room at once rough and rich. Because of my uncontained enthusiasm I was invited to stay there.

The energy of two dozen undiscovered stars, the mixture of grand and poor, mostly poor, the fact that everyone was nearly the same age, the lack of a principal or teacher to shake fingers or teach "academic precepts"—all of this made for a kind of hell. Anyone could try out for a part, suggest a play or criticize anyone else. Only the strong could live through this criticism because it was as hot as a baptism of fire. You didn't play the part badly—you *stank*. Your idea wasn't interesting—it was great or stupid. Physical fights were nonexistent, but belligerent standoffs could last for days.

But always we were totally involved, ecstatically alive. So, from this torment and apparently continuous disagreement, came beautiful, even masterful theatre. Each play seemed perfectly cast and vibrantly played, the costumes exquisite, the scenery and lighting seemingly too professional for college students. Even older roles were convincing because of painstaking makeup and great wigs.

It was in this group I discovered that good theatre is not collaboration. Artists cannot truly collaborate. To be good they must follow their inspiration, their urge, their ego to the limit. And that limit is when the venture will collapse if they push themselves one inch further. Only then *must* they make an adjustment—a creative compromise—but just enough of a compromise to avoid disaster.

Charlie and Windy made all of the casting decisions, deaf to the cries of pain. Windy directed and demanded discipline—even got it at rehearsal. The stage crew remained neutral so they could stay calm and build superb scenery. But inside, each member burned hot love not only for the theatre but for their company—yes, and for each other. We actually believed we were better than anyone. We would have challenged any company in the country. It was only this blind, idiot confidence that could make us accept minor parts, odd jobs with the crew, our meager salary of five dollars a week less laundry, our frayed clothing and our repetitious skimpy diet. It was an almost monastic life but it produced extraordinary results.

The town looked on us as wild kids having a crazy sinful summer together on the Cape. Would that that were true. Sin would have been welcome and relaxing. But learning lines, rehearsing, helping to build sets, plus lack of sleep and food, left little time or energy or even opportunity—to say nothing of privacy—for such bliss. Physical love had to wait in line.

On Monday night, July 9, 1928, the University Players opened with A. A. Milne's *The Dover Road*. Then followed O'Neill's *Beyond the Horizon*, a lugubrious play in which Charlie Leatherbee spent hours suffering from love and tuberculosis. As my professional debut, I made a short forgettable appearance as an old sea captain.

Then came George Kelly's wonderful and ridiculous *The Torch Bearers*, about amateur theatricals in Philadelphia. I read for and won the idiotic role of Huxley Hossefrosse, a fatuous old man. I invented a flat, human capon voice which I thought hilarious.

At the second performance, the moment I spoke my first line a high, strangulated sob came from the darkness. I thought someone was having an asthmatic attack. I said my second line and the wail came out again, higher and flatter this time. Some odd human animal out there found me funny. And, to my delight, it was infecting the audience.

When he screeched, they began to scream. That night I had my first triumph, but whose mad laughter had helped it along?

Bernard Hanighen, from Harvard, who did our music, came to our dressing room after the performance with a friend of his from Omaha who had been acting at the Cape Playhouse in Dennis.

"This is my friend, Hank Fonda."

Standing in the doorway was a tall, lean man in his early twenties. His head jutted forward over a concave chest and a protruding abdomen which made him seem to lead with his crotch. He wore skimpy, white plus four knickers, long black socks and black shoes. Either he had a daring tailor or he just didn't care. I was to find out it was the latter. His extraordinarily handsome, almost beautiful face and huge innocent eyes, combined with that roughhewn physique, made for a startling effect.

He was looking at me as though he were about to pop. "You were Huxley Hossefrosse, weren't you?"

"Yes," I answered, and he exploded with that same strangled sob laugh I'd heard all evening. At that moment I knew I would care for him the rest of my life. There's no one as endearing as one you can make laugh.

Fonda was fresh from the University of Minnesota. He had acted for Mrs. Brando (Marlon's mother) at the Omaha Community Playhouse and he wanted to join our company.

Unfortunately, our next play was *The Jest*, an Italian play full of semipoetic language, set in the fifteenth century. I was to play two parts: Tornaquinci, the noble host, and, in the last act, the headsman. I decided to share one of my parts with Fonda so I could hear him laugh some more. But I couldn't give up the headsman: I'd been looking forward to wearing black tights and baring my Charles Atlas chest. So I generously relinquished the dull role of noble Tornaquinci to Fonda. It almost ruined his career.

When the suave and verbal Italian host spoke with a nasal Omaha whine and moved like a human angle iron, we all wondered what we had gotten ourselves into. But Leatherbee liked him too, and decided to try something in Hank's American-boy style: *Is Zat So?* Fonda played a brainless young boxer and Kent Smith (who always got the roles I wanted) his manager. I played a wealthy young man who bankrolled them. Fonda wiped us all off the stage simply by seeming to do nothing. His understatement has become one of our national treasures.

At the end of the summer I was "chosen" by lottery to direct a mystery made of toothpicks and spit: *The Thirteenth Chair* by Bayard Veiller. None of us wanted to direct; we all wanted to be onstage getting laughs, tears and applause. I can't remember how I went about my first directorial task. I must have followed the original New York stage directions indicated in the script: "On line three, move left and look out the window; at bottom of page, move center and light a cigarette." I thought, what a dull life a director must lead. It was like making an omelet from a cookbook.

But I was slowly being transformed that summer, without realizing it. Up until then I'd been a half-assed opportunist. I'd gone to Princeton not for an education but for the Triangle Club. Before that, almost everything I'd done was to get a pat on the back. I still had no clear-cut vision of what I was or wanted to be.

I wasn't a director. I had never thought of being one, and yet I seemed driven to absorb the whole world with a director's eye. I began to be aware of my own taste, to appreciate the furnishings of a room, or shape of a house, or the designing of a set. I was stimulated by the choice of one color over another for a costume, or the perfection of a prop, or the subtlety of lighting. I turned into a visual animal. I became acutely conscious of the way an actor stood, or moved, or stopped, or sat. I found structure in great sculpture, the "twist" of the skeleton. And I discovered art in sports. I felt actors should capture the relaxed anticipation of an outfielder: living anatomy in repose but with a promise of instant action.

CHAPTER
4

Returning to Princeton for my sophomore year seemed a burdensome duty. I had worked myself up into a magic spell and everything, including college, was an intrusion. I knew I must hide my feelings. Outwardly I became a wax figure of a typical Princeton undergraduate—bloated by gin and beer. I made a token appearance in enough classes to avoid expulsion and the loss of the Triangle Club.

My 1928 courses were ingeniously chosen to allow me as much time as possible in New York. Charlie would come down every weekend from Harvard and we all gathered at his grandfather's huge Park Avenue apartment.

Hank Fonda was now unsuccessfully making the rounds in New York, looking for a job.

But Windy also met us each weekend. How very different we were. Where I was enthusiastic, Windy was calm and cerebral; when I said, "Yes, Yes, Yes," he said, "I'll think it over." He was maddeningly organized, I wasn't. He was shortish, with straw hair combed back flat, with silver-rimmed spectacles. I was bulging, sprawling and unkempt.

Saturday nights at the Crane apartment would begin with Charlie mixing the University Players' Cocktail—lemon juice, egg whites and an almond syrup called orgeat, all to disguise the taste of bootleg gin. Three cocktail shakers of the stuff and off to pick up the girls from the company, then for the latest Broadway hit, and winding up at Harlem's Cotton Club where we could listen to Duke Ellington and Ethel Waters. And watch young luscious beauties like Lena Horne in the chorus.

Erik and I were finally working in earnest on *Zuyder Zee*, but when we finished he pointed out that I had written the funniest part, Dick, for myself:

Act 1: Dick: "I'm just a raspberry seed lodged in the wisdom tooth of time."

Act 2: Dick: "I'm just a rolling collar button under God's great bureau."

The yearly Triangle tour of major cities got under way during our Christmas vacation. It was adventurous at first. Whether it was Pittsburgh, St. Louis, Kansas City or Chicago, we were dragged out of our sleeping car berths by jovial alumni, driven in ornate limousines to the local Racquet, Athletic, or University Club. We were plied with beer, fine bootleg liquor and a bite of dinner before being driven to the theatre. Our performance was only slightly affected by our semicomatose condition. After that, it was into white gloves, white tie and tails, and off to a huge, decorated hotel ballroom or country club for a formal supper dance where we had our choice of the finest debutantes and booze available. The local hostess who drew the Triangle Club Show night for her daughter's debut was at least assured of a stag line of sixty eligible if wobbly college men.

Midterm examinations were worse than I expected. I stayed in college by the barest margin. But my low grades made me ineligible for the eating clubs. I knew I wouldn't be chosen by a good club anyway as I had made up my mind not to play up to the social boys. I had my own brand of snobbery. My friends had to be funny, talented, original and brilliant, and these types are scarce.

By the next weekend, Charlie had plans for the new theatre he wanted to build with money borrowed from Cape Cod bankers. He had chosen a great site at Old Silver Beach in West Falmouth. The structure was to be of wood and Celotex and annexed to an existing tearoom and bathing pavilion.

But there was something else on Charlie's mind. She was nineteen, from Virginia, and had been a guest actress in a Harvard production. Windy asked pointedly if she could act.

"She's a great actress! You'll see. Her name is Margaret Sullavan."

That semester I directed *Othello* for the Intime. I loved the play and worked hard, but successful as it was I decided that new plays were the life of our theatre. I decided never to direct a classic again. Directors tend to put themselves above the author when the author can't defend himself. They bend the play to make it fit their own fancy. "Let's not do *Julius Caesar* in Civil War costumes. Yale did it that way. Let's do ours pre-Columbian." I made the decision against classics at nineteen and I have never regretted it.

Summer finally came. Sophomore year was over. Charlie met me at Woods Hole station with the news that the theatre lacked a roof and seats, but would be ready in time.

"What are we opening with?"

"The most charming, magical little play, *The Devil in the Cheese* by Tom Cushing."

When someone calls a play "charming" or "magical," look out!

With one week to go, we had to rehearse this complicated magical play and also help finish building the theatre.

We learned one thing at rehearsals. The new Virginia girl, Margaret Sullavan, was all Charlie had promised. She had a pulsing and husky voice which could suddenly switch, in emotional moments, to a high choir boy soprano. Her beauty was not obvious or even standard. It showed as she tilted her head, as she walked, as she laughed, and she was breathtakingly beautiful as she ran. One of my girlfriends complained that I talked too much about Sullavan, and she was right. We were all in love with her.

Three days before the opening, Windy appeared and said rehearsals were over. We were all to go inside to finish the goddamn theatre. The wiring was askew. The grid system, a complicated series of ropes and pulleys, had not been installed. We scattered. I was hoisted sixty feet in the air in a boatswain's chair to attach pulleys.

We wielded hammers and pliers. After three sleepless days and nights, we were giddy, frantic and bleary-eyed. Windy saw this, and called off all work four hours before curtain time. We were to shower, come back refreshed and "give a great show."

If that first performance had a theme song, it would surely have been "Nobody Knows the Trouble I've Seen." God has graciously let me forget most of it, but the points I remember still haunt me. It was a symphony in descending discords. The scenery was skeletal, the costumes incomplete. No props were where they should have been. Oh, yes, there was one: the flying fish in a twenty-gallon can of seawater, a sea robin with such nasty fins that Fonda had to dump out the water onto the stage floor to get it out, thus flooding the stage and footlights.

The only bright, competent figure—the only ray of hope in all that despair—was radiant, little Margaret Sullavan, who was making her professional debut. For the rest of us it was total failure, black despair, the grotesque end of the University Players.

But the audience must have interpreted our Tragedy as Comedy because they howled, and the theatre was just as full the next night and it stayed that way for four years to come.

We turned the adjacent tearoom into an after-theatre nightspot. Fonda painted some Gauguinesque South Sea murals. Bernie Hanighen got us a dance band and all of us took turns as waiters and cooks. The menu was modest—coffee and melted cheese sandwiches.

Charlie felt entertainment might attract more customers and asked for volunteers. Fonda, to my horror, volunteered the two of us.

"But I've got a date tonight," I said, lying.

"You can be Huxley Hossefrosse from George Kelly's *The Torch Bearers* and I'll be Elmer, the idiot boy."

The idiot boy was an Omaha import—a boy who did moronic imitations of birds and fish. I called off my date, and we sketched it out quickly. I was to be head of a summer camp and Fonda, a camper. I took off my shoes and socks and rouged my nose; Fonda rolled up his pants and put on a boy's beach hat. After a fanfare from the band, I padded onstage.

I improvised in Huxley's flattest tones about my camp for boys "between the ages of fourteen" (a line borrowed from Robert Benchley). The audience laughed and I felt suddenly confident.

"And now, our littlest camper, Elmer."

A spotlight hit Fonda hiding his head under one arm. I pulled the shy thing on the floor.

"Elmer, imitate a little bird."

Elmer began to puff and snort, and with tremendous effort crossed his left forefinger with that of his right and wiggled the fingers. Then a quick return to shyness. "Now a big bird!" (crossed hands flapping). And finally, the fish—big and little—ending with the spectacular school of little fish (all fingers wriggling).

We were an immediate institution and had to vary the act. Sometimes I would lecture with Elmer annoying me until, with sudden inspiration, I would put a hundred-pound cake of ice in his hands, surprising him into silence. While I continued with my lecture, the ice melted down, wetting his pants. It was a great success and excused us from making melted cheese sandwiches.

In a company where there were no stars, Fonda shone. I fell under his influence—to like what he liked and hate a bit too. Since he resented all authority, I began to view Charlie and Windy as bosses. We were fellow rebels. I don't think I ever felt as close to anyone as I did to Fonda in those days. But we were never sentimental. We clowned all day for the girls and improvised our jokes in pantomime which we called "rackets." I found myself constantly trying to think of some "racket" that would make Fonda give out with that bloodcurdling laugh.

Meanwhile, there were constant requests for Fonda and Sullavan. I kept after Charlie to do something truly romantic with them. They were both "naturals"—consummate actors but with an animal attraction that was quite apparent. Although they pretended to despise each other offstage, they caught fire when the curtain went up.

Charlie, who was obviously in love with Peggy Sullavan, decided we would do *The Constant Nymph* by Margaret Kennedy. Hank would play Lewis Dodd, the young composer, and Peggy would play Tessa, the Cinderella of Sanger's Circus.

They had to sing a Lewis Dodd composition, "Ah, Say Not So, Another Love Will Find Thee." Even though Hank was able to sing on key, his voice was described as an on-key whine. Sullavan was so insecure musically that she never settled on any key. It didn't seem to matter. Everyone melted the moment they appeared. Watching Fonda and Sullavan as they sang their duet, I became aware that Fonda was falling in love with her. It was beautiful and yet painful to me.

My partner was gone. I'd brought it on myself by pushing them together. The "nightclub acts" were a thing of the past. Now he was off with her—out on the beach with sandwiches, cuing each other, working out scenes. They grew remote.

I began to examine my changing moods. Was I really an actor? Did I actually want to be one? I couldn't bear anyone telling me what to do, and at a hint of criticism of my acting I'd sulk for days. But it wasn't only my own acting that troubled me. I began to question everyone else's acting while onstage myself.

"What's she doing so far upstage? No one on the side can see her."

And then I'd be conscious of an appalling silence and the cast looking at me. Good God, I'd forgotten my line.

I left Falmouth that year without a partner, with seven black marks against me for seven forgotten lines, and most of all with a deep concern about myself. Was I going in the wrong direction? Was I just playing at theatre? Was I a goddamn dilettante?

Back in Princeton, for junior year, the new Triangle show Al Wade and I had written was called *The Golden Dog*. The tour was very much the same as the year before—beautiful girls and bad gin. But one of the young accordion players who was in a number called "Blue Hell" had an attractive personality and I asked him if he ever thought of becoming an actor. "Good God, no. I'm going to be an architect." He walked away as if I had slandered him. His name was James Stewart.

Since the theatre seemed to be rejecting me on all sides, I decided finally to try and learn something at college. Why not be a professional student and do research in a sequestered academic community? I seriously considered skipping next year's Triangle show. I'd hole up for the year and write a great thesis instead.

But evidently the Triangle Club wouldn't let me. I learned I had been elected the next year's president unanimously. The news made the front page of the *Daily Princetonian* and Mother planted a holly tree called President of the Triangle Club.

I was catapulted at once into being a "big man on campus." At first I felt raw pride—pride that I had become as important at Princeton as the captain of the football team or the editor of the paper.

But mine was a tortured and confused reaction. I knew I should have been jubilant, done handsprings in front of Nassau Hall. But instead, I went to my new single room and sat in the dark, put my face in my hands and wept.

What the hell was I weeping about? Was I afraid of being called conceited? Was I afraid of being conspicuous on a campus where I had moved about unnoticed for so long? Maybe it was the job itself. Could I go hacking out another of those mindless plots or scouring the campus to find a new composer? Is being president of Triangle worth all this? Of course it is.

I had to do something. Get to work, for instance. I made notes. I could have some fun—light some firecrackers—shake up the stuffy clubs with my show. All I needed was to be outwardly innocent. I knew what to do! I'd write something for that lanky, drawling sophomore, Jimmy Stewart.

When the spring grades were posted, I realized I would flunk out of Princeton unless I took a summer reading course and wrote three acceptable papers over the summer. There was nothing to do but postpone going to the Cape.

I spent a month in Shreveport force-feeding myself on Montaigne and Spenser. Finally, I talked myself into feeling that the company was dying without me and took the train.

When I arrived, Goury, one of the Russian students, met me in the truck.

"Company in bad shape. Big split. Windy go one way, Charlie go other."

It was true! Windy, with the backing of the eternal rebel, Fonda, wanted the company to be made up entirely of college students, while Charlie wanted a freer system, accepting outstanding talents as well. I was appalled. The split might destroy the company forever. I sought out Windy and appealed to him. "Of course," I said, "college students must receive preference, but suppose one of our rejects turns out to be a Charlie Chaplin or a Greta Garbo?"

This seemed to disconcert him and he said he'd think it over. Then I dashed to Charlie and told him I agreed with him totally, but he and Windy should discuss their differences. I brought them together and jumped in and talked so fast that they agreed to postpone any drastic action. Plainly they had been secretly hoping for a compromise all along.

Charlie turned to Windy. "To keep this from happening again, I think Josh should be a director too. With three of us we can't have even splits. What do you say, Windy?"

"I wish I'd thought of it. What do you say, Josh?"

I wasn't sure. "What will the company say? They'll hate me."

"We're not asking them, we're asking you," said Charlie.

"All right, but I'm going down to the beach. You tell 'em," I said, and left.

Most members took my appointment indifferently, but Fonda, who had been most partisan in the Charlie-Windy conflict, was bitter because he hadn't been consulted. When I next suggested we do our act together, he said, "You're too big for that now. You're one of the holy triumvirate."

On the other hand, Miss Frances was radiant about it. I had saved Charlie's company. She told me quite seriously that I could easily turn out to be a great diplomat. And an invitation to Juniper Point, the Charles R. Crane house, arrived one day.

One frequent guest there was Thomas Whittemore, a Harvard professor who advised the Cranes on archaeology and was a trusted mentor and friend. After seeing me play the Count in our production of Noel Coward's *The Marquise,* he told Miss Frances that I bore a striking resemblance to the young Stanislavsky, in voice, stature and carriage. She leaped at this remark as some kind of omen. "I felt that way when I saw him last year in *The Czarina!* Shouldn't he be the one to accompany Charlie next winter to study with Stanislavsky in Russia?"

Norman and Elizabeth Hapgood had become close friends with Stanislavsky during the American and French tours of the Moscow Art Theatre, and Elizabeth had become his English translator. She had obtained permission for Charlie and a companion student to go to Moscow and observe Stanislavsky's rehearsals.

Stanislavsky and me? The mere thought was indigestible.

Charlie had just graduated from Harvard and planned to leave for Europe and Russia in the early fall. The early fall! That made my heart stop. I was committed to the Triangle Club as president. I couldn't shirk that. Crushed, I told the Cranes I'd have to turn down the offer.

But Charlie didn't want to go without me, and so it was decided that he would wait for me in Europe until I had finished the Triangle tour in early January. Then we could go together to Moscow, if my parents agreed.

The trip would mean delaying my graduation until the following year. When I called Mother to explain, she was so shocked that she could make no sense of what I was asking. I asked to speak to Father:

"And, of course, Father, I'll have to use my money for senior year on this trip."

In his brisk military tone, he asked, "Son, is it more important to you than Princeton?"

"There's no comparison. Thousands can go to Princeton. Only one or two can study with Stanislavsky. I'll learn something others would give the world to know."

"I'll talk your mother into it. But she'll make you promise to finish Princeton."

"I promise."

He got her agreement, and I have always been grateful to both of them, though it took longer to get a Princeton degree than we expected.

CHAPTER

If I work well under disturbed conditions, as doctors tell me, I must have learned how that fall at Princeton. As president of the Triangle Club I charged about seeing writers, lyricists, musicians, scenic artists, choreographers. But when suddenly I stopped and seemed misty-eyed and vague, my head was not in the clouds: it was in Moscow.

I was to join Charlie in Berlin after I spent a couple of days in Paris, but he made me promise to get my visa for the Soviet Union before I left America, so we could move fast.

My show was called *The Tiger Smiles*, and the juvenile lead was written for James Stewart, with his droll Pennsylvania drawl in mind. He spoke in a stately pavane even then. He still felt he was an architect. This stage "monkey business" was just fun. But he was so good I knew deep down he loved acting but was too embarrassed to admit it.

The Tiger Smiles opened at the McCarter Theatre and was well received. Stewart was gangling and hilarious singing and dancing "On a

Sunday Evening," which I had written for him. He winced as he sang my corny rhymes. But they were nothing compared to the songs of his boyhood friend Dutch Campbell, which Jimmy, with a few drinks, still does: "Itsy and Boo-Boo," "Flamin' Mamie," "Fat Phoebe and Ruth."

The morning I was to leave, I opened the *Daily Princetonian*. "Logan Goes to Moscow Today" was the headline. On the little train, the man across the aisle nodded and smiled. I recognized him with a jolt. André Maurois, the famous Frenchman of letters who had been a visiting professor at Princeton that year. He told me how witty he found *The Tiger Smiles* and talked about my forthcoming trip.

"In Paris you must meet my friend Louis Jouvet." He wrote him a note. Although I took the card, I knew I would be too reticent to use it. What a start—an accolade from Maurois and a card to prove it!

I sailed on the *Majestic* the eleventh of January. The voyage was luxurious but endless, giving me a chance to anticipate the wickedness of Paris and Berlin. I was a bit more experienced since the Kitchenette Apartments but not much. I longed for some extension courses.

When I arrived at the Paris hotel, my eyes latched onto a poster for the Folies Bergere. I knew my mother or even Miss Frances would want me to see an opera or a concert on my first night. My twenty-two-year-old mind agreed with them but my twenty-two-year-old body decided to see the Folies Bergere!

That night I realized the lyrical beauty of sex, of physical love. The simple and powerful effect of nudity—yes, even the awesome holiness of it. What all those poor Methodists had been taught was ugly or obscene, I found, along with the audience, charming and tantalizing. And so that the evening would never end, I went to a boîte called the Scheherazade where I met a delicious girl who asked me to dance. We danced and danced until the club closed. I reluctantly took her home, only to discover that the evening was just beginning.

As a consequence, I had time only for a quick dash of culture—the touristic trot, I called it: opalescent Ste. Chapelle, with a half-hour jog through the Louvre and, of course, the opera because it was Russian and Feodor Chaliapin was singing *Boris Godunov*. He gave a wonderful performance, but the Russian language seemed so turgid I was frightened. Would I understand it or like the people who spoke it? Even Chaliapin's huge bass and rolling blue eyes were as remote to me as the story he told.

In Berlin, I was met at the station by Charlie. His first anxious question was had I got my visa. I tried to excuse myself, but he was furious.

"Your neglect means we'll have to spend at least three weeks waiting in Godless and garish Berlin." I was openly delighted, as I wanted to see Berlin, and behind his fury so did he.

The first night, Charlie and I put on white tie and tails, as was the custom in thirty-one, and started for Berlin's most elegant and notorious nightclub, the Eldorado. Inside, cavernous and dimly lit, each table had its own phone for making dates at other tables.

As soon as we were seated, a lithe young mädchen came over to us offering to dance. Charlie leaped up. I was left to watch the stage where a heavily made-up chanteuse with a jib sail nose was fluttering high notes and an ostrich fan. When she finished her number, the ghastly singer started across the dance floor in my direction. Onstage she had appeared to have a bluish pallor to her chest. As she came closer I realized it was painted calamine white to cover a shaved chest. To my horror, he leaned coyly across my table and, batting his beaded eyelashes, pinched my cheek as if I were a plump baby, saying, "Coochie, coochie, coo" and then sashayed on.

I was paralyzed. My mouth sagged open and I knew someone was writhing on the dance floor nearby. It was Charlie. He had seen it all and was in uncontrollable paroxysms of laughter.

After we both had a stiff drink, another young girl joined us. She had worked at the Eldorado for two years—ever since she was thirteen. She wanted me to go "upstairs." I was very tempted, but since she was fifteen and I was from Mansfield, I hesitated. But soon all four of us took the elevator. In our room my fifteen-year-old instructor completed, in a short time, all the courses I had missed in Paris. I decided we should never leave Berlin.

It was January 1931, and Hitler had just made his first speech. H. R. Knickerbocker, Berlin correspondent for the *New York Journal*, with whom we had become friends, warned us of the impending power of this odd little man. "Look closely at Berlin now. Study it. Tell about it to everyone you see. It will change for the worse."

Knickerbocker took us to a riverfront saloon. Along the huge carved bar leaned giant, muscled men, thick-necked, tattooed and often with shaved heads. The scrawny piano player at the open upright dangled a cigarette from the corner of his mouth. On the dance floor, tough men were locked in embrace, grinding their lower bodies into each other. It was a scene from George Grosz.

Yet Berlin had greatness too. The theatre to begin with: *Liliom* with rugged Franz Albers, with its spectacular backgrounds projected on a vast cyclorama.

An enthralling production of Ferdinand Bruckner's *Elizabeth von England*. In the climactic scene, the aged Elizabeth is choosing a gown from one of eight faceless, wooden mannequins. She wears an unbecoming shift and her own scraggly hair when Essex, her young and virile lover, bursts into the room with news from the war. Horrified, Elizabeth tries to hide her hideous self behind the mannequins. One by one, young Essex pushes them aside in an attempt to look her in the eyes. Finally, she is revealed to him—a pitiful-looking, shriveled old lady. He is unshaken. He declares again his everlasting love. It was a moment of terrible pain and beauty for me.

Knowing food was scarce in Moscow, we provisioned ourselves with cans of pork and beans, corned beef hash, macaroni and cheese, plus a small stove which burned white Sterno pellets that looked like long aspirin tablets. In the same Berlin department store, we bought American sailor pea jackets, heavy blue woolen sailor pants and turtleneck sweaters. Knick told us that the exchange rate was unrealistic in the Soviet Union and urged us to buy our rubles in Berlin and hide them in our long johns. My visa arrived and we took off.

Russian railroad tracks are set wider apart than others; so after Warsaw, at the Russian border, we changed trains. It was an endless trip, and the gloomy dining car we were in had no food. Somewhere we managed to get a few shots of vodka. The flat landscape was broken only by an endless flicking of telephone poles.

On arrival in Moscow, our Intourist guide, a short, stocky girl called Tarasova, bounced into our compartment. She had a beaming smile, high spirits, a drab uniform and even drabber skin coloring. She spoke an odd, potshot English.

Like a top sergeant, she commanded the porters to carry our luggage, while we looked around the station.

Under the huge steel arches of the railroad shed which sheltered them from rain and snow squatted hundreds of poor men, women and children trying to warm their hands over small fires burning in pierced iron cans. Their clothes were familiar to us from paintings and photographs: straggly fur caps, thick, homemade felt boots, or, failing boots, long foot bindings of cloth. Their faces were gray. It seemed to be an entire nation of people made not of flesh but of gristle.

The Soviet Union was in the midst of Stalin's first five-year plan, the one enforcing rapid industrialization and collectivized farms. Nothing else mattered—comfort, food or even life. Those who refused collectivization were either sent to Siberia or shot. We had been warned not to remark on what we saw, good or bad, and Tarasova marched past the silent mass of paupers, pretending they didn't exist.

Out in the snow-packed street she had lined up two small droshkies. Charlie and I let out whoops as the horses' sleighs took off, skidding wildly over the white and icy streets. We might have been moving through a ghost town, as there was no one on the streets and all the stores were boarded up. The Grand Hotel was not.

The odor of the lobby still lingers with me: a smell of heat, oil and fetid, stagnant air trapped in one place for months. There was no ventilation in any Russian building during the winter. The cracks around the windows were taped shut from October to the end of May. In the smelly hotel lobby stood two enormous stuffed bears bearing trays. Their fur was rat-chewed and dusty. I said to Charlie, "Bet you think those bears are stuffed. Well, they're not—they're just dead."

We faced a greater olfactory hurdle in the hall on the way to our room, passing what our noses told us was the community toilet, with its wastebasket full of used bits of newspaper. We soon learned to run past it holding our breath, but even then the acrid smell made our eyes smart. Using it was indescribable. It required an insecticide spray gun to clear away the hundreds of cockroaches and double-quick action before they returned.

Next day we headed for the Moscow Art Theatre to meet Stanislavsky's secretary, Tomanseva. She was a small, sharp-featured, black-haired woman in her fifties. Her English was excellent, her voice kind and friendly. She closed the door behind us, pulled a ceiling-high interior monk's cloth curtain across the wall and put a finger to her lips as she did so. The entire room was enclosed. It was like being in a loosely padded cell. As we began to talk, Tomanseva kept her voice low. In the USSR, she explained, one must always act as if being overheard. Innocent conversations could be dangerously misinterpreted. I felt my skin crawl.

We learned that Stanislavsky's office was an enclave in a theatre full of rival Soviets, that a Red director had been installed recently above him—a man Tomanseva obviously hated but even to us pretended to respect. Stanislavsky was still nominally one of the directors of the company and many of his productions remained in the repertory. But three years before he had suffered a heart attack, leaving him virtually bedridden. Now he devoted much of his attention to his Opera Studio and classes were held in his own house. Vladimir Nemirovich-Danchenko, his cofounder, was still very much active.

The company had had its first success in 1898 with Chekhov's *The Sea Gull*. Still working in Moscow when we arrived were the great actors, Olga Knipper (Chekhov's widow), Leonidev, Kachalov, Moskvin, among others.

Recently they had been under pressure to "Sovietize" their productions. Tomanseva felt that Stanislavsky's illness was a result of being forced to direct the company's first out-and-out propaganda play, Ivanov's *Armored Train 14–69*.

Tomanseva said Stanislavsky was rehearsing opera students and wanted us to attend rehearsals. But the arrangements would take a day or two. We were puzzled. By the lifting and lowering of her eyebrows she indicated Soviet formalities. We mustn't seem hurried. It might be misunderstood.

Each night before we went to the theatre, Tomanseva briefed us on the plot of the play we were going to see. That first night it was Beaumarchais' *The Marriage of Figaro*, directed by a Stanislavsky we never knew existed. The curtain rose on an astounding production. Such joyous, wildly colored madness. A crazy story done with such broad, bold playing that it was often a bit like dance. Every time the love-struck young page saw a pretty girl he would point his whole body like a bird dog and erotically purse his lips into a rigid pucker. This automatic lechery was repeated throughout the play. What we call a "running gag." The audience began to wait for it.

Neither Charlie nor I had been prepared for Stanislavsky's flair for farce and low comedy. How could Chekhov think that Stanislavsky robbed his plays of their comic elements?

Our first meeting was set for one o'clock. We arrived punctually at the large, classic stone house with its weathered, orange-colored stucco facade. An ancient retainer answered the door and led us up one flight of stairs.

Our first view of the vast ballroom revealed at one end four huge round white columns, suggestive of the country estate in *Eugene Onegin*. Stanislavsky sat on a Madame Recamier-type couch, resting his back on several large pillows, his feet stretched out on the couch and covered by a crocheted throw. A thick sheaf of scoring paper lay on his lap, and he held a pencil in one hand. His large head, light beige complexion and white hair were easily recognizable from photographs. His features were large, with black almost piercing eyes and thick, full lips. In proper costume, he could have been taken for Kublai Khan, president of France, or the chief of an Eskimo tribe.

He clasped our hands and welcomed us vigorously in French. He did not seem a sick man. He introduced us with lordly charm to twenty or so students of the Russian equivalent of our Juilliard School of Music. To our delight, they seemed thrilled to meet Americans. Then the great man seated us in two chairs very close to him. We were about to observe Stanislavsky at work. He had just begun to rehearse *Le Coq d'Or*, Rimsky-Korsakov's opera of a Far Eastern court. Tomanseva had told us that sometimes these rehearsals extended over a period of years. Charlie and I found the thought a luxury after our frenzied stock experience. We were invited to ask any questions during breaks and then Stanislavsky settled down to direct.

I had seen great people before—greatness is easy to recognize—but I was awestruck by the man directing from that couch. Having successfully turned myself from Southern softy to Hoosier to Princetonian, I immediately decided I would become a replica of Stanislavsky. I would copy his gestures and use them daily, absorb his thoughts and think them regularly until they were mine.

Stanislavsky was determined to achieve exact truth in opera, to break down its formalism, to make its scenes spontaneous and human. He therefore bypassed the prima donnas with their solidified ways, and worked with the young, malleable singing students. But even these he found he had to "police" to rid them of meaningless posturing and the beloved standby of the classic theatre, the so-called "pear-shaped tone," the aggressive consonants and hooted vowels, the even more pretentious "birds' wing gesture," the downstage posturing that had been drilled into them by singing and diction teachers.

Stanislavsky was authoritative and tenaciously insistent, brooking little argument. But even with the greatest director in the world, the students showed that they considered themselves graduate artists, with

blue ribbons and gold medals to prove it. There were whimpering complaints, plus a bit of trial balloon temperament. Fortunately for Russian
opera, Stanislavsky always won the arguments. When he sensed he was
about to lose a battle, he turned into Dr. Johnson, who, as the story
goes, if his pistol misfired, would hit you over the head with its butt. At
the end of a minor verbal soufflé, he would turn to us and hiss viciously
in French, "Singing teachers!" and roll his eyes to heaven.

A plumpish girl playing the princess began the lovely aria with
which she eventually seduces the king. She began to plod slowly toward the throne. Stanislavsky called out to her to get down on all fours
and to move sinuously, like a cat. She refused, shocked at the suggestion. She couldn't make a good tone that way. He commanded her to
crawl while singing the aria perfectly. She threw up her hands. It was
impossible; it was indecent; it broke all the rules of singing.
Stanislavsky almost snarled: "Those rules are ridiculous! Just sing!"
And because he was Stanislavsky, and only for that reason, she did as
she was told. Perhaps it was anger's adrenalin that accomplished it, but
a beautiful tone plus a properly seductive attitude was produced. We
all applauded.

No matter whether they are lying down, standing on their heads,
fencing, descending a staircase, dancing, or physically fighting, he explained to us later, singers can sing and sing well. He had proved it in
performance time and time again. Beautiful tones do not ring forth
only from bodies in formalized attitudes. The girl on the floor was singing away happily now, and crawling like a cat. She and all about her,
for the moment at least, were converts.

As I watched the rehearsals day after day, I was intrigued especially
with Stanislavsky's use of all the musical detail in the orchestration:
the score outside of the actual singing. How he fused it to the thoughts
and emotions of the character. Most opera directors today let the actors
wait about in limbo till that music is over; the actions of these performers are therefore vague and shoddy. But Stanislavsky sought total
integration of actor and music. No detail was blurred or left to accident. Every transition, even the tiniest change of purpose, was meticu-
lously worked over with the actor and the accompanist, and fitted to a
suitable chord or phrase of music. But in no way was this part of the
world of dance where large sound is often accompanied by large body
movement, gestures, whirls or leaps. Nor was it close to the world of
mime, which seems to demand sweeping gestures, exaggerated hand

clasps, drooping heads and shoulders. Stanislavsky's opera technique demanded that large sound be accompanied by small, almost invisible, movement or by none at all. He instructed his actors not to move to music but to think, feel and even live to music, and at the same time to allow music to dictate those feelings. Change in the music would command change in the emotional state of the performer—from anger to happiness, from passivity to resolve. He fought flamboyant meaningless gestures because he wanted everything concentrated on the inner private emotion of the character. The singer was to become so familiar with the notes or chords of each theme, so conditioned by thinking and feeling the character's progress and the parallel music, that a web of naturalness would be spun.

What I was witnessing was not the well-publicized Stanislavsky "method" whereby an actor actually "lives the scene" by forcing himself to recall in detail a similar emotional experience in real life—the method Stanislavsky had laid out in his two great books, *My Life in Art* and *An Actor Prepares.* What I was observing here was that dirty word "technique"—and a technique rigorously insisted upon by Stanislavsky. Yet to me and to Charles, as well as to all us University Players, the name Stanislavsky meant one thing: the Stanislavsky method. I finally worked up enough courage to talk to him about it.

"Back home they are planning a company," I said, "called the Group Theatre, and they expect to practice the Stanislavsky method. If an actor is required to feel sad because his wife in the play leaves him and if he can't seem to summon up any feeling of emotion, he makes himself recall something from his own personal memory, something else that made him sad. Perhaps he saw a child run over in the street. He concentrates almost self-hypnotically on his emotion at the street incident and soon he begins to feel so sad that he produces tears. Then he quickly transfers those tears to the memory of his dear departed wife in the play. When he does it well, he soon has the matinee audience sniffling along with him."

"Oh, I see. You've read my books. Well, that method can be helpful. It was very helpful during our beginnings as actors, when we were breaking away from the classic form. But theatre is an ever-moving, ever-growing art. We have extended ourselves past that. Now, that's for the bathroom."

"Bathroom, sir?" asked Charlie.

"Yes. My method is for the bathroom, the back porch, deep in the woods, where you can make all the resounding racket you want or all the mistakes you must make to find out what's good. There you can re-call memories to your heart's content. You can perfect something you've found by repeating it till it suits you. Then you can bring it full-blown to rehearsal without ever having to show your personal and embarrass-ing experiments. We never ask anyone to practice my method in public."

We were truly jolted. "You mean that, sir?" I said.

"Yes. It mustn't be an end in itself or it becomes self instead of art. Now we are always experimenting and changing. You should, too. Ev-eryone should. At the moment we are using this conditioned reflex to music, to broaden our experiments in acting and directing. You may ob-serve what we do as long as you keep in mind that we are different from you. We have different national goals, a different society. You like whiskey, we like vodka. You're only allowed to rehearse a play for four weeks; we sometimes take as long as three years. To be truly cre-ative you must find your own way, you *must not* follow some old Stanislavsky method. Create a method of your own! Make your own private traditions, and lest they grow stale, break them. Nail unimaginative singing and diction teachers behind oak doors. Cherish the fresh. Avoid the rigid, the formalized—yes, including that which you are learning from me now, if you are learning anything. Keep working on yourself to learn what is inside and whether it is good—and don't worship fame. Love the art in yourself rather than yourself in the art."

Day after day, I followed these rehearsals like a sniffing beagle never losing his scent. I was determined to discover his way of getting the musical effect he wanted. I am still discovering Stanislavsky. Today, when I prepare a musical sequence, I think of those white pillars, the uncovered parquet floors, the music students in their rough clothes sit-ting about on the floor, the lady accompanist who knew that every note she played could be inspiring an actor to find his way. I see the half-reclining Stanislavsky, as though painted by Michelangelo with the face of an enormous God and the eyes of the devil, exploring, delving, searching out everything meaningful, finding an emotional change and setting it along with the actor and musician so that it can be re-created instantaneously at the drop of a baton, for instance, and repeated year after year.

*   *   *

The house on Polk Street.

Joshua Logan's mother
(Susan McHenry Nabors),
at age sixteen,
Mansfield, Louisiana.

His father,
Joshua Lockwood Logan,
around 1908.

Josh and Mary Lee
in May fête on the grounds of
Mansfield Female College.

Joshua Logan, age four.

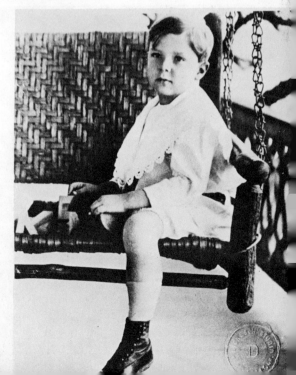

Colonel Howard Frank Noble.

A lieutenant at Culver
at eighteen.

When we saw the Stanislavsky opera production of Moussorgsky's *Boris Godunov*, we felt we had never seen opera before. Chaliapin's portrayal of Boris paled in comparison as I found myself under the spell of the performance of a young man I'd just seen working in rehearsals. There he had been rather nondescript with a daytime pallor. But that night, with elevated shoes that lifted him six inches, black-socketed eyes and a Mephistophelian wig, he was astonishingly effective as the hero-devil Boris.

One scene shall remain with me forever. Boris, crazed by an aggravated guilt, actually believes he sees the walking figure of the child, Dmitri, whom he has killed in order to seize the throne for himself. As the apparition of the child closes in on him, Boris lets out a gasp of terror to the exact beat of the music, leaps backward onto the canopied bed to appropriate chords, tears down the drapes in rhythm, still moving to the beat and still singing in full voice. He throws the drapes at the vision in vain, hoping to erase him, but cannot, and falls back screaming, rolling over on his side, cringing in terror to hide himself—always singing and acting. The music was truly wedded to the actor's feelings—and I was having the most exciting theatrical night of my life. I realized then what direction can accomplish.

We saw a charming production of *Princess Turandot* by Eugene Vakhtangov, a loyal follower of the Art Theatre, and Vsevolod Meyerhold's new, revolutionary production, *The Last Decision*, which had harsh lights flashing into the audience's eyes, cannons bursting and happy Soviet workers waving flags to surefire applause.

We met Meyerhold after the performance. He was a former pupil of Stanislavsky but lacked his Old World charm. He was a devoted Communist and seemed suspicious of us. Ironically, he and his wife would suffer a dreadful fate at the hands of his beloved Soviet government several years later.

Like all young people of that era, we considered ourselves liberal thinkers and had often wondered how susceptible we would be to Communism. Although we were both from conservative families, we were certainly interested in change, especially if it provided a better way of life. Here in Russia we tried to keep an open mind, but we began to feel threatened very early on, starting with our teatime talk with Stanislavsky.

Stanislavsky was worried about his old cook-housekeeper. She had given up the chance of another job to care for Stanislavsky and his wife and to allow them to share her food rations—two loaves of bread a week. As an artist, Stanislavsky was entitled to less rations than she was as a worker. The architect of a building got less of a ration than one of his bricklayers.

From the moment we crossed the border I had begun to feel a sense of suffocation. It was the feeling of being watched and having our rooms searched and not being allowed to take one snapshot. I suddenly had a desire to run. I wanted to get out, and now. But Charlie said I was foolish. Why leave before we saw everything we came to see? I agreed in order to make him happy, but I still felt imprisoned.

Meanwhile, we had become minor celebrities. One night, after seeing a Moscow Art production, Charlie and I went backstage to visit members of the cast, who had asked to meet us. Tomanseva acted as hostess and interpreter. I noticed a short, roundish man with a white beard watching me. When I turned to him he smiled and walked over. In halting English he said, "I know that you are observing Stanislavsky's rehearsals every day, but I think you should know me also."

Puzzled and somewhat embarrassed, I asked his name.

"I am Nemirovich-Danchenko."

I clasped his hands and poured out the most profuse apologies. This man had been as instrumental as Stanislavsky in the creation of the Art Theatre. He had introduced Chekhov to the company. We had seen his spectacular and shattering staging of *Resurrection*. In Moscow, today, there are two streets close together—Nemirovich-Danchenko Street and Stanislavsky Street.

The Russian play that stirred me in a deep, atavistic way was Chekhov's *The Cherry Orchard*. It had opened in this same theatre in 1904. In 1931, I was seeing it with a major part of the original cast, including Olga Knipper. I took for granted that the play would be familiar as I had seen it in New York. I scarcely recognized it. The ladylike translations of Chekhov's works which I had read or seen had never captured his humor. But here in the original production was the broad, almost pratfall comedy that Chekhov liked. It was integral to his showing the painful absurdity of life. During the fourth act, with the great house lost and the old cherry trees falling to the axes, Epihodov hammered away at a crate clumsily, missing the nail repeatedly and hitting his knuckles instead. The audience howled. It was never subtle: it was low, Mack Sennett humor, most welcome and most touching.

But there was something else about the play that stirred me—the omnipotence of the servants, always dominating their masters, even treating them like children. In this play, the lowly coped with life while the aristocrats let it slip through their fingers.

We found that art was a welcome pastime of the Soviet populace. It was in the theatre or a museum that people gathered, as though in clubs, since there were no bars, no nightclubs. The theatre was the only place accessible to all and it was a happy place. That strange, cumbersome government had learned what we here in America still don't know—that art is a powerful force. That art can be stronger than money or guns or treaties. Art is the personality of a country.

We paid a farewell visit to Stanislavsky and his dear little birdlike wife, Lilina, at chocolate candy and teatime. With warm personal feelings we sat together and took our parting hot glasses. Stanislavsky presented us each with a portrait photograph of himself. On mine he had inscribed in French what he knew was my favorite quotation: "To Joshua Logan—*Aimez l'art en vous meme et non pas vous meme en l'art.*"

The next morning we headed south by train, planning to take a boat across the Black Sea to Constantinople, where we would join Charlie's mother—now divorced from Jan Masaryk—and his two brothers for a short trip to the Middle East.

At Batum, on the Black Sea, our last Russian city, we squandered our remaining rubles on jewelry, gold cloth (for costumes for the University Players) and icons, none of which interested the customs officials as we boarded the small French paquet line freighter that would take us from port to port until we reached Constantinople.

After settling in our cabin, we went back on deck to watch the ship pull away from the dock. Like lunatics, we whooped and yelled. There is no single pleasure in life, I decided at that moment, that compares with the utter joy of leaving the Soviet Union.

But that night I woke up suddenly in my cabin and looked around me. As my eyes rested on the half-emptied suitcase, an emotional reaction set in. I was leaving this high peak of my life and sliding reluctantly back to normality. I saw Stanislavsky's photograph poking out among the papers.

"Aimez l'art en vous meme et non pas vous meme en l'art."

Back home, art was a fancy word. I didn't know much about art in the cities, but in the dust bowl if a man was called artistic, it was almost always said with a leer. "Oh, these artists, there's nothing they won't do."

How dare my country look down on art? I thought. It was very upsetting. I had seen great art in Moscow. I had felt its force affect me personally. Art is virile, tough, lean and muscular, soft and infinitely beautiful all at the same time. I had fathomed the Russian mind through art—its humor, its eccentricities, its lyric beauty, its vulgarity. I hadn't learned much of its language but I had absorbed this country and its people mainly through its art. Of course, I thought smugly, I must have a bit of art in me to take it all in!

That night I knew what I must do for the rest of my life. I must love the art in myself. I must work for it to grow, but above all, I must care for it so that it becomes a part of the powerful art of the world.

CHAPTER

I was on the Grand Canal in Venice, reading my mail. From the *Daily Princetonian,* the results of the senior voting for class favorites.

"Most likely to succeed." Leonard Firestone, '31. But of course. His father's the tire king.

"Best all around athlete." Trix Bennett, '31. Naturally!

"Wittiest." Who? Who? Logan, Joshua, '31.

Next category: "*Thinks* he's the wittiest." And I won that too. Damn. Plus "Most original," along with "*Thinks* he's most original." Oh, hell. I didn't mind. It was perhaps the last accolade that Princeton would probably ever give me. It might as well have flair.

I opened another letter and a check for fifty dollars fluttered out. A short story I had written for a course assigned last fall at Princeton had won the Jesse Lynch Williams Prize. I was so excited that I immediately splurged all of it on some beautiful Venetian glass figurines for Mother.

Venice had been a side trip I had made alone after the trip through the Near East. Now it was time for Falmouth and the summer season.

While we were in Russia, Windy had been stage manager for the Theatre Guild. Margaret Sullavan had caused a sensation on Broadway in a third-rate play entitled *A Modern Virgin,* but she had still arranged to take the two months off for our summer season. My sister, Mary Lee, announced she had joined the company. She began as a box office underling and with her fresh beauty and entertaining ways she soon became very popular. She even scored a success, to my surprise, with sophisticated Miss Frances.

The season really started when Sullavan arrived for *Coquette.* Since this play was set in the South, I was assigned to direct it. Sullavan was at her best as the impulsive Norma Besant, a young female animal always on the brink of tears or laughter. Fonda played Michael, her lover, and projected an intensity and masculinity that galvanized the romance. And there was a Cracker Jack-box surprise: my irrepressible sister, Mary Lee. She gave an extremely funny and endearing performance as Norma's squeaky-voiced friend, Betty Lou. Charlie thought she was entrancing. But she immediately holed in with the box office staff and was mostly seen with Tom Smith, a Harvard business student.

During rehearsals I was as fascinated with myself as I was with the cast. I was caught up by the poetically tragic quality of the star-crossed lovers and directed their scenes as if I were Nemirovich-Danchenko working on *Resurrection.* At first, the actors were suspicious, then astonished at my new-found intensity. To my surprise, for the first time ever, they welcomed my help. And I thoroughly enjoyed my role as director. My Moscow experience had borne fruit, at least for *Coquette.*

Windy, Charlie and I talked constantly about a permanent company: *our* Moscow Art Theatre. But we were nervous. A similar purpose had been announced by the Group Theatre, a new and rival organization. They were summering in Connecticut, preparing Paul Green's *The House of Connelly.* And they seemed to have Broadway connections. But at least we felt superior to their claim that Stanislavsky was their mentor. None of them really knew him personally. Besides, our actors were equal to any of theirs: Fonda, Sullavan, Kent Smith, Elizabeth Fenner, Myron McCormick. And Windy was a solidly grounded director. (Deep down, I hoped someday I could be as good or better.) All we needed was a place to try our Art Theatre wings before we swooped down on New York.

It was the sister of our costume designer, our true witch, Joy Higgins, with her parchment face of ancient Ireland, who told us she heard voices calling us to Baltimore. She had worked there with an amateur group, The Vagabonds. With eyebrows arching in rhythm, she told us how she knew the *socially* powerful. Through her, we were visited by the manager of the Maryland Theatre, who saw us perform and then offered the theatre to us. It was settled quickly: Baltimore would have the honor of presenting us to the world that fall.

And a true art theatre we would be! A new play every night! We hurried to plan our repertory.

We got through that summer season at Falmouth well enough, even though our heads were in Baltimore. Between the two seasons, in order to save expenses and transportation, we decided to sleep on pallets in the tearoom and so rehearse our planned repertory of five plays without having to move anywhere. The crew used the stage and the workshop in the back for the huge task of building four complete sets of scenery. We set up mattresses around the dance floor for the girls, and in the foyer, separated by a decent doorway curtain, mattresses for the boys.

Our first week of repertory was set: the accursed *Devil in the Cheese,* which Charlie insisted upon for luck; next a mystery, *The Silent House* by John G. Brandon and George Pickett; then *Hell-Bent Fer Heaven* by Hatcher Hughes; *Mr. Pim Passes By* by A. A. Milne; and finally, *The Constant Nymph* by Margaret Kennedy and Basil Dean. To replace Sullavan, who had returned to Broadway, we hired Merna Pace, and for more heroic roles, a lovely actress who had been recommended by George Pierce Baker of Yale, Barbara O'Neil.

We loaded the train, climbed in and with uncontrollable yelping enthusiasm set off for Baltimore. As soon as we dropped our bags at the Kernan Hotel, we rushed next door to see the Maryland Theatre. Our happiness was short-lived. The stagehands' union was picketing the theatre. They had insisted we carry a full crew of union men, but since we couldn't afford to pay union wages we had voted to go openly nonunion.

In this moment of crisis, a mass war cry arose from all of us, and we marched through the picket line into the theatre like a noble Soviet poster, only to find that the union flymen had snarled the stage ropes until the fly gallery looked like huge black spaghetti. We worked all Saturday night and Sunday straightening the ropes, cleaning up, and unpacking the productions. The pickets kept marching.

On November 10, 1931, we opened before a distinguished Baltimore audience with our least distinguished play, _The Devil in the Cheese_. To Charlie's delight, it went well and received good notices. The next night we changed productions and shifted to our thriller, _The Silent House_. Again, the notices were good and it was only Wednesday. That night we performed _Hell-Bent Fer Heaven_. I had a good part in it—a Southern mountain boy. I thickened and flattened my Louisiana accent and in a flagrant attempt to look as handsome as Fonda, I utilized all the makeup secrets of the Russians, including a Greek god putty nose. The next morning one reviewer wrote: "Mr. Logan, who started out well, soon allowed his enthusiasm to get the better of his self-control." The history of my life.

We had a repertory theatre but unfortunately we didn't have an audience. The Baltimore theatre audiences would come to see one play only to find another one playing. It was too confusing. Russian audiences, European audiences, were used to such programming, but repertory simply drove Baltimore audiences wild. They couldn't understand all the shifting of plays. Since they didn't know exactly when to show up, they didn't show up. But we were unshakable. We swore to educate them whether it confused them or not! So we went doggedly on with our repertory program, ignoring the constantly decreasing attendance. The only sure line at the box office was the union picket line.

In the nick of time, Sullavan's play closed on Broadway and she rejoined our company. The manager of the theatre used this opportunity to demand that we change our policy to stock, which meant running a play a whole week. We had to give in. We became a stock company overnight.

The Constant Nymph was our first full week. Slowly, the audiences began to catch on. The turning point came when we received rave reviews for _Death Takes a Holiday_ by Walter Ferris, starring Sullavan and Kent Smith, and at the same time cut our prices to fifty cents for matinees and a dollar for evening performances. It was resurrection day! Ticket buyers appeared from holes, from cellars. We had the thrill of "selling out" for the first time. And Smith, Fonda and Sullavan became Baltimore stars. Crowds waited in the alleyways for autographs, newspapers carried feature stories about their romantic lives. Those rhapsodic reporters were never to be allowed on the top floor of the Kernan Hotel where we each had a rather shabby room for a dollar a day. And no one saw our marble-lined, once grand, dining room in which Marie, our cook, had set up a soup kitchen.

It was through a newspaper item that we first learned that Fonda and Sullavan had applied for a marriage license. And Sullavan even denied it at first. But on Christmas Day at eleven in the morning, the company gathered in that large, dreary dining room and witnessed the marriage performed by Horace Donegan, an Episcopal rector of Christ Church and an old classmate of Charlie's. After the ceremony, Windy played the love duet from *The Constant Nymph*, and Peggy and Hank managed a few strident phrases. We all choked up. We had to. We were their family.

That day there was a matinee of *The Ghost Train* by Arnold Ridley. Fonda played a bridegroom in it. The news of the wedding had spread via the lady ushers, so that when Fonda accidentally scattered rice by pulling a handkerchief from his pocket (part of the plot), the audience applauded, then everyone choked up again, especially the ushers.

Overnight we had vanished from the theatrical sections of the Baltimore press. Our place had been usurped by our arch rival—the Group Theatre—who had been forced by bad business to close its Broadway run of *The House of Connelly* and had decided to invade our territory. After all, their beautiful ingenue, Margaret Barker, was the daughter of a prominent Baltimore family. So all Baltimore would flock to her opening and the papers would continue to ignore us until the Group Theatre left town. It was disaster!

We held an emergency mass meeting. It was Charlie who came up with the great diversionary tactic. A few weeks back in Los Angeles, a bawdy version of Aristophanes' *Lysistrata* had been closed by the police and the cast forced to spend the night in jail. It had made front pages all over the country. Headlines, sex scandals, that's what we needed. Great shouts of agreement rang out, except from Sullavan and Fonda, who pretended to be horrified that the company would even consider doing a dirty play. Or was it that they wanted time for a honeymoon? At any rate, they took off in a borrowed car.

We had only four hysterical days to prepare and rehearse this monster of a play, which had a cast of over one hundred. We also had to build a towering production that should have taken weeks. Every amateur company, actor, model, debutante in town was recruited. Costumes were dyed in caldrons fit for *Macbeth*. Gilded papier-mâché shields and helmets were constructed; strong wooden swords were carved and then painted silver. Dance teachers from the Denis-Shawn troupe in Washington came over and staged the extensive bacchanal which would end the evening to a recording of Stravinsky's *Le Sacre du Printemps*.

On opening night a beautiful sign greeted our eyes in the lobby: Sold Out. Nine hundred seats plus eighty standees. And our triumph was complete when spies reported that the Group Theatre had an audience of less than two hundred. Suddenly the vengeful turned to the magnanimous. We decided we should really be grateful to the poor old Group Theatre. Had they not come to Baltimore we never would have been spurred to reach such magnificent heights. That whole week was sold out and we extended the run for another week. We didn't walk, we strutted around town.

The honeymoon car Peggy and Hank had borrowed broke down before they reached Washington. They began to feel so lonely for the company, they turned back. We welcomed them with much hugging and kissing and then practically locked them in a room in the Kernan. They remained there for days incommunicado except for messages which appeared from under the door rebuking us for the smut we were selling the Baltimore public.

The demand for tickets was so great we had to play *Lysistrata* a third week, so we moved it to the Auditorium Theatre nearby. At the Maryland we continued our season with James M. Barrie's *Mary Rose*.

I directed Fonda and Sullavan in this delicate play of a young girl caught between reality and a strange world beyond that.

During the dress rehearsal, I was engrossed in fitting some ethereal music into a scene. I was so full of myself, I scarcely heard Sullavan shouting in a querulous voice.

"What did you say, Peggy?"

"Do you expect me to play this scene in this horrible set?"

Norris Houghton, the designer of the production, had planted real birch trees and berry bushes in a wood base. I thought it made a natural and appropriate effect. But something was upsetting Sullavan which even she didn't understand. Feeling panicked, she had arbitrarily picked on the set.

Charlie and Hank had made me aware of her tantrums, but this was the first time that one was aimed at me. I didn't know what to do. I only knew what Stanislavsky would do—be very, very strong. I heard myself saying, "If you don't like the set, why don't you go home? Just pack your bags and leave Baltimore. We can't change the set, but we can change you. Merna can learn your part overnight." I was trembling inside. I had never spoken to her or anyone else like that before and, to be honest, I was talking nonsense. She was irreplaceable. But I needn't have worried. Just as abruptly as the tantrum began, it ended. I will never know why. She turned away and continued the scene as if there had never been a break.

We in the theatre work with a harnessed yet dangerous fury that can easily break its bounds. Something deep inside me understood this. I found my anger at Peggy Sullavan turning into sympathy. I didn't try to analyze it. It was just there.

Mary Rose was a real achievement. I have seldom seen anything better. Peggy and Hank were unsurpassable and again there were standees the entire week. Baltimore loved us more than ever.

My direction and handling of Peggy Sullavan had given me an underground reputation for strength which I really didn't feel I had. I could withdraw now and settle back into playing small parts or, in other words, fade into the background. It would have been more peaceful, less chancy. But it was not to be.

Our next play was S. N. Behrman's *The Second Man* and our four big guns were cast in it under Windust's direction: Kent Smith, Elizabeth Fenner, Fonda and Sullavan. It was a *class* production— University Players style.

Early in the morning, Charlie woke me with a call. "Get over to the rehearsal room. Windy is very sick with TB and will be in the hospital for an indefinite period." When I arrived, Hall Basset, the stage manager, handed me a script. Charlie said, "You've got to take over right now." I had never seen the play or read it. I protested to Charlie that I couldn't start directing a play I didn't know. The cast wouldn't believe in me.

"Just do the best you can. They know as well as we do that we've got to have a show next week."

Perhaps being honest was not the way to start. I said I didn't know anything about this play. The cast said nothing. They only looked unhappy, which in the theatre generally means afraid. Charlie urged them to be patient with me and left for the office. I tried to follow the moves which accompanied the printed script—the one used by the original New York company. I had no ideas of my own. I just read from the script. "Hank, move to behind the sofa," "Peggy, sit on chair stage left," and so forth.

Finally, Hank protested. Actors shouldn't be made to move when the director doesn't know why.

"That's not fair, Hank," I said. "Let's just blunder through the business indicated in the script today, and after I've read the play tonight I can make some sense." With a lot of foot-dragging, they moved through the play, followed the printed directions and took a few of my tentatively offered suggestions. Every now and then I caught an exchange of dark looks among them.

I was about to dismiss them when Fonda said quietly, "Just a minute. I don't think anyone should leave until Charlie gets here. We've sent for him." A stern Charlie came in and Fonda rose in a formal manner. "This is a protest and I am speaking for all of us." As he spoke, he avoided looking at me. "We want you to send to New York for a decent director. If Windy is sick, we've got to have someone who can direct the whole company. Josh isn't experienced enough for that. It's all right for him to direct a single play once in a while, but not our entire season. To put it bluntly, we won't work with him."

I urged the cast to reserve its decision and give me the chance to work on the play that night. If my work was still unacceptable tomorrow, then they could do what they liked. Betty Fenner and Kent agreed and Charlie showed a fixed stubbornness. He said, "Come hell or high water, I'm not sending to New York for anyone. It would disrupt our whole company. Josh can handle this and so can you if you try. If at the end of the week it isn't working out, we'll talk about other arrangements."

Throughout that week I felt a strong urge just to get on a train and disappear. I would never direct like Windy. I couldn't. I would never give an actor a definite reason I didn't believe, but Windy could—and immediately and convincingly—to maintain authority and keep rehearsals moving along. And I was never afraid to say, "I don't know," and "What do you think?" which I knew Windy would never do.

I urged the actors to let their imaginations go to work and I'd stand by ready to edit. The cast slowly began to thaw. They liked the freedom and the confidence. I found I had acquired some authority. The next two plays were easier.

For *The Trial of Mary Dugan* by Bayard Veiller, I was to deal with a new company member, a magnificent actress Fonda and Smith had met in a children's theatre. Her name was Mildred Natwick. It was her first appearance and Margaret Sullavan's last with the company. We were still great box office attractions but a feeling of decline was in the air.

Our next play fell during Lent. The theatre manager urged us to do a religious drama showing the last days in the life of Christ, *The Dark Hours* by Don Marquis (yes, the author of *archie and mehitabel*). On hearing this, I thanked God Windy had recovered sufficiently to direct it. The dye vats were out again as it was another backbreaking spectacle requiring dozens of Baltimore amateurs, debutantes and volunteers weaving around and about Norris Houghton's dramatic circular setting. Fonda was St. Peter, and since he had to appear only once and in profile, he removed the makeup from the upstage side of his face. I suspect it was his last burst of comic defiance at our coming catastrophe. His last "racket."

Even with costumes and makeup, we were surely the most unlikely group of Hebrews ever. The dominant accent of the crowd was cornpone Southern. The audience howled when they heard a voice from the crowd cry out, "He say-uv-ed othuhs, led Him say-uv Heumseyeff."

Naturally, it was a financial disaster. Even the blind children to whom we offered free matinee seats never showed up. Before the winter was over our Baltimore venture received its death knell. There was nothing to do but repair to Falmouth, long before the summer colony would appear.

We had learned to live with each other. We had played for seventeen weeks. We should have felt better than we did.

To utilize the waiting time, we "landscaped" the outside of our theatre by transplanting small scraggly juniper trees from the nearby dunes to our lumpy brick terrace. It seemed skimpy to me. Why not try just digging up one big tree and giving the terrace some class? I recruited the whole company for the project. We cut a deep trench around the roots of the giant tree I had found. Without a single sprained back, we managed to sweat and groan it up planks and onto a truck and onto the terrace. With more sweat, cheers from me and much more grunting, the tree was lowered into place.

We drowned it in water daily, fed it everything, talked about nothing else. Feverish and dry, it hung on for two weeks, then curled its leaves and gave up. Not since Little Nell had there been such public bereavement. It became known as "Logan's Folly." Our costumer sprayed it with green paint, giving it a counterfeit semblance of life that lasted a full season. To me, it began to symbolize our company. It looked green and healthy but it was only pretending.

Fonda had never been the same Fonda after Baltimore. With a declaration of discontent at the way the University Players was being run, he left the company to find his way alone. He was a tremendous loss. He was the heart of the company. But I had been thinking of a possible replacement: lanky, drawling Jimmy Stewart, who was just now graduating from Princeton.

While casting for new people in New York, we became involved with a newly arrived producer, Arthur J. Beckhard. He had just produced and directed a great Broadway success, *Another Language* by Rose Franken, starring Dorothy Stickney. Ten years our senior, owlish, seemingly benign, with a soup-strainer black moustache and puckish ways, he convinced us to try out two or three plays for him the following summer. We were flattered; a real Broadway success was interested in collaborating with us. Before we knew it, he was swallowing our company.

Our opening bill in June 1932 was Booth Tarkington's satiric comedy of the South, *Magnolia,* with newcomer Jimmy Stewart howlingly funny in it as a lanky Southern slob. Later, in *It's a Wise Child* by Laurence E. Johnson, he proved to be a fine actor—honest and talented. Perhaps he could carry us all on his shoulders—as Fonda and Sullavan could have done.

But Beckhard's "participation" began in full force. He used our "facilities" to try out the road company of *Another Language* while we kept busy preparing the tryout of a new play that had been offered to him, *Goodbye Again,* by Allan Scott and George Haight. It was a comedy about a touring lecturer, and for the main role he imported from New York Howard Lindsay, a man who would later become both my mentor and trusted friend. The play was witty and amusing. For a short time we thought our Broadway connection would help our beloved company. We even began to dream of moving to New York and having a permanent repertoire.

But then came the ax blow: *Carry Nation* by Frank McGrath. Beckhard was passionately interested in this play which required fifty actors and an elaborate production. Beckhard felt it was the perfect vehicle for his wife, Esther Dale, a sweet woman and a successful concert lieder singer. When we worried about her lack of stage experience, he said she would have firm guidance from Blanche Yurka, the star turned director, who had just come in from New York. We delivered a formal protest against the entire venture, including the use of an outside director. He read our protest and cackled.

The play was a groaning bore at Old Silver Beach, although Esther was, for a nonactress, quite good. But Beckhard, who had demanded fifty-fifty control, insisted the play be revamped for the second week of our upcoming Baltimore fall season. When we objected, he coolly informed us he was taking the play directly to New York from Baltimore with most of our actors, and we could all come with him or stay in the sticks forever. It was checkmate. We were financially and emotionally busted. Our only hope was that New York might look past the play and see the actors.

Carry Nation opened at the Biltmore Theatre on October 29, 1932, starring Esther Dale. Among the supporting actors making their Broadway debuts were James Stewart, Myron McCormick, Mildred Natwick, Barbara O'Neil and Joshua Logan.

The reviews were deservedly lugubrious. I remember reading them in the flickering light of a subway car, crumbling them into the corner before getting off.

It was the end of our company. I was more than saddened—I was furious—with me, with us. My great expectations, my vision of theatrical exploration, had been stolen from me—from us—and with our eyes wide open. Now I was just an out-of-work actor—a predicament we all shared, including Fonda and Sullavan. We had nothing left but our insignificant names: Mildred Natwick, Joshua Logan, Myron McCormick, Bretaigne Windust, James Stewart, Cynthia Rogers, Kent Smith, Barbara O'Neil, Norris Houghton and Charles Leatherbee.

Beckhard was a bit guilty. Besides he needed additional theatre people in his office who would work cheaply. His staff consisted of an accountant, young Kermit Bloomgarden, Victor Samrock at the switchboard, and, as publicity manager, George Haight, coauthor of *Goodbye Again*.

I forced myself to work as casting director for fifteen dollars a week, though I never managed to keep the money since Beckhard was always short of cab fare. He would giggle each night as he borrowed it from me. I was too embarrassed, too angry and too afraid I might lose my job to ask for it back. Jobs were nonexistent during those Depression days. And besides, Beckhard had come up with a larcenous brain wave. He would use Windy and me as what he euphemistically termed "white bodies." Since he was in great demand as a director, he would contract to direct more than one play at a time, and then pop in after we had done the actual work and make a suggestion or two. He took full credit for the first play, *Goodbye Again,* although Windy had done the directorial work in Falmouth and in New York.

It opened to hit business, and I suppose we were lucky to be in it. Again to save Beckhard money, I was given two jobs in this production: as company manager (working at night) I received twenty-five dollars a week, and as assistant box office man (working all day) I received another twenty-five dollars. Two men would have cost twice that. And, as usual, half of my salary found its way back into Arthur J.'s pocket for the everlasting taxi, when I wasn't lucky enough to see him coming.

With Jimmy now making thirty-five dollars and Myron thirty dollars, we took a small, smelly apartment on West Sixty-third Street just off Central Park West. It consisted of a soot-colored bedroom with twin beds, a living room with two sprung studio couches, a bathroom with a mildewed shower, and a huge kitchen stove out in the hall.

Although we needed additional money from a fourth person, we invited unemployed and totally broke Fonda to move in. He and Sullavan had agreed to part without bitterness. It was inevitable. Her career was streaking across the sky. Fonda had been living on a box of rice for the past three weeks. In accepting our invitation, he vowed he would share in the expenses just as soon as he got a job.

"The elevator man told me 'Legs' Diamond lives two doors down the street," Stewart announced the day we moved in.

"Oh, yeah, this whole street's full of gangsters, whores and pimps," was Fonda's reply.

I tried to defend our new home. "There's a nice clean YMCA across the street with a free gym. We could get in shape and fight 'em all off."

McCormick sniffed the air and winced.

The stench in the bathroom was from a mildewed rubber shower curtain, but we didn't dare take it down for fear of being evicted. So there it hung, at least keeping the bathroom mainly available. We took turns cooking—mostly bacon and eggs, except for Fonda, who in addition to his other accomplishments was a great cook.

We cheered when finally he got a job as leading man with a stock company in Jersey City. He proudly announced he was to receive "ten percent of the gross." We were flabbergasted. Only the biggest stars— the Lunts, Ethel Barrymore or Katharine Cornell—rated ten percent. That could amount to three or four thousand dollars a week.

"Well, I guess we're in clover," Fonda stated matter-of-factly. But the admission was so low and the attendance so poor that the most he ever pocketed any week was seven dollars. Suddenly I was furious. This fine actor who had great talent, youth, a handsome and expressive face, an outstanding range, a lean, muscular body—all the ingredients for a successful leading man—had never even been noticed by a Broadway producer or director, although he made the rounds dutifully and daily.

Our friendship had drifted back into shape, of course, but I was still deeply envious of him. Anything he touched, he mastered: acting, carpentry, painting and now cooking. Lithe as a tiger, he could turn on that young, innocent *Merton of the Movies* look and melt everything in sight. And to give the knife in my side an extra twist, I soon learned he was also a born acrobat. He could actually walk on his hands. That was really too much. Since childhood, my greatest passion was to walk on my hands, but I was always too heavy, too weak, too chicken or too something.

Over at the Y, my blood drained as I watched Hank bend palms flat on the floor and push his feet into the air, then without strain pad around on his palms, legs either bent or stretched straight. I got into such a fever of envy that I pointed to a thick two-story rope suspended from the gymnasium ceiling, and with sudden bravado asked if he would like to see me climb it. I can still hear the Omaha corroding sarcasm of his reply. "I *certainly* would." It sent angry juices gushing through my veins, which must have also given me a flash of superhuman strength because I marched over to the rope and climbed it smoothly, hand over hand, to the very top. Unfortunately, once I got there, my chronic vertigo got the better of my false courage and I felt the strength draining from my hands. In terror, I managed to inch myself jerkily down, desperately maintaining my grasp to avoid crashing at his feet.

When I finally got down, I said, "Well, did you see me go up?" He shrugged and answered casually, "I didn't think you could do it," and then walked away.

The next day, I went back by myself, clasped the rope and started to pull, straining with everything I had in me—but not one inch of me got off the ground, then or since!

Stewart was the opposite of Fonda. He had had the least experience but the shortest wait for success. Day after day he would come home with a new script and a new offer. The theatre was fast becoming the sole ambition of his life. McCormick, too, was having little trouble finding jobs. Only gifted Fonda, with five years of playing leads in our company, remained unnoticed. The fine young firebrand of Baltimore had almost lost his flame.

About this time, Charlie and Mary Lee announced their engagement. It came as a complete surprise to me. Here was my closest friend and my sister, and I hadn't realized they cared about each other. They had been nervous as to what my reaction would be. What would I say? I did find myself subconsciously hesitant about it. Still, they seemed to love each other and I was confident Charlie would eventually become an important producer. I decided to concentrate on that and bury my feelings that there was something hurried and even a bit forced about their decision.

Miss Frances was delighted. She loved Mary Lee's drive and independence, which she felt the family needed, her capacity for fun and her scrupulous honesty. These were important qualities for her son's wife to have. Although she always professed that her son was perfect, it was almost as though subconsciously she counted on Mary Lee to strengthen that perfection.

The wedding took place in the fashionable and beautiful St. Thomas Church on Fifth Avenue. Although Mother had been ill for a long time with a lingering bronchial condition, she summoned enough strength for the trip to New York with her Colonel Noble, who appeared in good shape physically, if not financially. I'm sure they stretched themselves to the breaking point to make the wedding appropriately elaborate. There was nothing else to do—not if you're Southern.

After the frantic rush of the engagement and marriage and leave-taking, I stood all day at my job in the box office of *Goodbye Again,* trying to sort out my real feelings. They were both so headstrong—she so pell-mell and he so set—there were bound to be collisions. I could only hope their sense of humor and intelligence would overcome the rest.

After *Goodbye Again* closed, my turn as a "white body" came up with a play by Elsie Schauffler entitled *Peep Show.* Peggy Fears, the singer, was the producer. When I arrived for work, Peggy informed me that the plans were changed. Her fortuneteller had told her the night before, "Only in London will you have a hit." No sooner said than half the cast was fired and the scenery, Dorothy Hall, the star and I were on the way across the ocean. The play opened at the Globe Theatre under the title *The Day I Forgot* and closed the next day.

Pleading telegrams to Beckhard brought no response, so I cabled my mother for the money to come home, and got it.

Mary Lee and Charlie met me at the dock with news that Father had suffered a heart attack. They skipped over any questions about their honeymoon, which naturally stirred up my old apprehensions. Charlie had grown a bushy moustache at Mary Lee's insistence. She thought it gave him a more mature and sophisticated look. And Charlie was now able to play bridge and loved it. She had wanted to vary their social life with the aid of some of her friends from Wells instead of relying on the endless stream of theatrical people. It seemed unlike Charlie to agree to this, but he had.

Charlie planned to reorganize the University Players, if he could make it work. He planned to get the financing himself, as he had no faith in Beckhard.

At dinner one night, I foolishly told Beckhard of our plans to revive the company. "I'd like to see that," he cackled, and pulled his moustache. "I'd be willing to work with you."

"That would be great," I said, without too much enthusiasm.

"There'd only be one condition. I don't think Charlie Leatherbee is worth his salt. I'd have to take over his spot."

Enraged, I sprang to my feet. I couldn't talk, so I turned and left the apartment. I never spoke to him or saw him again. I knew I had no respect for Beckhard, but I wondered at my anger. Why was it so intense? Why couldn't I accept his remark as the rude and asinine comment it was and pass it off? We all held him responsible for the destruction of the University Players. But with our eyes open, we had let him destroy us.

Slowly, I began to acknowledge the responsive chord he had struck that night. Charlie was a determined idealist. Even on New York streets he seemed to be traveling the "golden road to Samarkand." I, too, must have often questioned whether he had enough of a practical business sense to sustain his visions. Beckhard had crudely put my own fears about Charlie into words. And if Mary Lee had heard Beckhard she would probably have reacted even more violently than I did. What a strange revelation that silly man's statement had produced. And yet deep down I know I still believed in Charlie's taste and producing talent—no matter what anyone said.

I was back living on Sixty-third Street with Stewart, McCormick and Fonda. We drank, laughed, listened to good jazz, rotated our sleeping arrangements so as to leave the living room couches to those who had dates.

Then came a blow, the effects of which I wouldn't realize for years to come. Father died. Mother begged us not to come south as we were both working and she was hysterically worried about money. Mary Lee and I sent a telegram to Mother: "Think of fields of daisies." The funeral was scarcely over when we learned that Mother had worked herself up into a frenzy to get out of Louisiana. She claimed to resent bitterly the way some of the family had neglected Colonel Noble and herself since their move to Shreveport. I have always doubted whether this was true. Above all, she said she didn't want ten-year-old Marshall to continue schooling in that benighted place.

Without consulting me, Mary Lee pleaded with her on the phone to come to New York where she could afford to live if we all pooled expenses. I explained to Mary Lee that I was a grown man and did not want to live with Mother again. She shouted vehemently that this was the only honorable course for a dutiful son. I was so shocked by the idea, I found my knees buckling. Mary Lee couldn't move in with Mother since she was married, but it made no sense to her that I should refuse. She found the "perfect" place for us—a cheap apartment near Columbia University on 114th Street with four bedrooms, a dining room, two baths, a living room, and no daylight whatsoever.

Mother must have charmed the packing company, as her furniture arrived before she did. Mary Lee and I began to get the place in order. No matter how I disparaged it, she kept pumping up enthusiasm. "Mother will love these high ceilings. Now, it isn't so dark in *this* room, is it?" I made no effort to hide my feelings, and Mary Lee lashed out at my despair. "You'll just have to look cheerful. She's been sad enough without your long face to look at."

Mother drove north in our old seven-passenger Franklin. Mottled and shineless, it still managed to carry Mother, my cousin Eleanor, ten-year-old Marshall, twenty-four-year-old Lizzy, mother's maid of all work, and just for the ride, Mother's ninety-year-old Aunt Bena.

Mother loved the flat before she really saw it. She'd hang a bit of curtain here and there "to hide the lack of view," the dining room was perfect for the huge table and twelve mahogany chairs "which once belonged to Jerome Bonaparte," the living room for her Victorian couches and high-backed chairs. But her main happiness, she said, stemmed from the fact that she had two wonderful sons who wanted to make a beautiful home for her.

My friends began to drop by for one of Lizzy's good meals—turkey or ham and coconut cake. Jimmy Stewart would sit on the floor and play his accordion. But they'd always leave early. When I would try to go with them, Mary Lee always stayed late to stop me. And whenever I did manage to go out, Mother couldn't resist calling out from her bedroom, "Where have you been?" whenever I came home. Or on the way out, it was "Please don't spend any money. We're going to end up in the poorhouse if you keep going out." Every time she said that, I immediately went out and spent money, even if all I had was a quarter for beer.

My distressed state of mind was deepened by another blow. While I was kicking the sidewalk on Broadway and cursing my fate, a friend ran up and said, "Josh, they've been looking all over for you. You have to go to the Crane apartment immediately." Charlie had contracted pneumonia and was in the hospital. What had seemed a simple cold had rapidly grown worse in his new but drafty penthouse apartment. Mary Lee had come over to Mr. Crane's. Her face was white, her eyes glazed, and she kept muttering, "Don't let him die. Don't let him die. Don't let him die. Don't let him die."

To Miss Frances, Charlie's death was the end of all faith, hope and dreams. She was inconsolable to the degree that pushed all comforting away. Mary Lee kept wondering, in a rush of grief and guilt, why she hadn't been nicer to him. Why she didn't let him do all the things he wanted to do. Why hadn't she shown the love she now felt so strongly?

I had lost my best and closest friend, the one who would have stood behind me whatever I did. I despaired. Death had not allowed him to prove himself either the great man I found my heart believing he could have been or the impractical dreamer others thought him. It seems ironic that this was the only way he got to travel the "golden road to Samarkand."

I went with Miss Frances to select a casket. She suddenly impulsively wanted something that would preserve his body forever. She chose the most massive, the heaviest, and surely the most overpriced hunk of copper.

He would have hated it.

CHAPTER

Jesus, how I needed a job. It was 1933, the open, hot belly of the Depression. The theatre was my only hope of survival, but I was like a mosquito trying to bite its way into success. My credentials were ridiculous: the feckless Beckhard charade, the nobody-ever-heard-of University Players, the collegiate snobbery of the Triangle Club. Through the years of travail, I had become a kind of glorified nothing, a has-been that never was, plus the head of what I thought to be a haunted household. Mary Lee had moved in with us and I was now the official, if inadequate, breadwinner for everyone. I had allowed myself to be caught in a web that stretched in all directions to nowhere. It was as though I was starting all over again with a green spotlight on me, cackling, "I'm Nobody. Cackle Cackle. I'm Nobody."

I reached in my pocket and found a lone quarter. I flipped it in the air. Why not flaunt a little poverty for a change? I bet even Cyrano would flip a coin, stroke his white plume and test the temper of his trusty blade at a time like this. It was thinking about Cyrano's white plume that brought me back to reality. I made a swift and dramatic decision. I changed the quarter to five nickels. One nickel was reserved for a Nedick's orange drink, and the others would be used to phone four giants of the theatre. I planned to face TRUTH today. If none of the four offered me a job immediately, I'd give up the theatre. I took an oath right then. I'd become a Wall Street messenger boy, a package wrapper at Macy's or a ditch digger or something. We'd soon see whether or not the lofty gods of the theatre really wanted a great talent like me. They'd have to prove it.

The first call went to Samson Raphaelson, a highly successful playwright, author of, among other hits, *The Jazz Singer*. We had met on shipboard when I was returning from *The Day I Forgot*. "I know exactly how you feel, Josh," he said, "but I'm just finishing a play and haven't the slightest idea whether anyone will even produce it. If I hear of anything, I'll let you know." And he was gracious enough to take my address. But my white plume began to droop.

The second call went to actor-playwright Howard Lindsay. Both he and his darling wife, Dorothy Stickney, had been good friends since Falmouth. At this moment, his new play *She Loves Me Not* had just opened to great notices, and although the production staff would surely be set, there might be something coming up. "But, Josh," he said, "old boy, you ought to hold out for a job as a director. I'd hate to see you just take anything now. Whatever I could offer would be beneath you."

I almost jumped through the receiver. "I accept," I said. "Nothing's beneath me."

"Please, Josh. I'm embarrassed to admit that we have one very, very insignificant job open. It pays minimum. Oh, God, how can I tell you what it is?"

"I want that job and at your salary."

"But it's sixth assistant stage manager."

"*Sixth?*"

"This is a complicated show with six small curtained platform stages, each manned with an assistant. The other unfortunate thing is that the job cannot pay more than twenty-five dollars a week."

To a man with three nickels in his pocket, it seemed an astronomical amount and I told him so.

The company of *She Loves Me Not* was exhilarating to work with. Every night there was a running bridge game in Burgess Meredith's

Age nineteen. When he first joined the University Players.

Jimmy Stewart and Josh singing in *The Tiger Smiles*,
written by Josh, his last year in Princeton.

Scenes from a movie on the University Players, 1931-32.
(CHARLES E. ARNT, JR.)

Josh Logan with Barbara O'Neil at a first reading.

Margaret Sullavan and Henry Fonda,
a few minutes after their marriage.

The University Players Theatre
on Cape Cod.

Bretaigne Windust directing
an actress at Falmouth.

Charles Leatherbee in Arab
skullcap and sailor suit.

On Borrowed Time. Frank Conroy as Mr. Brink,
Dudley Digges as Gramps, Peter Holden as Pud.
(LUCAS & PRITCHARD STUDIO)

dressing room, but I was too busy as a sixth assistant to join. I was attending understudy rehearsals. Searching for opportunities to improve my foothold, I had discovered that all the roles weren't covered. So I offered myself, and since there seemed no one in charge I soon promoted myself to the understudy of eleven roles. After I had learned them, I took a deep breath and went to Jack Del Bondio, the company manager, and explained to him that I was saving the company about fifty dollars a week. Wouldn't it be fair for me to get at least a ten-dollar raise? He consulted Dwight Deere Wiman, the producer, and I got my raise.

Wiman was heir to the John Deere plow fortune. He had gone to Yale and was very gung ho about it. He approved of me at first because I had gone to Princeton, so I pretended I was as hot for my alma mater as he was for his. In time, he and his wife, Steve, became close friends of mine.

Accepting that menial job had been the turning point in my theatre life. Everything else that followed came from that nickel phone call. In a very short time I was to become a well-known stage manager. Among the shows I managed for Dwight Wiman was *The Distaff Side* by John van Druten, with Sybil Thorndike and Estelle Winwood.

Del Bondio was convinced he had discovered me, and I would make his fortune. He was therefore ambitious to produce and to use me as his director. He loaded me down with dog-eared scripts which only the most desperate would consider.

When I turned down a play, he asked, "Why, for Chrissake?" and I answered, "Because it's no good and I want to protect my name."

"You stupid son of a bitch, you haven't *got* a name!"

"No, but I will one day and I don't want this son-of-a-bitching lousy play to besmirch it."

My attitude seemed only to fire his persistence. He came to me one day. "You want to direct something distinguished, right? You like John van Druten, right? Okay. If I got Van Druten to find us a play, would you direct it?"

"Of course; I respect John. He's a gentleman and all his plays are literate and witty. If he approved a play, I'd do it."

"Okay, I have one. It's called *To See Ourselves*, by E. M. Delafield. It just missed on the West End, but Van Druten feels it has a chance here, and do you know something else beautiful about it, you son of a bitch? It has *two* interior sets!"

"What's that got to do with it?"

"Stoopido! Do you think I'm a schmuck? *I didn't just ask* him for a good play. I said I wanted a good play that had two interior sets. Get my drift? *The Distaff Side* has two sets and it's ready to close. I'll book it to tour the country, then *bring it back* to New York for a three-week engagement like a farewell salute to Sybil Thorndike before she returns to England. Then when it closes, we don't touch the sets—no trucks— we can leave the whole production onstage. We won't even rehang the lights. We can use everything for *To See Ourselves,* don't you get it? We'll just paint the sets another color. I figure we can bring it in for two thousand dollars. The average play costs about thirty thousand dollars."

"You're out of your mind! Two thousand dollars? Sure, if we don't have good actors."

"Actors—we'll give them a minimum guarantee and a percentage. We got a Depression. We should take advantage of it. Good actors need jobs just as much as bad actors. You'll have good actors. Now read the play and if you like it you'll be a Broadway director without spoiling your goddamn name, and then you can go fuck yourself!"

And, so help me God, it worked. We toured *The Distaff Side* and then came back to New York for three weeks. I found Delafield's play a delicate, witty comedy about the mousy wife of a neglected country manufacturer. To my surprise, I persuaded lovely Patricia Collinge to play the wife, Reginald Mason the bullish husband, and Earl Larimore played the young lover.

The opening night party wasn't at 21 or Sardi's but at Childs. We rushed to Times Square for the first editions of the papers. Brooks Atkinson of *The New York Times* and Percy Hammond of the *Tribune* weren't ecstatic, but they liked the play and performances. Atkinson even had a kind word for the direction.

To See Ourselves was not a hit but it certainly wasn't an embarrassment. And most important for me, I finally had my name as director on a Broadway play at twenty-six.

The play ran for two weeks, with Jack passing out "free" tickets for which the bearer paid forty cents. It was a shady box office trick but paid off a fraction of our losses.

To my surprise and delight, a call came from the great Gilbert Miller. "I'm presenting Helen Hayes in Laurence Housman's *Victoria Regina.* Rex Whistler is designing the sets . . ."

"Oh, my God!" I said. "A distinguished combination." I was dizzy with the thought of directing a great play at last.

"Are you free? Helen wants you very much and my wife, Kitty, and I heard you did a fine job on Sybil's play."

"Oh, you want me to stage-manage?"

"Of course. What else?" he asked with a touch of impatience.

Here was a sure smash hit. I'd probably get a hundred and fifty dollars a week minimum, maybe two hundred dollars. It would pay the rent, Marshall's schooling. I'd get to know Helen Hayes well, and working for such a distinguished producer as Gilbert Miller, why it was almost better than an annuity.

"Mr. Miller, it breaks my heart to say this, but I've given up stage managing. I'm a director."

"Of plays?"

"Yes, sir. If anyone will ever trust me with one. I recently directed *To See Ourselves*."

"I must have missed it. But good luck. Helen will be disappointed."

I felt exhilarated for a second. I had made a life decision. I knew I was right! But then the doubt began to set in. Maybe the phone would never ring again. Maybe I should call Miller back. No, that's weak and wavering. I'm a director and that's that. But the doubts persisted until I did get a call. It wasn't quite what I had in mind. I was asked to direct the next Triangle show at Princeton, *Stags at Bay*. An amateur show—just my speed! They wanted a professional to direct and it paid fifteen hundred dollars. Not a bad salary! Anyway, I'd be technically fulfilling my ambition, and it might be fun to relive a bit of my not-too-distant youth. I said yes.

No sooner had I started rehearsals for *Stags at Bay* when I was offered a Broadway directorial job for the play *Hell Freezes Over*, written by an unknown named John Patrick, who turned out to be a delightful guy and a great playwright. It was to go into production immediately, which meant I would have to handle both assignments at the same time. But I had to accept.

We gathered a talented cast for the Patrick play: Louis Calhern, John Litel, George Tobias and Myron McCormick. The play was a grisly melodramatic shocker about seven explorers who survive a zeppelin crash at the North Pole. It included murder, suicide and death in the frozen North.

I rehearsed *Hell* all day, caught a train for Princeton where I rehearsed *Stags* until midnight, slept on any available couch until the eight o'clock morning train took me back to New York. To save money, Mother met me at Pennsylvania Station in the old Franklin with a pint jar of grapefruit juice, and drove me to the theatre.

The pressure was so great that, exhausted and dizzy, I developed uncontrollable hiccoughs. The only way to quiet them was to stretch out flat on my back in the aisle and direct looking skyward. That's where Jack Wildberg, the play's producer, found me two days before the play opened. The actors took my prone position for granted, but Wildberg didn't. Enraged, he ordered me to direct standing up or he'd get a director who could. Fear is a powerful medicine. I staggered up, and lo and behold I managed to hide and space the hiccoughs. Back to Princeton I went that night, where I could hiccough all I wanted to without complaint.

The reviewers attacked *Hell Freezes Over* as a contrivance. It closed after a few performances. But now I had *two* Broadway plays to my credit, and I had a good friend in John Patrick.

Stags at Bay, the Triangle show, on the other hand, was a triumph and is still remembered, in its annals, as the best ever. It even had a memorable song, the creation of Brooks Bowman, an undergraduate: "East of the Sun and West of the Moon." How I wished the New York critics could have seen it instead of *Hell*. Buddy Lewis, who choreographed the dances, was now my confrere.

Again, no one was discovering me. There were no offers, no activity, no money and plenty of poorhouse predictions from Mother. I was in total desperation when I got a call from Kay Brown, David Selznick's East Coast representative. Selznick wanted me as dialogue director for his next movie extravaganza, *The Garden of Allah*. Everything about it would be "distinguished," she said. It was based on a 1904 novel by Robert Hichens. The epic production would star Marlene Dietrich, Charles Boyer, Joseph Schildkraut, Basil Rathbone, C. Aubrey Smith, John Carradine, and there would be a dance sequence with the great Tilly Losch. The director would be Richard Boleslawski, formerly of my beloved Moscow Art Theatre. And if all this wasn't enough, this romance of the desert would be filmed in the new three-color process, Technicolor.

I wanted to call everyone to share in my good fortune. But I had no time. They needed me on the Coast immediately. I was drunk with excitement. So were Mother and Mary Lee.

Clutching my contract for three hundred dollars a week and a fat copy of the novel, I rushed into a Ford trimotor for the night flight to California. I stayed glued to the window watching the lighted cities fly by. I even got off at each stop the plane made and walked about on the ground so that I could say I had been there. Between looking and napping I managed to read five pages of the turgid novel.

Descending the gangway in the morning, I noticed my arrival was being photographed. This was real Hollywood, all right. But no! The photographer was Hank Fonda using his 16 mm., and with him, waving hands and laughing, were Margaret Sullavan and Jimmy Stewart. They had preceded me to Hollywood with movie contracts arranged by their manager, Leland Hayward, whom they had bullied into handling me. A decision he wavered about for years. We piled into Hank's car and went off to Peggy's house for breakfast, everyone talking at once.

I was to share a house in Brentwood with Stewart, Fonda and John Swope, Gerard Swope's son and a charter member of the University Players from Harvard, but there was not time to leave my things at my new home. A chauffeured limousine was waiting to deliver me to the studio for a story conference already in progress.

Selznick's offices were in a white-columned version of a Southern mansion, only bigger. His enormous office had enough English casual furniture to fill a hotel lobby. Twenty or so men and women were sitting on the printed linen upholstery. Selznick, a puffy-faced man in his early thirties, introduced me in a commanding voice: "This is Logan." And in the same breath. "Now, Logan, we're talking about the first scene to be shot at the Black Pool oasis. Now, I want your opinion. Listen to the discussion and join in." He indicated my chair.

I sank down into it, trying to get a clue from someone else. From hearing things about what the "monk" says to the girl and what the girl says to the "monk," I soon gathered there must be a monk in the story who jumps a wall and marries a beautiful girl.

They handed me some pages of the scene I was to direct. It was almost incomprehensible. Boris and Domini get off their horses at the Black Pool oasis and she says to him, "But if you are not accustomed to riding, Boris, why must you pick the most fiery horse in the entire Sahara?"

Boris (laughing): "It's all Batouche's fault" (and then, imitating Batouche), "Forgive me, Monsieur Androvsky, if instead of the horse you ordered, I bring a lamb. It is with the greatest difficulty it can be persuaded to run. It prefers like the swans on the lake of the Prophet, to float, Monsieur, to float."

Selznick was watching me read.

"Great scene, eh?"

I was so astounded by the naïvely fancy writing, I couldn't answer.

I was saved by a secretary who whispered in his ear. Selznick turned white. Then his eyes settled on me.

"Logan," he spoke sotto voce, "Dietrich's out there. Go talk to her. She'll tell you she doesn't like the script and blah, blah, blah. Listen to her ideas carefully, then tell her you think the script's great, and keep at it till she believes you. Now, get going."

I started for the door with some hesitation. A year before I had melted into a pudding the first time I saw her in *Morocco*. Her brand of smoldering seductiveness had such an erotic effect on me that I trotted excitedly across Times Square immediately thereafter to see her in another theatre in *The Blue Angel*. The thought of seeing her in the flesh now had my body trembling and my mouth dry.

In jodhpurs and a thin silk blouse, one eye covered by a lock of silken hair, she leaned casually against a door. She was the most beautiful thing I had ever seen. In a quiet, breathy voice, she spoke first.

"Who are you?"

"I'm J-Joshua Logan, the dialogue director."

"Oh, you're the one fwom New York. I love people fwom New York. They're so bwight, so tasteful. Tell me, have you wead the scwipt?" She had trouble pronouncing R, as some Germans do.

"Well, Miss Dietrich . . . I . . . er . . ."

"It's twash, isn't it?" She spoke so quietly I had difficulty hearing her, and her eyes disturbed me deeply.

"Well . . . er . . . I can see how it might seem . . . er . . . lightweight at the moment. But it's still in work." I continued desperately, "Lynn Riggs is a very fine and poetic writer. After all, he's the author of *Green Grow the Lilacs*. I know him from New York. The other writers are talented men, too, I'm sure. And Mr. Selznick, who is practically an expert on style and construction, is dedicating a great deal of his time too."

"It's twash, that's what you are saying. Garbo wouldn't play this part. They offered it to Garbo and she said she didn't believe the girl would send the boy back to the monastawy. She is a *vewy clever* woman, Garbo! She has the pwimitive instincts—dose peasants have, you know."

The last remark took several seconds to penetrate my starstruck brain. I was so befuddled and inarticulate.

"Miss Dietrich, let's promise each other that we won't judge anything until . . ."

"Look me in the eye and tell me the twuth." I began to sweat. "Tell me the twuth, now. It's twash, isn't it? You're a tasteful New Yorker. Admit it. It's twash."

I stared helplessly into her one visible and lucid eye. "Well, maybe it's a *little* trash, but it's going to be improved." I felt I had lost something, but didn't know what.

"Go tell Mr. Selznick how you feel," she said as she dismissed me.

When I returned to Selznick's office, all eyes were on me. He asked, "Did she complain?"

"Not a bit. I wouldn't allow it." I sat down, hoping no one could see what was going on inside me.

Boleslawski, a big, soft bear of a man with blue eyes and a heavy Russian accent came in dressed like Teddy Roosevelt at San Juan Hill. Selznick introduced us, saying to me, "Boley's off to the desert. Now, Logan, remember this. Boley is the general and you are the lieutenant. Do everything he tells you and everything I tell you. Above all, I want our beautiful words spoken clearly. Remember, this is 'desert poetry,' and I want that poetry heard! Now, Boleslawski doesn't speak a goddamn word of English. Right, Boley? *Dietrich* doesn't speak English. *Boyer* speaks no English whatsoever. Schildkraut speaks bad English. That's why we brought you out here—to make them speak and pronounce every syllable. Every syl-la-ble.

"Monday morning a car will take you to our location camp in the Mojave Desert near Yuma, Arizona. So study your script. The first scene at the Black Pool oasis is tricky for you because in it Boyer has to imitate the epicene Arab guide, Batouche, played by Schildkraut, son of the great Jewish actor, Rudolph Schildkraut. He is a desert poet, a powder puff young man who wears a fez, but now get this—*he also wears a hibiscus flower in his ear*. Oh, he's some character." He laughed and everyone joined in. "Now, I'm sending Schildkraut down a week early—it's costing an extra three thousand—so he can read the line in character so then Boyer can hear him and speak in the flowery way

Batouche does. It should be a riot if you coach it right. And you better. We need all the laughs we can get in this lousy picture."

I was growing weary. The story conference lasted all night long and I hadn't slept in two nights.

At daybreak, I was driven to Fonda's house. Having no key, I crawled through a window. There, in an upper bunk, was the vast body, face and nose of John Swope, groggy from sleep. He pointed to the lower bunk. I dove in and slept. At five in the afternoon, I was awakened by Jimmy Stewart holding out an old-fashioned. "Get up. We're going to Ginger's for dinner." Ginger was Ginger Rogers, with whom Jimmy was involved at that time. I was so excited at the thought of meeting her that I downed the old-fashioned and two others in quick succession before I realized I hadn't had anything to eat.

Jimmy and I started to talk about Max Reinhardt's film *A Midsummer Night's Dream,* which I had liked.

"I saw it and it stinks," said Jimmy.

"How can you say that? It's a work of art!"

"It won't make a nickel."

In my fuzzy condition I decided it was time to save my friend from this insidious Hollywood commercialism.

"How could you change so quickly from a man of ideals? You sound like a crass distributor who can only think in picture grosses."

"That's the way they judge films out here—and anyway, it stinks."

Our violent words continued over more old-fashioneds all the way to Ginger Rogers' house. There, I found myself accosting people and accusing them of selling out for money. They just laughed and walked away.

Then I spotted Ginger Rogers dancing with someone. I cut in, but feeling woozy, I had to cling to her to steady my weaving feet. She extricated herself from my grasp and I decided it was a good time to go to the bathroom. Down the hallway I wobbled to a likely door, opened it and plunged down a ladder twelve feet into the basement. Heaven must protect drunks, for I got up unharmed, climbed back to find Fonda and Stewart waiting for me.

"Come on outside, Josh."

I followed them, thinking they were going to drive me home.

Fonda said, "We don't like the way you're behaving."

"Well, I don't like the way Mr. J. Hollywood Stewart talked to me. I think you've all sold out for the money. I'm gonna move out of your money-tainted house. You go your way and I'll go mine."

"Okay with me." Fonda shrugged.

"And with me," said Jim.

Johnny Swope drove me home. I growled and grumbled and sniffled all the way home. Some place, Hollywood—desert poetry—that peasant Garbo—every syllable—twash—and no home—ole friends are gone and Ginger Rogers can't even dance. John pushed me into my bunk. In a few hours, at 6:00 A.M., a limousine would pick me up to take me on the seven-hour ride to the Black Pool oasis where I would have to teach those illiterate goddamned stars that stupid desert poetry.

The car arrived promptly and I crawled inside with my throbbing hangover. Joseph Schildkraut was stretched across the back seat, allowing a minimal space for his cousin, a skinny, red-necked man who turned out to be his stand-in as well. They kicked down the jump seat for me. I felt properly insignificant.

I introduced myself. Disdainfully, Schildkraut said, "Yes, I know all about you," and closed his eyes. There was silence for about an hour. It was broken when Schildkraut dramatically announced, "I'm going to fuck Dietrich."

"Are you sure?" his cousin asked with awed amazement.

I withheld any of the acerbic remarks that came to mind.

We arrived at the production camp hours later. It was an astonishing sight. Not a blade of vegetation to be seen—only ripples and ridges of pink sand. Set down in this desert was a vast network of newly constructed streets and wood and canvas bungalows. In the valley close by was an immense tent for camels, water buffalo, sheep, pigs, geese, chickens, peacocks and every other photogenic animal imaginable. The horses had their own vast tent still farther on.

I found my bungalow complete with hot and cold shower and bathroom near a huge mess tent that was used both for eating and for screening the rushes. I couldn't sleep that night. I was in the fabulous land of the movies and it was all just like *Photoplay* had said it would be!

At three in the morning I sat at one of the acres of tables for breakfast and met a fellow Princetonian, Ring Lardner, Jr., who was in the publicity department. He wished me luck in such a wry tone that I wished he hadn't. After breakfast, we were herded like Okies into the back of a truck which took off for the Black Pool oasis set seventeen miles away.

Allah be praised, there it was! A concrete pool three inches deep (its bottom painted black), surrounded by live palm trees transplanted from Los Angeles along with little desert grasses and blossoms. Electricians were rolling out cables, camera assistants were pushing camera equipment into position, propmen were loping about with boxes in their hands.

I wandered around like a newly arrived soul in purgatory. Wherever I moved, someone shouted, "Out of the way, big boy," or "Look out, big boy, you're gonna get it right in the . . ." I decided to circle around the set to find Boleslawski. He was easy to spot in his big campaign hat and uniform. He was peering through a view finder and saying, "Move dose camels a little right. No, too far, too far, move back. Move one camel right, one camel left. Good! Keep Arab in middle. Okay. Tie dem down."

"Mr. Boleslawski . . ."

"Vat? Vat?"

"It's me. Joshua Logan. Remember?"

"Yes, yes, Logan. Vat you doing here?"

"I'd like to know what I should do."

"Do? Do vat you came for. Direct de scene."

"But I thought you were going to do that."

He started to yell. "Vat you tink, I got fife hands? Goddamn dose camels, dot lousy Technicolor—you tink I vant to take on Marlene too? Go to tent and direct de scene."

I managed to find her pyramidal tent and knocked. To a breathy "Yesss," I entered the dark tent. Dietrich sat in front of the traditional dressing table mirror ringed with pink bulbs. She looked like a Burne-Jones heroine as she carefully squirted gold dust onto the marcelled ridges of her hair from a rubber bulb with a long stem which I learned later was a baby enema. Nellie, her hairdresser, a sharp-featured old parrot with bleached blonde hair, hovered over her, pointing to each unspurted ridge with clawlike fingers. Dietrich froze like an Irish setter, took careful aim—and puff, another bull's-eye.

They finally decided to acknowledge me. "Oh, hello, Mister New York."

"Er, Miss Dietrich, Mr. Boleslawski told me that I should come and, er, rehearse the scene with you."

Astounded, she turned to Nellie, who rolled her eyes to heaven in disgust.

"But that's the cwaziest thing I ever heawd of. They won't be weady for hou-wuhs yet."

"I know, but it's a very complicated scene and it's damnably wordy."

"But Chawles is not even here."

"Oh, right. I'll go find him and bring him back."

I waited for Boyer up by the Yuma road. It was an hour before sunrise and hot as hell already. Shortly, a powerful open phaeton, gleaming with brass fittings, appeared with the obligatory uniformed chauffeur and a terrified-looking young man in the back seat. For some reason, he was pressing his fingers frantically to his upper forehead. Even from a distance, I could see his skin had a corpselike pallor. It was Boyer. He was breathing hard—almost snorting. I realized what his fingers were up to as he stepped out of the car. They were trying to keep his small hairpiece from becoming unglued in the intense heat. His mordant pallor was due to his makeup, known as "Technicolor gray." In the early days it was thought that Technicolor film exaggerated the red in a man's complexion, and the mud makeup was to blot it out. The fact that it also made the man look as if he had a liver condition was immaterial.

I said, "Mr. Boyer?"

He drew back as if I was going to attack him and dropped his hands from his forehead. Rivulets of perspiration dripped through his hairpiece and on down his nose and chin.

"I am Joshua Logan, the dialogue director."

"*Deealog?* Oh, dee-a-log. No, no, Horr-ee-ble! A-a-m-poss-ee-bluh!"

Obviously, even a Frenchman couldn't understand the desert poetry of that Black Pool scene.

"You're so right, Mr. Boyer. But I'm going to help you. We'll take it very slowly. I'll get Mr. Schildkraut to read it for you first. You're supposed to imitate him, you know."

"Je ne comprends pas."

"Of course. Just wait here."

I found Schildkraut spread-eagled across a canvas chair as two female extras on either side of his outstretched arms applied ice bags to his wrists to keep him from fainting.

"Mr. Schildkraut," I said, "Mr. Boyer is here and I'd like you to read some lines in your manner of playing the part so that Mr. Boyer can imitate you."

"Is this man out of his mind?" he asked the girls.

"What do you mean?"

"I wouldn't think of insulting an actor of Mr. Boyer's stature by telling him how to play a scene."

I felt my blood rising. "Mr. Selznick explained this to your agent and your agent explained it to you. You have been brought down here early at a great deal of extra expense for this purpose. Now, *get up* and come along. *And be goddamned quick about it!*"

He got up and followed me like Mary's lamb. I was afraid to look back—it might be considered a sign of weakness.

Boyer, Schildkraut and I entered Dietrich's sand-streaked door. She was still aiming the baby's enema at her hair with Nellie guiding. She looked up.

"Chawles, oh, Chawles," and she immediately switched to French. Schildkraut smothered her hands with kisses and I arranged chairs.

"Er, please. Everybody quiet. Mr. Selznick wants every syllable spoken clearly. Would you all please sit down and start to read the scene?" I realized this was a historic moment in my life. My movie career was about to begin. "Miss Dietrich."

Dietrich started to read the first line. At least I think she did. She moved her lips but only a slight whir came out.

"Er . . . is that the way you plan to read the line, Miss Dietrich?"

"Yes, I do not think Domini would be co-wuss."

"Oh, not *coarse,* no! But the sound man *should* be able to hear you and so should Mr. Boyer because it's his cue."

Slightly annoyed, she began again, raising her tone one-thousandth of a decibel. It sounded like this:

"But if you awuh not accustomed to widing, Bowis, why must you pick the most fieh-wee howus in the en-ti-wah Sahawa?"

For one who could not pronounce R, it was unfortunate that her opening line contained seven of them.

"Would you go ahead, Mr. Boyer?" I said.

He was so transfixed by Dietrich's reading, he had to shake himself together to read his line.

"Ees oll Batouche's foll. Forgeev me, M'sieur Androvsky . . ."

"Excuse me, Mr. Boyer," I said, "but Mr. Schildkraut is here to demonstrate how he's going to play Batouche so you can imitate him. Mr. Schildkraut?"

With a supercilious smile, Schildkraut said, "Certainly you don't want me to tell a man of Mr. Boyer's accomplishments how to act . . ."

"Just read the line, Mr. Schildkraut. Mr. Boyer understands. And so does your agent. And so do I."

Schildkraut grabbed the script and began to shout in a rough, guttural accent complete with street-vendor gestures, "Forgiff me, Monsier Androffsky, eef instad off dee hawss you ordurred, I breeng you a laaam." Then he pulled out all stops. By the time he got to the end, his low-class accent was thick as mud and he was howling like a banshee, the tent was flapping and the rest of us were in a state of shock.

I pulled myself together and said as quietly as I could, "Is that the way you plan to play this flowery desert poet, Mr. Schildkraut?"

"Yes. In my opinion, Batouche is a kike."

Boyer's mouth fell agape. Dietrich turned back to her mirror and caught Nellie's eye. They reached for the baby enema.

Still trying to make sense, I said, "Does Mr. Selznick know you plan to play Batouche in this coarse way?"

"I don't give a damn what Mr. Selznick thinks. I am an artist and he is a film merchant."

I said, "Thank you for your help, Mr. Schildkraut. You've done the job you agreed to do. Go now, and you don't have to come back." I urged him to the door and hurried back to Boyer, who had grown grayer than his makeup.

"But thees ees— I cannot— But thees ees—"

"Forget him. It's ridiculous. And never mind the imitation. Just play the part your own way. I'll explain it all to Mr. Selznick."

At my urging, Boyer started to read: "Forgeev me, M'sieur Androvsky, eef instead of zee hawss you or-daired, I breeng you a lem."

I jumped in. "No, that's la-a-a-mb. Flat a. Laaam."

"Ah, yes, leh-eh-em. Eet ees wizz ze greatest deefeecoltay zat . . ."

"It's not 'wizz ze.' It's 'with the.' "

"Oh, non, non, non. I weel not. I will say, 'Eet eez *wizz the*'—or I will say, 'Eet eez wi*th* ze,' but 'with the,' non, non, non!"

He continued, and when he said "lick" I said "lay-ke." He tried to stretch it out and flatten the sound; he was making an enormous effort to please me. I suffered with him. He was a superb actor and a fine man. But these lines were a match for anyone.

Eventually, we were called to the set for rehearsal. I huddled over by the side of the camera. The die was cast. Now, everyone would see the result of my first Hollywood labor. I hoped, by some miracle, it would all make sense.

On the opposite side of the black pool, Dietrich and Boyer were led in on horseback. Each horse was held by four men. On top of the enormous Technicolor camera next to me sat a little man in a hat with its brim turned up. He had a turned-up nose, a turned-up moustache and even turned-up toes. Later on I learned he was Hal Rossen, future husband of Jean Harlow, and one of the finest cameramen ever.

Boleslawski took over, shouting, *"Rehearsal. Action!"*

Boyer and Dietrich, in character, laughing, dismounted and moved to the edge of the pool. I could see Dietrich speaking and I could see the sound man desperately twisting the microphone around in the air, trying to locate her voice. When Boyer spoke, I heard those valiant, incomprehensible and embarrassing imitations of me: "La-a-a-mb," "lay-ay-ayke," "ruh-uhn."

When they finished the scene, Hal Rossen, not knowing who I was, looked down from the camera at me with a turned-up smile and said, "I didn't understand a fucking word they said."

Back at camp after supper that night, a uniformed and grinning chauffeur came to my cabin to deliver a note. It was written on the stationery of a Yuma hotel and had one sentence: "Are your ears burning?" It was signed by a single initial, "M." I was so distraught, I couldn't remember what "ears burning" signified. Was it bad or good? An inheritance, an accident, a surprise? It was exciting.

Before dawn the next morning, Boyer and Dietrich were sitting on the set chatting. They beckoned excitedly to me. Marlene said, "Wuh you-wah ears buwning? When I wote that note, we wuh talking about you." Charles nodded in agreement with a smile.

"Well, that's very flattering. What were you saying?"

"Only vewy nice things. We both feel you helped us with that ho-wibble scene."

I was encouraged, but somehow had a niggling fear there was something else behind it—at least on her part. As for Charles, he had decided that I owned the English language and only I could lease it to him bit by bit.

But I had an immediate problem. I had to warn Selznick of Schildkraut's guttural Batouche and I had to do it secretly.

I learned of a pay phone in a shed some miles across the sand in a tiny train stop called Sidewinder (the name of a local snake). I borrowed a truck and drove there between setups. I dug away the dust and cobwebs from the phone and then peered about to make sure there were no snakes and eavesdroppers. When I reached Selznick, he spoke with that touchy impatience characteristic of great men in a hurry.

"Yes, what is it, Logan? I'm very busy, you know."

"So am I, sir, but you should know something I consider crucial."

"Marlene sick?"

"No. But I rehearsed with Schildkraut. Did you know he plans to play Batouche with a thick, guttural, Russian accent?"

Selznick answered angrily, "Joseph Schildkraut is a great actor, as was his father. Whatever he wants to do has my approval. And don't interrupt me anymore except for something important."

"I don't want it to be a surprise, Mr. Selznick." But he had hung up.

If that's what he wanted, fine. I'd step aside. But I knew it wasn't what he wanted.

We moved to a date grove to rehearse the first Batouche scenes. Schildkraut's guttural rantings were even hammier than before. I told Boleslawski I agreed the accent was terrible but that Mr. Selznick knew about it and approved.

The next short sequences dealt with the sand-blown honeymoon of Domini and Boris, Dietrich and Boyer gazing dreamily out at the sand. Examples: Boyer (intensely): "Isn't ze desert beautiful?" Dietrich looks at him lovingly. Fade-out. Dietrich, after pausing to allow unheard music that Max Steiner would dub in later: "Listen, that song again. The slaves sang it when they wah set fwee." Boyer nods. Fade-out. And still another: "Listen, that stwange song. I cannot get it out of my mind." Fade-out. Then another for Dietrich: "Ah, theey-uh is that slave song. It weally haunts me."

Dietrich read all her lines in a rather flat, toneless voice which she felt was ladylike. I decided I should earn my salary by offering a bit of directorial advice, so I suggested, "Marlene, there are so many lines about that slave song, couldn't you for variety read one in a different mood? You know, as if the song was beginning to get under your skin, to almost get on your nerves. As if you were slightly disturbed by it, annoyed at how it was affecting you?"

She read it again. I honestly believe she tried to achieve the variety I suggested, but I couldn't be sure. It was still ladylike to me.

Rumors flew through the camp that Selznick had arrived with his staff and was encamped in a Yuma hotel and was out for blood—anybody's. Fear swept the camp when twenty people were summoned for questioning. I was not among the first group, which might be a bad or a good omen.

Boleslawski and Schildkraut returned from Yuma first, looking like whipped bears. They walked past me without a word. Schildkraut took his sullen face in front of the camera and Boleslawski rolled the cameras. Miraculously, Schildkraut's performance had lost its guttural accent. Batouche was now our languid desert poet with singsong phrasing and a hibiscus flower over his ear.

My triumph was short-lived. At the end of the day, came my call to Yuma.

The hotel room was a makeshift producer's office, with Selznick behind a desk. He looked at me superciliously for a long time and then said, "What are you trying to insinuate into this picture, Logan?"

I felt the adrenalin beginning its trip through me. "To put it simply, Mr. Selznick, I'm trying to make this picture as good as I can."

He roared, *"Did you or did you not tell Dietrich to read her lines as if she was annoyed with them?"*

Enraged, I tried to hold on to myself. "Annoyed with the lines? Ridiculous. I told her to read the line as if the song was getting under her skin, as if it were deeply disturbing. Quite frankly, she was getting so goddamned monotonous, I was trying to keep all of those little honeymoon scenes from sounding exactly like each other."

"Exactly like each other! I don't like snide remarks about this script! Do you understand?"

I lost control. "Mr. Selznick, may I leave for New York tonight? I want to get away from this overwritten script, Dietrich and her buckpassing and you with your quick suspicion. The whole setup makes me sick. Let me get back to serious people and tonight. Good-bye, sir." I did a military turn and marched to the door.

Selznick yelled bloody murder after me. *"Oh, no, you don't. You can't get away with it that easily.* You're staying on this picture, goddammit, and don't dare try to sneak out of it."

"I'm not sneaking out, I'm walking out. And do you know any good reason I should stay?"

For a moment he looked confused. "I don't know. There must be some reason. I don't change my mind without some reason. Oh, yeah, you warned me in advance about that awful Schildkraut accent. You even had the balls to try to make Marlene act. You've talked me into making you stay. Now go back to work and phone me."

The next day, Selznick's caravan wandered off and things returned to the routine.

Charles and Marlene were extremely nice to me, especially Marlene. One day, worried about my overexposure to the sun's rays, she spent a half hour personally covering my back and chest with oil, to the smirking delight of the crew. "You must stay out of the sun. You'll get tewwibbly buwned." From that time on, badly concealed leers and knowing looks followed me everywhere I went.

One night she even invited me to her room after dinner. As we walked down the hall, she confided to me of her love for John Gilbert. Upon entering the room, we were both dumbfounded to see Joseph Schildkraut sitting there.

"What are you doing heuh? How on eawuth did you get to my woom?"

"Your maid let me in." He smiled guiltily. "I told her I had an engagement with you." He was speaking to her and glaring at me.

"As you can see, I have a fwiend with me. Will you kindly leave this woom this minute?"

"Marlene, I'm a great artist. I'm not used to being treated this way in front of the crew and I'm not going to forget it."

"Nowuh am I. Get out, you Middle Euwopean chawacter actuh. Get out."

As he left, he gave me a wild, threatening look.

But as if there had been no interruption, Marlene cooed on about John Gilbert. There were pictures of him all over the room. Each picture, unbelievable as it may seem, had a votive candle burning before it. She explained the candles were there because she worshipped him.

When I looked for a chair that wasn't under a votive candle she said, "Oh, just sit on the bed. It's vewy nice. I'll join you." I should have been cool and sophisticated. After all, I was halfway through my twenties. But I sat rather gingerly, feeling like Holofernes and wondering if the drink she was fixing was going to drug me. She sat beside me and I could feel her warmth and smell her perfume. I tried to think of fields of yellow daisies.

"I asked you tonight because you seemed so bwight, so attwactive, so clevah." She put her hand on my forehead and smoothed it. "Don't winkle the fowead like that. It's nothing to wowwy about. You'll make the wight decision about this. I know you will."

"About what?"

I was startled when she said, "You don't weally like Boleslawski, do you? Do you weally think he has talent?"

"Of course I do, and more than that, I think he's a nice man."

"Oh, no, no, no. Oh, please, that's not twue. He's a tewwible man. He's Wussian. No sensitivity. He can't diwect women. He is not like you." Then she changed her tone to a soft German purr. "Wouldn't you like to see him wesign fwom the pictuah?"

"Resign? Good God, no. I think it would be dangerous for the whole project if he left now, but . . . well . . . may I go now, Miss Dietrich. I've been up since two this morning . . ."

"Call up Selznick wight now. Theuh's the phone. Tell him you think Boleslawski is not the wight man for this pictuah. He wespects you. The mowah people we get to call him, the bettah."

"Miss Dietrich, are you trying to get out of the picture, I mean if Boley left?"

"If he left—we could get a good diwectuh—like Josef von Stawnbawg, who just happens to be available. He'd be exactly wight fowah this, and fowah me. Call Mr. Selznick now. Do it fowah me."

Von Sternberg had directed most of her movies.

"Let me think about it for a minute," I said. She poured another heavy Scotch for me and we talked and talked. She kept getting closer and seemingly more affectionate. Finally, I did what ended up as an embarrassing footnote to my Hollywood experience—I dozed off.

I woke up a few minutes later, my head cradled in her arms. "Is not sleep lovely? When you feel peaceful with someone you like, you can sleep."

"Please, it's terribly late and I'll be no good at work tomorrow. Thank you so much for a wonderful evening."

"Think ovah what I said; only think fast."

"Oh, yes, of course I will. I'll think very fast." I kissed her hand and backed out the door.

Boleslawski remained on the picture in spite of her efforts, and I very much doubt whether another director could have saved it.

We returned to Hollywood to complete the interiors and I moved back with Swope, Stewart and Fonda. Our argument was never mentioned.

The Garden of Allah was previewed, and it was an artistic catastrophe. No one could understand a word of the desert poetry in the Black Pool sequence, nor did anyone have a clue that Boris was a monk. It was then that Selznick suddenly became the champion he could be. He excised the Black Pool and, more importantly, filmed an opening sequence which made it clear that Boris had escaped from a monastery. He cut down Schildkraut and some of his uncomic patter. In short, he established order and showed himself as a thorough professional. The photography won an Academy Award, but that desert poetry inspired one critic to say, "The dialogue was obviously written by Alf Landon."

My new agent, the legendary, tough-talking Leland Hayward, who was soon to marry Peggy Sullavan, called just before I was to return to New York. In his overcasual manner he informed me, "I just sold you to Walter Wanger."

I went off to Wanger's office with no confidence in Hayward or myself.

Wanger, lounging in a polo uniform, a booted foot on his desk, was toying with a polo mallet. Leland was flat on the couch, swamped in pillows. After a muddled introduction, Wanger snapped at me, "What do *you* know that I don't know or everybody else out here doesn't know?"

"Well, nothing—that is—I just came because . . ." I looked plaintively over at Leland, hoping he would bail me out. He didn't.

Wanger continued. "You lousy Theatre Guild guys come out here and tell us what to do. Well, you can't tell me anything. I don't need you. Is that clear?"

"Of course it is. Let's go, Leland."

Leland pulled himself perhaps one inch out of the pillows. "Well, Walter, I thought that maybe you could give him a job in the cutting room and let him learn . . ."

"You think this is some goddamn SCHOOL? I don't teach. I want people who can teach me something. What the hell do I need amateurs from the Theatre Guild for?"

"Mr. Wanger, I absolutely agree with you," I said. "I think you make fantastic pictures here, and don't think twice about me. I have plenty of exciting jobs waiting for me in New York." I started out. Wanger shouted to me. "Boyer says you're a dialogue director. I might be able to use you to coach him for *Wuthering Heights. If* I do it and *if* he does."

"And *if* I'm not too busy. Good-bye, sir," I said.

Leland followed me out and I closed the door. I was ready to strangle him for putting me through all that. He smiled, clapped me on the back and said, "See, he's crazy about you."

Back in New York, I did a stint with a summer stock company in Suffern, New York, playing Captain Flagg to Broderick Crawford's Sergeant Quirt in *What Price Glory?* Another Princetonian, Jose Ferrer, who wanted to be an actor but who was now driving the station wagon for the company, played the French girl's father.

Leland came up one night with Peggy Sullavan and began to shout at me for being so wishy-washy. Why should I work in Hollywood as a lousy dialogue director for Wanger? "You stay in New York until you direct a hit play, then I'll sell you to Hollywood for real big money."

I pointed out that hit plays didn't come often and working for Wanger was his idea, not mine.

"I know. I could kill myself. Didn't I say that, Maggie? I was wrong, absolutely wrong. Now let's get this clear. Direct a hit here. *You are not going to Hollywood, come hell or high water.*"

A week later, Leland, back in Hollywood, called me. "Josh, I just sold you to Wanger. Now forget these crazy, wishy-washy Broadway play ideas. This is a big picture with Charles Boyer and Jean Arthur. Frank Borzage is directing. They're calling it *History Is Made at Night.* I had to work my ass off selling you, but I told Wanger you'd be right out there. Come tomorrow." He hung up before I had a chance to answer.

Before I knew it, I was on the Coast, wondering how it all happened.

When I saw Boyer in the commissary, he gave me a warm hug. "Oh, am I glad you're here. I told Walter zat eef he didn't get you, I wouldn't do ze picture! But he deedn't tell me you were cooming." Good old reliable Leland.

All that existed of *History Is Made at Night* was a fifty-two-page script being written by the two latest hotshot writers around, Gene

Towne and Graham Baker, who were said to make Hecht and MacArthur look like snails. The story opened on a Paris hotel balcony with Boyer climbing through a window to save Jean Arthur who is being attacked by her chauffeur. Gallant Boyer punches the dastardly chauffeur who falls and accidentally cracks his head on an andiron. To escape Jean Arthur's madly jealous rich husband, Colin Clive, whom she wants to divorce, Boyer and Arthur slip out and spend a night of revelry on the town. By the morning, they are in love. Meanwhile, jewelry czar Clive enters the hotel room. He expects to find his wife in the arms of the chauffeur, which according to French law will make her unable to divorce him. Instead, he finds the chauffeur dead. Aha! She must have a lover. Close-up. He will pursue the man who killed his suddenly beloved chauffeur and pin the murder on the unknown bastard and thus get his wife back. That's where the script stopped—on page fifty-two.

"Gene and Graham are going to give me another ten pages today," said Wanger. "Wait till you meet them. They're dazzling talents."

At least they were great salesmen. They barged into the office and started "talking the story." If the thinnest boredom appeared to cross Wanger's eyes, they pepped up the story by sexing it up.

I named their improvisations The Ballet of the Genitals. Gene Towne would begin with high laughter that almost commanded Wanger to laugh with him. "Here's the great scene, boss. This big, handsome prick charges into this beautiful cunt's bedroom, grabs her by the tit, then throws a fuck into her. Ha, ha, ha. When she grabs him by the balls, the door opens and Mr. Soft Cock husband enters, yelling, 'Shit, shit, shit!' Some scene, eh, boss? Ha, ha. The big prick cornholes the husband's fat ass out of the door. Then the two sex hounds climb out of the cocksucking window and take a hotel room." Gene and Graham would laugh maniacally, rolling on the couch. Then, with a "See you later, boss," they would shoot out of the door.

Wanger's face was flushed. "There goes genius," he'd say to me in a husky voice.

But their story line got so snarled up that they couldn't find a logical ending. They came up with a slam-bang, sand-in-the-eye twist. This was the era of "physical finishes." Ridiculous and unbelievable plots were solved by sweeping them up in some all-engulfing disaster: the San Francisco earthquake, the Chicago fire, a Goldwyn hurricane, a Pearl Buck plague of locusts. Towne and Baker had a convenient seizure: they decided to sink the *Titanic* in our picture. I asked what the *Titanic* had to do with a jewelry czar.

"It's a cinch," said Gene and Graham. "And it's beautiful. We switcheroo Colin Clive into an owner of ocean liners. And get this fantastic twist. He builds a special ship named after Jean Arthur to bring her back to him from America—across the ocean. Why does it crash into that sweet old iceberg? Because *he's got those old hot nuts.* By radio from London, he forces the captain to go faster than he should—in a big fuckin' fog—and crash. Thinking he's drowned her, he shoots himself. Happy Ending: Jean's in a lifeboat with Boyer."

It seemed ridiculous to me but it certainly was impressive, especially when I watched the construction of the huge model of the ocean liner in the carpenter shop and the life-size decks going up on the sound stages.

Not only was I dialogue director, but now I became second unit director. I was to stage the shipwreck sequences with a new face, Arthur Ripley. Ripley was a long, lean, roughshod man with shaggy hair and a moth-eaten moustache. His face was heavily lined and pockmarked. He had been hidden at a desk up in the writers' building by Towne and Baker because Wanger would have been offended by such an uncouth scarecrow. Wanger had his fingernails and toenails manicured weekly by the world-famous Perc Westmore. Ripley didn't.

But there was another reason Gene and Graham hid Ripley. He was the only one doing the real writing. To me, Ripley was a true movie man. He had written and cut for Mack Sennett. He had a beagle's nose for film. He knew everything there was to know. An inspired man, almost a clairvoyant, it took careful knowing to appreciate him. When he grew enthusiastic, he would shout crazily, truculently, as if all listeners, including unseen demons, were fighting his idea.

Ripley solemnly predicted to me that this film would collapse and at the first preview it did—completely. Wanger was in despair. The next morning I asked Ripley if anything could be done to save the film. He said, "Yes, but Wanger's too chickenshit to do it. Back in the Sennett days we would put in a scene where the villain 'kicked a dog' so the public would know who to hate. You got to make the public feel the way *you* want them to."

"What does all that have to do with this picture?"

"Everything. Nobody knows who to hate or who to root for. Boyer's killed the guy; intentionally or not, he did the killing. So why *shouldn't* Colin Clive, an understandably jealous husband, go after him? Why should an audience be expected to hate Colin Clive for *liking his wife?* Wives in the audience don't. To them he's a nice guy in spite of all his evil smirks, and he's rich as hell, too, and women love rich guys."

"You mean you could fix it so that they would be guaranteed to hate Clive? How?"

"Simple. When Clive comes in to compromise his wife, shoot another scene where the chauffeur gets up, rubbing his head, and tells Clive what happened. Clive gets furious at the chauffeur for bungling it, picks up a poker and cracks his skull. That way *he's* the *murderer* and he's trying to pin it on a poor innocent man, Boyer."

I went straight to Wanger. At first he winced, looked seasick and said, "That's terrible. Harebrained and melodramatic. I suppose that ghoul Ripley thought it up."

"Oh, no. It's mine. Straight from the Theatre Guild who've had nothing but successes. Whether you have the sensitivity to appreciate art films or not, this is great."

Since we had very little to lose, we tried it. It worked—and brilliantly. The picture made a fortune for Wanger and three lifelong friends for me—Jean Arthur, Boyer and Arthur Ripley.

While Wanger wouldn't be caught dead admitting it, he knew that scene had been the catalytic agent, and on the strength of it offered Ripley and me the chance to codirect and write a film. It was based on a slick magazine short story called "Summer Lightning" about a young mother who returns to her New England small town after her husband's death and falls in love again with her childhood sweetheart. It was pretty banal but perhaps we could give it some bite.

Wanger had bought it for his beautiful young wife, Joan Bennett. As the male lead I suggested one of Wanger's young stars, Hank Fonda. I thought of a new title, *I Met My Love Again,* and to save money we shot the whole picture in the studio. I directed scenes and Ripley planned lenses and the movement of the camera.

Wanger had no faith in us. Every time the sound stage doors opened for air, he would appear in the doorway, look in at what we were shooting, look at his watch, shake his head direfully and leave. Each afternoon he would shake his finger at us. "One day of bad rushes and you're both *out!*"

The first preview was pretty good. Everyone liked it, except Wanger.

He asked one of the world's greatest directors, George Cukor, to shoot some retakes. Cukor saw it and said, "All it needs is a little work. Why don't you get the original people to brush it up?"

Wanger said, "No, no. I don't trust them. They're idiots. You do it."

I didn't mind accepting help from such a great director, but it was rough on Ripley. He had hoped this would be a step up for him, but Wanger barred him from the lot, fearing an outburst. The other writer on the film, David Hertz, had left for another assignment, so Wanger, to save money, asked me to write the new scenes Cukor wanted. I was surprised until I realized he still had a few more weeks left to my contract. Cukor liked what I wrote and filmed it.

Nevertheless, my option was not taken up. As they say, Hollywood was not ready for me. Still I swore to return, and soon. It would take seventeen years to get me back there.

All those years later, I visited George Cukor in his beautiful but lavish Hollywood Hills house. "Everything here is wonderfully original, but I think my favorite thing is that superb marble fireplace," I said with admiration.

"Oh, really. You gave that to me."

"I did?"

"Wanger sent it to me for doing the retakes on the picture you made. You really should have had it, but I'm not giving it to you."

CHAPTER

The day I got back to New York in June 1937 an extraordinary thing happened. I was offered a play that had not been turned down by Guthrie McClintic, Jed Harris or George Abbott. I was the first choice.

There the script was, stuck under the door of my mother's 114th Street apartment, the envelope marked "Joshua Logan—By Hand."

I read the title page: *On Borrowed Time*, a play by Paul Osborn, submitted by Dwight Wiman. What a true and believing friend I had in Dwight Wiman.

I locked myself in my room and began to read. The play was a modern fable with magic and supernatural overtones. Set in the backyard of a small-town American house, it was the story of eighty-nine-year-old Gramps and six-year-old Pud whose parents had been killed in an automobile accident. Death appears in the shape of a strange man named Mr. Brink, to take Gramps to "where the woodbine twineth." Pud saves him by remembering what Gramps did when a boy was trying to steal an apple. "My book says if you do a good deed, Gramps, then anything you wish will come true. *You did a good deed* by letting that boy have an apple." So Gramps takes a flier and asks Mr. Brink to climb up the tree to get him an apple and once he is there, uses his wish by shouting, "By God, Mr. Brink, you gotta stay up there till I let you come down." At which point the apple tree shakes and Death is caught in the tree by Gramps's wish. Gramps plans to keep him there forever so he can be with Pud.

The last twenty minutes, except for the final curtain, were weak, feckless. Nevertheless, the play had tremendous possibilities. I called Dwight Wiman and thanked him warmly. He set a date for us to meet Paul Osborn at Tony's the next day for lunch.

When I entered Tony's, it was dark and virtually empty, save for a man sitting alone in a booth in the far corner. I placed myself at a table near the door so that Dwight would see me when he came in. I waited nervously for a half hour. I was terrified that Paul would not like me. And where was Dwight? Could he be locked into some conference? Had he had a few too many prelunch cocktails?

The man in the back booth seemed to be expecting someone also, for he constantly peered from his watch to the door. My God, could that be Osborn? I got up and walked over to him. When I got up close, I saw panic streak across his face. He was dark and handsome with night-black eyes and patches of matching black beneath them. In a tentative manner, I said, "Excuse me, but by any chance, could you be . . ."

He jumped up and shouted, "You're Josh Logan?"

"Yes. And you're Paul Osborn."

"What do you think of the script?"

"It's one of the most marvelous I've read in my life—that is, up to a point. Then it suddenly dips and is ridiculous. And then, goddammit, it becomes great again at the very end."

"That's exactly right! How did you know that? I mean, that's the way I feel, but the novel goes that way."

We sat talking for two hours about the script and what was wrong with it and how it could be fixed. Dwight never showed up and we never missed him. We were too fascinated by our ideas. We had all kinds of things to settle, including how long we could suspend Death. We decided twenty-four hours was our limit.

For four months Paul and I agonized over the play, day and night, trying to solve the last third. We worked in Paul's railroad flat where Paul's wife, Millicent, a beautiful actress who had given a vivid performance in Elmer Rice's *Street Scene* a few seasons before, shared our excitement and torture.

As the search went on, Paul, Millicent and I grew closer and closer to each other and further from the solution. One day, Paul said, "When it comes right down to it, this is a love story between Gramps and Pud. Their life looks rosy. They've gotten Mr. Brink up a tree. Gramps will live forever, and so will everyone else. Nothing can part the lovers now. In all great love stories at this point, something has to happen. Now, what happens at this point in a famous love story?"

"Well, I saw Garbo's *Camille* last week. Marguerite and Armand are living happily in the country, just like Pud and Gramps, then *Armand's father shows up and tells Marguerite that she must let Armand go.* She's an embarrassment to his young sister and she's too old for him."

"The father comes in." Paul was smiling.

I said, "You're right. Only for us the doctor comes in and bawls Gramps out for keeping old and terribly sick people from dying." Then I went on. "So Camille leaving Armand is like Gramps leaving Pud by thinking he should die. Pud screams at him, 'Gramps, you don't love me anymore' and runs away."

And we both shouted: "Into the arms of Mr. Brink, who grabs at Pud, who then falls and breaks his back. Now both Pud and Gramps can die together. And that ends the play."

The words started tumbling out of Paul in such a rush I moved out of the room.

The next day we ran into Dwight Wiman's wife, Steve, and we told her it was finished. She had read the novel and hadn't liked it, but she insisted on reading the play right away.

At eleven that night, Paul and I arrived at her apartment. Paul's eyes had grown blacker with fear. Together, we approached stern-faced Steve. She had a reputation as a strong-willed, bright individualist with a too-honest tongue.

"It's absolutely marvelous. I never read a better play in my life. I laughed and I cried. I couldn't put it down. It will be a huge, huge hit."

Her enthusiasm and Dwight's and all of Dwight's staff got us through the nerves of the next weeks. I felt Gramps mustn't be an ancient country bumpkin stereotype; he had to have a romantic nobility. One actor and one actor alone seemed perfect: Richard Bennett, once a great leading man, with leonine, roughhewn looks, and an air of deep intelligence. We had heard he had difficulty memorizing lines, but he was too perfect for us not to take a chance on.

We thought we'd have a particularly difficult task finding Pud. But *two* Puds appeared. The first was a boy I'll remember all my life. He was the six-year-old son of the distinguished director, Worthington Miner, and the fine actress, Frances Fuller. He had a perfectly round head, like one of those little Japanese doll pencils, with strong round black eyes that peered out from the whitish expanse of his face, a piping voice somewhere about high C, a tiny nose and a wide, wide smile.

The other Pud was a New Jersey farm boy named Peter Holden whose ruddy cheeks and robust little body made you think he climbed apple trees every day of his life. He had no trouble with the scene where Pud climbs the tree to test its magic power. He could have hung there for hours. From the first rehearsal, Peter Holden thought Peter Miner was the funniest kid he had ever seen in his life. When it came his turn to play the part, he read the lines exactly the way Peter Miner did, a decision totally his own.

For Granny, we persuaded the talented and youthful Dorothy Stickney to don a white wig.

The actress I admired most for the role of the evil Aunt Demetria, Jean Adair, was far too sweet looking. She had one advantage, though: her thick eyeglasses looked like the bottoms of bottles. We decided that with some Paul Osborn color under her eyes she would scare anybody.

Bennett rehearsed like an old-time star. He mumbled his lines. He was "saving" his performance. There is a theatre phrase for it: he's a "money actor"—he'll only give when the audience has paid to see him. To avoid the harsh glare of the single, unshaded pilot light used in rehearsals (it is too weak to read by and too painful to look at directly), Bennett pushed an old, beat-up felt hat down over his eyes while he murmured. Obviously, he was studying the part and thinking of the many things he might do with each line. But it was disconcerting for the rest of us. There was no guessing what his performance would be like. He did, however, open up when he performed with the little boy. I convinced him that otherwise the boy would not be able to learn how loud to talk or how fast to move.

Soon a tiny worry spot appeared. Without a script in his hands, Bennett almost froze with fear. And Gramps had many lines that were similar in content, such as "Mr. Brink, you can't come down now," and "Mr. Brink, if I let you come down now, will you take Demetria?" and "Mr. Brink, I've decided to let you come down." The similarities drove Bennett mad. I fully sympathized, since I have never been able to memorize well myself.

For the New Haven opening, I had put a prompter on stage left in addition to the regular prompter on stage right. Bennett started off by stumbling on lines that had never bothered him before. He grew frantic and angry with himself. Finally, he forgot one line completely. With a sinking heart, I heard both prompters feed the line to him. Bennett roared, "One at a time, one at a time!" The audience applauded vociferously. At another point, during a conversation across a table between Pud and Gramps, Bennett floundered. Although little Peter Miner knew the play by heart, he had never even heard of prompting. He just felt sorry for Dick Bennett and he went around the table, crawled into Bennett's lap and whispered the line into his ear. Bennett smiled and said, "Thank you, son. That's real thoughtful of you." Once again the audience applauded.

In the back of the theatre, Paul, Dwight and the rest of us were in terrible pain. At each moment we expected the worst, and that's what we got.

When Bennett was in control, he was still vitally touching, virile and funny. There must be some way to save him. I thought of having the script written on the backs of all the chairs, on the tree, on Bennett's cuffs. But Dwight, John Wharton, his lawyer, and Kay Brown, who in this case represented Jock Whitney, a large investor in the show, all insisted Bennett be replaced before the opening in New York and by the following week. And I agreed—as long as I didn't have to tell Bennett personally.

Dudley Digges took over the role after reading the play and seeing a performance in New Haven. He learned the entire script over the weekend. I rehearsed him all day Monday and that night we had a run-through. He was only a tiny bit insecure. He did not play the role as Bennett had. He was worried about the age. Since he was younger than Bennett, he wore a white wig and bent over in a stoop. In the first run-through he stooped, and as the play progressed, he got lower and lower. I said, "Dudley, if the audience doesn't realize you're an old man by the third act, it's too late to remind them."

"I should straighten up a bit, eh?" he said, and he did.

But then he gave me another jolt. He decided not to play the Tuesday and Wednesday preview performances, as he wanted more time for further study. Parker Fennelly, the understudy and a very clever actor, took over. But this meant that when we opened on Thursday night, Digges would have played only one performance of the play.

On Monday, Peter Miner caught a cold and the role of Pud was played by Peter Holden who, at his mother's insistence, took over the part from then on. I wondered what else could happen.

Leland Hayward showed up. He liked the play and decided it *was* a hit, but he warned, "The only thing that can hurt you is the Jed Harris show, *Our Town* by Thornton Wilder, which opens the night after yours. Let's take a look at it." He dragged me there the next night. Halfway through, I said to Leland, "This is a masterpiece. How can anybody like our play if they've seen this?"

"Are you out of your mind? This is terrible!" He continued to growl, "They haven't got a chance. It'll close in two nights." And as the third act began with the townspeople gathering under umbrellas by the gravesides, he pulled me up and said, "Come on, I'm tired of this dreary crap. Let's go back to a good play." I found it touching and theatrical, and I will always be grateful that *Our Town* opened the night after *On Borrowed Time*. Whether Leland really hated *Our Town* or pretended to bolster my spirits, I'll never know.

Thursday, February 3, 1938, was my first proper opening night on Broadway. I came to the theatre early, went backstage to shake everyone's hands and make bad jokes. The important first-nighters began to arrive and Dwight, with too many cocktails showing, rattled off their names to me with machine-gun rapidity. There were the critics, agents, backers and movie studio officials who might be interested in buying the film rights.

We had gone through so many frustrating experiences with this play that I wasn't quite sure what was going to happen, and yet I had a deep confidence in it. I had seen a preview audience accept the fact that Mr. Brink was caught up in the tree by Gramps's wish, and I had heard at least once or twice the huge laughs and moving applause that the play had when adequately played. Tonight, I knew Dudley Digges would give everything he had; I knew Peter Holden would be perfect because little boys always are, and even though the benefit audience the night before had found the play ridiculous, I was sure that it was well enough constructed to please a sophisticated Broadway audience.

So, instead of being a trembling boy from Mansfield waiting to see his first Broadway play open, I was a rather smug, arrogant young man who had the attitude of, "You lucky people—just you wait till this play hits you." And the curtain went up and the old man was sitting there working, engraving a watch fob, and I heard the audience buzz start when Pud's head appeared behind Gramps's chair about one foot from the floor and then continue as Pud climbed over the arm of the chair, knocking Gramps only slightly. With that commitment of the audience, for the first time I realized that it was giving a signal which told me the play was becoming a hit.

As I became more experienced and directed more plays, I learned that during tryouts there was always—like the "click" in Tennessee Williams' *Cat on a Hot Tin Roof* which signals to Brick that he has got drunk enough to face the evening—a click to tell me a play is going to go. There is to me one moment in each of my shows that acts as a signal that the audience understands what the play is saying and it is going along with it. It generally happens early in the play—though sometimes not until very late. But in *On Borrowed Time* it was mercifully early.

The laughs came naturally after that audience commitment. Dudley was completely at ease—and magnificent. Peter Holden was, I had to admit, as bright and delightful as Peter Miner would have been.

Still, we were afraid to be certain of success before the reviews appeared. Paul and I congratulated the actors and then went over to Mother's new apartment at Fifty-sixth Street and Park. She was a Southern hostess to all Mary Lee's and my friends: gumbo, corn bread, coconut cake and ambrosia. She had even hired Galli-Galli, a small Arab magician who took baby chicks from behind your ear. But Paul soon begged off, and I followed him to Dorothy Stickney's and Howard Lindsay's house for their opening night party. When some members of the cast who had waited at the Times Square newsstand rushed in waving the papers, we crowded around and shouted, "Read them aloud." Dwight read Brooks Atkinson's first. Great round phrases poured forth and when Dudley Digges's name was mentioned, a loud, rooster-like crow came from him. He had had a few nice, strong whiskies and was in a high Irish mood. He crowed all through the notices and soon we joined in with him. We jumped up and down and kissed each other—in a celebration more special than Christmas or New Year's or the Fourth of July because it was for us!

But with all the mentions of Peter Holden and Frank Conroy, I was still waiting for some hint of my contribution. After all, this was my debut as a Broadway director. Why wasn't anyone saying that a discovery had been made, that the theatre had had an amazing stroke of fortune last night when, unannounced and unheralded, a young backwoodsman from Mansfield had blinded the public with his special brand of fireworks? But no one did. In fact, my name appeared in only one review. I decided that I had been paid the highest compliment a theatre director can get. Isn't the final result of a production a knitting together of playwriting, directing and acting? No one element should stand out above the other if it is to be a perfect evening.

Next morning I picked up the phone and called Paul. "How do you feel?"

"All right, I guess."

"Heard from anybody?"

"Nope. Have you?"

"Nope. Well, what are you going to do?"

"I don't know. What are you going to do?"

"Maybe we should go down and see if there's a line at the box office and then have lunch."

I picked him up and we wandered down to the Longacre Theatre, where we found twelve tasteful, clever people lined up. I had been told that if you had a real smash hit, there would be fifty to one hundred people lined up.

We went to lunch at La Hiff's Tavern where we had eaten all during rehearsals. We were hoping the waiters or the manager or the girl at the cash register would say, "Great work. Congratulations. Here's a special table. How about a drink on the house!" But we got nothing except the usual nods.

I said to Paul, "Do you realize that we're two of the most famous men in New York and nobody knows it?"

We complimented each other on the fine job we had done on the play and on how cooperative we had been with each other and how hard it had been. After lunch, we shook hands with a sure, firm grip and went our respective ways home.

* * *

The fact that I had a Broadway success made Leland think that I was now ready to go to Hollywood at an enormous salary. I quickly disabused him of this by accepting an offer from Dwight to direct another play for him.

"You're going to love it," Dwight said. "It's the new Richard Rodgers and Larry Hart musical, *I Married an Angel.* Dick Rodgers is delighted, and he's not easily pleased."

Had Rodgers forgotten our first unfortunate meeting? It was at Ciro's during my *Garden of Allah* period. I had downed too many martinis and had settled myself comfortably on the floor. Roger Edens brought Dick and his wife, Dorothy, over to meet me. I made a feeble effort to stand up. Rodgers bent over and patted my shoulder. With the smile one gives nice drunks, he said, "Oh, no, sit right there. Nice to meet you. Hope we'll have the chance to work together someday."

I didn't believe he wanted a drunk in the middle of a nightclub floor to direct a play of his then, and I couldn't believe it now. Dwight laughed. "He wants you all right. And he'll probably want you to go down to Atlantic City with Larry Hart."

"What's he doing there?"

"He's at the Traymore writing the second act. The score's mostly finished. I bought the show on the strength of the songs, but I'm not worried about the book. Dick and Larry will take care of that."

I met Dick and Dorothy Rodgers at their lovely apartment and was introduced to their daughters: tiny Linda whose turned-up nose made her father warn her never to go out in the rain lest she drown, and the older and quiet Mary with her curious, searching eyes.

As the evening progressed I saw that Dick was worried. He asked me to go to Atlantic City but warned me that Larry was rather eccentric. "He disappears. A will-o'-the-wisp. Just put your foot on his tail and get him to write that second act."

Larry Hart met me at the Atlantic City station. Not as short as Toulouse-Lautrec—he was just a bit over five feet—he did share certain similarities with the French master. He was slightly balding and his eyes darted about like a bird's. He puffed away on an oversized cigar and spoke in staccato phrases. It was easy to talk to him if you had him captive sitting beside you in a car, but walking down the boardwalk, conversation was catch-as-catch-can. Should you glance away for a second, he could vanish. After a few of these disappearing tricks, I learned to search for him in the nearest tobacco shop where he had gone to relight his cigar.

His imagination worked endlessly, but only to make you laugh so he could laugh louder himself. Perhaps his pressured laughter covered something deeper. I never tried to penetrate it, I just learned to respect it.

He was always referred to as lovable—so diminutive, so antic—something to play with, like a frisky pup. Yet in truth, he was a colossus. Larry was a master at the art of lyrics. His rhyming technique is being attacked now by a popular and garrulous rival, but Larry Hart's catalog of songs is stupendous and will always be. He had a still-unmatched flair for telling jokes in rhyme gracefully, then being able to switch quickly into poignant poetry. His unrequited love lyrics to Rodgers' music are now classics. To put it bluntly, he was the biggest little man I ever knew.

During our entire week at the Traymore, Larry gaily avoided work. At our first session, he began with "Let's play some cards."

"I'm not much of a . . ."

"Anybody can learn this. It's called 'Cocksucker's Rummy.'"

"How do you play it?" I asked carefully.

"Any form of cheating goes. Steal, put a card up your sleeve, pretend it's another one, point out the window and grab my cards and put them on yours. Anything nasty is fair."

Puffing his cigar, he started to deal. He had a dazzling number of ways to cheat and a childish delight in all of them. After an especially diabolic action, he snapped out, "Boy, if only the principal could have seen that."

"Who's the principal?"

"A certain five-foot-eight character back home with a sour-apple face." It was the only reference he made to Richard Rodgers that week.

It seemed to me Larry envied and therefore hated Dick's rugged self-discipline, his ability to be punctual, efficient and to bring a show in on time. It was agony for Larry to sit down to work. Perhaps it was his fear of being less than perfect or just the painful fact of being Larry.

I cared deeply for Larry. I wanted to protect him from hurt, to help him cope, to go enthusiastically along with all his crazy schemes. All that week, I tried to make him happy by joining in his daily search for a new restaurant. Once there, we would examine the food in the kitchen before ordering and consider every item on the wine list. And then we would go back to his room for more games of Cocksucker's Rummy.

The day we were to return to New York, I found him for the first time at his hotel room desk furiously scribbling away on an oversized pad as fast as I've seen anyone write. Three or four scratched lines were enough for each sheet.

"Look at me. I'm writing the second act."

On the train back, he continued his frantic scratching away. Halfway to New York, he folded the mountain of papers, stuffed them in an envelope, and pulled out the playing cards. He made no offer to show me what he had written.

When I delivered the manuscript to Dick, he looked sick and he said, "What is this all about?" There was nothing to do but tell him what had happened. There was no flicker of change in his face. I had not given him any news.

"We'll have to go into rehearsal in two weeks without a second act. I hope you can wing it."

The plot was set in Budapest and dealt with a jilted banker, Willy, who swears he'll never again decide to marry unless an angel comes down from heaven. Down she comes, feathered wings and all. Unfortunately, she manages to offend Willy's phony friends by her heavenly but blunt truthfulness. This angers Willy too.

Dennis King played Willy. Walter Slezak played Harry, a rival banker. Vivienne Segal, whom Larry Hart adored above all women, played an American friend, Peggy. Audrey Christie was Peggy's wild cousin and Charles Walters was Audrey's young lover. For the crucial role of Angel, Dwight and Dick had found one of the most beautiful women ever to appear onstage or anywhere else. She was a Norwegian girl, born Eva Brigitta Hartwig. Wanting a ballet career, she had adopted a Russian-sounding name, Vera Zorina. Her husband, George Balanchine, the brilliant choreographer, had been persuaded to create our dances.

Jo Mielziner, the set designer, and Dick and I wanted a set that would give the show the flow and grace that musicals never seemed to manage. We voted against those cumbersome curtains that "closed in" after each scene. Instead, we'd have "open changes" in a dim blue light and thereby melt from one stage picture to the next while the furniture traveled on and off on treadmills. But all the action had to be perfectly planned and rehearsed if we were to achieve this flow.

At the first rehearsal, Dick played the score and then the cast sang it. Larry listened to the lyrics with intense concentration. Every so often, he would scratch down a change on a yellow page. He needed the live performance to stimulate him.

By the fourth day, I had put the first act on its feet, but the second act was still not in evidence. While Balanchine was working out a dance number, I sidled over to Dick and Larry. "We're ready for the second act."

Dick said, "Okay. You and I will go to Larry's house tonight. If it takes all night, we'll have a second act."

"But what about the second act songs?"

"Oh, we'll do those tomorrow night," said Larry.

Larry and Dick paced the floor all that night dictating lines while I sat at a desk writing them all down in my laborious scrawl.

The next night, Dick and Larry carried out their promise by finishing the songs.

In the second act, Harry, Willy's rival, gives an all-night party at the end of which all of them are to go to Willy's Budapest bank and withdraw their deposits, thus causing Willy's ruin. Yet the song Rodgers and Hart wrote for the revenge party wasn't about angels, Budapest, banks, parties or anything even remotely connected with the show. It was a wild Larry Hart conceit, "At The Roxy Music Hall," to be sung by Audrey Christie and to be acted out by the whole cast as a takeoff on a Music Hall show. Bewildered and completely at a loss as to how to stage it, I asked them what it had to do with the plot.

Larry began, "Oh, you can't just keep writing about old Budapest all night, so we thought we'd do a takeoff on Radio City—you know, a divertissement. First, we'll have a big symphony orchestra with stages going up and down, then the Radio City male chorus behind Dennis King, a specialty for Slezak, Vivienne and Audrey as Rockettes, the ballet corps for Zorina."

"But how do we explain it to the audience?"

Dick said, "The less you explain, the happier they are. Let's just do it."

That was an astounding theatrical lesson for me. When you have no reason for putting something into a musical show, then for Christ's sake, don't give a reason. Just do it.

As Larry explained "divertissement" to me, it had been a custom for years in Europe toward the end of a musical play to allow all the stars to kick up their heels, clown, be *themselves* for a madcap moment, rather than the characters they were portraying. In other words, a breather from the strict plot, a diversion, yes, a divertissement.

Of course, the ballet part of our Music Hall divertissement gave Zorina her chance. And Balanchine had an evil brainstorm for it. All New York was awaiting Salvador Dali's first visit to America. Balanchine stole his thunder by revealing, in the ballet, all the tricks of surrealism before Dali arrived.

In despair, I asked Larry, "What's surrealism got to do with the Radio City Music Hall?"

"Absolutely nothing. Why?"

"Well, then, why is it in the show?"

"So Zorina can dance and Balanchine can fry Dali's ass. What the hell are you trying to do? Make this Ibsen?" I slumped away.

The ballet was puzzling enough and even more so when Balanchine told me it was based on *Othello*. One man carried his head under his arm throughout it. I asked Balanchine who that man was supposed to be, Othello or Iago. With his usual sniff, he answered, "Both."

"You're as crazy as Larry Hart," I told him.

"Larry Hart is baby. I'm grown man," he said.

I kept telling myself all this is a scene in a Budapest living room. And when we go back to the plot the audience is coming with us because we damned well tell them to.

I was back in New Haven dress rehearsing, but it wasn't like the New Haven of *On Borrowed Time*. Now there was a battalion of help: a composer, lyricist, orchestrator, choral arranger, dance captain, set designer, costume designer and many others, all working like hell.

Not believing I was contributing enough, I worked twice as hard. I tried to make crosses smoother, readings a bit easier to understand, Larry and Dick's divertissement wilder. I wanted the show to be great for them and for my first fan, Dwight. It just had to be.

Balanchine showed the nearest thing to rage during one rehearsal of the ballet. "I am going down on dot stage and geeving dose leetle ballet girls haaal!" With a fierce warrior's face, he marched down the aisle, up the stage steps, and with no transition whatsoever spoke in the sweetest, gentlest tone. "Leetle ballet girls, please leeft legs *leetle* higher."

Late one night just as we were about to rehearse the Roxy number on stage, I heard a slight noise in the back of the theatre. There was

Larry Hart, staggering back and forth, his hip hitting the seats at his side, trying to light a cigar. He seemed to be serene enough so I started to rehearse. Audrey entered and started to sing:

> Now come with me,
> And you won't believe a thing you see . . .

A tornado broke out—a thrashing machine had been let loose in the aisles. It was Larry Hart shouting out incomprehensible phrases.

"Hold the rehearsal. What is it, Larry?"

He kept screaming hoarsely, but I couldn't understand the words.

"Slow down, Larry. Say it a little slower."

Then he said very slowly and carefully, "No now-singers in this show! No now-singers in this show! No now-singers in this show!"

"What are now-singers?"

"*She's* a now-singer! Did you hear how she began my chorus? It's 'Come with me' and she began '*Now* come with me'! No *now-singers!*"

Audrey apologized. "Oh, I'm sorry, Larry. I forgot. It's something I . . ."

"Don't forget! Don't forget!" And he climbed up and sat down on stage below the left side of the proscenium so that no one would put in any more "nows." In a few minutes, he was tight asleep and the rehearsal continued.

Walter Slezak came out front to look at the set and started to grin. I said to him, "Beautiful, isn't it?"

"I don't know. There's something asymmetrical. There should be another little Larry Hart on the other side for balance."

Opening night in New Haven, I positioned myself at the back of the theatre with Larry, Dick and Dwight. Dick turned to me with a stern, dour expression. "Josh, you've done a wonderful job on this show."

I was taken aback. "But think of all the help I've had," I said, expressing my genuine feeling of inadequacy.

"Josh," he said impatiently, "if you think you contributed nothing, then you're plain crazy and there's nothing I can do about it. But I still have the right to my opinion." But his eyes seemed to have a hint of softness. What a strange personality. When he sounded extra tough or disapproving, he might be thinking nice things or negative things or even getting a good idea for a song. It was always difficult to tell.

The overture, filled with promising Rodgers tunes, was applauded. The curtain rose and the audience greeted Jo Mielziner's magical set with gasps. Everything was gauze and mist and clouds. Even the tread-mills worked like film dissolves. When King shouted the line, "I will not marry unless an angel comes down from heaven," celestial music filled the air and through the gauze from high up, a gleaming angel appeared with tiny bare feet, a thin flowing gown and widespread wings. She touched the ground behind a scrim cloud. Then Vera Zorina stepped into the room and quietly said, "I am an angel. You sent for me?"

The audience fell in love with her on sight. But soon King, who up to then had been at his smooth, British best, started to do things he had never done in rehearsal. When Zorina turned front as directed and batted her long lashes, King poured water into a glass. On her best lines, he paced the floor making grimaces. He sat beside her on a bench as he sang from the title song, "Have you heard? I married an angel," but he rolled his eyes at the audience, ignoring her existence. It was clear her success was driving him mad.

At intermission, I tore backstage and burst into King's dressing room. "What on earth are you doing, Dennis? You're not only hurting Zorina and the play but you're hurting yourself. Why are you carrying on like a lunatic while another actor is talking? Please play the scenes the way they were rehearsed."

He turned white, then red, then white again, and started to scream so loudly that I was sure he could be heard out front. "Get out of here, you inexperienced bastard. How dare you come into my dressing room at intermission, when I should be calm? Get out of here before I kill you!"

Shaking with frustration, I slammed out. But I must have made an impact, for he played the second act beautifully and never again tried his distracting antics, or at least not when I was watching.

At our next stop, Boston, two important things happened to me. I met Elliot Norton, the drama critic of the *Boston Post,* a bright, wise, sensitive man who taught me what a critic can mean to the success of a show. Not only was Norton able to write literate judgments, but he could interpret a work to its creator as well. I made it a lifetime habit to have lunch with him two or three days after he had seen a show of mine to hear further thoughts.

And from Dick Rodgers I learned a useful thing: when a show is set and no further major changes are possible, make use of all the time left to put in laughs.

* * *

I had felt a hint of success during the previews—the way the audience seemed to be ours the moment Vera Zorina emerged from behind that cloud. So I had only one worry on opening night in New York: what Brooks Atkinson would think of the Roxy Music Hall number. So I sighed with relief when I read the opening lines of his review. "Musical comedy has met its masters," it said, and then he noted that the divertissement was the high spot of the evening, and Zorina the Angel that Broadway needed.

CHAPTER

I had directed two successive hits for Dwight Wiman, and my friends were reporting that he was praising me extravagantly. "Dwight couldn't stop talking about you last night. Of course, he was a little high. Still, he says here you're not yet thirty but you've already become one of the all-time great directors."

I wanted to feel joy at such praise, but instead I perversely transformed it to almost tearful pain. I was having the same reaction I had when I was made president of the Triangle Club. I could hear my mother's Polk Street friends saying, "Mustn't let it go to his head. No gentleman gets his name in the papers."

Soon, I could feel a tightness developing under my diaphragm. It was as though a boa constrictor were trying to swallow a mongoose whole and had the little animal still alive inside him, caught halfway down waiting to be digested. I felt that I was going through the same process and wasn't quite sure which animal I was. I understood the ingredients of my feeling: what made me happy, what made me hurt, but I couldn't control it.

Along with these fantasy pains, I felt threatened by a real one. Dwight had recently taken over the role of my "best friend" in earnest. Over the tables of Tony's he had become quite simply my lord and master. After all, who had discovered this fellow Logan?

He summoned me to him with the news that he had a great new musical for me which we would start immediately, something called *Great Lady*, which would have the most beautiful costumes and music and . . . I stopped him. "Could I read it please, Dwight? It sounds a bit old-fashioned to me."

"You let me be the judge of that, my boy. I'm putting up the money, and I tell you that Lucinda Ballard is a genius."

"Who's she?" I said.

"Stop talking like that. She's a costume designer. Now this is my show, and when I say—"

"Dwight, Dwight, I'll read it. I'll consider it carefully, but you see, I've had a call this morning—"

"From the Playwrights' Company. I know. John Wharton's their lawyer, but don't forget, he's mine too. Unfortunately, I had to refuse them because you're going to be busy with *Great Lady*."

I began to splutter. "How dare you decide my life for me! This Playwright project is *Knickerbocker Holiday* by Maxwell Anderson. It's the first production of a company formed by our greatest writers, Robert Sherwood, Sidney Howard, S. N. Behrman, Elmer Rice and Max himself—and they want me for their very first production and you *refused* it for me!"

Nevertheless, I read *Great Lady* and listened to the music which was by a wonderfully gifted young man named Fritz Loewe. I remember that Loewe's mouth fell wide apart when I said I couldn't do it because I didn't like the book. "This Logan's a great man. He knows this show is lousy before we do."

By the time I saw Dwight he had guessed the outcome and had already taken it upon himself to arrange for me to hear the score of *Knickerbocker Holiday*. "I told them I was sure you'd be right for it," he said blandly.

I thanked him and went out to New City where I was to meet Kurt Weill, the composer, whose *The Threepenny Opera* had been the rage of Berlin when I was there. Kurt's wife, Lotte Lenya, had sung Jenny in *Threepenny,* and was to help Kurt sing the score for me. Kurt sat at the piano, staring at his manuscript paper through the two hunks of thick glass he used for spectacles. He was a little musical juggernaut. Nothing stopped him once he launched into a song. He caterwauled the melody in a toneless tenor with an accent so thick it hurt him as much as it did us. Lenya just smiled her pearly bear-trap smile. Kurt banged insistently on the keyboard to emphasize the bass rhythms. He had created the songs himself out of Max's little verses which he could scarcely understand.

My head was rattling a bit with what I'd heard. It wasn't Dick Rodgers, and Max wasn't Larry Hart, but everything about Kurt Weill was talent and enthusiasm. And Max's lyrics were poetic and funny. I knew I wanted to do the show and told them so. There was a small celebration consisting of clasped hands and squeezed shoulders. I was amazed by how much my approval meant to them. But again, I was swept with a malaise of doubt. What had I done to them by agreeing to direct before I had even read the script?

In Max's plot, based on Washington Irving's stories of early Nieuw Amsterdam, the old fat Dutch burghers were pure Weber and Fields and the boy and the girl were pure coy. It wasn't until the new governor, peg-legged Peter Stuyvesant, entered, flashing his silver-encrusted stump of a leg, that things began to crackle. He was obviously a dictator and less obviously, a satire of Roosevelt. I hesitated to tell Max what I thought. After all, he had written *What Price Glory?,* the high spot of my life at fifteen.

"Josh, say anything you want to. You know musicals, I don't. I had to follow *The Mikado* as I would a cookbook to find any kind of form."

I made some suggestions, particularly regarding the opening, which he snapped up like the pro he was. Soon, he and Kurt and I were as close as Larry and Dick and I had been. We knew that we needed a great star for Stuyvesant, and also that it was a comparatively small part which made attracting a big star difficult. Someone suggested Walter Huston, but I cut the discussion short. We had offered the part of Gramps in *On Borrowed Time* to Huston and he had sent it on to Max Gordon, his producer friend, for an opinion. Max hated any play with "death" in it, so Walter had turned it down.

Kurt said, "Call him, Josh, call him now. Maybe he's sorry now that it's such a big hit. Only tell him not to send ours to Max Gordon."

Kurt was right. Walter was in California at Lake Arrowhead and wanted me to fly out to read the script to him. He said acting on a peg leg as well as singing and dancing might be a challenge.

Two days later, high up in the California mountains by the lake, I turned the last page and sang in my frog's voice the last lyric. Walter and his lovely wife, Nan, made enthusiastic sounds.

"He's an old scoundrel," Walter said.

I began to knot up inside.

"Oh, I like the nasty part, except that the character's pretty skimpy."

"It can be longer," I said.

"Not longer, just better. It's too one-note, too cool-headed. Couldn't this old bastard make love to that pretty young girl a bit? Not win her, just give her a squeeze or tickle her under the chin, and she could even consider him for a fraction of a second when she hears his song."

"Song?" I said, not realizing I was making history by the question.

"Sure—something nice I could sing to her. I like the other songs, 'The Scars' particularly, but I mean something, you know, a moment for the old son of a bitch to be charming."

And that, my children, was how "September Song" was born.

"No problem, Walter, you'll have the song you want. I guarantee it."

Before returning to New York with Walter's requests, I stopped off in Hollywood to see my friends. Jimmy Stewart was being skittish about the lavish attentions of the studio queen, Norma Shearer, Irving Thalberg's widow. In a moment of alcoholic gallantry at a Marion Davies costume party, Jim had told Shearer, with blazing eyes, that she was the most gorgeous creature he had ever seen. Jimmy's remark hit her like a thunderbolt, which was more than he reckoned on. Since then, she had taken royal possession of him. She transported him about town openly in her yellow limousine, even though he slumped down in the back seat hoping his friends would not recognize him in his thralldom. As proof of her ownership she gave him a gold cigarette case sprinkled with diamonds, so that she could ask for a cigarette in front of others, hoping her gift would advertise the giver. But Jimmy, not wanting to see sly looks, would fumble in every pocket until he came up with a crumpled pack of Lucky Strikes—his badge as a free man. The long, shy, former architecture student was shuffling and stuttering his way through the gaudy glamour of movie city.

* * *

We sang "September Song" in New City over the phone to Walter at Arrowhead. Kurt played and sang it with his inch-thick accent and his faltering accompaniment, and then I sang it with just as bad a voice but emphasizing the lyrics which I loved.

After a pause, Walter said, "Yes, yes, yes, yes, yes—play me the tune again."

Then, amazingly, he sang the whole thing back to us.

During rehearsal, Walter made only one request—that he be allowed to experiment with using Stuyvesant's peg leg in private, so that "people won't worry when I'm worrying."

At dress rehearsal, to the bug-eyed excitement of all, he thumped onstage, up and down steps, flashing the silver leg, then he twirled on it, constantly swirling his long cape which was held out in back by his sword. In this way, he always covered the lower half of his right leg, which was strapped up against the back of his thigh.

In my entire professional career I have never seen anything to equal the dexterity, the professional ease of Walter Huston. He charmed the world.

Since Huston was a close friend of President Roosevelt, Roosevelt decided to go to the theatre when our pre-Broadway tour reached Washington. That night, the theatre was crawling with Secret Service. It was a historic time, not long before Hitler's invasion of Czechoslovakia and just after Roosevelt's letter to Hitler—the famous Munich letter. Max had satirized this by having one old Dutchman named Roosevelt say (about a war threat from Connecticut), "Maybe ve send dem a letter—maybe dey go vay."

When the president arrived in his box, Kurt Weill struck up "The Star-Spangled Banner" and Roosevelt rose to his feet, standing, it seemed to me, like a caped statue of victory. The house applauded and cheered him till he sat, and then the curtain went up.

Of course the play went to hell that night, for the entire audience turned compulsively to FDR's box at each funny line to see if he was laughing. Since he howled at each joke, they didn't have time to follow suit, so they turned silently back to the stage. To a blind man, it must have seemed like an empty auditorium except for one crazy, laughing fool.

In honor of Walter's play, some of us were invited to the White House after the performance. Max stayed away: he couldn't go to a party given by the man his play was attacking. As we arrived in the

Oval Room, Roosevelt, already seated, put us at our ease by shouting out demands for our drink orders, and then began telling us in a loud voice how much he had enjoyed the play—with a certain exception.

"That 'letter' thing wasn't funny. In the first place, it was a *telegram* I sent to Hitler and I sent it personally. The important thing about that was the fact that that bastard's secretary didn't throw it into a wastebasket, but rather put it on top of the important mail to be answered. If it hadn't come from a *powerful* United States it would never even have gotten onto that desk. We've simply *got* to stay powerful enough to stay out of the wastebasket."

Someone asked if he thought that war was unavoidable.

"Unavoidable. Doesn't everyone know it? It's only a question of when. Maybe six months, maybe a year. If I hadn't sent that telegram, we'd be at war now."

He fixed his eyes on me and pointed his finger.

"*You* can do something too."

"Me? What?"

"Put some warnings in that play of yours. Make people know we are in danger. Stick a pin in them. We are going to be attacked, and the longer it takes us to know it, the greater the enemy's advantage."

The president's attendance was reported by all the national magazines, wire services and the radio. *Time* even had a cover picture of Huston as Stuyvesant. Before we reached New York we had a solid advance, which was a help since the reviews were not very good. Nothing, not even "September Song," was praised. Someone once said that critics have tin ears. They never recognize a hit tune. This was never so true as their first brushing aside of "September Song."

New York's opening night audience, however, loved the show, though I didn't relax until I heard my signal of success when Walter Huston stumped on as Peter Stuyvesant. After a week or two, "September Song" had become such a hit that the audience insisted on an encore. Walter, hating to repeat the same chorus, asked Max to write another.

It was working closely with Max Anderson—a man dedicated to the craft of playwriting—that taught me something that has been useful to me all my professional life. One day he casually mentioned that he had arrived at a theory for making a play a hit.

My ears perked up. "You mean *any* play?"

"Any literate play, yes. I've made a study of what kind of story an audience accepts and what kind it rejects. I set out to discover if there is a single element in successes that isn't in failures. I started by examining my own plays. They were after all conceived by the same talent, yet some survived and the rest died quickly. Why? I searched for my answer in Aristotle and I reread Shakespeare, the great Greek masters and hit plays of the present. Eventually, I arrived at my little personal rule. I'm going to write about it someday and I'll send it to you."

"Max, you're going to tell me *now!* What is it?"

"Well, it turns out that it was *in* Aristotle all the time. And it's also in *all* of the great Shakespeare plays, in *all strong plays* anywhere, any time."

"What is the rule, Max?"

"A play should take its protagonist through a series of experiences which lead to a climactic moment toward the end when he *learns* something, *discovers* something about himself that he could have known all along but has been blind to. This discovery comes as such an emotionally shattering blow (and that's the key word, *emotionally*) *that it changes the entire course of his life*—and that change *must* be for the better. If he's changed for the worse, the audience will reject the play, as they do *Troilus and Cressida,* and all other failures. The audience must feel and see the leading man or woman become wiser, and the discovery must happen *onstage in front of their eyes. And that doesn't mean a happy ending.* If the hero is to die, then he just must make the discovery *before* he dies. Of course, the classic example is *Oedipus.* But it's true of *Hamlet* and *Macbeth* and down the line even to Jeeter Lester in *Tobacco Road* and De Lawd in *Green Pastures.* You'll find it in every successful play. For when the protagonist has this revelation, one which raises his moral stature, the audience can grow vicariously along with him. Thus people leave the theatre feeling better, healthier-minded than when they arrived. It's an exciting experience. And that excitement makes plays live."

I've used this Golden Rule, to some extent, on every play and film I've done. It has strengthened the strong ones and quite often saved the weak ones from disaster. George Axelrod, who did the fine screenplay when I directed Marilyn Monroe in *Bus Stop,* still calls it Logan's Law.

* * *

Despite my three outstanding successes, there remained my childlike home life with Mother, who still complained if I spent the evening out. I longed for any jobs that would take me away from New York for a road tour, and as though my prayers were being answered, Dwight called me for another show.

In the discussion stage, it was known as *The McEvoy Show*. The tousle-haired J. P. McEvoy's plot line for this show was based on a young boy genius, like Orson Welles or Pare Lorenz, going to Hollywood. Only this boy would be leftist, which was a popular theme then. It was McEvoy's thought to mix Hollywood with left-wing radicals. The score Dorothy Fields and Arthur Schwartz were composing already had two songs about union troubles, and they planned to write more.

Nothing on the red side sounded funny to me. I told Dwight so, quite emphatically, but he was on fire to have a big musical on Broadway in time for the upcoming 1939 World's Fair, and had already signed two supergreats, Ethel Merman and Jimmy Durante. He told me, "If you don't like it the way it is, change it; only make sure it's a hit."

"All right," I said. "Let's throw all the unfunny Communist stuff out the window and just do a show about the crazy way Hollywood people mix sex and movies."

"For instance?"

And one second later I had an idea that just might be wild enough for a start: Jimmy Stewart hiding on the floor of Norma Shearer's limousine! What if the young director was someone like Stewart, all wide-eyed and virginal, and Ethel Merman (the studio big star and owner because her husband had left it to her) was hot for him. Jimmy Durante? He could be "Hoppe," the M-G-M "idea" or "weenie" man who was a genius at physical finishes (he was famous for cornering studio executives outside the commissary with lines like, "I'll give you two quick ideas—Gable, Tracy, San Francisco!"). And Dwight had found another beautiful dancer whose Broadway career he was going to launch—Tamara Toumanova. She could be a black-eyed Russian waif whom the young director really loves.

McEvoy started rewriting the show at once and we christened it *Stars in Your Eyes*.

By the time we went into rehearsal we were all tired and harassed. The script wasn't completed and I worked frantically on weekends and

I Met My Love Again, Josh's third picture,
the first as director. Josh to left of camera,
co-director Arthur Ripley to right.

Dennis King with Vera Zorina in *I Married an Angel*.

Walter Huston and peg leg in *Knickerbocker Holiday*.
(COSMO-SILEO CO. LENT BY THE MUSEUM OF
THE CITY OF NEW YORK.)

Right: Mildred Natwick
and Jimmy Durante
in *Stars in Your Eyes.*
(LUCAS & PRITCHARD STUDIO)

Below: Ethel Merman in seduction scene of
Stars in Your Eyes. (RICHARD TUCKER)

Jo Mielziner's magnificent setting for *Morning's At Seven*.
(LUCAS & MONROE STUDIO. LENT BY THE MUSEUM OF THE CITY OF NEW YORK).

Charley's Aunt. Nedda Harrigan in the costume she hated. With her are
Arthur Margetson and Katherine Wiman (Dwight's daughter).

after rehearsals with McEvoy, Dorothy Fields and Arthur Schwartz. Often I had to break rehearsal to ask Mac to rewrite the very scene we were rehearsing. There was little time for sleep.

Extracting the Communist slant was trickier than brain surgery. I urged everyone to follow a straight line, until Mac dubbed me "Joe Construction." But he always dutifully went away to try new scenes. Dorothy and Arthur were such great talents that I let them talk me into keeping three songs they had written though they didn't belong. One was for Merman, a plaint about the nonunion working girl, "Just a Little Bit More," and their favorite, "My New Kentucky Home," in which the sun, stars and grass functioned only on union hours. As often happens, it was such a bright, witty song that we didn't realize it was killing the show until almost too late.

Stars in Your Eyes had everything in it but the M-G-M lion; I considered it my most fantastic, fabulous, exciting and funny show, but when we opened in New Haven we found that it ran an hour too long. We had to chop fifty minutes by the next night, and I think that as a result the show was never quite as good as it should have been.

One scene was the wildest I've ever tried. It had Merman and Durante singing a duet of a good song, "It's All Yours." In the middle of each chorus, with the music still going, Durante would stop singing and do one of his notorious jokes. He'd grab a phone from the footlights and shout, "Hello, is dis de meat market? Well, meet my wife at six o'clock!" Then he'd throw the phone to the floor and continue the song, with Merman never missing a beat. This went on for ten choruses, but the audience was so happy we could have gone on for twenty-four.

The sex scenes were so successful that I finally persuaded Dorothy and Arthur to write a more appropriate song than "My New Kentucky Home." They did: "The Lady Needs a Change." It was bawdy and wonderful and turned the show into a hit.

The reviewers welcomed Durante back to Broadway and hailed Merman as a newfound actress, a side of her great talent that she had not been able to show before. In fact, during rehearsal I was so thrilled at her great natural talent that I dubbed her Sarah Bernhardt, Jr., and gave her a silver cup with that inscription on opening night.

During the out-of-town tryouts we had had trouble with the dances. There was talk of changing the choreographer. We should have looked right into the ranks of our own chorus, which included the soon-to-be-famous Norah Kaye, Alicia Alonso, Maria Karnilova, and a very shy kid named Jerome Robbins.

When *Stars in Your Eyes* opened I was cross-eyed with exhaustion. I suddenly didn't want to work. I felt terribly low as though I had been used. I realized I had done more work than anyone else and for much less compensation.

I baffled my friends and family by suddenly boarding a ship with Johnny Swope, bound for South America, and gave no set date for my return. Johnny had got an assignment to photograph South American debutantes for *Vogue* and *Harper's Bazaar*, and I was going to watch. In Valparaiso and Santiago, because of the famous "magazine photographer," we were treated like visiting royalty, and we went crazy about the women, the food and the wine. We started the long drive south to Tierra del Fuego.

Then we went back north to Buenos Aires, across the pampas. There were no roads, only mud tracks, and at that time of year the Chilean land was frozen while the southern Argentine was beginning to thaw out. Many a night we spent on a frozen ridge of mud with the crankcase straddling that ridge, unable to get traction. The trip took three fascinating weeks. Seal beaches, penguins, ostriches who raced our car, and beautiful huanacos, a cousin to the llama, and always mud, mud, mud.

Johnny and I parted six months later after a stay of some weeks in Buenos Aires. He was going back to Chile to sell the car, while I flew to Rio de Janeiro. I was still in a kind of mood. I had resolved not to return to the United States unless I was offered a play that I really loved, and one that was already finished. While I was away *Stars* had closed and my income was dwindling to almost nothing. Only Paul Osborn's new play might be the solution. The script of *Morning's at Seven* arrived in Rio, and it seemed sour-pussed, cranky, funny and touching enough to make me want to go home, but I went the hard way, booking myself on a Brazilian freighter that stopped at every port along the Brazilian coast. Then I boarded a flying boat from Trinidad to New York. Since I had gained some weight in Rio, I determined to take it off on the return trip.

The food on board was so bad and the sight-seeing so interesting that I arrived in New York weighing a hundred and sixty pounds, twenty pounds less than I weighed when playing football at seventeen at

Culver. Though Mary Lee and Mother were appalled at the gaunt sight of me, I was so proud of my new physique that at every chance I stripped to the waist to show off my taut stomach. There is nothing more exciting for a fat man than to be able to see his own stomach muscles.

We cast *Morning's at Seven* in two weeks: Jean Adair, John Alexander, Enid Markey, Tom Chalmers, Russell Collins. My six months away had obviously reinvigorated me; at least, I was in high spirits for the first seven days of rehearsal, and then I collapsed.

One evening I was showing Arthur Schwartz and my family films of my trip when I was overcome with a dry dizziness. They found I had a high fever and called an ambulance. I was taken to St. Luke's Hospital where that night my fever reached 106. Whatever disease I had couldn't be diagnosed, and my delirium was treated with sulfa drugs.

It took at least ten days for me to rally, though by this time I was being treated for sulfa poisoning. The original illness remained a mystery. About two weeks later I was released from the hospital, and everyone agreed that my sudden weight loss had probably weakened my constitution.

While I had been sick, Dwight had been directing the play, or rather, keeping it frozen as I had left it. The play had opened, and not successfully, in Boston, and some of the cast had been changed. Dorothy Gish had taken over one role. I was unsure of the new actors and I didn't even know what had been wrong with the old ones, but I worked hard.

By the time we reached Philadelphia everything looked better, but as far as I was concerned the play had suffered from the same kind of illness that I had had. Undiagnosed. Dwight should have replaced me with an excellent director instead of loyally leaving the play hanging in suspension. The natural growth that happens during rehearsal—the day by day adding of new ideas, new feelings, new comic thoughts—had not been allowed *Morning's at Seven*.

I was left with my tired old toothache guilt for having become sick, and no one could reassure me that this superb play's shakiness was not my fault.

In New York, the play got poor to moderate notices. My heart sank, and the stomach tightenings I had had before going to South America began again, only worse. This time I felt I had let my dear friend, Paul Osborn, down. Paul was the one I had leaned on most. He had really started me. I saw the specter of my own failure. I dropped into the depths of self-pity and became so boring that I hid from people.

Time has justified my faith in that play. It has had belated success in stage revivals and on television.

Dwight completely ignored my morose state and began planning a new musical by Rodgers and Hart in which Vera Zorina would make a triumphant return to Broadway. He wanted a show about the Butler's Ball, an annual event in which the servants, dressed to the nines, hired a big hotel ballroom and had a fling.

After several conferences, I realized that there was no story, something Zorina must also have been aware of because she took off for Hollywood to make *The Goldwyn Follies*. I suggested we bring a playwright friend of mine, Gladys Hurlbut, in and they accepted her.

After Gladys and I had worked together for one afternoon, she said, "But you're not a director—you're coauthor. I'm going to use all your suggestions, and I'm not going to continue unless you are officially named my collaborator."

While we were working, I was offered the additional job of directing the sketches for *Two for the Show*, the Nancy Hamilton-Buddy Lewis revue. Buddy had done the dances in the Triangle Club's *Stags at Bay* with me. Buddy played me the score and I fell in love with their chief song, "How High the Moon"; in fact, I loved it so much I agreed to work with that show each morning and with Gladys in the afternoon. It was another bad decision.

The title for the Rodgers and Hart show became *Higher and Higher*, and in spite of my misgivings we got together quite a good cast: Jack Haley, Shirley Ross, Marta Eggerth, and a trained seal Gladys discovered at a country fair, Sharkey. She was sure it would steal the show.

I plugged on, but never recovered any enthusiasm. By the first day of rehearsal I was in such a deep state of despondency that I could hardly sit through the reading. I had no faith in what we had written. But there was no way of getting out of it. If I left now, Broadway would consider me a deserter. I put the blame for my despair on the poor play. While in my mind there was a hint that something more dangerous was wrong, I suppressed it. If I had known there was such a thing as curable mental illness, I would have welcomed the chance to go to a mental hospital, knock on the door and say, "Let me in." At that time, all I knew was that some people were well and some were crazy.

Even in my despondency I knew that Dick's music was superb, that Robert Alton had devised some amusing dances, and Larry Hart had supplied brilliant lyrics. And so I worked on as well as I could to put *Higher* on its feet.

Jack Del Bondio tried to keep my spirits up. "Buck up, Josh," he said.

Jo Mielziner was so concerned about my behavior that he suggested I join the Catholic Church and see a priest.

On opening night, the final curtain gave me the only laugh I had had for months. Sharkey the seal was on his little stand, stage center, and when the audience applauded, he slapped his fins together, which caused the audience to applaud and laugh more. The house lights came up and the audience started out, and as usual the center aisle was blocked by the several hundred people trying to exit.

Everyone was quiet for a moment. Then an enthusiastic voice rang out: "Darling, zat ees zee muss wanderful fuck in zee worl."

Many people turned to see who was talking. It was the young French wife of an American lawyer. She was using the French word for "seal," which is "phoque." Her husband tried to keep her quiet, but she protested. "I deed not say zee *show* wass gud—I shuzz say zee *fuck* was good—zee *fuck*, only zee *fuck*, and oh, how I loved zat *fuck*." By this time the whole aisle was laughing.

I stood in my box, saying to myself, "At last—a funny scene. But it's not onstage."

Next morning, the notices were as gruesome as I knew they would be. The show ran as long as the advance sale lasted, a few months.

Meanwhile, *Two for the Show* with its promising young cast—Keenan Wynn, Alfred Drake, Eve Arden, Betty Hutton, William Archibald—was a hit. But even that did not erase *Higher and Higher* from my stubbornly morbid mind. Everyone gave me the one piece of advice: "Buck up, Josh."

And then, my blue funk passed. Passed? It shot by me like a rocket and dragged me with it. I started sailing.

Mary Lee and Mother went to Louisiana in April for a visit, and I was suddenly balloon high: wild, ribald, aggressive. It was as if the world had been moving too slowly for me and I had to get twenty miles ahead of it. Every night I haunted the clubs, talking back wildly to the entertainers, who answered with the wisecracks they save for drunks and hecklers, but sometimes I went too far. And after the clubs I stayed up the whole night with friends or simply walked the streets.

It was during this time I started seeing Barbara O'Neil regularly. I had been fond of her since University Players days, when I had dubbed her the statue of Athena brought to life. But now I pursued her in earnest, lavishing presents on her, taking her to clubs and restaurants, sending gifts to her mother. Barbara had played the part of Scarlett O'Hara's mother in the movie of *Gone With the Wind*, and together we went to the exciting New York opening.

It was an intense and hasty courtship—too intense, too hasty—but it was in this fevered atmosphere that I proposed to her.

After setting a June date I broke the news to Mother and Mary Lee on their return. They were astonished and also confused at the swiftness of it all. And I became unreasonably rough with them, as I was rough with anyone at that time who opposed my will. What I didn't know was that this seeming happiness was in fact illness. And a far more dangerous illness than my former low and depressed state.

Barbara and I were married on a foggy day in June. I had bought a white suit for the occasion, but it was so cold and dank that the ceremony took place not in the garden as planned but in the O'Neils' large living room. The yellow forsythia was shrouded in weeping mist; the whole day seemed to weep. That night we flew to Cuba: Barbara wanted to arrive at night so there would be less likelihood of the bellboys snickering at newlyweds. Just the thought of them disgusted her.

I had sent my Packard down by boat and I had booked a beautiful suite in the Nacional. But before we lost sight of the fogbound forsythia we both knew the marriage was a mistake. It was as though it were all mad pursuit and no calm facing of facts. We liked each other and that was all. On the third day, as we sat near the sea in my open car, she said aloud what we had both been thinking: "Why have we gone through with such an empty marriage?" But then she decided we must stay there a few weeks, because her mother would be shocked if we returned too quickly.

And so we spent three weeks in a cottage at the beach. We soaked up the sun and drank daiquiris at noon so that we would be good and sozzled by the steamy afternoon when we would sink into lovely oblivion.

Back in New York, we covered the truth, because Barbara had to fly to California to secure her role as Charles Boyer's patrician wife in *All This and Heaven, Too*. I urged her to go. I wanted her to have success, and I knew my salvation was work.

When Barbara came back she stayed with her family in Cos Cob while I, to keep up a front, settled in the hotel room we had selected. For both our sakes I prayed that she would soon have the courage to tell her family the truth.

Before our marriage, I had been offered a revival of *Charley's Aunt* with my old Princeton and Suffern friend, Jose Ferrer. I had doubts about doing an 1892 farce, but none about Ferrer.

My first meetings with him had that wild excitement we always bring out in each other. We struck gold when we ran Sidney Chaplin's 1924 silent film of *Charley's Aunt*, which was packed with elaborately comic and fantastic visual routines, all of which were conceived by Sidney's brother Charles and the pratfall geniuses of early two-reelers. We decided to graft them all onto the old play, and for scenes not in the movie we invented wilder routines.

But I had never worked so happily and so well. In fact, I seemed to have an overdrive. Although I had never even heard the term, I was in a high state of manic elation. As a result, we completed the work on the play in two weeks (instead of the usual four). I was so stimulated I couldn't sleep at all. Ideas piled upon each other, gag on gag, routine on routine, the funniest scenes I had ever directed.

For the real Charley's Aunt I desperately needed someone of fulsome womanly beauty and immediately recognizable sexuality. And I found her in the office of the producers: an astoundingly beautiful woman, darkly radiant, with an exciting body.

"Holy Christ," I said, "who are you?"

Her name was Nedda Harrigan, and nothing could stop me from having her play the part—nothing, that is, except Miss Harrigan herself.

"What? Play that old chestnut? Why, Jane Darwell played that character part when we did the play in stock! Of course, I might put some money in it because it's a good idea."

She had just come from Hollywood after the death of her husband, the famous Walter Connolly, and she had brought her spectacularly beautiful fifteen-year-old daughter Ann with her.

I persuaded her to let me stop by her apartment at the Lombardy, across the street from Mother's where I was now living, but when I got to her hotel I found a note: "I am very sorry. I have gone to the Stork Club." Off to the Stork Club I went, forced myself on her table, kept at her until the club closed, and she agreed at least to come to rehearsal the next day.

For two days she rehearsed, then quit. I searched her out and dragged her back. This time she stayed. Without losing comedy, I wanted the whole thing played with a romantic passion. I wanted above all to rid it of that chicken-without-a-head flopping about with which farce is generally played.

All farces have complicated plots because they are based on one major and many little offshoot lies. The first twenty-five minutes of *Charley's Aunt* are loaded with essential exposition and therefore tricky to make interesting. But without this solid basis the lunatic heights can never be reached.

In addition, I had five producers, and from them came a geyser of advice. As I sat directing, there were so many crackling whispers that I became quite unnerved. I made it a rule that no one could sit within earshot of me during rehearsal and that all suggestions must be written down and handed to me at the end of the day. But I didn't really have to read them, since they were all complaints about those tedious first twenty-five minutes.

Producer Day Tuttle's notes began in a professorial manner: "The essence of farce is speed," he wrote me.

When I saw him the next day, I answered, "The essence of farce, my dear Day, is not speed, it is *desperation*. It is the desperate, the almost cataclysmic attitude the characters have toward what the audience finds a ridiculous subject that makes it funny. Not, I repeat *not*, the speed. If it's desperate enough it will seem to have speed."

I decided to practice what I preached. I would slow things up! I was certain that the audience hates muddy confusion and hysterical hurry, especially in the opening moments. What they want is security: the feeling that they are in the hands of professionals. The wisest thing, I decided, was to have the first scene spoken with quiet, attractive, yes benign arrogance. Above all, I would avoid a sense of apology, that mincing, rattling tone that seems to say to the audience, "Please, dear audience, do excuse us unimportant folk for being here. Unfortunately, we *have* to go through this boring preliminary bit, but . . ." At that point, unconsciously, the audience flies into a rage: "Get off the stage, you bums!" they would like to say. "Bring on someone who knows his business."

When I was a stage manager it was the accepted practice after a show had been running for a while to tell the cast, "Keep it moving! Give it pace—get a little tempo there." But I have learned that "pace" and "tempo" are umbrella words beloved of amateurs. I never use them. They embarrass me. And I never ever say simply, "Speed up." I go point by point. If you make your point and then make the next one and the next, speed and tempo will grow naturally. The moment you tell actors, "Tempo, children, pace," they rattle like typewriters. They stop thinking—and so does the audience.

So, in *Charley's Aunt* I tried to make that first twenty-five minutes as funny and strong as I could. And above all, audible, to give the author, Brandon Thomas, a chance to tell his story. I was sure he had intended the opening to be as amusing as the rest of the play, and soon ours became so.

Joe Ferrer is an actor of taste, intellect and protean technique, and he has a matchless sense of humor. In addition, he is a natural athlete, a fact which allowed us to do feats that had never been tried onstage. At one point he ran across a crenellated ten-foot wall, jumped from that into a tree and climbed to the top, swinging a concealed ladder in the flies, giving out a Tarzan yell. All this to avoid putting Donna Lucia's dress back on and thus be forced to continue his disguise as Charley's aunt. His pals tempted him down with a bottle of Scotch held at the neck of the dress. While they held the dress like a tunnel, Joe dived horizontally through the dress, his arms slipping into the sleeves and his hands grabbing the Scotch—all this without touching the floor.

But his real success with the audience was that flashing, lecherous leer of his. It was hilarious coupled with those gray curls, especially when his big rolling eyes fixed a little too long on the well-developed Phyllis Avery's breasts.

Nedda Harrigan was being extra careful about her appearance because the play marked her return to Broadway after many years in Hollywood. On dress rehearsal night, a night of nerves, I was told that

Miss Harrigan was standing in front of her pier-glass mirror ringed with pink lights and that she absolutely *hated* her costume and would not appear on stage in it. I sent for her, knowing John Koenig had designed her a beautiful costume. It was a full-skirted dress of chartreuse moiré silk, trimmed with an eight-inch border of rust-colored velvet which matched her rust Empress Eugénie hat, gloves and muff. As she came storming onto the stage in a fury, those extraordinary colors in their proper lighting drew gasps and applause from all of us in the theatre. And I witnessed my first instant metamorphosis. Racing motors and driving temperament reversed themselves without even a screech of stripped gears; at once she was all gentle smiles and glowing charm.

I think that ridiculous moment was when I fell in love with her.

All during the preparation of *Charley's Aunt* I was in that seemingly enchanted state—never sleeping, always working, going, always going. I kept making small polishing changes up to twenty minutes before the doors opened on the night of the premiere. The mental manic state which I did not realize I had was working wonders.

Mother gave another gumbo, cake and ambrosia party after the opening. Again, with Galli-Galli and the chicks behind the ears. But I was too restless to stay long. I went to Times Square and waited for the morning papers.

If any single production made me famous, it was that one. The reviews were filled with extravagant praise for me and for Joe Ferrer. Everywhere I went, people came up to speak their enthusiasm. I was dizzy, of course, with happiness and excitement, but I did wonder, why *this* play? I had done just as good a job on four others. Why hadn't the critics and public noticed me then?

I was told that it was because "You've taken a tired old turkey and made it a work of art," and I answered that it wasn't a turkey but a great, almost classic, play—surely the best farce written in the English language.

Over and over, I tried to explain to people that some of our best laughs came from Sid Chaplin's movie, that the play itself was marvelously substantial, that Joe Ferrer improvised some of his own business and so did the cast. But it either didn't register on outsiders or they thought me mad—as most everyone did by that time.

They thought I was just fishing for compliments.

* * *

At my urging, Barbara and I met in my family's apartment to talk over our suspended marriage. I asked her point-blank if she was interested in remaining my wife.

She said she was.

I asked her if she wanted to have children with me.

She said no.

I asked why, but she refused to answer. I pressed the point. I wanted the truth. She answered that she wanted to stay married because a divorce would break her family's heart, but she would never have children by me, and that I should know why. I looked at her blankly, and she added:

"I have no wish to bring insane children into this world."

I was stunned. Then I tried to collect my thoughts. I had just done my best job in the theatre. How could I be insane? Insane? She didn't know what she was talking about. She couldn't mean it. But I could see in her eyes that she did.

Since there seemed nothing more to say, we left each other.

CHAPTER

10

If anything, Barbara's words made me spend more nights on the town. I closed nightclubs, made friends with strangers with whom I could drink until it was time to make an attempt to sleep. But sleep never came, so after tossing restlessly, I showered and readied myself to go out again.

Charley's Aunt continued to be my entree everywhere. My checks were accepted easily. I gave tickets out like handbills—to a shoe salesman, a stenographer . . . Scripts came to me by the dozens and I didn't stop to read them, but rather relied on the opinions of others, mostly those of my wonderful secretary, Anna Erskine. I sent flowers by the carloads and I began investing in plays, which merely increased the script load and seekers of advice. I had a self-assurance that was incredible even to me, and I seemed able to convince anybody of anything. It was as though I were speaking someone else's lines. I'd say to a girl in a store, "You're coming to bed with me tonight at eight—here's my card."

And she came. My wishes were granted almost too easily. Life was a fantasy of utter freedom. But that ecstatic fantasy life was to turn sinister soon, become a nightmare world from which I would flee in terror.

Finally, at one nightclub when I had begun to slow up and stagger a bit, I ran into Dr. Lawrence Crawley, our family doctor and the man who had treated my high fever at St. Luke's. Seemingly very casual, he invited me to his apartment to meet some friends. Longing for fresh audiences, I went. I spent that whole night haltingly answering their questions about the theatre, napping at intervals, and talking about everything until I wore them out, and after they left I continued talking to Dr. Crawley, regaling him with anything that occurred to me.

Early the next morning, I went back to change my shirt, but a short time later my mother came in to tell me that Dr. Crawley had arrived with two friends who wanted to talk to me. I combed my hair and rubbed cold cream on my face, since people had begun to tell me that my skin was dry and my eyes unfocused. Surely that was because of improper grooming.

In the living room, Dr. Crawley and Mother sat with two gray-faced men whose very drabness made me hate them immediately. I walked in nonchalantly. In a slow, nasal drawl, one of them said, "Mr. Logan, you are suffering from a severe nervous breakdown and you need immediate hospitalization."

I sat down and assumed a carefully modulated Basil Rathbone tone. "How can you say such an extraordinary thing when you've never seen me before in your life?"

"It doesn't take more than a second to diagnose a nervous breakdown, and besides, we know your recent history."

"Will you kindly tell me what you want?"

He answered in that same slow, raspy manner. "It isn't what *I* want, Mr. Logan, it's what *you* want. You do want to get well, don't you?"

"If I'm sick, yes. But I would prefer to get well my way, not yours."

"That is a sick remark."

Overcome with fury, I wanted to yell not only at this smart-ass doctor but at my mother for allowing him in the room. But I held myself in, afraid to give them further proof. I knew nothing about mental illness, although I had read of the horrors of psychiatric wards in *Asylum*, William Seabrook's book. If that was the kind of place they wanted to put me, I'd have none of it. And if the word "insane" was ever breathed about me around Broadway, it would be the end of my directing plays or movies, the end of trust, the end of my entire career.

"All right then, Doctor, just what is it you have in mind?"

"I want you to enter the New York Hospital in Westchester and begin treatment." Such an ugly drawl.

"How long would I have to stay there?"

"That depends on the severity of your illness."

"Will I be able to leave when I want?"

"Of course not."

"What about the padded cells?"

"Oh, come now, Mr. Logan, they're only for extreme cases."

"How do you know mine's not extreme?"

"I don't know, Mr. Logan."

"What about electric shock?"

"That depends on what the doctors recommend after you've been examined."

"What about the rest of my life? What happens to that?"

"That's entirely up to how you conduct your life. All we try to do is cure your illness, no matter how long it takes."

"And how long is that? The truth now."

"Four months, six months, maybe a year. Of course, there have been people who have been there for more than twenty years, but those are very rare."

I stood up and excused myself, to cover my raw panic. A large bathroom adjoined the living room, and I went in, locked the door behind me, then drew down the shade. I stood there in the darkness, shaking violently. For the first time in my life, I felt abandoned. My doctor had called these men, my mother had called my doctor. The evening before had not been a social one, but a sneaky examination. Obviously, friends or enemies had been complaining about my behavior. I felt as though the bathroom walls were inching in around me. I suddenly wanted to pray, but I didn't believe in God so I searched my mind for some symbol—some deity that had nothing to do with the God of that man out there. Who was the god of yellow daisies, the god of beauty? Could it be Apollo? I heard myself praying aloud in a tight, strained voice. "Apollo, are you there? If you are save me, Jesus Christ, Apollo, save me. I'll do anything you say, only save me now."

Nothing happened, but the mere fantasy of a god of beauty there in the dark made me feel a little better, and I went back to the living room.

"Mother, Dr. Crawley, I'll go to the hospital on one condition: that I be allowed to look it over before agreeing to stay. If I don't like it, if it is the color of this man who represents it, then I have no intention of staying."

Everyone seemed to consider that reasonable, and I was urged to pack quickly. All I would need would be pajamas and a toilet kit. The hospital supplied everything, it seemed. In my rush, the only book I managed to throw into my suitcase was a copy of *The Oxford Book of English Verse.*

Dr. Crawley drove Mother and me to Westchester County, to a severe-looking building that had always been known locally as Bloomingdale's.

In the reception room, we were joined by a doctor who quickly put a paper agreement in front of me. I told him I wasn't going to sign anything until I had looked the place over.

"This is most irregular. We don't allow this generally," and he spoke in the same flat tones as the other doctor.

Certainly, it must have been slightly maddening to follow me around as a male nurse did while I darted all over the place, inspecting window shades, pictures on the wall, the carpets, deciding whether I could remain in a place so atrociously decorated. I planned pleasurably to object to everything.

I was shown the Men's Ward, and another white-coated giant led me through some locked doors—I carefully noted their clank—on to a more modern section which housed the recreation room. It seemed comfortable enough: a Ping-Pong table, some card tables, lounging chairs covered in plastic, a piano, books, a radio. As I was studying all this, my eyes met those of two men who were peering out of their rooms at the newcomer. They studied me, and I was fascinated by them. I had a terrible flash of terror that the entrance door behind me had been locked, and I rushed back, but it was still open. My gigantic guide gave me a small, knowing smile. I wondered if it would count against me.

On the way back to the reception room, I stared down at the turkey-red carpet.

The admissions doctor said, "Well, Mr. Logan, now that you're satisfied, just sign here."

"I wouldn't think of staying in this tacky place."

"What's wrong?"

"The color of the hall carpet to begin with—it's revolting."

Mother and Dr. Crawley wearily stood up, barely glancing at each other, and the three of us walked outside to the porch. The moon shone through the trees surrounding the building, and I began to sing softly a song Colonel Noble had taught me and which had been my favorite during Culver days: About the moonlight on the Wabash . . . and the sycamores revealing the gleaming candlelight.

Then I said, "I know there is a marvelous restaurant around here— either in Mount Kisco or Pleasantville. Let's have champagne and caviar and everything expensive."

But Lawrence Crawley had a determined look. We got back in the car and he drove to the nearest drugstore. He was inside for a long while. I spoke to Mother of Culver and Indiana, and of life with Colonel Noble. I was sure there was no chance of my being put into a hospital, for I had her promise that I wouldn't go anywhere I didn't want to.

"I've got him. I've got him!" Crawley came running out of the drugstore. "The greatest neurologist in the world. You're not going to a mental hospital, just to a regular hospital, and the great Dr. Foster Kennedy is going to take over your case. He's Churchill's doctor."

"Where is Churchill's hospital?"

"In New York. Doctors Hospital. Anyone would be willing to go there."

"But I'm not sick. Why should I go to any hospital at all?"

"Josh, you're sick, very sick," he said.

"How can you tell? You don't know anything about mental disease."

"I've no need to. It's obvious. You're manic. You can't stay on any one subject."

"That's because one subject bores me. So I keep moving to the next."

"But underneath you are still depressed. The manic state covers depression when it becomes unbearable."

There was no way I could make him understand that this high whizzing feeling I had now delighted me. It was true that when people crossed me I turned nasty, but as long as I got my way I considered myself the nicest guy in the world. I was full of extra warmth for taxi drivers, waitresses, clerks, anyone who was helpful—and I kept talking nice, no matter how nervous my behavior made them. I kept at them until they liked me. I was forever offering everyone free dinners or seats to _Charley's Aunt._ If this sense of freedom and expansiveness was manic, then manic was what I'd been hoping for all my life.

But my head whirled as I kept asking myself, did Mother send for Dr. Crawley or did Dr. Crawley come to Mother? Who started it? Who told whom that I was out of my mind? I don't know why I never asked my mother and I don't know why she never mentioned it to me. Perhaps she felt that talking about it made it more of a fact.

It was ten in the evening by the time we reached Doctors Hospital, and we went to a small waiting room on one of the upper floors for our meeting with Dr. Kennedy. I left Mother and Dr. Crawley there and restlessly roamed around, peeking in pantries, talking to the nurses, but keeping one eye on the elevator door. Soon, a tall, slender young man stepped out and I followed him to the waiting room. He was Dr. Kennedy's assistant, Dr. Lawrence Poole, an intelligent, charming man, but too well-trained to give any indication of anything until Dr. Kennedy arrived. While he asked Dr. Crawley about my case, I went back to the elevator and continued talking to the nurses. The elevator door opened again and out stepped a portly, white-haired man with the look of a statesman or college president. I asked him if he was Dr. Kennedy.

"Yes. I'm very pleased to meet you. I came as quickly as I could . . . You _are_ Dr. Crawley, aren't you?"

"No, I'm the patient."

His composure dropped from him as though he had shed his skin. He stuttered out, "Come, let's go talk to Dr. Crawley."

When the two of us came into the waiting room, Drs. Poole and Crawley sprang to attention. Even Mother's smile was frozen in mid-terror.

I asked to be excused. "You probably have a lot to talk about. I'll just go back and fool around."

With a searching look, Dr. Kennedy said, "Yes, go ahead, but come back in a few minutes."

All they were going to say I knew by heart already; my only question was what Dr. Kennedy planned to do about it. When I came back, he said, "Mr. Logan, I want you to spend the night here. I assure you that if I were ill, this is where I'd stay. You'll be treated as a regular patient, not a mental patient."

"Are there any locked doors?"

"All doors will be open."

"Doctor, do you know what's wrong with me?"

"I don't think anyone knows that yet. Certainly, you're in an over-wrought state. Not only have I been told that by reliable people, but I observed it myself when I came out of the elevator."

"In that case, why did you think I was the doctor?"

"Doctors get disturbed too, you know."

He had all the answers, and there was nothing to do but stay. Within a few minutes I was in a hospital bed in my own pajamas, feeling absolutely awake, healthy and happy, and only puzzled by why I was on the seventh floor of a hospital.

In the morning I had a light breakfast and then wondered what to do all day. My only book was *The Oxford Book of English Verse,* so I browsed through the index: Byron, Keats, Shelley—John Logan. My eyes focused on that name and a thrill of excitement went through me. Could he be an ancestor of mine? If so, perhaps he had a sign for me, a secret, personal message. I turned to his page and at the top was the name John Logan, and under it his poem, "To the Cuckoo."

I burst into wild laughter. I rolled around on the bed, got up still bent over from laughing. A nurse hurried in to find out what was the matter, but I couldn't stop laughing long enough to explain it to her.

Old John Logan's message had come through the years clear as crystal. It had made its mark. Now for the first time I really believed I might be mentally disturbed, though I certainly felt fine. I remembered how dark blue I had been during the rehearsals of *Higher and Higher.* At that time I was in a different frame of mind. I knew I was in trouble. But why now when I felt so soaringly happy? Yet according to Dr. Crawley my state of mind was just as dangerous since it was covering the same disease.

I wanted to tell Dr. Crawley about John Logan's poem, and so I went into the corridor outside my room. I asked an orderly where I could make a phone call.

"Dr. Kennedy doesn't want you to make any calls yet. You are to rest."

"In that case, I want to call Dr. Kennedy and tell him to change his orders."

"I'm afraid I can't allow you out in the hall where the phone is."

I looked down the hall and saw a barred iron gate in a barred iron wall. "Just a minute," I said with shock. "This is a locked section, isn't it?"

"Yes, it is."

"I was promised I would not be locked in. Otherwise I would never have come here."

Two nurses hurried over as I began screaming fiercely at the orderly to unlock the door.

"We're not allowed to. That door has to remain locked."

I ranted on. "But there's got to be some mistake. Dr. Kennedy promised me . . ." Over my left shoulder I noticed that the upper half of a window had been lowered, and I dove to the window. Before the orderly and the nurses could even move, I had climbed out over the lower half and was clinging to the window frame. "Don't move, anybody. If that door is not opened this minute, I'm going to climb down the side of this building and go home."

My room was on the seventh floor, and I have a terror of falling—as my children say, I have "the heights"—but on the ledge I forgot that. I was all-powerful—a human fly. My only fear was of being locked in, and I had every intention of following through with my threat unless that door was unlocked.

The nurses begged me to come back in. "Look! Look through the window. The door's open."

"How do I know it's going to stay that way?"

"We promise. Honestly, it will stay open. Please come back."

I looked below me. It would be difficult, perhaps impossible, to get down to the ground and still be alive on arrival. So I climbed back inside.

To fill the time until Dr. Kennedy arrived, I read poems. Time and time again lines struck me as having been written for my eyes alone. Those old boys, I thought, must have written these poems in their manic periods. Maybe I should write my manic feelings. In about as fast as it takes to read it, I wrote an attenuated comic, jingling work, my "Ode to The Oxford Book of English Verse," intended to state my case humorously so that Dr. Kennedy would laugh and say, "Logan, I've been wrong about you. You're all right. As a matter of fact, you're brilliant."

When he arrived, I said nothing, just handed him my effort. Slowly, carefully, he read it. I knew there were riotous lines on the first and second pages, but he gave not a flicker of a smile. He handed it back and said, "That's very interesting."

His humorless reaction made me swear secretly that come hell or high water I would never do anything, ever, that he suggested. He assigned me two elderly male nurses, one for the day, the other for the evening, Leslie, an Irishman, and John, a Scot, both of them amusing, personable old men.

I asked that I be allowed to spend some days at my author friend Freddy Finklehoffe's country home in Bucks County, which he had offered to lend me. John, Leslie and I were driven down, and for a day I wandered in the fields, looked through Freddy's library, cooked, and according to my guardians, behaved in a calm, collected fashion. Soon, though, I was bored, and asked to spend a day in nearby Bethlehem, just to look around the stores.

A taxi was called and off we went. With my uncanny instinct for the best place to spend a lot of money, I found a gift shop loaded with elaborate boxes of exotic foods, perfect for Christmas shopping. As the bill mounted, John and Leslie grew more and more disturbed. Evidently to the medical profession my extravagance was a symptom of my illness, for, after John and Leslie had given their report, I was carted back to New York and Dr. Kennedy, with John at my side.

Kennedy had a stern expression as I came into his office. Then he placed his hands on my shoulders and tried to appear benign. "Cultivate equanimity," he said.

I suppressed the four-letter word that rose within me.

"Thank you, Dr. Kennedy. I know that's quite a hunk of thinking."

He gave me a smug smile. "Mr. Logan," he said, "you've gone too far. You are unable to control yourself in the free world. You must go to a mental hospital for a while."

"Really, Doctor? Would you excuse me now?" I bowed out of his office, saying, "Come on, John."

My mind was in a whirl. I wondered if Kennedy had called the police already, whether in fact they weren't at this very moment stationed downstairs, ready to grab me. Maybe there was a car outside, with a chauffeur with handcuffs in his pocket, or a straitjacket in case I tried to get away. But I wouldn't go; they couldn't make me.

Nice old John said, "Don't worry. It won't be so bad."

"You're not going to take me now, John, are you?"

"No, of course not. It'll be arranged later."

In the elevator going down, I thought of putting into action every escape I had read about, from Dumas to Galsworthy, and as we stepped into the lobby I noticed a florist shop. John knew how much I liked flowers so he didn't mind waiting while I ordered some. Luckily, the florist had forget-me-nots, and out of John's sight I wrote a note to Dr. Kennedy: "Thank you and good-bye. Joshua Logan." I asked the florist to send them to Dr. Foster Kennedy in about fifteen minutes.

John and I got into a taxi and I told the driver to head down Lexington Avenue. When John asked where we were going, I told him I wanted to find a shop that I had liked.

"But you're not supposed to buy anything."

"This'll cost peanuts."

In fact, I was headed for a coffee shop that adjoined the passageway from Lexington Avenue to Grand Central Station. When we got there, we sat at the counter, near a door that led to the station passageway. Through its window, I saw the crowds of people hurrying for their trains.

John and I ordered coffee. I was still in terror that I was being followed, and I checked the front window to see if any car had drawn up. There was none, but I didn't dare waste a minute. I told John I'd be right back, I was just going to the men's room. I stepped out the back door, and in a second I was swallowed up in the crowd.

Afraid to look back, I kept walking until I saw a gate sign announcing a Boston-bound train. It was leaving in two minutes. I pushed along into the rush of people boarding it, and only when the train pulled out did I begin to feel safe.

All during the journey I tried to imagine what was happening with Kennedy and his crew, poor John, Dr. Crawley and my mother. By now they would all be talking it over. They might figure out I was headed for Boston, and therefore I must take special care not to be seen.

Since I usually got off at Back Bay when doing a show in Boston, I got off instead at the South Station. And I knew the last place I could register would be the Ritz Carlton. I took a taxi to the Public Gardens, and from there walked to a Turkish bath that Larry Hart had once pointedly told me to avoid because it was so dreary. That made it a good hiding place. As soon as I got in my tiny cubicle, I decided to stay there until the possibility of people searching for me in Boston was over. But as Larry had said, it was pretty gruesome—dank, dark, stained, with weird-looking men wandering about in various stages of undress. I was able to stand it for only about two hours.

I left for a walk. It was November 1940.

Two days later, when I was standing at the back of the theatre watching a rehearsal of Finklehoffe's *Hi-Ya Gentlemen,* in which I had invested ten thousand dollars, I heard from behind me a quiet, male, Southern voice say, "It's uh interestin' show, isn't it? You know 'bout shows too, don'cha?"

If I had had any premonition of what was going to happen, I would have run as fast as my legs would carry me. Instead, I turned and found a big, oddly shaped creature.

He was tall, balding, with a protruding paunch. His eyes were close together and his cheeks pushed far apart by layers of fat: he was a perfect Modigliani subject. He appeared to be a few years older than I, and I could have well believed it if someone had told me that he was a fugitive from an asylum.

His remark had been so clumsily amateur that I figured he was some kind of spy.

"Oh, I don't know much about show business," I said.

"Yes, you do. I'd like you to come out to mah boathouse and tell me all about it. I love hearin' about shows. Dwight Wiman's comin' too."

"What?"

"Oh, yes, Dwight Wiman said he'd go anywhere you'd go, so I invited him to mah boathouse."

I gave him a careful look. "You don't look it, but *you're a goddamned doctor.*"

"Well, blass mah soul, ah *am* a kind uv a doctuh—but a good one. Ah teach psychiatry at Harvard Medical School. Have for twenty-five years. Ah'm mostly a lecturer. Why don't ya come over to the Ritz Carlton and talk it over with Dwight Wiman?"

His approach left me in such confusion that I didn't know what to do. The mysterious circuit had been at work. Someone had sent this man. He had gotten in touch with Dwight. Plans had already been made for me. I was panicked.

"I want you to understand right now that I'm not going to be locked up in a mental institution, and *you're* not going to tell me what to do."

"Oh, no, nuthin' like that. The only thang ah thank you ought to do is to take *advantage* of this elation of yowuz." Astonishingly, this idiot had plucked just the right, magic string. It stopped me dead in my tracks. "Take *advantage* of it," he continued. "Not many people are able to have an elation. During elation yo' mind is free of censorship. It wipes out all fear and doubt. Without the obstacle of doubt, you're able to learn in a way that you could never learn in a normal state of mind."

"Learn what?"

"Anythin', everythin'. Your mind is a white piece of papuh and it hasn't got the dark shadow of your fear over it. You can learn languages, athletics, you can memorize instantly. I would be more than happy to help you cash in on this elation."

No one else had ever said anything like that before, though it's true I had believed my elation was a gift and not a curse. Others had simply looked in horror and said I should hurry and commit myself. Testing this man further, I reached into my pocket and got out the poem I had written for Dr. Kennedy: "Ode to The Oxford Book of English Verse." I gave it to him and watched his face while he read it.

On the first page, he smiled, laughed on the second, laughed loudly further along. At one point he said, "This is absolutely marvelous, rhyming the words 'Klaxon' and 'Anglo-Saxon,'" and when he finished, "Publish this in *The Atlantic Monthly*. Call it 'Verse Written During a Manic Elation.' It will cause a sensation."

Phony or not, every word he said was what I wanted to hear.

"Who are you?" I asked.

"Is that important? We've met, we've gotten to know each other, and the next thing to do is to see Dwight Wiman. You know, he's up here with that new show of his, *Letters to Lucerne*. He'll tell you all about me."

"At least tell me your name."

"I can't without seemin' to brag, but since you've been braggin' so much, well, it's Merrill Moore. And I've written more sonnets than there are days in five years. They're superb sonnets. I'll give you a copy of my books so I can brag too."

His looks were too grotesque for me to take him seriously, and there was something shifty about his eyes. He seemed nutty enough to have written more sonnets than there were days in five years, but could he have been associated with Harvard's psychiatric department? I doubted it.

I agreed to go to Dwight's room, and when we arrived it was clear Dwight had been expecting us.

"How did you know I was here, Dwight?"

"Everybody knows. Everybody knows everything you do. Half the bloody telephone calls in New York are about you."

"I thought I sneaked up to Boston."

"You sneaked up here on a streak of lightning. You could be seen for miles. I even know that you're staying at a Turkish bath. Come on, Josh, let's get to this very nice man's house and spend the night. We'll have a long talk. Okay?"

Merrill Moore took over my life. I stayed at the Ritz Carlton and went to see Merrill twice a week, or rather, I was turned over to Merrill's youngish so-called therapist, Bernice Roberts. She seemed to have no plan. Just freewheeling, like Merrill. During the consultation hours, Merrill would lope in and autograph one of his books with an elaborate inscription to me. The one with a thousand sonnets was entitled with the Roman numeral M. I avoided reading them, but I couldn't avoid his reciting them to me, which he did constantly while walking down halls or going up in elevators. He told me he composed his sonnets while crossing streets or climbing stairs or while he was starting his car.

"Gee, Merrill, that's remarkable. I've never been able to write a play that way. It takes me months and months. I wish I had your facility."

"Just let things go. It will happen. Go over to the Boston Museum and look at the miniature collection. By this afternoon you'll know more about those miniatures than I do or anyone."

Instead, I chose to go to the Y for a workout—with Moore's agreement. I decided this was my chance to test Merrill's theory—to try the impossible. I would stand on my hands with my feet stretched straight up. Ever since I had first watched Hank Fonda do it, I had been wracked with jealousy. No matter how long and hard I tried, I always fell over. In that Boston YMCA I went through the preliminaries, stood on my hands and, so help me God, held myself there, my legs straight up. I got back on my feet, and then tried again. Perfect. Then again. It was one of the greatest thrills of my life. Merrill Moore was right: I could do anything! I asked Merrill why I had waited so long to have a manic attack and he said they seldom show up until the late twenties.

As Christmas of 1940 grew closer, I felt restless and asked Moore if I could spend the holidays with Miss Frances Crane on the Cape. He said yes, and told me that if I got into any trouble I could reach him on the twenty-eighth of December at the Bellevue-Stratford in Philadelphia where he would be attending a psychiatrists' convention.

Charley's Aunt.
Nedda Harrigan and
Jose Ferrer.

Josh directing
Jose Ferrer.

Dick Rodgers, Larry Hart and Josh
between rehearsals of *By Jupiter*. Dwight Wiman
and Forrest Haring are talking in back.

Ray Bolger and his mother (Bertha Belmore)
in *By Jupiter*. (VANDAMM STUDIO. LENT BY
THE MUSEUM OF THE CITY OF NEW YORK.)

Mandy number in *This Is the Army*. (VANDAMM STUDIO. LENT BY THE
MUSEUM OF THE CITY OF NEW YORK.)

Josh in Harrisburg.
Resplendent in gold
Spanish dolphin chair.

Wartime reunion. Josh, Mary Lee, and Marshall
at Fort Bragg in 1943.

John, my old Scot nurse, had rejoined me in Boston (only growing a trifle wary whenever we passed a coffee shop). The two of us drove down to the Cape in a rented station wagon, arriving just after dark.

Our old theatre had burned down two years before, and without the summer people the place seemed desolate. I hadn't been to the Cape for a few years. Miss Frances' superb white clapboard house was still as lovely as I had remembered it, but the contrast with what was no longer on the Cape saddened me. I told John I was going to join Merrill in Philadelphia, and sent him on his way. I pushed on to New York, and once there I took a penthouse suite in a midtown hotel that no one would associate with me.

My incessant wandering through the streets began again, and to cap it all I decided to have a Christmas party in my suite. Any and all helpful strangers were invited: redcaps, taxi drivers, a young saleslady who accepted on the condition that she bring her husband. And then I took a deep breath and sent a message to the entire *Charley's Aunt* company, inviting them all.

It was the weirdest Christmas party of my life. Only those I didn't know showed up. The cast of *Charley's Aunt* never came, afraid, perhaps, or warned not to be around me. I was the chief stranger there, the true uninvited guest. Just as I decided I'd never be able to see anyone I knew, in walked the beautiful Nedda Harrigan with her daughter, Ann, who had just come from California. I was so touched that I was unable to talk for a few minutes. Not only was she not afraid of me, she had brought Ann. It was the only reassuring thing about that Christmas.

The next day I began my tired trek by train to Philadelphia in search of Merrill Moore and possible salvation, a complicated picaresque journey that was to grow ghastly. I knew I looked as odd as I felt, for my face, for no physical reason, burned painfully, and the only relief was to cool it with ice. I stood at the water cooler in the tiny men's room of the train, taking ice from the cooler and pressing it against my fevered eyes.

Hours seemed to have passed before the conductor called out Princeton Junction. I got off, staggered into a cab and asked to be taken to my friend "Chink" Warfield's house. He wasn't there. His wife, Charlotte, was leaving for her job—she taught dancing at Arthur Murray's—but to my only slight surprise asked me to go along.

I watched her giving lessons for a while, and then I decided I must continue on to Philadelphia. But for some reason she wouldn't let me go.

"You must wait and see Chink. He'll be disappointed if he doesn't see you. Wouldn't you like to learn to tango?"

Suspicious of her and with my mind on Philadelphia, I took what must have started as the most pitiful tango lesson ever given. But once again, Merrill was right. In a moment I was dipping her to the floor and gliding with the proper hesitation. I was Valentino.

She said, "I don't need to teach you. You're wonderful!"

"I'm Valentino," I replied.

Nevertheless, I boarded the next train for Philadelphia, and again stood in the men's room, pressing ice to my face. The trip lasted for hundreds of years, and each time the train stopped or slowed down I thought, This is going to be the end of me. I'm going to die before this train gets there. Please, someone make it move faster! Please! Please! It didn't. It crept on so slowly I couldn't feel it move. Then I thought, But what if Merrill isn't there, what if he never went to that meeting, what do I do next?

I had left New York in the early morning; when I got to Philadelphia it was dark. From the station to the hotel would be a short easy walk. I thought I knew the way, for the Bellevue-Stratford was near City Hall. But I became unsure of my way. I tried to stop people to ask them for help, but they seemed to make a wide circle to avoid me. Finally, I was able to corner a thin, leather-faced old man. As he studied me, he jerked his head high and narrowed his eyes to slits, as if he were taking cover behind them. He pointed out the way, and I trudged off uncertainly. My sense of balance and direction was gone. My feet dragged behind me.

The long, heavy stone stairs from the street to the lobby were like Calvary. At the desk, Merrill Moore was talking to a clerk. My savior. Later, he claimed he had been leaving a note for me. If he noticed anything peculiar about my appearance or behavior, he didn't show it. After I registered, he told me blithely that he and his friend, Bob, were going bowling. I hadn't come to Philadelphia to bowl; I needed him to save my life. But he insisted.

"Bowling is relaxation. Come along. Healthy, glorious!"

"Okay, so we'll go bowling." Of course, I planned to stand by and watch—I'd never been much good at it.

"Here, you take the first ball, Josh."

And down the alley it went. A strike.

Merrill looked smug. "You see, Bob? See what good condition he's in? We're not as elated as he is. He's going to beat us both, you watch."

When they bowled, they would knock down one pin, maybe two, but I consistently made a strike. Oh, this game's too easy, I thought, and on my next turn I put my back to the pins and bowled through my legs. Another strike. People from the other alleys crowded around, and they cheered and applauded me as we left.

I never bowled again.

Merrill headed me back to the hotel. He would join me after he was through with an official banquet. On my way to my little room, I stopped in the lobby drugstore. I was fed up with people telling me how bad I looked. As a theatre man, I knew how to use makeup. I bought various shades of brown skin color, red jars for lips, pink for cheeks, a dark brown liner and cold cream.

In my room I practiced applying it all in front of the bathroom mirror. But making up exhausted me. It was much too difficult; it was impossible. I cold-creamed it all off and scrubbed my face clean. I lay down on the bed, defeated, and tried to rest.

Then it began. First, a kind of chill that seemed to shoot tiny quivers through me, then that same chill mixed with a knotting diaphragm and bursting, gushing hysteria. My body shook so violently, it shook the bed; I couldn't hold still. All I could do was try to live through it, survive it and when I did, wait breathlessly and pray it wouldn't start again. But it did, over and over. Oh, my God, what was I going to do? I knew Merrill's solution would be the same as everyone else's: I must be institutionalized. But that was too terrifying. I couldn't bear the idea.

Eventually, he turned up, and switched on the lights. Seeing the vestiges of makeup on my clothes, he asked me what had happened. As best I could, knowing I sounded feeble and unclear, I tried to explain it all, then broke down with, "What am I going to do? I just can't go to a hospital. I have so much to do . . . People are counting on me. I've made a lot of promises."

"Listen to this." He turned out the room lights, and only by the glow that came through the transom could I make out his amorphous bulk.

He sat on the side of the bed and recited all of Robert Frost's "Stopping by Woods on a Snowy Evening," ending with:

> . . . the woods are lovely, dark, and deep,
> But I have promises to keep,
> And miles to go before I sleep,
> And miles to go before I sleep.

The aptness and simple beauty of those words hypnotized me. I had tears in my eyes. I asked him where the hospital was.

"It's the Pennsylvania Hospital in West Philadelphia."

"How do I get there?"

"Take a taxi. Go on your own, Josh. Then no one can ever say you were committed."

I was moved by his complete trust in me and I told him he could leave me, promising I would do as he suggested. But the moment he was gone I was left alone again with my recurring terror.

I knew what to do. Since the world had deserted me, I would desert it. I would become a tramp, like Charlie Chaplin, and spend the rest of my life walking down roads. I felt better for that decision. I crumpled my jacket, trousers and topcoat and rubbed them on the floor until they were wrinkled and filthy. I covered my face with what was left of the makeup, hoping it would look like encrusted dirt. But I was weak. I could scarcely lift my arms to my face.

Dawn was breaking and I had completed my stupid disguise. To avoid any inquisitive glances from the elevator boys, I sneaked down the back stairs. Outside, I found an old taxi parked at the curb. The driver was fixing something under the hood. I slumped in the back seat. At first I thought of asking him to drive me to Bucks County, to Freddy's house, but when I got in I realized I wouldn't be able to stand that trip. All I could manage was to ask him to take me to the Pennsylvania Hospital—yet in my sick mind I was still trying to find a way out.

When the cab reached the brick gate, I read the copper plaque on the post: "Pennsylvania Hospital for Mental and Nervous Diseases."

I was shaking violently. "Back up," I said to the driver. "I can't go through that gate. Head for Bucks County. I have a friend there who— No! Never mind. Is there another entrance—without a sign about mental and nervous diseases?"

"The rear entrance doesn't have any sign."

"All right. Go back, but through the rear entrance."

We drove up to the door. I had no money to pay the driver and instead gave him my watch—which he later returned.

In the receiving room I was met by a Dr. Howard Rome, who spoke to me as if we were old friends. In my confusion, I thought he was the composer Harold Rome. But no, he knew me from my Triangle days, for the year I was president he had been president of the University of Pennsylvania's Mask and Wig Club. He chatted on as if we'd known each other always.

He asked me to sign some papers, and on one I filled in with marginal provisions that if either my mother or Merrill Moore wished, I could be released. He whipped out one final duplicate—a mere formality, he explained—and I signed it without reading because I was too tired, too anxious to get on with it. That last one, as I found out later, committed me to stay there as long as the hospital thought necessary—which could mean forever.

A male nurse led me through a locked door, and I found the rest of the hospital decorated with superb antique furniture and fine drapes. It had a distinctly Southern feel about it, as though it were Monticello or Westover. As the door clanked closed behind me, I felt immediately at ease. I knew deep inside at that moment that I was starting to get well.

In Ward D in the men's section I was put into pajamas, and I sank down into a white bed.

Though I woke at least six times for a few minutes, I slept for over two days. Each time I woke, a different young man was sitting at the foot of my bed: a short one, then a tall one, a dark one or a light one. All of them seemed friendly, and it was a comfort to know I was being watched over and cared for. I must have been wanting this all the time I was resisting it.

When I finally woke up, I found that my clothes had been cleaned. I went for a stroll around the ward. My fellow inmates were unembarrassed about being there. Some were even proud of their manic exploits and were like bragging fishermen swapping whoppers.

As the days passed, I waited for some word from Merrill, a visit or a letter or a call, some acknowledgment. But nothing came. I kept writing him letters which I left in a box in the night nurse's office. When I checked the box the next day, they were always gone. But after a while, I wondered whether my messages had left the hospital grounds. In a panic, I grabbed Dr. Rome's lapels one day and asked, "What are you doing to me? Who decides which letters to mail and which ones to put in the wastebasket? Where is Dr. Moore? I told you when I arrived he was my doctor, that he's the one who sent me here. Is he being kept from me?"

Once again, I heard that dry, cool, professional voice—he too held one in reserve. "Why don't you settle down, Josh, and stop worrying? This is the time for you to relax and rest. That's what you're here for. Why don't you write a play?" He left me with my mouth hanging open.

I asked one of the nurses what was going to be done to me, and his answer came casually. "They're not going to do anything. You're just going to stay here and get well."

"How can I get well if I receive no treatment?"

"That's the way to get well. When you learn to live a normal life. Get up, eat, do exercises, go to sleep. You'll be well in no time. They all are."

I noticed a line of disturbed men in bathrobes growling resentfully at life, at each other, and at the male nurses who were escorting them through a door.

"Where are they going?" I asked another patient.

"For shock treatment. You know, they fix you up like they do for the electric chair, and they run some juice through you. Supposed to be good for what ails you."

Forty minutes later, these same men came out, but now they were serene, better looking and happy. One even seemed younger. He passed me and gave me a smile, and then went into his room. He sat down and began looking out the window in perfect contentment.

At the first opportunity, I cornered a young doctor.

"Dr. Jordan, I want some shock treatment."

"I'm sorry, but you can't have any. Your mother won't allow it."

"My mother? What the hell has she got to do with it?"

"She's your next of kin, and her permission is needed."

"Why the hell won't she give it?"

"She's afraid it will impair your talent. She says your genius is your fortune."

"Naturally." I smiled. "But is there any truth in what she's afraid of? Would it change me?"

I was furious that she had taken it upon herself to make such an important medical decision, but at least I had learned something heartening. It was proof positive that *someone* knew I was in that hospital.

But who could have asked her? No one seemed to care what I did, where I went, how long I slept, whether I had a temperature. Everyone I encountered—patients, orderlies and the occasional doctor—all wore that bland, indulgent smile which said, "Please don't spoil my lovely mood."

Most of the male nurses were former coal miners, not always brainy, but good fellows, easy to get along with, fun to talk to, and so grateful to be away from the mines that their present job seemed like cheating. They even persuaded me to go out and play catch one morning, something I hadn't done since I was thirteen, and then badly. But I was still fundamentally in my extraordinary elated state, without fear or censorship, so I caught, pitched and caught again. My absence of self-criticism, of self-doubt, again made everything come easily, except access to the outside world.

When I heard two of the evening male nurses speaking Spanish, I tried out some Spanish phrases I remembered from Chile. To my surprise and delight, they answered, and I found myself rattling back phrases to them, though I had no memory of ever being able to move easily in that language before. My incredible fluency lacked any grammatical form, but that didn't seem to worry my new friends or me. With this achievement under my belt, I then tackled free-form French with the dietician, also ignoring those cumbersome verb endings, the exact use of which had hampered me for years. I was instantly trilingual.

In the afternoon was Shop: we could practice any craft we wanted. In fact, the beautiful furniture I had noted on entering the hospital had been made years ago by inmate-craftsmen. So, too, had the fine rugs and handsome lampshades. I began fashioning a Greek theatre out of small stones and papier-mâché, and in my room worked on a hooked rug and place mats of white string. I have always enjoyed Santa's workshop—my pet name for occupational therapy.

Through it all, I wrote reams of doggerel, and in the print shop I set it all in type. Some of it was full of anger with those I thought

had locked me up, and some was my first nostalgic attempt at verse auto-
biography:

> Mansfield is a lazy town,
> And melancholy too.
> It has a kind of haze about it,
> Made of smoke and honeydew.

In a short while, I found myself looking forward to each day, playing
catch in the morning, swimming before breakfast, then working on my
ancient Greek theatre, trying conversational French, or setting my
rhymes in type.

I was willing to try anything, even to playing the piano, though I
had given it up at eleven, just when I started to read music. Taking for
granted that I recalled it all, my lady music teacher commanded me to
play a duet with her. I looked at the page of music and plunged right
in. I went through an entire page and continued on with her as she
turned the page. Finally, I reached the end in bewildered but happy
surprise.

"I don't believe I'm reading music. I haven't done this—ever."

"Oh, you'll be doing much better than this soon. Let's start over." And
off we went again.

It wasn't quite the same experience with sculpting because I had
never done it before. The instructor told me to do a head of a young
lady, and showed me how to pack clay around an armature.

"Now, take this instrument and cut away until it looks like the
model." The model was a pretty young social worker.

"What do I do about the hair?"

"That's always a question. Well, you must do what you *feel* about
the hair, what seems right to you."

Day after day, I carved away. The instructor finally told me to stop
working on the face, that it was finished; all that was needed was something here and there on the hair. I cut away, and finally liked my cuts.
By the end of that afternoon it was done. I secretly found the head
beautiful, and I keep it to this day.

In the gym, I shied away from the boxing mat and watched the
wrestlers in a corner. The instructor, another tough young man from a
mining town, asked if I would like to try it.

"Sure, except I know nothing about it."

"Who does? Would you like to have a go?"

"Without any instruction?"

"That's the only way you'll learn. Now, take off your clothes."

"Why?"

"Because you haven't any equipment. The Greeks never wore anything. Besides, that's the roughest way."

Soon, we were stark naked, and I was amazed at what great physical shape I was in. He told me to stop admiring myself and get down on my hands and knees, then try to throw him. For a while we slithered past each other, but he finally managed to grab me around the neck and throw me. All my competitive energy got to work, and quickly I had him on the floor. After fifteen minutes or so, with each of us having tumbled the other to the mat three times, I marched off to the showers feeling like a champion. Did I really want to get well?

At seven in the morning and three in the afternoon the Pennsylvania Hospital seemed a happily functioning country club, all its members playing ball, exercising and wrestling. But at two in the afternoon, after lunch, and particularly at six in the evening, when the day was over, the personal shadows closed around each member of Ward D. High-pitched arguments were heard down the hallway, and sometimes word battles between the male nurses and patients. At those times, I sat in my room and felt the dark, hazy, purple mood settle over me. I was forgotten, and terribly lonely.

But it helped if I got out my loom and worked on a place mat or wrote some more comic verse. Or even better, I could continue with my hooked rug, stabbing at the drawing I'd made on a large piece of burlap, a cartoon copied from the program of *Charley's Aunt*: a caricature of Ferrer as the aunt, with the girls, Kitty and Amy, all done in the brightest of Walt Disney colors. It would never blend into a room, but it made me laugh.

Still, none of that shook off the dreariness of having an illness that didn't seem like one, of not knowing how or when I'd be rid of it, of not knowing even why it had happened to me, of having iron bars on the windows—even though those bars were fashioned like curlicued decorative devices. Was I ever, ever, going to get out? And if I did— what would I do? Where would I go?

* * *

Five months after my arrival, Dr. Jordan surprised me by telling me
that Dr. Moore was coming down to see me to talk about Barbara's request for a divorce. I was startled. Not that I cared, but she had always
been so courteous. Why hadn't she written or called me directly? But
there was no telling what she had been told of my condition. If she
were refused a divorce, she may have feared some mad, manic revenge.
Her parents must have wanted the divorce even more than she did. No,
I knew well that she was the one who wanted it. She had wanted it
one-half second after we were married. And, my God, why hadn't I?
Was I just being a goddamn Southern gentleman? Or did I really still
care for her in some vague way?

On the morning before Easter Sunday, an attendant brought me a
salmon-pink azalea in full bloom. It was my first gift from the outside
world, my first link with it, in fact. I knew my mother and sister had
been told not to write. I opened the card and was flooded with gratitude and joyous happiness and hope and all the things I'd missed. It
read: "Get well. With all my love. Nedda."

I wrote Nedda fifteen poems of thanks, tore them all up and finally
arrived at one that seemed fairly good and sent that.

When Merrill showed up, he suggested we take a drive, an invitation I jumped at since I hadn't been off the hospital premises since I
had arrived. In the car, he broached the topic of Barbara's settlement. I
told him, "Let her keep what she wants. I will never make any
demands on her or try to see her. Tell her not to worry."

Before Merrill left, he gave the hospital doctors his orders for the re-
mainder of my treatment. I was to spend a month at the institute, a
huge compound nearby, which was under the same aegis as the hospital,
but which treated outpatients. I was to live in a downtown hotel and
come to the institute daily for physiotherapy and continue with sculpting, music and language lessons.

But at the end of that month I was still to be forbidden to return to
the theatre or even discuss it for six more months. Instead, I would
spend my time in Boston, seeing Merrill or his assistant, Bernice
Roberts, two hours a week. Only after that might I return to work. I
was condemned to seven more months of dreary pretending.

How had I gotten into all this? This man I'd met only a short time
before was now emperor of my existence. I would have to spend more
interminably boring hours with him (was my own life never to begin
again? Was my freedom gone forever?) and be forced to appear inter-

ested while his assistant asked me inane and inhibited questions about my early sex life, hinting with most arch delicacy at masturbation. I should have told her I began at three years old and did it eight times a day. But would that have satisfied her?

That evening, Dr. Jordan, the one doctor who still had my complete faith, came to my room, and I asked him if he had spoken to Merrill Moore.

"Yes. We all agree his plan is the best way."

"But be honest with me. How can I go back to the theatre after all I've put my friends through, after all the galloping whispers and all the people who've seen me in this strange state? How will anybody, as long as I live, believe that I'm well again?"

And Jordan, a handsome, husky young man who to my great sadness was killed two years later in the war, said, "They'll look at you, Josh, like I'm looking at you now, and they'll know that you're well. It's that simple."

The Warwick is a hotel where theatre people stay when they play Philadelphia. I'd been there many times and was comfortable with the staff, the facilities, the rooms, the location. Most of my day was spent at the institute, though, and so both at the Warwick and the institute I felt like a transient stranger. That month was a footless and mindless one for me, a time out of time. I was neither sick nor well. I had a room but not a home. At the Institute every one was impersonal. When I put clay between my fingers in sculpture class, I no longer had a particularly creative urge, and during the French and Spanish lessons I began searching for verb endings, and soon began to stutter again, as in the old days. My blissful freedom from censorship, that sure symptom of my illness, was leaving me. And I was convinced that old acquaintances had forgotten me and that my theatrical career was finished.

Late one afternoon, returning from the institute, I bumped into a tall man hurrying out of the Warwick lobby. He backed off, then gave me a look of surprise and cried out, "Josh!" It was big Louis Calhern, and if I'd been reading the papers I would have known he was in town with the touring company of *Life With Father*. He was playing Father to Dorothy Gish's Mother. We hadn't been in touch since the disaster of *Hell Freezes Over*, but I had kept track of his important career.

Lou clasped my hand and for a second I searched his face, worrying what he was thinking. With an easy, unstudied calm he said, "You know, I don't have much to do here during the day. Have you any free time?"

"Yes, a lot."

"What about the day after tomorrow? Let's drive out to the country-side and go for a walk."

"Of course. That would be great."

I got permission from the institute, and on the agreed day I waited for Lou in the lobby. Perhaps he hadn't known about my breakdown, and then again, perhaps he was covering up so as not to embarrass me or himself. I was determined to find out.

He arrived, and we drove in his car to a lovely section of the country where he pulled up beside a small bridge which crossed a stream.

"Where are we going?"

"Come on," he said, and we crossed the bridge to the opposite bank where a man was renting flat-bottomed rowboats. Obviously, Lou had been there often. We climbed into one and steered the boat slowly down the small, still canal. It was a bright day and I had the sense of being in the middle of a Monet. Lou told me of his childhood and his leading ladies, and he never once asked me how I happened to be in Philadelphia or how I was feeling. I swapped tales with him, but couldn't work up courage to ask him whether or not he knew about my illness. His sensitivity and tact made that question an unnecessary in-trusion on a grand, comradely afternoon.

I never did find out what he knew that day. Perhaps his under-standing, his knowing just what we should do together, came from what he had learned through his own rough experiences, for only after his death did I learn that Lou had been a confirmed alcoholic. When I think of him my first remembrance is not of his great performances, but of an old friend with whom I spent a lovely afternoon. Lou Calhern led me back to life.

Mary Lee and Mother rented a cottage on Cape Cod for the sum-mer. I slept on a big swing on the screened porch. I seldom talked, ate very little, and the only way I could get through the day was by doing simple crossword puzzles.

Once a week I went to Boston by train, and stayed overnight at the Harvard Club. The first day I would have my session with Bernice

Roberts, and the following day with Merrill, whom I might have still found funny if I hadn't been so low. I should have seen that he was my personal Keystone Kop. He was the affable boy who had just moved into the neighborhood and was trying to impress me with the fact that his scout knife had more blades than mine. He continually behaved as if I were challenging him, and he dropped names all day long, trying to impress me.

After the summer I still had three endless months to go before being allowed to return to New York, so my sister volunteered to sublet with me a Beacon Hill apartment on Louisburg Square. We had never discussed my illness. During those months there was a cessation of hostilities between us—she concealed her critical scrutiny of everything I did, maybe fearing that if she spoke out she'd bring on another manic attack.

To fill the days we took courses in the Extension Division at Harvard, one in the history of music and another in the history of art. The courses turned out to be another step in my return to life, for one day after class I returned to the apartment and browsed through the owner's books. I took down *Nicholas Nickleby* and began to read, stopping after twenty pages with a start at the realization that this was the first book I had read since the beginning of my illness. Enjoying it tremendously, I read it all the way through in two days, and when I saw Merrill next, I said, "Don't you think that's a good sign?"

His thick Tennessee intellectual voice took over and he pronounced, "It's an excellent sign, Josh. It shows that you no longer feel that your mother is trying to take your penis away from you."

I had no idea what that meant, but I had learned to tune out early when Merrill began one of his junior Freudian discourses. He had a way of treating me as if I were a lecture hall to be filled with the sound of his voice.

Bernice Roberts had her own characteristic brand of reaction.

"Tell me about the shows you did," she said. "Didn't you work with Rodgers and Hart?"

"Yes, on two, and I hope to do more."

"What are they like?"

"Well, Larry Hart is a darling little man."

She stiffened and said sharply, "What did you say?"

"I said Larry Hart is a darling little man."

"You *mustn't* say *that!* A man must never refer to another man as 'darling.' That's, well—it would be misunderstood."

"Only by a boor. If you knew Larry, you'd think he was a darling too."

"Please! I know you know what I mean."

Way down deep I heard voices in disharmony chanting, "Sissy, sissy, don't be a sissy." I flew into a rage. "You are supposed to be a psychotherapist, and you're educated. I would imagine your work with troubled people might give you some sophistication. How dare you associate the word 'darling' with homosexual? Larry is a darling man and will remain a darling man to me until my dying day. Why I—or anyone— should change his mode of speech for your repressed thinking is beyond me."

I told Merrill about Bernice's reaction to "darling" and he said, "*Talk* to Bernice, Josh, don't, for God's sake, listen to her. She's—that is, she has problems. And don't get upset like that. Let women be hysterics. You've got to learn composure, my friend. We don't want this to happen again, do we?"

"Good God, this isn't going to happen again!"

"Not if you keep calm. Not if you keep coming to me anytime you feel like it. It's a thousand to one you won't. Now, buck up."

And I left the office, wondering how long it would be before I could get back to the normal people of the theatre.

Six months to the day Merrill had given me on his timetable, he told me I could go back to New York, though I would continue therapy with him in Boston when I needed it. "I think we've all learned a lot from this experience, Josh." I was happy that I had proved instructional for Merrill.

Anna Erskine met me with my car at the airport in New York, and the drive from there into the city at dusk was one more step to freedom. New York with its lighted windows looked like a wizard's city, and as I was about to turn off Park Avenue I saw a woman, wrapped in a full coat with only a bit of nightgown showing, walking a taffy-colored dog. It was Nedda, pulling at her cocker spaniel because he wouldn't behave. I stopped quickly and she put her arm over her face and began her lifelong and needless apology for her appearance. She looked great to me. Indeed, it occurred to me that Apollo had heard my prayer and, though a little late, was answering it in his own handsome way.

She asked me to stop by her apartment at the Lombardy for a drink, where she would fill me in with the latest theatre gossip.

Later, in her living room, after she had changed into a hostess gown, we talked and laughed and remembered for hours. *Charley's Aunt* had been made into a movie with Jack Benny, and the film company had stolen the stage production in detail.

"Why shouldn't they?" I said. "I did a bit of stealing myself."

I was back in the world I loved most. I felt so at ease with Nedda's warmth and beauty that I didn't want to leave. I told her that Barbara and I were getting a divorce and asked if she would have dinner with me the next evening. And then I went over to her and kissed her.

In a short time, we became an item, as they say, seen together so frequently that friends began coupling our names—Josh and Nedda, Nedda and Josh.

And it wasn't so very long after my return that I got a call from Dick Rodgers.

He came immediately to the point. "How would you like to direct Larry's and my new show, *By Jupiter?*"

Without hesitating, I said, "Sounds great. When can we talk? Is there something I can read?"

Not until after I had hung up did the impact of what had happened hit me. I had actually been offered a directorial job right after a year's mental illness. Obviously, neither Larry nor Dick nor Dwight had any vestige of doubt concerning my ability. If they had, they would have asked to see me before making an offer.

Yes, I had had a nervous breakdown, but I had gotten over it. I had won out over it. People love a winner.

Working again could be the best therapy of all, for work crowds out all other problems—there is no room for them. *By Jupiter* was going to be a personal joy.

The contracts were signed and several meetings were held. Even Larry, who had been stepping up his disappearing acts lately, appeared at one.

My enthusiasm for the show was growing when I received a letter from the War Department.

"Greetings," it said.

CHAPTER

11

"Greetings" meant one thing then: "Hello, sucker. I'm your draft notice." I was to report in two weeks.

My first reaction was relief, as I had begun to feel another musical might stir things up. Military service would be KP therapy, barracks therapy and mostly anger therapy, as I was infuriated by Hitler and the Japanese and wanted to go after them myself. But would the army take me after being in a mental institution? I asked Merrill, who said, "Jes' don't tell 'em a damned thing, Josh. They're lucky to have you."

Dwight, however, hit the rafters and persuaded my draft board to give me a deferment.

None of the fear I expected at facing a cast was there at *By Jupiter*'s first rehearsal. As Dr. Jordan had predicted, everyone just looked at me and knew I was all right.

The show was based on Julian F. Thompson's play, *The Warrior's Husband*, about the powerful Amazons and their weak husbands. Our cast was first class: Ray Bolger, Benay Venuta and Constance Moore. The one and only Bob Alton, who had choreographed *Higher and Higher* and *Two for the Show,* did the dances, Jo Mielziner the sets, and the costume designer was the fantastic, imaginative Irene Sharaff.

Larry and Dick wrote a big, bold song for Benay, "Jupiter Forbid," and there was a comic love-by-insult number for Benay and Bolger, "Everything I've Got." My favorite, however, was a rueful little song that turned out to be the last ballad Larry ever wrote, "Nobody's Heart."

Dick was forced to cover a lot for Larry, who kept on disappearing. Once when I asked Dick where Larry was, Dick shrugged, "God knows. I've asked his most disreputable friends, and even they're worried." There were even times when Dick was compelled to write the lyrics himself. He didn't enjoy it; he just did it.

Near the end of the Boston tryout, we still had two problems: we needed a good first act curtain and one song didn't work. Bob Alton turned four chorus boys' backs into a bed on which Bolger preened himself seductively. Presto! our first act curtain.

Our second problem seems ludicrous today: we all loved a song but couldn't fit it into the show. First, it came before Connie Moore's entrance, then it was moved to the second act as a trio. In a last-ditch effort, Bob Alton turned it into a big dance number for the New York opening, but we knew the song was still wrong. The day after the opening, we *eliminated* it altogether. The irony is that of all the songs in *By Jupiter* the most famous is that one. It is "Wait Till You See Her."

By Jupiter was an immediate commercial hit, and Nedda and I felt it would have a long run.

Few people knew I was headed for the army, so at a party given by the Theatre Guild, Theresa Helburn asked me to direct an old play of the Guild's which was being turned into a musical for Rodgers and Hart. It was Lynn Riggs's *Green Grow the Lilacs,* set in Oklahoma as it became a state. I had to beg off because of my draft.

I told Dick how sorry I was, and asked that he and Larry think of me in the future.

Dick said, "Josh, I don't know how to put this, but Larry doesn't want to work anymore. I don't know if it's some kind of boxed-up panic, or whether it's me. You know how he calls me the high-school principal."

"You mean you will work with another lyricist?"

"I'll have to, Josh. Oh, I'll do something with Larry again. Maybe the only way to scare him out of this is to find someone else. What would you think of Oscar Hammerstein?"

Just hearing that name made my heart beat faster. The *Show Boat* lyrics were one of my early enthusiasms.

I said, "Dick, you and Hammerstein would be unbeatable."

"Can he do comedy songs? Larry was always able to get big laughs. I don't know. I don't know."

Months later, I heard that Dick and Oscar were collaborating. The show became *Oklahoma!*, which incidentally boasted the two biggest belly-laugh songs ever: "Pore Jud Is Daid" and "I Cain't Say No." On *Oklahoma!*'s opening night, Larry sat alone in a box, howling with laughter and calling out, "Bravo!" He really loved it, which I'm sure made it all the more painful to him.

I learned of Larry's death while I was in Europe. A week after Rodgers and Hart's revival of *A Connecticut Yankee* opened, Larry was found dead in a gutter, having drowned in his own regurgitation. It was such a grotesque, ridiculous death, I could almost hear him laugh.

Everyone had his own juicy theory of what Larry did on his midnight prowlings, but does it really matter? His lyrics explain everything anyone needs to know about him, and for those lucky enough to have been his friend he was a delightful man. And also, yes, indeed, a *darling* man.

A month after *By Jupiter* opened, I had to report for military service. My divorce from Barbara had been set, but I hesitated about asking Nedda to marry me. I wanted to be a combat soldier, which meant not knowing where I'd be stationed or what chances I'd be taking, or how long we'd be separated. My commission from Culver had lapsed, because I had not attended final summer camp, and so I would be a private. I explained it to her and she said she understood. I knew she didn't, and I knew I didn't either. I was just following my nose.

At five A.M. one morning I lined up in a street with other grab-bag civilians, some ten years younger (I was thirty-four). We were ferried to Governor's Island for a bare-assed physical examination, with the insulting proddings, pokings and coughings—and finally, for me, came the moment of truth: the psychiatrist. He gave me a glance, then rattled off a list of diseases to which I could happily answer no. When he got to "nervous and mental" diseases, I said, "Sir, I'm sound as a nut." Which God knows was the truth.

We were shipped to Fort Dix, then a separation center in New Jersey. My first assignment was dear old KP. But the next morning I went through an experience that would haunt my career for a long time.

I took some kind of test with five hundred other men and instructions blared out over a loudspeaker. I didn't realize the test was against time, so when the bell rang I was only halfway through. I begged for another chance but all I got was, "Sorry, soldier." I'd blown my IQ. I ranked low among the idiots.

At that moment, my name boomed over the loudspeaker. I staggered to some office and picked up the phone.

"Hello, Josh?"

"Who is this?" I didn't recognize the high-pitched, slightly hoarse voice.

"It's Irving Berlin."

He might as well have said George Washington. Berlin! My God, I'd worshiped him since I was a kid, when his song "Lazy" was published in *Judge* magazine. Berlin was a legend.

"You know, I like your work, Josh."

"Thanks, Mr. Berlin, but I'm in the Army now so—"

"That's why I'm calling you. All you need is a transfer, and we've taken care of that. My show, *This Is the Army,* is going to open in a few days, but we're not ready. You've got to get it in shape. You'll be here tomorrow. Looking forward to meeting you." He hung up—just when I was ready to tell him I didn't want to come.

In a matter of hours I was on special assignment, and that afternoon in my suntans I arrived back home, giving Nedda a turn.

Later, at the Broadway Theatre, I was led down the aisle to meet the fabled Irving Berlin. He grabbed my arm and pulled me conspiratorially out into the lobby. Not as short as Larry Hart, he was a black-haired, lean man who did, however, resemble Larry in his bubbling enthusiasm. Berlin was at once excitement, glitter, comedy and melody. I fell for him immediately. But at that moment he was in a black panic. The show, he said, had good things, but it was a badly arranged jumble. He gave me nine days to take it apart and put it back together into a hit. He had told everyone I was in complete charge as of now. I winced and asked who had been directing it before.

"Anybody who wanted to. Ezra Stone and Bob Sidney mostly, and, oh, lots of others. You've just got to make it work, Josh. We're putting on the whole show for you in fifteen minutes."

The idea of working on something others had directed, choreographed and routined didn't make me too secure, and I wondered how the cast was feeling, having to please someone brand new. And how the directors were taking it.

I was probably the first outsider to see This Is the Army, and the size, emotion, melody and comedy of it left me weak. Ten rows of bleachers stretched all across the stage, filled with soldiers, all seemingly great talents. Then song after song, end-man-type jokes, big choruses, acrobatic acts. Then, for the smashing first act curtain, an inundation of men dressed in Navy whites pouring down the aisles and up onto the stage, singing "How About a Cheer for the Navy?" It was stupefying, and when I turned to Irving, overcome with enthusiasm, he said, "It's not right, it's not right. You've got to fix it."

How could I fix a show that to my mind was bulletproof perfection? But, urged on by Berlin, I saw it again and again, and found a few songs that could be reprised, dialogue that could be snipped a bit, an order of playing that might help. Once when the vast geometrical pattern of soldiers was singing the plaintive song "I'm Getting Tired So I Can Sleep," I broke their rigid pose and asked them to lean back or sideways on an elbow while the lights dimmed. It was a change of mood and Berlin seemed delighted, so I kept working. I rearranged the acrobatic scene and put orchestral reprises under it. Not very much to be called the "additional" director of This Is the Army, yet Berlin felt I had saved his neck.

This Is the Army opened to the biggest roars of applause and laughter I have ever heard. That the performers were soldiers made everything better. Many of these same men had performed as civilians to no recognition; now, in khaki, they were budding Chaplins or Carusos. Berlin killed the audience toward the end by singing his World War One song, "Oh, How I Hate to Get Up in the Morning" in skinny breeches and rolled cloth puttees. If any show ever took the town, this one did. And why not? It was conceived and written by the astounding theatreman of his time.

But after it opened there was little for me to do, and I became restless again for combat.

I had heard of a Colonel Harold Adamson who was organizing Hollywood directors and photographers into a unit called Combat Photography, which would photograph for historical purposes all maneuvers and battles. It sounded perfect. I'd be in actual combat and still do something I knew how to do—tell a story.

I called Adamson in Washington, identifying myself and said I'd like to be with him. He seemed delighted and advised me to get transferred back to Fort Dix. Once I was there, he would be able to put through my assignment papers.

Berlin hated to let anyone go, but finally he gave in and in a few days I was back at Fort Dix and called Washington with new enthusiasm.

Colonel Adamson's secretary said, "But, Mr. Logan, haven't you been reading the papers? Mr. Rickenbacker is lost somewhere in the Pacific on a raft."

"Oh, yes, that's terrible, but—"

"Colonel Adamson is with him."

"No! Oh, my God!"

Now I had truly reached nowhere. How could I get into combat now? With a theatrical and movie background, I'd surely get Special Services or the Signal Corps, and in neither of them would I ever see combat. What about the Air Corps? Even its ground personnel were in combat. But how could I conceal my theatre background enough to break in?

It would take larceny. I bribed a personnel sergeant with tickets to *By Jupiter* and soon found myself on a filthy overcrowded train heading for a great Air Corps base: at Miami Beach.

The Miami area seemed to be a combination of all the road companies of *The Student Prince.* The streets were overrun with marching, singing airmen. Their general had said, "I want a singing army," and that's what he got. You couldn't turn a corner without having to step back to let Squadron 13 pass as it sang aggressive parodies of popular tunes.

The Miami barracks were requisitioned hotels, grand ones for the officers, middle-class ones for us.

Standing in line with my open mess kit one day, I waited while a slow-witted KP tried nervously to plop a few canned cherries into my tin cup. I said, "Just pour it all in."

"No, you don't, big boy! You only get five. Hold that thing still while I count them again."

The familiar voice of the KP soldier turned out to belong to an old friend, Alan Campbell, Dorothy Parker's husband and one of the country's more unlikely soldiers.

"Josh! Look, meet me after supper at my hotel and I'll give you some ashtrays."

"What do I need ashtrays for?"

"Everybody needs ashtrays in this place. I've been hoarding them just for friends—but you're the only friend who's come along."

Soon I learned that all my new friends were applying for Officer Candidate School, even Alan. I was too embarrassed to admit why I didn't particularly want to be an officer. I was still edgy about bringing up my medical history. But as a gesture of comradeship, I put in my application too.

The subject of OCS was rife with rumor, superstition and old wives' tales. For prospective officer candidates there were several "musts." The first was Frankie the Fix, a sergeant on whose desk all applications landed. He had the power to pull one from the bottom of the pile and place it at the top.

Frankie liked Scotch, so it was Standard Operating Procedure to slip him a bottle of Ballantine's with your name carefully written on it. We all dutifully made this contribution and then sweated it out.

Then each of us bought four extra sets of suntans which were starched and hung in a friend's room near where the OCS Board interviewed applicants. This was insurance lest back-of-the-knee sweat marks or bottom-of-the-seat wrinkles appear when we stepped before the board.

But Frankie dealt me the blow I was unconsciously waiting for. "You haven't got a chance, Logan! I almost feel like giving your bottle back. You got less than ninety on your IQ. And you got to have more than a hundred and fifteen. See the officer in charge of IQ's. Maybe you can con him."

The officer I saw was skeptical. No one, he said, ever improved their scores when retested—but he agreed to give me the test again.

At the examination I went through the questions thoroughly but fast, answering immediately all the ones I knew on sight. Then I went over it again, and a third time. My score was 167, far above what was needed. I gave another Scotch to Frankie, just for the hell of it.

Alan and I both passed easily. Alan was surely helped by four years at V.M.I. and I by Culver. We knew how to speak in a military manner. That's all that was wanted anyway: appearance and zest.

Classes were held in rows of identical screened-in huts in Biscayne Park. We were taught some rarefied courses.

Military Hygiene and Sanitation class provided one memorable Army day for me. The officer instructor lectured in a singsong tone. A group of backwoods Southern boys were constantly raising their hands and whispering among themselves for fear that they had missed some hot dope.

The instructor said, "And you must be very careful, gentlemen, about the disposal of the urine and the feces. In case anyone does not know what the word 'feces' means, feces, gentlemen, is just plain, ordinary shit."

A Southern boy waved his hand frantically. "What wuz that ughin, suh? What wuz that ughin?"

The boy next to him half whispered, "He said it was just plain shit."

"Ah *know*, but what did he say shit *wuz*?"

The last day of underclass, we gathered on a huge field to hear the officer appointments for our upper class term. When the adjutant called out, "Squadron commander for Squadron 24, Joshua L. Logan," my knees nearly buckled in surprise. And my next in command was Alan Campbell! Good Christ! We were both upper class officers.

Alan and I attacked a major problem immediately. Food and drink. We rented, across the alley from our barracks hotel, a small apartment with a stove and an icebox and stashed it from the nearest grocer, butcher and liquor stores.

Nedda and Dorothy came down for ten days and we used the apartment to meet. But the days grew harder as we neared graduation, and we didn't draw our first calm breaths until we were able to put on officers' uniforms and second lieutenants' bars. We had come through what was surely the worst part of the war.

Most of our group, including our roommates Bruce Cabot and Robert Preston, went to Air Force Intelligence School at Harrisburg, Pennsylvania. It was the nearest thing to combat we could get without pilot, gunnery or navigational training.

As officers, we could live as we pleased. Larcenous Bruce Cabot got us an ornate Spanish house in the best residential section. Bob Preston called it Casa Gangrene. The lumps in the stucco made the outside look like gigantic peanut brittle and the inside was infested with gold cupids and dolphins. Bruce also owned the local MPs who supplied us with girls.

There was always a new and ravishing girl parading down the stairs or taking a nap on a gold sofa. With some accuracy, our Harrisburg stay could be called a three-month-long dirty houseparty.

I applied for a troop carrier unit, whose mission was to drop parachutists into enemy territory. I was accepted and told to go to Camp Mackall in North Carolina, where I'd be an assistant intelligence officer.

I drove my car alone to Camp Mackall, which gave me time to think. I felt fairly sure my mental illness was forgotten and that no one in the service would bring it up. I was in the war at last.

I felt serene, realizing I didn't have to top one success with another. I was down to just plain me, starting from scratch this time, without any trumped-up publicity. Could I really learn a new life? The life of a soldier? Why not? It was this promise of discovery that excited me.

Nedda. What about Nedda? She was the loveliest woman I'd ever known, the easiest companion, the most fun and beautiful beyond belief. She had an endlessly fascinating range from the gracious to the wickedly charming, with flashes of fire and of great generosity and—I had to admit it—more sense than I had.

I knew she wanted to get married, but I couldn't help hesitating. I was free of the demands and responsibilities of others for the very first time in my life. I didn't want to change that too soon—and above all I didn't want to give her a bad time, as I'd done Barbara.

Could we hold on to our present feelings after years of being apart?

Besides, what was the truth about me?

I had talked my way through every school I'd gone to. I'd pretended, cheated, lied, said I'd read books I'd never opened, repeated remarks of others as my own. But now was the time to end all that fakery. I mustn't make any decision until I'd found out the real truth about me—me at this age—me in this particular world. And maybe I'd find out soon.

* * *

Exeter, England. D Day-1. Josh, second from left,
top of picture, near Intelligence map.

Josh and Nedda,
Paris.

Annie Get Your Gun. First performance of
There's No Business Like Show Business.
William O'Neal, Marty May, Ethel Merman,
and Ray Middleton. (RICHARD TUCKER).

Working on *Annie* with Irving Berlin.
(ZINN ARTHUR)

At Wing Headquarters, fuzzy old Colonel Frank G. McCormick, the head of the Intelligence Section of the wing, welcomed me warmly. I wondered then, and always will, how this slightly inarticulate, avuncular, former football coach became an intelligence officer. He was jovial, kind, and even hard, but he was just bad casting.

Speaking of bad casting, I became the aircraft identification officer. I had had a bit of it at Harrisburg, but since I had never been able to tell a Buick from a Dodge, how could I spot aircraft whizzing by? But, as with Colonel Mac, the Army works in mysterious ways, and not only did I become an expert on aircraft, eventually I was the top authority in all our squadrons.

Our commanding officer, Colonel Julian M. Chappell, feeling my theatre contacts belonged to the wing, arranged business trips for us to New York so I could get show tickets for his staff. Most of them wanted to see *Oklahoma!* My credit with Dick Rodgers got to the stretching point, but I didn't object because it gave me a chance to see Nedda.

Even scarcer than *Oklahoma!* tickets was liquor. Resourceful, persuasive Nedda made friends with liquor distributors and began hoarding bottles for me to take overseas.

Mary Lee, my vibrant, athletic sister, had joined the WASPS and was in Jacqueline Cochran's group of girl pilots who ferried fighting planes between bases, relieving men for combat. Mary Lee loved adventure. And her adventures continued even after the war: crossing Holland in a balloon, going down rapids in the Amazon.

She wrote that my young brother Marshall had been drafted and was stationed near me at dusty, sandy Fort Bragg in North Carolina. Mother had written her: "Isn't it wonderful for Marshall to be in North Carolina just during rhododendron time?"

There was one last family reunion. Mary Lee sent a wire saying, ARRIVING POPE FIELD IN B-25. PLEASE CORRAL MARSHALL AND MEET ME. As Marshall and I waited, the huge B-25 bomber appeared, circled the field and landed. Mary Lee was so relieved to have landed such a monster that she quickly downed a whiskey, and then off we drove to the beach for a picnic of whiskey in oranges—what else?—with some other officers.

Just before the war shortages started, Mary Lee had bought a little three-storied Dutch farmhouse in Bucks County. That farm was Mary Lee's personality. She gave it her entire heart. With all her adventuring, I still think of the adult Mary Lee with a backdrop of masses of roses, or bridal wreath, or Japanese magnolia.

During the war, Mother lived alone in that house, and every day worked on the grounds with one or two old men, planting trees, and several million forget-me-nots, and tiny little flowers called Chinese houses. Mother redirected the little stream with rocks so it would make an attractive noise, and gardened around the hunk of concrete which had been the floor of a former pigpen. Mother preserved those first letters of pigpen by calling it Pleasant Place. In this way, guests would be reminded of how charm covers all.

Soon our wing was sent to Camp Kilmer in New Jersey. In New York, Nedda and I had a few final days together. She told me, "I've arranged to have all that heavy liquor delivered to Camp Kilmer tomorrow so you won't have to carry it."

Nedda had sent to Kilmer a full case of Scotch. Since I could get only one bottle into my B-4 bag, the other eleven would roll up in my bedroll, then be strapped horseshoe-wise around the knapsack, and hoisted on my back. With it there, I was unable to stand without four people pulling me to my feet. Then I could just manage to stay upright as long as my legs were absolutely rigid, but if I bent my knees slightly, they buckled under and I sank to the floor. But I was not going to sail without every precious bottle.

I did knee bends and leg lifts for strength to withstand the weight as I had visions of losing my balance and falling off the gangway. When the final call came, eight friends strapped me up, hoisted me upright, and headed my faltering feet for the *Queen Mary.*

Almost collapsing under the weight, I trudged stiff legged up the gangplank. The Frankenstein monster goes to war.

CHAPTER

12

The *Queen Mary* zigzagged her way at full speed, knocking us all off balance every thirty seconds, but there wasn't room to fall. It was as crowded and giddy as Mardi Gras. Our course changes were to confuse submarine torpedoes. We were in the war from the moment we sailed until we docked at Glasgow (Greenock).

Soon we were in our first station, Cottesmore, and I was on weekend to London, which was all blackout and queues for buses, for food and for the theatre. A soldier I knew ran up to me. "Irving Berlin wants you," he said. *This Is the Army* had crossed the Atlantic before I had and was ready to open in London, except Irving wanted to see me first.

Berlin seemed almost supercharged when I went to his hotel room. He had convinced himself that he had brought me there—conjured up my appearance in London personally because he wanted to put a new and bawdy scene in the show which was going to play to GI posts around the world and I was the only director with the evil mind to do it.

Julie Oshins would play a private who ached to spend the night with his wife, a lieutenant in the WACS, but who had to go "through channels," via his mother-in-law, her huge WAC first sergeant, to be played by burly, pop-eyed Hank Henry.

I wanted to do it, but I was sure my CO, Colonel Chappell, would not let me. Berlin waved that aside with a "poof-poof"—he'd handled my transfer via the highest channels, namely General Eisenhower.

Since the invasion of the Continent was imminent, commanding officers had final say about shifts in personnel which might weaken their units. Berlin's request went through to Eisenhower, who approved it and sent it down to Colonel Chappell. Chappell, as a good combat commander, immediately disapproved it.

Berlin couldn't believe his ears. Up to now, his requests for talent had been law.

He heatedly called overseas to General "Hap" Arnold at the Pentagon. The approved request went winging back to England only to again hit the immovable object, Chappell. "Request disapproved." And that was that.

Berlin was furious with Arnold and Eisenhower for being such weaklings. He called Chappell directly. The call went right through.

Berlin said, "Colonel Chappell? This is Irving Berlin." There was a long pause and Berlin called out, "Hello? Hello?"

Finally, Chappell said in a strained voice, "Did you say you were Irving Berlin? *The* Irving Berlin?"

"That's right. Now, I want Logan for three weeks, and no more beating about the bush."

"Of course not. Anything you say, Mr. Berlin. Irving Berlin, huh? Jesus Christ, *Irving Berlin!*"

For three weeks I worked with my raunchy theatrical pals and put in a new scene. Taking Berlin's theme, we improvised laugh upon laugh until it was the riot Berlin had dreamed of. The opening night at the Palladium must rank high in London theatrical history. The audience seemed to cheer half the night. Berlin was deeply moved.

That brief taste of theatre was fun, but soon I headed, according to plan, for the most important aircraft identification school in the United Kingdom. It was a few miles from Liverpool at Southport, one of the grayest, saddest of British sea resorts.

One weekend I went alone into wartime Liverpool. I wandered

about the colorless city and stopped at a poster on a theatre where a new play, *The Druid's Rest* by Emlyn Williams, the author of *Night Must Fall* and *The Corn Is Green,* was to premiere the following night. I noticed that in the cast was an old friend from the Dwight Wiman days, Gladys Henson. Since there would be a dress rehearsal that night, I went to the stage door.

Gladys was excited to see me, and introduced me to two of the closest friends I would ever have, Emlyn Williams and his wife Molly. Emlyn said I could watch the rehearsal.

This one was about Emlyn's childhood in Wales, and an eight-year-old boy played the lead. Gladys Henson played his mother, but the greatest talent shown was the blue-eyed, seventeen-year-old actor playing the brother. It was young Richard Burton, who would be seen by the public for the first time the next night.

With the spring of 1944 whispers accelerated. The invasion was near. The wing was moved south, to the very lower edge of England across from Brittany. We now occupied a fine house called Gypsy Hill near Exeter.

At Gypsy Hill was the map room which only senior officers could enter. It showed the exact invasion plans. When I, as an intelligence officer, was finally let in, high-ranking officers were being instructed on D-day plans from huge maps that papered the rooms. All spoke in subdued voices, and I studied the plan for our planes to cross the Channel and the Cotentin Peninsula, where we would drop the 506th Paratroop Infantry and return to our bases. My tasks included briefing pilots on German positions and knowing enough to interrogate the pilots afterward.

A young colonel called me over on something "of utmost importance."

"Now, keep your voice down," he said. "Get closer. And don't for God's sake change your expression. Listen, Josh, Janet is pregnant. Now, you know all that theatre crowd in London. Please find out where she can get an abortion, and fast."

Was this going to be my only involvement in the war, that my "theatre crowd" would take care of a knocked-up Army nurse? At any rate, my friends came through and the girl was all right after one morning in London.

The exact date of D day was unknown: Eisenhower was deciding it with one eye on the location of German forces in France and the other on the weather. To be ready for a quick decision, we were moved to our D-day spots. I was sent to Upottery, an airfield close to Exeter, where the 506th were encamped. Our planes would drop them near Sainte Mere Eglise three hours before midnight on the eve of D day, D Minus One.

The first man to parachute out of each plane was to light a flare, then organize the men who followed him to make sure the bridges to the beaches were not blown up by the Germans. Paratroopers equipped with electric torches would have formed themselves on the ground in the shape of a T, showing the pilots safe places to drop their groups.

On June 5, 1944, we were told that at 2100 hours our planes would take off. There was a final pilot briefing at seven. As the pilots filed in, they looked like sober schoolboys going to class.

First, the commanding officer explained their mission. Then I pointed out on the map locations of German guns and troops, after which the operations officer carefully traced the flight pattern on the map. No pilot was to return with a single parachutist in his plane. If he could not spot the T on the ground below, he was to drop the men anyway.

Everyone was thinking the same thing. These men would parachute out with no idea of where they were or how they would join the others. How would they find each other in the darkness? What a paratrooper dreaded most was to be dropped in unknown water, and that night a huge percentage of them would be.

The chaplain, a huge, burly, red-haired Irish Catholic, offered the send-off prayer. When he finished his blessing, these men were going to walk to their planes and launch the invasion. Overcome with excitement and emotion, the red-faced chaplain began his blessing in sober-toned Latin. But soon his voice rose an octave as he forgot the litany and started screaming, "Now get out there and kill 'em, murder 'em, kill 'em! Kill! Kill! Kill! In Jesus' name, Amen!"

For a moment the white-faced boys sat in shock. Then, not much comforted by God's words, they pulled themselves together and moved out.

At the loading area I watched the paratroopers climbing into the huge troop carrier planes. They had blackened faces so they'd be harder to see at night. Each soldier was in battle dress that had been sprayed with antigas liquid, giving him a wild, mottled appearance, had pockets bulging with grenades and bullet clips, and a pistol pushed within his belt. Some stuck their chewing gum on the plane's wing for good luck. One tall, black-haired, stringy but powerful paratrooper was kneeling in the center of the plane, praying desperately. But most of them sat in dumb stupor, almost blending into the gloomy night with their makeup and spattered uniforms.

From a low building near the base tower, I waited with a large group for the historic takeoff. On the strip, the signal man swiped a red electric torch through the air and the engines began to roar. The first plane's wheels started to turn and the big hulk bumped slowly along, gathering speed, seeming so heavy it couldn't bear to part from the ground, then with more speed the wheels gradually inched up off the runway. I'll never forget the sound I heard. It was a primitive yell from the men around me. There were tones in that yell of triumph, of vengeance, of pain and of relief. It was so loud that my ears hurt with the mixed sound and emotion.

For close to three hours we waited, pacing, speculating, and when they returned home some planes were flashing their lights to indicate that they were crippled mechanically, and there was one rocket indicating a wounded man aboard. Wounded?

A stretcher drew out from it a paratrooper who had been shot by antiaircraft before he'd had a chance to jump.

During the interrogation, I heard the ghastly story from the pilots. There had been no T, not one, no indication as to where the men were to be dropped. At the eight-hundred-foot height specified by the weather officer, a shallow but crucial strata of cloud kept most of the pilots flying blind. The weatherman had failed them badly. A few hundred feet above or below would have been clear. Less than fifty percent of the paratroopers dropped were able to carry out their mission. Most were drowned in the sea, and many were captured by the Germans because they landed too close to them and walked right into their arms.

The infantry would be landing from boats in a few hours on the French beaches dubbed Omaha and Utah. They would be counting—and mostly in vain—on our paratroopers to clear out Germans and secure vital bridges.

My participation in D day made me want to remain close to dramatic action all the more. I wasn't able to imagine when paratroopers would be used again, and since I couldn't stand the thought of waiting at some outstation, I applied for a transfer. Fighter pilots based in England were flying fast strafing missions over the French countryside. There was little room for an intelligence officer in these outfits, but they did need a public relations officer to help morale by writing "hometown" stories. I accepted the job and boarded a train for the town of Christchurch, near Bournemouth, by the sea. I was to become P.R. Officer for the 405th Fighter Group.

I had made a firm resolve that in this new chapter of my life no one would break through my anonymity. I would rid myself of associations with the theatre or of where I'd gone to school or college or where I'd been brought up. I wanted to be Mr. Nobody for the rest of the war and observe others.

The Quonset hut I entered was empty and I looked around for a cot that wasn't stacked with equipment. I was delighted to be in this remote building. No one would ever spot me.

A beady-eyed, beaky-nosed, brash young man in flying clothes walked in.

"Hello. I'm Jake Nielsen. Who are you?"

I braced myself.

"My name's Logan."

He dubbed me with a nickname that stuck for the rest of the war.

"Logue," he said, "where'd you go to school?"

I gave a carefully vague answer. "In the Midwest."

"No college, eh?"

"Of course. A place in New Jersey."

"Rutgers?"

"No, God damn it," I said. "Princeton."

"Oh, folks had money, eh, Logue?"

Except for the fact that my folks didn't have money, he managed to learn an awful lot from Mr. Nobody in thirty seconds. I tried to brush him off by starting to arrange my equipment.

"Hold it, Logue. Don't get eager. What did you do in civilian life?"

"Oh, I was in New York."

"Yeah, you were probably a millionaire stockbroker." I shook my head disgustedly. "Well, what *were* you, Logue? You did something, didn't you?"

"Sure, I, uh, I was in the theatre."

"Were you an actor?" Again I shook my head. "Well, then what the hell *did* you do? And speak up—I can hardly hear you."

"I was . . . um . . . a director and a writer and . . ."

"Oh, big shot, eh, Logue?"

Mr. Nobodys couldn't exist in that place. I was thrust into being the group's most exciting new acquisition. I figured the best thing to do was to relax and enjoy it.

The others in the hut were P-47 pilots whose average age must have been twenty. Their eyes were clear, their skin a baby's, their spirits so high that they yelled rather than talked. And they were thoroughgoing cynics. Their sense of fatality was so great that they never allowed the word Death to connote anything sad or sentimental. It was only allowed to be funny.

Jake Nielsen was Damon and Gene Gray was Pythias and the two of them strenuously avoided saying anything slightly serious or calling anything by its proper name. The King's Arms Pub became The Queen's Legs. Jake always said of a pilot who had been killed in action, "He's flying wing on the great white leader," and he said it so often he forgot there was any other term for it.

One day he came in, and just stood there by the door.

I asked him what was wrong.

He started yelling in a high-pitched voice. "You know what? Just before Gene took off he asked me where Airy was and I said Airy was flying wing on the great white leader. And no time later, while I was taking a piss, I hear that *Gene* is flying wing on the great white leader. *Did you hear what I said, Logue? Gene's* flying wing . . ." He turned and ran out the door.

Almost daily one or two pilots were shot down and their cots taken over the next day by replacements. There was one replacement whose memory haunts me still. His arrival shook the entire compound with an enormous blast.

He had been sent up without the chance to get used to his plane. He was nervous, and in gunning the engine prior to takeoff he hadn't adjusted the wing flaps properly. So he took off late, his plane scraped the roof of one of the little brick houses that were close to the air strip, a bomb was ripped off his wing, and it exploded—killing all the people in the house. Miraculously, the green young pilot survived and came back to the hut to try to rest. But he was called to report to the operations officer.

An hour later, while I was in the middle of one of my fancy pilot-hero stories for a Chattanooga paper, there was another blast, far worse than the first. Instantly, I knew it was the same boy. As if flying were like riding a horse, the commanding officer believed that if you got thrown, the best thing to do was to pick yourself up, brush yourself off and mount the horse again. In this case the second ride was even more disastrous. He hadn't been able to take off at all. He just plowed into another house and exploded, killing or destroying everyone and everything around.

Omaha Beach was cleared, and two weeks after D day we were all to be moved by boat across the Channel and marched to a Normandy airstrip. The Allied Forces were still fighting bitterly in the northern orchards and had not been able to reach the crucial town of St. Lo.

We camped for weeks in octagonal tents by the perforated aluminum portable landing strip—with occasional strafing visits from German planes.

After mass bombing at St. Lo, the infantry broke through and moved fast. In a short time, we learned that Paris had been liberated. We were to move on to a major aircraft position at St. Dizier, just east of Paris.

Unlike the primitive Normandy airfield, St. Dizier was a real town, much nearer to the front, with citizens waiting to see if we were worse than the Germans. In short order, we commandeered a large building to serve as an officers' club—one of the holy rituals of every outfit was to create a clubhouse. The town was near the champagne country, so the colonel appointed me "champagne officer," since I looked decadent enough to know what champagne was.

I returned with a bulging truckload of the finest vintage champagne (it cost something like seventy cents a bottle), and those adolescent pilots broke open the cases while I conducted a short course in twisting off the wire and gently pressing out the cork.

In the rush, some corks popped, showering bubbling fountains. It took these growing boys no time to realize that by putting a thumb on top of the bottle and shaking, they could create stinging jets to squirt into each other's faces.

I had started the great champagne war. I thought someone might stop it since it ruined uniforms, tablecloths, walls and floors, but when I looked at the young colonel, he was busily shaking up a bottle too.

I soon became the most popular man in the 405th, not for personal qualities or champagne, but because I wrote stories about these callow egomaniacs for their hometown papers. I was loaded with gifts of whiskey and chocolate any day I went with my photographer and posed a pilot climbing into his cockpit with his trusty mechanic standing by his wing. When the clippings came back from proud parents, there was always a celebration at the officers' club.

One day, my commanding officer came to me. "Logue, why didn't you tell us you were in the theatre?"

"What do you mean, sir? A lot of the guys know it."

"Well, you're being transferred to Paris even though there's no record of your theatre experience."

It seems the commanding general had called my colonel personally and said that when the European war came to an end there'd be a lot of soldiers stranded with nothing to do—soldiers who would need entertainment.

"He figured there must be somebody in Theatre of Operations who could head such a . . . so I told them to look through all those personnel files again. And that's what they did, Logue. And some lousy PFC recognized your name."

In Paris I was assigned to Special Services. My job was to encourage soldier shows and organize French civilian shows. One group of shows didn't need much attention as it was organized back in the States: the Jeep Shows. Three men went to the front lines in a jeep and put on an hour's entertainment. All I did was send them off to their assignments. All the men were surefire entertainers. It was instant theatre. They could pick up their instruments—guitar, accordion or banjo—throw them in the jeep, and move. One of those Jeep Shows was headed by Mickey Rooney, who did everything—sang, danced, pantomimed, played sketches.

Alan Campbell had got himself stationed in Paris and had wangled an office two floors below mine. At the end of each day we met friends in a nearby bar. There was nothing to drink but brandy, but it did the trick—and led to heated artistic discussions.

One memorable time, someone said, ". . . and then you take Monet's absinthe drinker . . ."

"What?" shouted another. "*Monet?* You don't know your ass from third base! Monet never painted any absinthe drinker!"

"Well, then, for Christ's sake, who did?"

"Toulouse-Lautrec."

I said, "Oh, wait a minute. Degas painted the absinthe drinker. I happen to have it in a book at home."

Pretty soon, every Impressionist painter had been proposed. What we needed was an authority, and I said, "I'll bet Gertrude Stein would know."

They all started daring me to call her. "But I don't know her."

"Who cares?"

So, loaded with two more brandies and a few francs, I went to the phone and, much to my horror, found her number in a telephone book. A voice answered that could have belonged to Alice B. Toklas.

"Miss Stein?"

"Yes, who is speaking, please?" She sounded extremely cordial.

"This is Joshua Logan. You wouldn't know me, Miss Stein, and I feel very presumptuous in calling you at this time of . . ."

"Oh, that's perfectly all right. You're an American, aren't you?"

"Yes, Miss Stein. I'm stationed here in Paris."

"What can I do for you, Mr. Logan?"

"Well, some friends and I are having a very violent argument about that painting *The Absinthe Drinker*. Some say it's Degas, some Monet, and somebody even said it was Toulouse-Lautrec. I thought that you'd be the one to know. Who did it?"

For a few seconds she said nothing, then she judiciously murmured, "Well, they *all* did, didn't they?"

"Of course they did. Isn't that ridiculous of us? Thank you so much, Miss Stein. It's really great of you to help us out."

When I hung up, I was ecstatic. I had reached the highest rung of artistic Paris—and all on brandy.

A French liaison officer named Captain Medrano was assigned to work with us. He had run his grandfather's circus for years and knew every circus and vaudeville act in the world. Any French acts, he said, would be happy to work for the American Army. Just appearing in an American camp meant they had been investigated and cleared of any possible collaboration with the Germans. And he was right: we got the very best talent for our civilian shows, including French girls, a guarantee of success with a GI audience.

Nedda had written me about how she'd gone to the USO and urged it to send out plays instead of just vaudeville shows, since plays were more of an escape from a lonely life. She took a comedy to Nova Scotia and Newfoundland and it was such a success that the USO opened the floodgates, sending hundreds of plays in all directions. Soon, the biggest stars in the theatre were touring Army camps—the Lunts, Katharine Cornell—and all because of Nedda.

The news of the German surrender reached me in Rheims while I was on a jeep expedition to requisition scenery and costumes from German towns. People were dancing in the streets, and I discovered that the Armistice had been signed directly across the street from where I had by accident spent the night.

When I returned to Paris, I found a letter from Nedda. She had orders to travel to Europe with a company of *Three's a Family*. They would start in Liége, after a stop in Paris. She said she would bring me two bottles of Scotch to celebrate her arrival.

At seven-thirty in the morning I waited outside the Gare St. Lazare in my jeep. Leaving it would have risked it being stolen. I saw a group in new green uniforms, and among them was Nedda. She waved and began to run, and when we embraced she wept. I helped her into the jeep and piled her bags in back.

"Darling," she said, "you have only one bottle of Scotch because, well, we drank one on that ghastly train. We had to; seven hours in the dark in that little cubicle. And anyway, we needed the empty bottle later to, you know, relieve ourselves."

I was trying to start the motor, which finally caught, and I pulled away, and making a sharp turn I heard a nearby crash of glass. We stopped.

Nedda said, "Oh, dear! Your bottle of Scotch was in my raincoat pocket. Now they're both gone. Oh, and I carried them all this way for you."

I assured her we could find some cognac.

The tourist guide in me took over and we went everywhere and ate great but limited food. At night we found romantic views on Montmartre. I took her to her train for Brussels.

Her cast returned to Paris on a very dramatic day—the bombing of Hiroshima.

And the weirdest day of all followed—V-J Day. The war was over, and Paris was befuddled. For the French, their war had ended months before. On V-J night there was an emptiness in the town. Nedda and I walked to Montmartre, looking for some signs of jubilation, but there was none.

Nedda returned to New York and I hoped I would be following her soon.

I had received a flattering letter from Lawrence Langner of the Theatre Guild, inviting me to join its board of directors. And even before that, Dick Rodgers had written that he and Oscar Hammerstein had taken an option to produce a musical for Ethel Merman, with a book by Herbert and Dorothy Fields, based on the life of Annie Oakley. Dorothy could write the lyrics and Jerome Kern, the music.

Dick said he had "reason to believe" the war would be over and I'd be back in the States in time for rehearsals in the fall. The letter had come before the Japanese surrender. How did he know the war would be over? Had someone slipped Dick Rodgers a hint about the atomic bomb? But, he was right. I just might be back in time.

CHAPTER

I found myself standing in an endless line of returning GIs waiting to use a Camp Kilmer pay telephone.

I could only make one call, so I made it to Dick. "Hello, Josh. Are you out of the Army?"

"Except for some medical examinations. How's our Annie Oakley show coming?"

"Josh, it's falling apart. Jerome Kern is terribly ill. The doctors think he might die tonight."

"Oh, my God!" I said. I was shocked, and at the same time felt a selfish loss. At the moment, my whole life seemed to hang on that show.

"Call me tomorrow. We might know if we're going ahead. I'll call Nedda for you."

Jerome Kern! My spirits dragged me to the dreary barracks for no sleep.

I was back next day at the phone. "Any news?"

"Jerry died last night."

"Holy Jesus—and poor Dorothy Fields, all set to do his lyrics. She loved him so."

"It's pretty grim. But there's still a chance, if we can find another composer who will accept Dorothy's lyrics, and vice versa."

As I headed for my medical checkup, the Logan "worryscope" surfaced—my personal periscope that scanned the horizon trying to find something to fret about. Who would dare follow Jerome Kern? And who would now want a doddering thirty-seven-year-old has-been. There must be hundreds of cheap and young directors coming back from the service. How could there be jobs for all of us?

A medical officer was looking over my Army history. I knew he was reading about some eye trouble I had had in Paris. "Read that eye chart for me—with your _left eye only_." I tried to peek a bit with my right eye, but he quickly put a card over it. With my left eye I couldn't even see the huge E at the top of the chart. "You're trying to cheat, aren't you? Why?"

"I want to get out of the service, and quick."

"But I'm not going to let you out. You must be examined thoroughly —which will take two, maybe three weeks."

Three weeks! "I've got a job to do; at least, I may have."

"You've got a life to live, and without the sight of your left eye."

"But the doctor in Paris told me that when the macular hemorrhage I was having in my left eye stopped, the scar it left in the back of the eye would eventually shrink, so I could see a bit more."

"A bit—a very little bit—but you will never see with the center of your eye. Only the periphery. But you can function almost perfectly without front vision in the left eye. You can work, you can drive, you can—"

"But I can't get out of the Army. Why?"

"Because I won't let you out until your discharge is properly processed. With the loss of an eye, as with the loss of a leg, you are entitled to captain's pay for the rest of your life."

"Suppose I told you I didn't want it?"

"I'm sorry, Captain, but you're going to get it anyway. It's my decision, not yours. All you have to do is stay in the Army three more weeks."

* * *

Waiting in that mile-long telephone line hating to hear more bad news, I tried to think of other producers who might let me work for them.

"Hello, Dick? It's Josh. I was wondering—"

"Can you sit down? Oh, no, you're in a booth. Well, lean against something. This morning, we were going down an alphabetical list of composers, and of course at the top of the list was B—Berlin—Irving, you know."

"Don't tell me that—"

"Wait. Everyone agreed there was no point in asking him. He's a boss. It's got to be his show all the way—his ideas, his money, his songs. He doesn't work for other people. So, we started on down our list, when Oscar said, 'Wait! How can a man say no until he's at least asked to say yes?' So, we asked him and he said yes."

I yelled so loud the whole line heard me. Then I remembered something.

"What about Dorothy Fields?"

"Oh, Dorothy doesn't mind giving up the lyrics to Mister One-and-Only. Don't you realize this little show just turned into a giant? Get out of that goddamned camp and let's get going!" I'd never heard Dick so enthusiastic about another musician's work.

The next few weeks I shuttled by car between medical officers and New York. I'd spend the early mornings being tested and the afternoons with Dorothy and her brother Herb, working on the book of *Annie*. It was salty and funny but had some holes in it. I also spent time with my old Army buddy, Irving Berlin, who was a geyser of excitement but needed someone, he said, to "splash against."

He would grab me by the collar and sing a lyric into my face the moment I stepped into the room. Only by fixing his eyes on the listener could he sense if the song worked. If one blinked too often or one's eyes glazed for a second, Irving was apt to toss the song away.

And Oscar Hammerstein and I were getting to know each other. He was an enormous, seemingly benign man with a pitted face, of the same cut as Maxwell Anderson. But his warmth was so apparent it was hard to see the glints of steel in his eyes. He had a way of judging songs, scenes and people that seemed completely sympathetic, yet contained. And he was able to make me laugh whenever he wanted to; there was an incipient smile, almost a wicked one, at the corner of his mouth. I discovered he enjoyed preparing very personal practical jokes, and I'm afraid they were designed to make people squirm a bit—but he was so delighted when they were a success that he was forgiven immediately.

When my discharge came through, a delayed surge of power swept through me. As I drove up through New Jersey I fantasized. From now on I wouldn't wait to be offered plays. I'd dig them up myself—be my own producer, collect a stable of composers and lyricists, buy stories, have them dramatized, then hire myself to direct them. I had the experience to do that, but did I have the business head, the cunning, the gall, to raise backing?

As I drove along, dreaming of grandeur, I became conscious of a sweet melody coming over the car radio. The lyrics were fresh, yes, and literate. It had to be by two budding talents. "Hello," I told myself, "this is a sign of my future—a nudge from the gods, telling me to get these unknowns to write me a show." Yes, that tune was to be my new start. I stopped the car to write down its title.

Soon, I burst into Nedda's apartment and poured out all my new resolves, and announced I was going to sign a new composer-lyricist team. But when I started to sing the song, she said, "Why, that's 'It Might As Well Be Spring.'"

"Yes, that's the title. I'm going to sign up whoever wrote it to a long-term contract."

"It's going to be difficult, dear. That song was written by Rodgers and Hammerstein for the film *State Fair*, last year, while you were abroad. They're already signed up. As a matter of fact, they've just signed *you* up."

We had an emotional dinner as we talked over our lives apart and our Paris meeting, of her daughter's marriage to John Lester, a young officer then with the USO in Germany. He was a general's aide and they had gotten married in a magnificent castle. But Nedda was worried that the marriage might have been a mistake: "He can't be very bright."

"Why not?"

"He laughed at everything I said, even when it wasn't funny. Does that sound bright to you?"

That evening was crucial. I knew that Nedda and I should talk about our much-delayed marriage. I felt that we should level, find out just where we stood.

After a few hours and more than a few glasses of wine, Nedda began to ask casually about my love life overseas.

Because of the airy way she asked it, I foolishly thought she was fishing for an excuse to confess a few flings of her own. I knew she'd been on long USO trips with men to remote all-male outstations. So, to remove any guilt she might feel, I started to tell her of the girls I had known and explained that in wartime things were mixed up emotionally for everybody—both for men and for women.

"Oh, really?" she said brightly. "Were any of them pretty?"

"One of them, a French girl who lived in the apartment next to mine in Paris, was stunning. Tall and golden, like a Petty girl. I inherited her from the former tenant, a captain who presented her to me via his first sergeant."

"Presented her?"

"Yes. His CO was being transferred and he didn't want her to be lonely."

"How thoughtful of him."

"Yes, it was just great, until another girl I knew caught us together and—"

Nedda's face had turned light blue. Within seconds, we were in the midst of a terrible fight, I defending myself by saying she had asked for it, and she aghast at my being such an "animal." I marched out and decided to sleep in my family's apartment a few doors away. For days I tried to speak to Nedda on the phone, but she cut me short, saying she was dated up for a week. Her dates must have been unsatisfactory because on the tenth day, Nedda granted me a short interview. By the time it was over, we had decided to get married the very next day.

We drove to Greenwich, Connecticut, where there was no waiting period, and the most forgettable ceremony became the most joyous event of my life: I married Nedda Harrigan. We had a lovely, tasteless lunch in a nearby hotel, drove back to New York, and lied to my mother, telling her we'd been married a long time. We didn't want parties, gifts and congratulations. There was an air of shock in the room, but it didn't prevent Mother from pulling herself together and saying gallantly, "This calls for a little sip of sherry."

We never gave out the exact date of our wedding, even to my sister. We just explained, "We couldn't tell you before because we got married against Army regulations." It sounded properly ambiguous. It was not until our tenth anniversary that we revealed the date.

There were still problems with the book of *Annie Oakley*. The first act was funny, but there were crater-like gaps in the second. I worked with Dorothy and Herb for days rearranging scenes, writing new ones and, because I insisted on it, giving Annie some character growth before the curtain came down, as Max Anderson had taught me. The important character growth for Annie would come when she—who could do anything better than anyone—decided to lose the shooting contest in order to get what she really wanted, Frank.

Berlin took short jaunts to his country place or worked in his rooftop apartment. One day he brought the verse and chorus of a song for Buffalo Bill, Annie and Frank called "There's No Business Like Show Business." While we never guessed it would become the theatre anthem of the world, we knew it was a great theatre piece. Then with amazing swiftness Irving brought us the beautiful "They Say It's Wonderful," and the fantastically funny "You Can't Get a Man with a Gun." This song, plus "Doin' What Comes Natur'lly," was the essence of Annie and of Ethel Merman.

One morning, Irving played for Dick, Oscar and me, "Who Do You Love, I Hope?" which he had written for the young couple. It sounded so fresh, that I'm afraid we were overenthusiastic about it, glad for someone besides the stars to have a number.

Surprised but happy at our enthusiasm, he started out, then turned. "Oh, by the way," he said, "I brought the second chorus of 'Show Business.'"

"Fine, fine," we said, and he sang it, as he had done before, right into our faces, draining us for reactions. Since we had gone quite crazy about the first chorus of "Show Business," it was hard to show greater enthusiasm for the second chorus.

"What's the matter?" he said. "Don't you like the song? Have you gone cold on it?"

"No, no," we said. "It's fine, great. But that song's already a smash. And this chorus wraps it up. Get after those new songs."

"Yes, but the way you looked, so skittish like." And he left the office, worrying.

Every afternoon, to test the score, Berlin would play it for a different professional friend while I listened. That day it was for another composer, Hugh Martin of "Trolley Song" fame. After a lot of songs, Berlin said, "Well, that's it." Martin was most impressed but I was astounded.

"Irving, you didn't sing 'Show Business.'"

"No, no, that's out," he said. "I can take a hint. I've thrown it away."

"What!" I yelled. "That's one of the greatest songs ever written!"

"I didn't like the way you three reacted."

"We had heard the song before. We yelled our heads off the first time. We can't scream louder every time we hear it. You've got to play it for Hugh. He's got to hear it."

"I don't think I could find it now. It's in a pile. My girl would need quite awhile to dig it up."

"Go try, please."

We followed Irving out and he said, "Do you remember that music I gave you this morning that I told you to file?"

"Oh, dear, Mr. Berlin, I'm afraid I don't. What was it like?" The poor girl began fumbling through stacks of paper near a file of thousands of Berlin songs. We all joined in the search. The girl finally discovered the lead sheet under a telephone book and handed it to Helmy, Irving's accompanist. And then Irving sent Hugh into an ecstatic tailspin with one of the world's greatest songs—the song that almost got lost.

While Irving was completing the score, we held progress meetings in Oscar's living room. At the last of these meetings we discussed Lucinda Ballard's costumes, Helen Tamiris' dances and Ray Middleton, who was to play Annie's true love, Frank Butler.

Berlin was talking to a group off on the far side of the room, so I whispered to Oscar, "I'm worried. There ought to be another duet for Merman and Middleton."

"Another song?" whispered Oscar to me.

"Another song?" whispered Berlin, whose head appeared beside Oscar's.

Berlin can smell anything, anywhere, at any distance. He shouted to the room, "Listen, everybody, Josh wants another song. Josh, where do you see this song?"

"I don't know," I said, "except the leads should have a duet in the second act. They never sing together after 'Wonderful.'"

Irving said, "If they're not talking to each other in the second act, how can they sing together?"

"Could they have a quarrel song or a challenge song?" Dick asked.

Irving jumped at the idea. "Challenge! Of course! *Meeting over!* I've got to go home and write a challenge song."

Nedda and I took a taxi a few blocks, and when we got to our apartment the phone was ringing. It was Irving.

"Hello, Josh? How's this?" And he started singing:

> Anything you can do, I can do better,
> I can do anything better than you.

And he carried right on through to:

> I can shoot a partridge with a single cartridge.
> I can get a sparrow with a bow and arrow.
> I can do most anything.
> Can you bake a pie?
> No!
> Neither can I."

"That's perfect!" I shouted incredulously. "When in hell did you write that?"

"In the taxicab. I had to, didn't I? We go into rehearsal Monday."

I am a total fan of Irving Berlin's, and I enjoy every moment we are together. He is the funniest, the most exuberant, most astute of men—and talent glows from him like the northern lights. It is impossible to be with him for any length of time without becoming drunk with the stimulation of him. Although some may find him self-servicing, he has always been wonderfully generous and thoughtful with me.

We changed the title and *Annie Get Your Gun* was announced. On the first day, I sat Ethel Merman down on a bench and brought Ray Middleton around the edge of the bench and into Annie's sight.

The script read, "She looks at him and in a second falls in love with him forever." I felt that the only way I could show such an abrupt change was to have her collapse inwardly and outwardly as if she were a puppet whose strings had been cut quickly. I told Ethel to keep her eyes fixed on Ray but to let everything else in her body and mind go. She tried it. Her mouth dropped open, her shoulders sank, her legs opened wide at the knees, her diaphragm caved in. It was an unforgettable effect. Later, we dubbed it the "goon look," and it won for me the eternal devotion of everyone, including myself. It seemed to be the catalytic moment—the moment at which the play became a hit.

During rehearsals, I was always concerned about our progress. Berlin, on the other hand, was dancing, almost skipping.

When *Annie* opened in New Haven it seems I was the only one who didn't realize it would be one of the greatest hits of all time. I remember sitting in a booth at Kaysey's Restaurant and listening to Dick and Oscar discuss the show as "one of the big ones." I distrusted their euphoria.

In Boston, after some juggling about with "the Brevoort scene," the show was fixed to my satisfaction, and after a three-week run we moved to New York, where we were to have two more days of polishing. But the scenery was being hung in the Imperial Theatre when the weight of it pulled down the brickwork of a side wall and a girder buckled. By some miracle the scenery itself was unharmed, but the theatre walls had to be repaired, requiring two further weeks. Moving quickly, the management was able to book *Annie* in Philadelphia.

I had begun to feel that an audience is not the disparate group of people it seems to the eye. Disparate on its way to the theatre, perhaps, but the moment it is seated and the curtain goes up it goes through slam-bang metamorphosis. It is transformed into a single being, a tremendous, almost terrifying animal—a behemoth that wants to be conquered and at the same time defies us to conquer it. It is one-hearted and one-eyed. It can be loving and docile or can turn and be quite noisy: coughing nervously, blowing its nose or sometimes even booing. Or, most horrifying of all, it can even close its eye and go to sleep.

The *Annie* audiences in Philadelphia were the loving, docile kind. They had heard great things from Boston, and entered the theatre laughing. As the saying goes, they laughed at the ushers, they laughed at the programs, they laughed at the curtain going up and they screamed at Ethel's first "goon face," and shouted "bravo" when she sang:

> You can't shoot a male in the tail like a quail,
> You can't get a man with a gun.

We got so used to this laughter coming at its exact times that we memorized it.

But the opening night audience in New York is a monster of a different kidney. It's Gamblers Anonymous watching that old roulette wheel, trying to preguess the outcome by each line as they do each spin of the wheel. "That's good. That one's bad. It's a hit. It's a flop. I told you so. The critics hate it. I've been watching Watts since the curtain went up. Why is that lady laughing? She must be a backer. Berlin's finished. Merman's lost her voice." They're so busy wallowing in almost sexual anxiety, hoping they're right and yet terrified they're wrong that they can't *see* the show, much less react.

Although all of us know this ugly phenomenon, we naïvely believe each time that our show will be the exception. I was standing next to Dick Rodgers that opening night as the audience sat mute through the first act. The laughs were polite or embarrassed at best. I was terrified Ethel would be thrown by this lack of response. When the reaction to the "goon look" was a few scattered "haws" and "hos," I half expected her to turn and give the look at the audience. But she played steadily as she'd always done, and when they didn't even make a sound at "male-tail-quail" I looked at Dick, who shrugged helplessly.

At intermission I rushed solicitously back to Ethel. "How are you able to play to them?" I asked.

"Easy," she said. "You may think I'm playing the part, but inside I'm saying, 'Screw you! You jerks! If you were as good as I am, you'd be up here!'"

I had gone back to make her feel better, but she had turned the tables.

The second act went roaringly. The audience during intermission had looked at itself in a cautious way and decided it liked the show. The gamble was over. Sexual anxiety turned to outright love. When this happens, a first night audience becomes the best in the world.

Annie has become a classic, surely one of the landmarks of musical stage history. It has always baffled me that so few people realized it when they first saw it. Brooks Atkinson, the dean of American critics, called the songs "undistinguished," with the possible exception of "I Got the Sun in the Morning." Yet that is the show with "Show Business," "The Girl That I Marry," "Doin' What Comes Natur'lly," "Moonshine Lullaby," "I Got Lost in His Arms," "I'm an Indian Too," "My Defenses Are Down"—all of which have become part of our musi-

Above:
Helen Hayes on giant
barstool in *Happy Birthday*.
Note legend over portal.
(VANDAMM STUDIO.
LENT BY THE MUSEUM OF THE
CITY OF NEW YORK)

Right:
Nedda and Josh
on delayed honeymoon
in Cuba.

John Loves Mary. William Prince, Nina Foch and Tom Ewell.
(ZINN ARTHUR)

With Tom Heggen. Finishing first draft of *Mister Roberts*.

The end of the Captain's palm tree. Henry Fonda in *Mister Roberts*.
(JOHN SWOPE)

Above: Mister Roberts (Henry Fonda) telling off
Ensign Pulver (David Wayne). (JOHN SWOPE)

Below: Testing the cargo net for *Mister Roberts.*
(JOHN SWOPE)

cal heritage. Now you know why so many of us wonder what most critics use for listening. But on the other hand, as Berlin said, "Aren't we
lucky that the critics only *write about* the music and don't try to *write*
it themselves?"

In the notices for *Annie Get Your Gun* the critics completely ignored
the book, the score and the dances. To read them, you'd think Ethel
Merman invented every line and song as it went along. Several of them
claimed, "This show could not be put on the stage without Ethel Merman." Now, admitting that Ethel is incomparable, the historical facts
are that *Annie* has been a hit for many years with dozens of other
actresses, and because it is so solidly constructed, its music so brilliantly
integrated, it can be done almost equally effectively by amateur or professional.

One member of one audience of *Annie* changed the course of my career. At the New Haven opening was Richard Halliday, an astute man
who instinctively knew his wife, Mary Martin, would make a wonderful Annie Oakley. Until then, everyone thought of Mary as the sex kit-
ten in a short fur coat who sang Cole Porter's "My Heart Belongs to
Daddy," or the gentle, witty goddess of *One Touch of Venus*. But
Richard knew that she could do more than that. So, when Mary agreed
that this show could change her image and broaden her range, the two
of them proposed to us that she take *Annie* on a national tour. But
Mary would do it only if she could audition for us first.

That weekend at Edna Ferber's, where Oscar and Dick and I were,
Mary was prevailed upon to sing a few songs. And the songs she chose
were "Doin' What Comes Natur'lly" and "You Can't Get a Man with
a Gun." What an explosion there was! The walls reverberated. When
she finished she asked, "Do you think I'm too demure?"

To stage the touring company and allow for the differences between
Martin's and Merman's interpretations, I found myself making a
change, albeit an almost infinitesimal change, in just about every line
and phrase of the production. Only the very broad strokes and the actual tempo of the music remained the same. There were different keys,
and often different rhythms. For instance, Mary's singing of "I Got
Lost in His Arms" was much more of a breathless young girl's than
Ethel's, and she moved about in the second chorus instead of sitting
stolidly on the steps of the circus wagon.

No one batted an eye about the restaging, and I realized then that one can never duplicate on the stage exactly what one has done before. But I was to learn later in a series of bitter experiences that not everyone felt the way that I did.

Oscar, openly impressed with my work on *Annie*, said he wanted to work with me again. That, I hoped, meant the next Rodgers and Hammerstein musical, but instead they asked me to direct a new play Anita Loos had written for Helen Hayes, *Happy Birthday*.

I found the script weak but original. The setting was funny: a Newark bar, over the entrance of which was emblazoned "Through this archway pass the nicest people in Newark." A straight-laced, prim librarian named Addie Beemis is drawn to this bar to see the man she worships from afar, a bank clerk. Here's where he meets his lady love, a flashy redhead. When Addie hears the redhead's baby talk, she accepts her first drink and is soon plastered. But in a fantastic way. The room turns into a glistening fairyland, and Addie sways about airily on a giant barstool, and plays a love scene with her young man under a table. When her drunken euphoria wears off, she finds to her surprise that she has not only won the interest of her love, but that she has also made him see how shallow his redhead is.

I wasn't on fire to do this flimsy piece, but I wanted to work with Anita and Helen. In her minute Olympian way, Anita said, "Helen is our greatest clown. What a chance we have to show that to the world."

But I warned Dick and Oscar that I wasn't sure I could pull *Happy Birthday* off. It needed some pyrotechnics to get it off the ground, and I suggested a small orchestra to cover some of the awkward transitions.

They agreed to anything that would please the two ladies, so I went to work. Helen's role was written in an odd schizophrenic way. In one breath she was mealymouthed, and in the next she was abrasive, sharp and bitchy. Throughout the play she zigzagged between the two attitudes.

Helen Hayes is a minor-sized monument, firmly planted on the ground, and from birth seems to have gotten exactly what she wants. Giants retreat and mighty redwoods fall at her bidding. As a professional, she is matchless. She can be tragic, funny, ridiculous, poetic and even sensual. She stands for no nonsense, and I would as soon give her a false reason for a stage attitude as jump from a cliff. She would determine by herself how a scene should be played and bring that attitude to rehearsal. Sometimes her ideas would click with mine—and sometimes not, in which case we would have to talk it over, which meant she would be moderately patient while I talked. I remained always on the alert and tried to dance slightly out of reach.

During the first rehearsals, I went through the painstaking job of cuing music, lights, and organizing the use of a set crammed with magic props: for flowers grew out of bottles on the bar and from the curved light over a telephone; the barstool mushroomed and rocked back and forth; one table rose in the air and spread out of its own accord till it became a bower in which Addie, the librarian, could recite Christina Rossetti's poem "Birthday" to her loved one.

But though the mechanics flourished, the play grew murkier and murkier. The schizophrenia was infecting me and the cast. It was a Nabisco wafer of a play and I had no idea what the first audience in Boston would make of it.

During that opening performance, everything on stage went as it was intended, but the audience seemed blanketed in despair.

I sought refuge in the lobby with Oscar, praying for it to be over. We could tell the final curtain had come down because of the humiliating sound of a few scattered handclaps. Soon the doors were flung open and the audience started emerging like imprisoned miners. Among them was my old friend Arthur Schwartz, in town with another show. He caught my eye, which gave him and me a shock, and blurted out, "Oh, hello, Josh, I just *hated* it." And then he stumbled away into the dark.

Anita, Oscar, Dick and I met in Oscar's suite at the Ritz, all of us equally stunned. I expected the worst—perhaps they would close it at once. But instead, Oscar said calmly, "Let's fix it."

And Dick added, in the same tone, "And by Monday."

To me, those words were straight out of Beethoven's Ninth. What had made me think they would abandon the play! I don't think I had ever seen dogged pride and fixed determination played in unison before. I vowed secretly to be always as emotionally tough as they were that night.

We all agreed that the audience was baffled by Addie's double-edged remarks. They never knew whether to like her or to hate her. I said, "Couldn't she be either bitchy or sweet, not both?" It would be a pleasanter evening if Addie were nice. Besides, who really believes Helen Hayes playing a bitch? It's like spitting on the flag.

Anita and I met early the next morning to excise the nasty lines. It was tricky, like pulling every other quill from a porcupine. At eleven, the cast was called. The great burden was to be on Helen. It was a long part and she had knocked herself out to make this two-pronged girl believable. But she saw our point, that the character should be softened, but it was going to be a brain-cracking job.

That morning, she would start a line and I would say, "No, Helen, that part's cut, but the next part's not." She would pull herself together and do it my way, and then say, her teeth on edge, "Let's go on." With the next line I would say, "No, dear, eliminate that first part—just keep part of this last part."

She not only had to memorize this detail but she had an audience to face that night and be word perfect. As we plowed determinedly along, Helen grew more and more unsteady. She kept thinking of that night's audience. We got to a crucial moment in the second act when Addie, drinking a pink lady cocktail, throws a nasty remark to the others in the bar. When I asked her to eliminate that umpteenth sarcastic line, she banged her prop glass down on the table and almost screamed, "No, *I won't cut it!* I need that line!"

"Why?" I said. "I don't understand."

"That's because you're down there and you don't have to play this maddening scene. You, my dear Josh, directed me specifically to drink an entire pink lady here, *and* I need one line to lift up the glass *and* I need another line to swallow it. If you try to force me to cut these lines, then in the interest of Anita's play and my performance, I'm going to have to refuse."

I said, "Helen, we're trying to salvage a very shaky show. These are two of the most damaging lines to your character. Anita feels it too. Besides, there will be plenty of time for you to drink the pink lady because you'll be getting laughs in this spot tonight—big and long enough for you to drain two glasses."

"Sweet, beady-eyed Josh, they will not be laughing. They didn't laugh last night and they won't laugh tonight."

"Please try, Helen, please at least try."

"*All right!*" she said with great heat, "I'll *try*. But you'll see. The scene will collapse. And it will be your own thickheaded fault. But I'll *try!*"

Her nerves were so frayed that I said quickly, "Do what you feel is right, Helen. Cut the lines, or don't cut them. This is your play much more than mine!"

It was a grueling day of niggling work, and at the end I was frazzled along with everyone else. But I had developed a big feeling of doom. For on Helen's small frame rested the fate of all of us.

At that night's performance, the laughs started within a few minutes of the opening. By slicing away Addie's abrasiveness, the audience began to see the funny, childlike story. Nothing heals wounds like an audience's laughter, but I kept watching Helen, who still showed signs of nerves. By the time she got to the scene where she lifted her pink lady, there were such full howling laughs that she could have slowly sipped twenty pink ladies.

The show became a hit that night—except to Helen.

I didn't go backstage after the performance as I didn't want to seem to crow. I simply went to bed, exhausted, having left a rehearsal call for noon the next day. There were still many bits and pieces to perfect.

At twelve, the cast sat in chairs on the stage of the dark theatre and I stood in front of them down on the auditorium level, with my notes spread out on the stage. Helen was late. While waiting for her, I nervously gave a few notes to the others, but all of us were uncomfortably conscious that our star was absent. When Helen arrived, almost fifteen minutes late, she walked in her little surefooted way down among the cast at the front of the stage. She nodded to everyone rather seriously and then spoke. "Please excuse me for being late, everyone. I was having a dreary breakfast of black coffee and humble pie."

In one second we were back in business.

We arrived three weeks later in New York and played a performance on October 31, 1946, which got one enthusiastic notice from Brooks Atkinson and almost unanimous scorn from every other paper. But even the worst notices included phrases like: "And in this God-awful play Helen Hayes gets drunk, dances, sings, recites poetry, climbs under a table and has an affair with a young man."

And whatever was said in dispraise of *Happy Birthday* seemed to intrigue people into buying tickets. *Happy Birthday* ran for a year and a half, and I think it could have run for another year had Helen been able to stay with it.

* * *

Nedda and I had a delayed honeymoon in Cuba at the huge Jaimanitas house of J. P. McEvoy and his wife Peggy. We met Ernest Hemingway for drinks, and he remembered that he had met me before when I was there with Barbara. He said, "I wish I'd put a few bets on you. Why didn't you tell me you were going to have all those hits? I could have made a fortune."

Back in New York, Leland Hayward, who was now a producer, brought me a play he liked but was not free to do. It was by Norman Krasna, very light but terribly funny. It was called *John Loves Mary*. To show my gratitude for *Annie*, I invited Hammerstein and Rodgers to come in with me half and half.

At the first cast call, I saw the basset-hound face of Tom Ewell, an out-of-work actor I had known for years. I was convinced he looked too much like a born loser for a part in this show, but he read brilliantly and so became Fred, John's Army buddy.

Nina Foch was a fresh choice as Mary, and William Prince, a clean-cut, stalwart John. Gertrude Lawrence's daughter, Pamela Gordon, a tall, gawky, but talented girl was chosen to play Fred's love from England. For Mary's understudy we chose a piquant girl named Cloris Leachman.

Norman Krasna was delighted with the cast, except for Loring Smith as Mary's father, the senator. Loring had been a vaudeville performer before turning legitimate.

Norman asked me, "Why does Loring hold his hand away from his chest with those two fingers sticking out so stiff?"

I asked Loring, who explained, "Don't let it worry you. In vaudeville, you see, a cigar was my trademark. I held it between my fingers here, away from my chest, while I told funny stories, and at the punch line I'd puff on the cigar. Well, Josh, the ghost of that cigar is still there, and when I'm nervous I clutch at it, but when I get calm I forget it."

But it was Loring Smith and Tom Ewell whom the audience loved the most.

The show went extremely well in New Haven and Boston, except that we had trouble ending the second act. Norman, Dick, Oscar and I went at it hot and heavy after every performance, trying to find an ending.

Sample suggestions: the boy goes out, the boy comes back, the father and the mother get furious, they don't get furious, there's a violent argument, there is no argument at all. And our tempers rose as we found no answer.

Then I had a flash of an idea. "I know what should happen! The father and mother see the boy out and go to bed, and the boy comes back in the room, kisses the girl and takes her off into the bedroom."

Oscar rose with a purple face and said, "Anyone who would make a suggestion like *that* is a *cad!*"

When we left, Norman said to me, "Everybody used to tell me that Oscar Hammerstein was cool as a cucumber. Well, he's the most belligerent cucumber I ever met."

We fixed it by bringing the curtain down, cutting the scene. The problems of *John Loves Mary* were small compared to those of *Happy Birthday,* but they were just as exhausting.

The play, which opened in New York in February 1947, didn't get distinguished notices. But one columnist wrote, "Folks will be laughing at *John Loves Mary* two years from next January." And some said I had taken a rickety play and turned it with my "magic touches" into strong entertainment.

Again, as with *Charley's Aunt,* I had received credit that was due someone else. Norman Krasna had written and constructed a brilliant piece of machinery; I had simply staged it. Because of my admiration for him, a guilt set in that kept me from enjoying my success. I began to drink a bit, and Nedda and I found ourselves going from one play to the other, and inviting a few of the cast to join us at Sardi's, where we would drink some more.

The drinking caught up with me at Sardi's one night when I saw Nina Foch there. I had heard a vague rumor that Bill Prince and Nina Foch were having an affair, and I had been shocked at the lie because I knew Bill and his wife cared deeply for each other. So that night at Sardi's, I decided to do what I could to save the marriage. I grabbed Nina, pulled her to her feet, and kissed her passionately in the middle of the room, proving to the whole world, I thought, that I was the lecherous culprit and not Bill.

To my surprise, no one else understood this, certainly not Nedda, who hustled me outside like a burlesque comic and into a cab. When we got to the entrance of the Lombardy I was still too shaken to go upstairs. I insisted on going for a walk.

Nedda said, "You're in no condition for that."

Outraged, I said I was going for a walk and maybe never coming back. I weaved along two blocks to the darkness under the Third Avenue el. Five men were standing near a store entrance.

One of them said to me, "Get off the street, bud."

Too full of drinks to let it pass, I said, "Why should I? It's my street just as much as yours."

The group walked over and circled me. "We said, 'Get off the street.'"

In a wild reflex I hit one of them in the jaw as hard as I could, and immediately I was clobbered by all five of them. After a minute or two, I found that I was on one knee in the street and that they had vanished into the darkness. With pain, I got to my feet and staggered down Third Avenue, looking for a policeman.

I weaved about for blocks, feeling hurt in my face mostly. Reading the words Fifty-second Street, I decided to go to my mother and sister's apartment nearby: I was too ashamed to go back to Nedda.

But Mary Lee, horrified at the sight of my bruised face, called Nedda, and she arrived within minutes and bundled me home in a cab. Out of chagrin, I didn't say much, and she asked few questions. She put ice on my purpling face and urged me to sleep.

For four or five days I stayed holed up at the Lombardy, while Nedda and I analyzed my strange behavior.

Three plays in less than a year's time (*Annie* in May 1946; *Happy Birthday* in October 1946; *John Loves Mary* in February 1947) had been a strain on me. Perhaps I had been overdriving myself again, hoping to make up for the years I lost during the war. Perhaps I was feeling old at thirty-nine.

Nedda thought we should find someplace where I could quietly consider my next move. I had to find out why each hit play left me so unsatisfied. And I was convinced I didn't need Merrill Moore's advice—not yet, anyway.

When my face healed we went to California where I did the brushup directing of a touring company of *Happy Birthday*, and from there we decided to go back to Cuba.

I took with me a short first novel sent to me by the agent Kay Brown. The book was called *Mister Roberts* and it was about the war. Although it concerned the Navy in the Pacific, it was talking to me about *my* war, the boredom and idiocy of it, and I felt it was written with a poetic lucidity seldom found anymore.

I told Nedda that I thought I might like to dramatize it myself, and she urged me to secure the rights, and quickly.

"Oh, no, I don't want to commit myself that much. I'll just try to write a bit of it, and if I'm on the right track, then I'll go into all that legal stuff."

"But you shouldn't even start something unless you have the rights. You might be wasting your time."

And then I spoke those fatal words. "Please, Nedda, let me do it my way."

After two days in Havana we drove to Varadero where we rented a small beach house with a cook and spent two weeks of uninterrupted bliss. I painted watercolors and Nedda read.

The McEvoys offered to rent us their great Havana house for six weeks. Immediately we wired friends to come and visit. The first to arrive were my sister, who was now working for *Life* magazine as entertainment editor, and her colleague and new friend, Tom Prideaux. Mary Lee never married after Charlie's death, but she did have a series of very attractive beaux. And the one who seemed to mean the most to her, and to us, was that delightful, witty and brilliant collaborator of hers, Tom Prideaux.

We had a great time swimming in the mornings off the coral-and-stone pier, napping in the afternoon, drinking rum and watching rumbas in the bars of "hot dog alley" at night. Most of the time I pestered them and our other guests with talk about what I should do next.

In the midst of all this, the prayed-for script appeared. Irene Selznick sent it with the note, "Please read this and tell me if you'd be interested in directing it." It was Tennessee Williams' *A Streetcar Named Desire.*

I became so excited just holding the script in my hand. I knew I was going to love it. I had admired *The Glass Menagerie* enormously. Certainly Williams had the quality I yearned to work with.

That night I read the play with mounting emotion and laughter. It seemed made for me. Not only was I raised in its Louisiana setting, but its protagonist was a woman who was becoming mentally ill, and I was an authority on that subject as well. Besides, it was full of poetry and sexual conflict. I became so charged just thinking about it that I sat up all night dreaming of a perfect cast. The obvious actress for it was Margaret Sullavan. Yes, she was Southern, she was vulnerable . . .

I wired Irene, saying I loved it. My sails were filled with joy and assurance, my life was back on course. *Streetcar* was the best play I had read in years; maybe the best play I had ever read.

Four days passed while my friends and Nedda listened to my ravings about people who send you plays and then don't respond when you say yes.

Unable to wait any longer, I called Irene. Her news hit me with tidal wave force. The day she sent me the play, Tennessee had sent it to Elia Kazan, and Kazan had said yes. The author has the say—and that meant no Logan.

I don't remember a drop as deep as the one I took on hearing those terrible facts. I wanted to put on sackcloth and ashes. I spent long hours alone on the beach, sitting stunned in the sand. I know why men tear out their hair. The world—at least my world—had come to an end. I felt no desire to work ever again.

Nedda said, "What about that novel you liked so much, the one about the war, and the ship and the awful captain. *Mister Roberts.* Why don't you find out about the rights?"

"No, Nedda, no! I could never make that work. This was a once-in-a-lifetime thing. Nothing will ever mean anything to me after this!"

CHAPTER

14

Bill Loverd, my friend and broker, mailed some interesting clippings to Cuba, and one almost exploded in my hand: "Leland Hayward has bought the rights from George Abbott to Thomas Heggen and Max Shulman's adaptation of Heggen's novel, *Mister Roberts*."

I yelled out in pain. Nedda came running, and was about to say, "I told you," when we both realized I could have got no rights since the play must have been written before I even read the book.

I tried to phone Leland, but he had gone to Hawaii to recuperate from a severe stomach operation. There was no telephone between Cuba and Hawaii, so I rushed off a cablegram: "Leland. May I coproduce or direct or coauthor *Mister Roberts*? Or at least be a member of the cast? Please answer." Two days later came the reply: "Delighted to hear from you. Many complications. Call me."

Everything frustrated me. I must return to the States to call him. Our Cuban idyll was over.

*   *   *

In Key West, with a hatful of coins, I called Honolulu. "What about *Mister Roberts?*" I shouted.

"It's a lousy play," screamed Leland.

"Then why did you buy it?"

"So nobody else would and make a flop out of it. I've told Tom Heggen to try and write it alone. I'll send you his first stuff as soon as I can."

"Leland, level with me. Can I do it with you?"

"Of course. Think I'm crazy? I mean, you can direct it and coproduce it, but I can't promise you can write it until I see what Heggen comes up with. He'll probably collapse again. Still, he must have the chance."

That's all I needed. Nedda and I headed north fast to our little house in Brookfield Center, Connecticut. When we arrived, on the doorstep was an envelope with Tom Heggen's first five scenes of *Mister Roberts.*

The dialogue was, as in the book, authentic and sometimes hilarious. But the scenes had no tension or even any connection with each other. I grew more and more discouraged. It was simply not dramatic. But in one scene he invented some conflict, and I suddenly saw the fulcrum of a play. In that scene, the ship has just docked at a liberty port, when the captain announces that the crew must stay on board. Roberts charges in to face the captain and demand that the crew be let off the ship. The captain uses Roberts' furious concern for the men to make a bargain. If Roberts will promise that he will *not send any more requests for transfer* (which are damaging to the captain's rating with the Navy Department), the crew will get liberty. In private agony, for all he wants is to get off that cargo ship and onto a fighting ship, Roberts agrees, and the captain announces liberty, to the crew's vociferous joy.

From this devil's pact, I could immediately visualize an entire play. The first act would lead up to the pact, and the second act give the results of it. I could see bad feeling grow between the crew and Roberts, because, not knowing he had wangled their liberty and hearing the change in his tone to the captain, the crew would feel he, like all officers, was just bucking for a promotion. The crew would hold Roberts in contempt until in some ridiculous way they discovered that he was responsible for their liberty, then in a burst of gratitude they would hold a drunken contest to pick the best forger of the captain's signature so they could approve Roberts' request for transfer. In my mind that night I called it "The Captain's Name-Signing Contest," which made me laugh so much I couldn't wait to suggest it to Heggen. If he didn't like it, I wouldn't like him.

I called Leland, who hated all of Tom's scenes. I told him my general scheme and he liked it, but told me I had to speak to Heggen directly.

Over the phone, Tom Heggen sounded wise and funny. I invited him to Connecticut and told him to bring along a wife or a girl, whatever, for we had plenty of room. I wanted him to feel at ease.

Alan Campbell was staying with us—he and Dorothy Parker were having one of their frequent wars—and he busied himself rearranging our furniture, a weekend specialty of his.

A telegram came: "ARRIVING WITH ONE RED HAT FRIDAY ELEVEN-FIFTEEN. TOM."

On Friday, Alan and I were at the little station when the face on the back of the book jacket stepped off the train, but the body below it was the thinnest thing I'd ever seen. He came forward shyly, his face suddenly scarlet and his body almost buckled with embarrassment. Immediately, though, he forcefully called us Alan and Josh.

"Why aren't you wearing the red hat you mentioned in the telegram?"

"Wearing? Oh, you mean red*head*."

He turned, and there stood a tall, beautiful, slightly freckled, flame-headed girl. She was Helen Parker, and she was quiet, reserved, almost diffident.

At the house, Nedda took over Helen and Alan while Tom and I withdrew to the little study to talk. I told him frankly what I thought about his scenes, then gave my general outline, and he agreed readily—almost too readily. He must have been frantic.

I told him, "I really love and respect this book, Tom, and we're going to have to work hard to keep a play close to your book." We agreed to get to work immediately right there in Brookfield.

Alan went back to New York and Helen returned too, to take care of her two little redheaded boys. Then began the happiest, the most hilarious, the most moving three months of my life.

Tom and I decided to get a male secretary so we wouldn't be inhibited in our language. We chose the first to apply, a young, spindly man with thick glasses named Jim Awe. He arrived with a formidable armload of books, all bearing the same title: *The Collected Works of George Bernard Shaw*. He had a dry, waspish tone and he explained to us that he was an intellectual rebel. This put us off him until we learned he had only pretended that he could type, and was forced to hide in his room while we slept to practice from his do-it-yourself typing manual.

Tom and I simply talked or shouted out a scene and then started tossing out trial balloons of dialogue. The only sure way we knew we had hit a good line was when Jim Awe put down his Shaw volume and started typing. It was the judgment of Solomon.

Since Tom liked to work at night, we started at five in the afternoon and dictated until six in the morning. Nedda was our sounding board. We would wake her politely and read her each new scene. She heard most of the play with her eyes closed, nodding affirmation, but delicately, so as not to nod herself awake.

For the first act, we were able to use numbers of scenes from Tom's book by tying them together with my almost invisible plot—the moves of an itinerant bottle of Scotch. Out of sheer boredom, Roberts goes to the alcoholic port director and bribes him with the bottle of Johnnie Walker Red Label to order the ship to a liberty port. As a result, the bottle is missing when Ensign Pulver tries to appropriate it for the seduction of a young Navy nurse. There's nothing to do then but to manufacture some Scotch out of grain alcohol, Coca-Cola and iodine, an invention of mine.

But the character of Roberts was a problem. "He's too perfect, he's almost a saint," I said. "In the book it's all right because he's shadowy, almost symbolic, but in the play we've got to see him, know something about his innards, his emotions. And above all, he must have some faults—a big flaw that can be cured at the end of the play. He must be able to grow, Tom." I started elaborating on the Maxwell Anderson discovery scene, expecting him to resist, but Tom was fascinated.

We thought of one humorous touch—to prove that Roberts was sexually human. After the crew uses binoculars to look through the open windows of the shore hospital to watch the nurses taking showers, Roberts waits until they run offstage, then picks up the binoculars and has a good look himself. And we decided to give this too noble character a burst of good-humored sadism toward Pulver. Though he likes his young friend, he also finds him exasperating. "You're scared of the captain," Roberts says, "and you sleep sixteen hours a day. You pretend you want to improve your mind . . ." He pulls out from under Pulver's mattress a dog-eared copy of *God's Little Acre* and says to Doc, "He's underlined every erotic passage—and after a certain pornographic climax he's inserted the words 'Damn well written.' "

After slogging away happily for three months, we reached the last scene of the first act—Tom's original scene—but in addition to the Roberts' bargain for the crew's liberty that he had invented, I added that the captain also makes Roberts give him his word of honor to be respectful of him in public and to keep their deal a *complete secret.* I knew this would help provide frustration for Roberts and the crew in the second act.

We had talked over the second act till we knew it by heart and had decided that Roberts' flaw was "snobbery." He feels combat officers are a superior race, and he despised those, including himself, who are not involved in combat.

Tom and I planned that his growth would come in the final scene when a letter from Roberts arrives, written from his fighting ship. Roberts has discovered that the men on the fighting ship need nothing from him, no help for their morale, since they are too busy fighting. He knows now there is another, an even tougher bravery—that of men who do not succumb to the most terrible enemy of this war—boredom. But in the same mail with Roberts' letter comes another, telling that Roberts has been killed.

Over these months Tom had become a part of our household. He loved our home in Brookfield Center and felt protected there. As brilliant as he was at the typewriter, Tom was incapable of sending out his laundry or of buying toothpaste. He found the world unkind in demanding cleanliness and other orderly pursuits. I believe that's why he clung to Nedda and me at first. We took care of these offensive and tiresome things.

And so he soon became "family." And yet, looking back, I think Nedda and I were always a little nervous around him. He was like a rare china cup, exquisitely made but definitely breakable.

Tom was as thrilled as I was about the progress of the play. But when we were ready to begin the actual writing of the second act, I realized that I had no definite understanding about my participation. And in the back of my mind I wondered, What if Tom is an ostrich and is pretending I don't exist, or what if he feels that all this help is due him, free? Certainly, the play was being based on his book, but every scene had been taken apart and rewritten to fit a dramatic frame. I'd invented the theme for the play, put the whole act together and had written most of the dialogue.

And I had made the character of Mister Roberts more visible, turned him from someone who was looked at into a verbal, active protagonist. He could speak, he had faults and had somewhere to grow.

I kept waiting for Tom to bring up the subject of my role as collaborator, but he never did. I called Leland and asked him what to do. Leland, who had been receiving reports and reading scenes, had felt from the first that I should be coauthor. He said if Heggen had accepted Max Shulman as a collaborator, then why should there be any question about me? Leland said he would talk to Tom personally.

Several days later, Leland drove out and I left him alone with Tom. After a half hour, Leland came across the lawn to me. "He's rough, Josh. He doesn't want to do it. He says he wrote the novel and he thought of doing it as a play, and he feels it should be his alone."

I left Leland and went across the lawn to Tom, who was curled up like a caterpillar in a canvas chair, his face half-hidden in his chest. Only his eyes were visible atop the hole in his sweater.

"What do you want?" he asked me in the nearest thing to a challenging tone he could manage.

"Leland tells me you want all of the writer's credit and percentage of the play."

"Leland's right. I do."

"You certainly know, don't you, that I've written a major part of the first act, that I've dictated it myself, with an occasional prompt from you?"

"That's right, you've had a lot to do with it—a great deal, in fact."

"Are you happy about the way it's gone?"

"Very happy."

I said, "Okay, you can have it. Free."

"What do you mean?"

I used as calm a voice as I could muster. "You can have the first act free, *if* you are able to accept it as yours and still look people in the eye. And then you can goddamned fucking well write the second act by yourself, Buster. You know my outline by heart. Use it—it's my going-away present. Because I'm going back to New York now to find a job."

I started to the house, about fifty yards away, and just before I got to the door he yelled, "Come back!"

I walked back slowly, holding my stomach in and breathing carefully. "What do you want?"

"I can't write this son of a bitching play alone. You know that."

"Why don't we throw the whole thing in the ashcan, because I won't write the second act with you and then keep passing marquees that say, 'By Thomas Heggen. By Thomas Heggen. By Thomas Heggen.'"

He said, "Of course not. You can have all the credit you want, as long as it's no more than half."

It was like a huge plane landing after a rough flight.

"Okay, and what about the money? Irving Berlin says, 'There's only one problem—the money. When that's settled, everything's settled.' What about fifty-fifty?"

He said, "What about two-thirds for me and one-third for you?"

"Okay."

Skinny, little, blushingly shy Tom had the great inner strength of Shylock. If he went fifty-fifty with Shulman, what had changed him regarding me? Had someone whispered in his ear—an agent, a cousin, a girl?

Though there was scarcely ten years difference in our ages, Tom seemed terribly young to me. Yet he could be older and wiser than anyone I knew. He had a constant gleam in his eye, and when he met someone pompous or too proper, he would nod curtly, while on his cheeks would appear the map of England in a pulsating pink, and explode with the loudest string of shocking words he could think of. It was Tom Heggen's scream of protest, I suppose, but very startling to the uninitiated.

Once, he was cajoled by his publisher into attending a literary luncheon in Boston, attended by proper ladies of the press and bookstores, many in Queen Mary hats. Tom was horrified when the lady president asked him to stand. In wracking agony, he forced himself to rise to the applause, which stopped suddenly when he was upright. He stood there, pilloried. Eventually, to save the embarrassment of an endless pause, a dear old lady spoke from the crowd. "Mr. Heggen, how did you happen to write the book?"

Tom spoke automatically. "Well, shit, I was on the boat." Then he sat down. His publishers never asked him to appear in public again.

Tom had indeed served on a Navy cargo ship, and it was while there that he wrote "Night Watch," the first of the series of stories that became *Mister Roberts*. His cousin, Wallace Stegner, had encouraged Tom to develop that story into a book, by writing similar sketches to add to it.

When Tom and I started writing the second act, I asked Tom if we should write an outline.

"No, let's just write it. I know what you think and you know what I think."

Nedda had gone to New York for a few days. Since the first act had taken three months, she figured the second would take two weeks at least. But she didn't know what charged energy had begun to fill that little room. Tom and I now knew the characters so well that they almost wrote their own lines.

We dictated the first and second scenes of act 2 and, since it was still early, we decided to barrel ahead. By three in the morning we had finished the third and fourth scenes. Why not do one more: the scene where Roberts leaves the ship? The men bring him, as they did in Tom's book, the sheet brass medal they've had cut in the machine shop, the Order of the Palm, "for action against the enemy (the captain) above and beyond the call of duty."

By now it was five in the morning, with only the final scene left to do. Might as well finish. We wrote the final letter from Roberts, the one telling what he had learned, the one which would arrive along with that from a fellow officer telling of his death. We wrote that self-realization letter together, using as much of Tom's prose from the book as possible, because I found it most touching. But of course we had to invent his growth, so to speak; that was the Maxwell Anderson in me. And I almost had to rope and throw Tom to get him to let us put in the lines, "From Tedium to Apathy and back, with an occasional side trip to Monotony," with which he had opened his book. He found it far too literary for Roberts and thought people would think him pretentious.

As in the book, Pulver, overcome by emotion at Roberts' death, throws the captain's two palm trees overboard and pounds his fist on the captain's door. "Captain, this is Ensign Pulver. I just threw your goddamn palm trees overboard." But I added, ". . . and now what's all this crap about no movie tonight?" I hoped to indicate that Pulver would take over Roberts' role as defender of the crew.

We were so wildly happy at having finished that we opened a bottle of Scotch and started to guzzle it. And we wanted to share our excitement with Nedda, so we called her up. Drowsily, she said, "I know. You finished the liberty scene."

Tom grabbed the phone. "Nedda, we finished the whole goddamn, fucking second act. Would you like to hear some of it?"

"No, I'd like to hear all of it."

It took over an hour and a half, but alternating, we read her, word by word, the entire second act, and she laughed and cried and cheered, and went to get a drink herself. Soon, all of us were crying and laughing and drinking.

After that, we couldn't think of sleeping, so I got out my projector and another bottle, and for the next two hours showed Tom and Jim Awe movies of South America. "Un'trusting composhishun! Unbuleevuble color."

I felt our next move was to read it to some professional for reaction and advice; I suggested Howard Lindsay, my friend and mentor. Tom agreed, and said he would like Helen to hear it also. I felt a deep warning bell toll somewhere near my prostate, but I said, brightly, "Of course bring Helen. I'd love to have her opinion."

I read it to Howard, his wife Dorothy Stickney, Tom and Helen at the Lindsay home. Dorothy and Howard laughed happily all the way through, but Tom seemed to be clutching his stomach in agony, and each time I looked up at Helen's once beautiful face it had formed sharper edges, as if she were suppressing an epileptic fit.

In the last scene, when the crew learns of Roberts' death, Howard let out a gasp. "Oh, no! Oh, no, Josh, you can't do that! Totally impossible! The hero of a comedy cannot die. You'll have to change that."

Roberts' death, to me, had always been a major part of the book, Tom's final comment. One of the truly worthless things about war. I tried to defend it.

"Sorry, Josh, but it just doesn't work," he said. "The audience will feel cheated at the hero's death after laughing all evening long. It's a great play, Josh and Tom. But it's a comedy. Just fix up that ending a little bit."

Walking home, I told Tom I would never change the ending, and he grunted. I avoided asking Helen what she thought for fear she might tell me, and she just as obviously moved in a mantle of portentous silence. Tom was a passive dormouse between us.

He and I both knew the gist of what he'd hear from her that night: I had bestialized Tom's beautiful novel by turning it into Broadway Comedy swamped with laughter. And she would be right about the laughter but not about the culprit. During the writing Tom had become a driving demon for laughs. When we thought of an especially bawdy line, Tom uncurled from the sofa and typed it himself to emphasize his approval. Whenever I tried to get in a bit of his poetic wordage from the book, Tom screamed in rage and pretended to vomit. He winced every time he heard that marvelous tedium to apathy to monotony line. And though he went along with Pulver's taking over Roberts' role as protector of the crew, he didn't think the audience would believe it. He was only relaxed in those days with huge laughter.

The next morning Tom and I read the play to Leland. His eyes shone with happiness the whole way. At the end, Tom asked him, "Well?"

Leland said, "Well, it's probably the greatest play that's ever been written in the history of the world, that's all!"

"What about Aristophanes?" said Tom.

"Aristophanes could never have written as good a play as that."

Both Tom and I found that a very satisfactory reaction. As a matter of fact, it's about the only kind of reaction that a playwright really accepts; one inch less than the superlative means disaster.

Once I asked Jean Kerr if she was writing a new play and she said, "Of course not. I can't stand those critics."

"But you always get good reviews."

"Never. They say awful things like 'the best comedy of the season' or 'the best laugh I've had in two years.'"

"Well, what do you want?"

"I keep hoping for a few decent lines like, 'Not since the eighteenth century has a playwright . . . and so forth.' And you know, they're never clever enough to think of things like that."

The casting of *Mister Roberts* was a major maneuver. Since it was shortly after the war, there were still many veterans who had read the novel and had felt as I did that it was their own story. Eight hundred young men crowded the stage door of the Alvin the first morning.

Ten to twenty men were lined up in a semicircle and Tom and I looked them over for age and type. Sometimes we had Leland's help and that of Maynard Morris, his casting expert, and always we consulted with my stage manager, Billy Hammerstein, Oscar's son, and his assistant, Ruth Mitchell.

What with the hundreds, the excitement, the keeping track, I don't know how we chose the crew, but all of a sudden we had one.

The leads—Doc, the captain, Pulver and Roberts—were still not settled, although I had a secret candidate to play Roberts.

Then Tom said, "Josh, I know it's crazy, but when I was writing *Roberts,* I was always thinking of Henry Fonda."

"That's a terrible idea," I said. "I ought to know, because I've had the same terrible idea for a long time."

Fonda was out of the Navy by then and preparing to start a new movie. But before his filming began, I learned that he would be coming to New York for a few days. Knowing he was committed, I asked Hank by wire if I could read him the play one afternoon. I told him I knew he wasn't free, but he should hear it. He agreed to hear it.

As another possibility, I had thought that perhaps the actor for Roberts should be someone close in type to Tom Heggen himself—a small, unobtrusive man rather than the big, handsome hero type—and so I asked David Wayne, so great in *Finian's Rainbow,* if he would attend the reading too. I told Wayne, "Fonda's not free to play this part, so you mustn't think you're second choice."

"With Fonda, I like being second choice."

With Tom at my side, wincing, I read the play to Hank and David. The second I finished, David, who had not changed his expression throughout, charged out of the room. The rest of us looked at each other and shrugged. I turned to Hank. "Hank, I'm really sorry you can't play Roberts."

"Don't be sorry. I'm going to play it," he said.

"But the picture! You've already made tests. Costumes have been fitted and—"

"They can be unfitted."

"But the contract? You've signed it."

"My agent, Lew Wasserman, is supposed to be a powerhouse. I'll just tell him to get me out of that picture because I'm going to play Doug Roberts."

For Tom and me, it was just too much to take in. Our play had just shot up into the stratosphere.

Within minutes, the phone rang. It was David Wayne. "Hank Fonda should play Roberts, not me. I want to play Pulver. In fact, I've got to!"

That was the shortest casting session I ever went through.

But the dry, droll Doc was harder to find. We saw one character actor after another. But when lanky Robert Keith shambled on stage with his bland eyes, hollow cheeks and bald head, Tom blushed violently and began nodding to me insistently. We had a Doc.

The part of the captain was the most troublesome of all. The captain had to have the murky authority to tyrannize Roberts and the crew, but he also needed enough boorishness to play a stupid, ridiculous man.

Nedda had heard me read the role aloud many times; I shone as the captain. When someone suggested her older brother, William Harrigan, for the part, the idea ran into some pretty stiff opposition.

"Oh, no!" And Nedda's voice, in panic, rose several octaves. "I couldn't go through that." She shivered in horror. "I'd be too nervous. No, no! Perhaps I shouldn't say this, but we don't always get along."

"Really? I never would have guessed it," I said. "What's the matter? Isn't he good enough?"

"Of course he's good enough—he's marvelous onstage."

We made an appointment with his agent, and on the day Bill was to read, I noticed before I left the apartment that Nedda, breathing heavily, her hair a bit askew, was just going out the front door.

"What's the matter? Are you sick?"

"No, no. I'm fine. I'm going out for a minute. Now you go along to rehearsal, you'll be late." She practically shoved me out the door.

That afternoon, Bill Harrigan gave an extraordinary, almost clairvoyant reading of the captain's role. He appeared to understand the play better than Tom and I did. Every reading, every phrasing, was on the nose. We all agreed that Bill *was* the captain. We didn't have to look any further.

Leland pointed into the auditorium. Nedda, who had been hiding, was coming down the aisle, and called to us, "Wasn't he good?"

"Nedda," I said, "he was marvelous, brilliant. How on earth could he get those readings so perfectly?"

"I gave them to him," she beamed. "I've been working like a dog all morning."

"I thought you didn't get along."

"We did today."

After finding the cast and okaying the scenic sketches, we had time for a week's vacation. Leland's marriage with Margaret Sullavan had broken up, and he was now planning to marry Nancy "Slim" Hawks. Nancy, Leland, Nedda and I decided to go to Florida, but the night before we left, Nedda and I went to the opening of *A Streetcar Named Desire*, as Jo Mielziner's guests.

The play was as beautiful as when I had read it in Cuba. Kazan's work was awe inspiring and young Marlon Brando as Kowalski left a mark in theatre annals. The pain of not doing it was still with me, but I could live through it because being the coauthor of *Mister Roberts* had been so fulfilling.

At Sardi's after the show, Jo's brother, Kenneth MacKenna, story editor at M-G-M, joined us. We talked about *Mister Roberts* and Kenneth said, "Oh, speaking of that, there's a book laid in the Pacific at the same time that we've just turned down. In fact, all the movie companies passed it, but you might glean something from it—some color for *Mister Roberts*."

I didn't feel we needed any more color, but to be polite I said, "Good. What is it?"

"*Tales of the South Pacific*," he said. "It's by James Michener."

Neither the book nor the author meant anything to me, but I bought a copy to take with me on the plane.

That night, in our Miami Beach suite, I flicked through the book, and started to read the story called "Fo' Dolla'." I was ensnared by the first few words.

The next morning at breakfast, Leland put me under his jeweler's eye and said, "You look funny. You've been reading something good?" I tried to look blank. I wanted to buy control of the book myself, so I stalled. "Oh, you wouldn't be interested in this book, it's for an opera."

That afternoon I stretched out for a nap with the book on my lap. When I woke an hour and a half later, the book was gone. I went into the next room and there was my honorable pal Leland just turning the last page.

"Where'd you get that?" I asked him.

"From your bed. I knew you were tired, so I thought I'd help you out by reading it. Josh, we're going to buy this son of a bitch!"

"What are we going to do with the son of a bitch?"

"We'll make some son-of-a-bitching movies, some musical shows, maybe a couple of straight plays—how the hell do I know? We'll just buy it quick, before somebody else does, and then make up our minds."

"But, Leland. We don't—"

"No buts. We've got to sew it up quickly. And no blabbing, you son of a bitch. Not a word until the deal is settled. Why let Aaron Copland ruin it when it could make a great musical?"

"Rodgers and Hammerstein would be perfect."

"Of course, but don't you dare mention it to them. They'll want the whole goddamn thing. They'd gobble us up for breakfast."

Sometime later, I saw Dick Rodgers at a cocktail party, and just seeing him made me know how Eve felt when she first saw the apple. Dick was forbidden fruit, but oh! he must write the music. Oh! what a show it would be. That bastard Leland was too cautious. I went over to Dick and said, "Don't tell anyone I've told you this, but I own a story you might make a musical of." He pulled out a little note pad and wrote in a very businesslike way, "*T of the S. Pacific*," and my recommended story, "*Fo' Dolla'.*" I was ashamed at having broken my word to Leland, but I felt an excitement that blotted out all regret.

On the first day of rehearsal of *Mister Roberts* the cast read the play aloud. They laughed and wept, and applauded at the end. We celebrated for a few minutes, congratulating each other.

I decided to put the play on its feet at once. For years I had followed the accepted tradition of perfecting line readings before letting the cast move, but soon I realized that I was robbing the actors of the fun of acting. They come alive on their feet; spontaneous things happen; moves, gestures, readings spurt out by instinct. It's also stimulating to the director, who then can approve, edit, lessen or make things more emphatic.

In my youth, directors made little marks and diagrams on the script margins to show where an actor is located during a line, and little arrows when he crosses. To me, it was third-grade stuff, mechanical, and deadening to the soul. What I do now is give a general idea of entrances and exits, chairs and sofas—and say, "Now take off and I'll try to stay out of the way."

But because the playing area for *Mister Roberts* was so confined, that day I suggested that Hank cross in front of a desk and sit, so that the

Directing *Mister Roberts*, Alvin Theatre. (JOHN SWOPE)

Above: Leland Hayward and Josh, watching rehearsals of
London company of *Mister Roberts.*

Below: Three Mister Roberts: Henry Fonda, New York company;
Tyrone Power, London company; John Forsythe, national company.
With director Logan at Bill Brown's, 1951.

South Pacific. Mary Martin washing that man right out of her hair. (RICHARD TUCKER)

Josh supervising the recording of *South Pacific.* Ezio Pinza and Mary Martin. (JOHN SWOPE)

Doing the dances for *South Pacific*. (JOHN SWOPE)

other two men could be seen. Hank gave me a belligerent look and said, "Didn't you just tell me to move after that line?"

"Yes. I'm not sure if it will be right eventually, but if you do it for now it would help me."

"I'm not trying to help you," he said. "I'm trying to play Roberts. Roberts wouldn't move a muscle on that line. Josh, this is not a Princeton Triangle Show. This is Broadway. We're going to face a New York audience."

"I know, Hank. I know New York. I've done a lot of shows since I handed you that cake of ice. So please let's get on with it."

"Do you understand the character of Roberts at all?"

"Understand Roberts, you son of a bitch! I *wrote* it! Of course Tom here helped some, but I was forced to write most of Roberts' lines since he scarcely spoke in Tom's book. I can talk for hours on Roberts."

"I certainly would like to hear you," he said sarcastically. "I'd be interested to find out if you know what the hell you're talking about." We were talking like twenty year olds.

"Then come to my apartment tonight. In the meantime, let's go on."

When he arrived that evening, Nedda discreetly left us alone with a supper she had ordered. I began to talk about Roberts and to eat and to talk, and when we finished supper I kept on talking. I told Hank how Roberts was brought up, went to medical school and the personal humiliation he felt being on the despised ship; how he felt about the crew, the captain, the world and the war. By eleven-thirty Fonda had scarcely said a word, but I finished by saying, "And that's Roberts!"

Fonda sat silent for a long moment, then stood up, looked at me curiously, choked back something and said very quietly, "I understand. I understand. Thank you very much." He took my hand, clasped it firmly, then walked out.

After that, he embarrassed me by accepting as gospel any hint of direction. I wish I could remember what golden words I used that night because they might come in handy later. But Fonda was now a believer, a convert, and what's more he was Doug Roberts—and he made our work together the joy of my theatrical life.

Fonda has deep within him a small but inextinguishable flame that burns in worship of the art of the theatre. He is one of the high priests of that art. When he feels laxness, insincerity, dilettantism around him, Hank can fly into short-lived tantrums and his votive flame can become a holocaust. He was giving me the best of himself during the rehearsals of *Mister Roberts,* but I was to see the searing Fonda fire again before many years passed.

After three weeks' rehearsal the show needed an audience; we couldn't perfect it without feeling reaction. So, we invited some five hundred friends to see a run-through, on a bare stage with no props or scenery.

The response was explosive, like something I had heard described but had never experienced. The silence between the laughs seemed charged with emotion, especially near the end, and with Pulver's words to the captain, "What's all this crap about no movie tonight?" there was the biggest laugh of all mixed with—yes, I'm sure—a cheer.

That spontaneous cheer was to happen every night throughout the years that *Roberts* played. When I first heard it, I was stunned by its ramifications. Tom and I had planned that moment to be not only a laugh but a violent cry of mourning coming from the whole ship. At this run-through we saw Pulver grow in front of our eyes. He was now a believable adult who had shuffled off the motley role of feckless clown. The captain was not off the hook, the crew was going to be protected. Pulver had become Roberts, and therefore Roberts would live— and take care of us all.

The applause began movingly as the cast took their bows and went offstage. Fonda, on the way home, had reached the street corner when someone ran after him and called, "Mr. Fonda, they want you to take another bow. They won't leave."

It was several minutes before he could get back to the dark bare stage, but the audience was still clapping, and when he finally appeared they rose and yelled until everyone was exhausted.

I prayed the audience would react the same with lights and scenery. Often a play is effective at the run-through because the audience is supplying the visual effects with its imagination. Would the play seem as emotional when their dream was walled in by fact?

And to me, *Mister Roberts* never did seem as powerful as it was in those stark surroundings. It was always a wildly funny play, but at that run-through the tragic, monotonous side of the war was more tactile and the play more like Tom's book.

I never thought I'd resent too much laughter, but I did. Leland would say, "What do you want? Blood?" There was only one answer to that: "That's right, Leland. Blood."

In New Haven, on the stage of the Shubert, stagehands were rigging the cargo net that would bring aboard the drunken sailors. As they were about to lift it for the first time loaded, I said, "Let me ride it. If it collapses with me, then it's unsafe." Several actors climbed in along with me. Packed in, I noticed a hand and arm that looked familiar. I turned and saw the face, scarlet with excitement, of Tom Heggen. He wouldn't let me get ahead of him. They hoisted us up and we swayed in the air.

During the next days of dress rehearsal I felt again what a giant talent Jo Mielziner had for atmosphere and mechanics. It all worked smoothly: the hatch that led below decks, the turntable which moved the staterooms quietly into place.

We opened to an audience of mostly student veterans, and they acted as if they were at a victorious Yale football game.

Some New York pilgrims gathered afterward in my suite at the sad old Hotel Taft to celebrate, and, as I feared, also to give their opinions. Sidney, a former agent of mine, took me aside and said we were in trouble. The captain's character was unbelievable. He needed a different background to motivate his behavior, like his having worked on the Yangtze as captain of a slave ship or, better yet, having been a prison warden. As he was pumping theories into my ear, I saw someone lecturing Leland, and I spotted another friendly adviser haranguing Tom.

The next day, the few local papers seemed happy, but an advance copy of *Variety* complained about the dirty words.

After our last performance in New Haven Saturday night, there was another save-the-show party in my room. As Robert E. Sherwood said, "Deliver me from constructive criticism." Carping criticism, negative thoughts from a fellow professional can actually stimulate new ideas if you do not let them depress you. It's when the criticisms are accompanied by worked-out solutions that they are indigestible.

Dick Rodgers saw the first Philadelphia matinee and told me *Mister Roberts* was one of the best shows he had ever seen, then went back to New York. Oscar saw it that evening. After giving me a few niggling suggestions, he apologized for changing the subject to himself. "Dick and I can't find anything to do next."

"Didn't Dick tell you about *Tales of the South Pacific?*"

"No, what's that?"

I said, "Get a copy. It would make a great musical."

Two days later, he telephoned from Doylestown. "Josh, you're so right, that Michener book is wonderful. When I mentioned it to Dick, he said to me, 'Oh, I was crazy about it, too, but some son of a bitch I met at a cocktail party owns it, so we haven't got a chance.' Then I asked, 'Was that son of a bitch, Josh?' and he said, 'Logan! *That's* the son of a bitch!'"

Of course, now I had to tell Leland that they wanted to do the show. I steadied myself for his reaction. Leland really lit into me. "Bastard— you idiot bastard. You *couldn't* have told them about it! You're a decent human being. You *couldn't* do that to me—or yourself."

"I knew it was dangerous, but I couldn't help it. They wanted a show. I was scared I'd lose them."

"But Jesus, Josh, we haven't finished negotiating the rights! With their power they'll have us over a barrel."

The next day, Leland told me, with a dark gray face, "Rodgers and Hammerstein won't do it unless they own fifty-one percent to our forty-nine, which assures them the final say and us no say. All this, thanks to you."

"I realize that, Leland. But let's give it to them. They're not the fairest but the best."

"Josh, you can't, you simply can't. These stories are our property. You and I found them. We mustn't give anything away—certainly not the controlling share. There are other composers—let's go to someone else."

At that moment I had such an adolescent worship for Rodgers and Hammerstein that I didn't care what they demanded, and foolhardy as it was, I forced Leland to give Dick and Oscar the final say on *South Pacific*. I don't think in his heart Leland ever forgave me. Later on, I couldn't forgive myself. But anyway, we signed a contract that Oscar was to write the book and lyrics, Dick the music, I was to direct—and all three were to have one hundred percent billing.

Mister Roberts was fifteen minutes too long and costing a fortune in stagehands, whose wages doubled after 11:30 P.M. I whined that I didn't know what to cut. Emlyn Williams was down from New York. He said, "Give me the script and a pencil and I'll have it out for you by morning." Right on schedule, he appeared with his edited script and said, modestly, "I was only able to do a minor superbrilliant job. I've cut sixteen minutes and I haven't eliminated one scene."

He demonstrated to me what I now call "Emlyn Williams cutting." He had axed nearly every adjective, adverb and needless dependent clause. He cut any repeat of the same idea. He found the shortest way to say something—for instance, the briefest verb form. It certainly worked for *Mister Roberts*. Leland, Tom and I gave Emlyn a pair of gold scissors engraved with our names.

From Philadelphia, *Mister Roberts* moved to Baltimore, and after Baltimore there was a week of previews in New York. Before the first performance, Lew Wasserman, head of powerful MCA, who were now my agents as well as Fonda's, came to me.

"Josh," Lew said, "the language is dangerous. There's one line that has to go before the opening or the police might close the show."

I was furious. "What line?"

Before leaving to make a big firecracker, Pulver tells Roberts he'll use fulminate of mercury as powder. Roberts says to Doc, "That stuff's murder! Do you suppose he means it?" Doc says, "Of course not. Where could he get fulminate of mercury?" Roberts answers, "I don't know. He's pretty resourceful. Where did he get the clap last year?"

Cutting that would eliminate our biggest laugh. I screamed, but Lew was relentless and he had convinced Leland, so we made the cut.

It was taken as a tragedy by the whole cast, and most particularly by Hank. Later on in the run, on the night our old buddy Jimmy Stewart was coming to see the play, I asked Hank if he would put the "clap" line back for just that performance. Hank glowed in the great rocking sound that came at the line, and from then on we slipped it in often, until a lady complained to the police and they threatened to close the show for good. So it was out for good.

The day of a Broadway opening is like an extra Christmas with telegrams, flowers and presents from close friends. I got one great present at the opening of *Mister Roberts:* a bound copy of Tom's manuscript of the novel. On the flyleaf was the inscription "To Josh and Nedda. I may sound mushy but I love you both. Tom."

Standing there, waiting for the curtain to go up, is an exciting time because it's a mysterious time. Almost anything can happen. It's very much like the first time you make love. It can be wonderful if you're loved back, and maddening until you find out whether you are.

Theatre isn't merely giver; it's giver and receiver. It's lover and loved. That's one of the reasons I feel that the theatre will never die—I mean the live theatre. Because there is a sense of immediacy about being in an audience, feeling yourself played to by live actors, that can be found nowhere else. Everyone knows in live theatre that every syllable spoken can be heard by everyone on either side of the footlights. If an actor gets extra applause or a bigger laugh, he is subliminally inspired by that sound to give a slightly different, perhaps better, performance of the next lines, and then on through the evening, and just as silently the audience knows it has helped.

All this love, this mutual affection, is of course subconscious, but it's there in one vast room, and it's exciting and it is the reason for a feeling of constant spontaneity. It is when this spontaneity becomes tired and worn, it is when, for instance, a romantic leading man after a year's run is kissing a girl onstage and at the same time deciding whether he can get the 11:15 or the 11:35 or will have to wait for the 12:01 that night—that's when plays are in trouble and need directors and creative rerehearsal and, if possible, unorthodox as it may sound, a few even arbitrary changes to force the actor to think again freshly.

But back to the opening night in New York—the night when all of it may go completely berserk.

At the performance, Nedda and I stood behind the boxes and watched many of our friends howling. We had no time at all to wait for reassurance with that show. It came the minute the curtain rose— the moment Chief Johnson entered, checked over his shoulder and then spat tobacco juice onto the captain's palm tree. There were too many curtain calls to count.

Nedda and I gave an opening night party at the Lombardy, and soon the place was crowded.

The morning newspapers were suddenly passed above heads all over the room. Nearby, someone was reading from the last line of Brooks Atkinson's review, "Thank you, Mr. Heggen and Mr. Logan, for a royal good time!"

Tom seemed to be pouring a bottle of champagne down his throat, while Helen stood by with a gloomy face. I figured she had read the notices too. I toasted her across the room, and she barely responded. She will always be a mystery to me.

A close friend of mine, the publisher Bennett Cerf, took Sinclair

Lewis to the second performance, and reported that though Lewis had laughed throughout, at the curtain his face became troubled. Bennett asked him what was wrong.

"This Heggen, he's twenty-nine, isn't he? My God, how terrible."

"Terrible? His play's a huge hit."

Lewis shook his head. "It's too much for him to stomach at this stage in his life."

Nedda and I wanted a holiday in Europe, but we worried about leaving Tom Heggen. Tom solved it by deciding to take a freighter to Europe himself with some of his old Navy friends. It was the only decision in my memory he had made on his own since we had met him. Was he finally taking charge of his own life? Had he stopped floating?

As for myself, I noticed there was a strange absence of that Logan "worryscope" that usually scanned the horizon each morning. I ascribed this temporary recess to the actual playwriting I had done instead of just helping other authors anonymously. For all these years I had been suppressing what I most wanted to do—write—and now I had done it. Of course, Tom had been the fountainhead, the gusher from which everything in the play flowed, but as he readily acknowledged, I had contributed some strong mountain streams of my own. In the midst of all the excitement, I felt a blissful serenity.

I knew that any success in the theatre depended first on the script and that, following Stanislavsky's words, my direction was determined by the author's intentions. But even the best plays I had worked on could use help—the author needed an indication from the director as to what theme could be further developed or what gap filled in or what muddiness clarified. But it seemed to be the author's divine right to collect any ideas that might be lying about and call them his own.

And it was after too many of these self-negating experiences that I had felt I must stop being the invisible man.

My state of mind made me realize that the strong stand I took with Tom Heggen should have been taken years before.

Nedda and I toured Sicily with John and Dorothy Swope, picnicked under Greek ruins and around the slopes of Mount Etna.

Before going to London to stay with Molly and Emlyn Williams, we went to Paris for the Flea Market and the restaurants. Besides food, one of my uncontrollable vices is collecting things, especially antiques, and more especially objects from the nineteenth century, both Victorian and Napoleon III—anything that suggests the prejet, preplastic, prepoured-concrete age. The real problem was that there wasn't much room for anything in our small Lombardy apartment.

My secret wish was to be able to afford to move to a large apartment which I could fill with Impressionist and pre-Raphaelite paintings as well as nineteenth-century furniture and rugs.

When we were headed for home on the *Queen Mary* we met Virginia Peine, the beautiful wife of Quentin Reynolds. She was going to sell her apartment at River House, which overlooked the East River. She felt it wasn't big enough for her grown daughter to receive young gentlemen. Another friend, George Schlee, who lived across from River House, said it was ideal for us. Ginnie shook hands with us on a deal.

I was in a state of glowing achievement that we were able to afford that beautiful apartment, and we were getting ready to move in when I came home one night to find that Mary Lee, my personal Cassandra, had harangued Nedda into believing it was too big for us, and they had gone to look for another place. Fortunately, I was able to trace them and pull them back to the River House before we lost the apartment.

Mary Lee felt in general that we bought too much and spent too much money. When we invited her to come see the three or four more Napoleon III chairs we had just acquired in France, she entered the room and in her sweetest tone said, "Oh, I see you're giving a party for chairs."

In less than two months, despite Mary Lee, we moved to River House, but the first night there I couldn't sleep. I walked from room to room, looking out the windows at glistening strings of lights and the lilac shadows of New York sprawled out there fourteen stories down. I knew again that I belonged to this city and that I must work extra hard to make our lives here comfortable and permanent. Oh, God, I thought, nothing must go wrong, not now that life has excitement and shape. A couple of flops, an illness, an accident, would shatter this mood like a machine gun in a hall of mirrors. I was, for a second, so terrified that I couldn't see the pale city below the windows anymore. I couldn't move or breathe. How could I keep what I'd earned? Could I keep well—mentally well? It was too early for it to start working, but there it was scanning the room, the windows, my eyes and my weakening heart. The worryscope was in full action.

CHAPTER
15

I was hoping that Oscar had finished the book of *South Pacific*. Instead, Dick called to say that Oscar, after working for months, had only finished the first scene and an outline.

As for songs, Dick said, "Well, we've done those for the first scene and Oscar's written some scattered lyrics. But God knows where they'll fit." I could feel Larry Hart's old school principal in his voice.

"Aren't you committed to a schedule?"

"You're damned right. We've booked theatres, drawn up ads. Oscar generally works fast. But now we're in trouble. I want you to drive down to Oscar's farm. Maybe you can help him."

I called Oscar, who said, "Josh, I know absolutely nothing about Army behavior or how a sergeant talks to a general, and vice versa. What do sailors do when young Lieutenant Cable comes onto the beach? I had them snapping to attention. But that seemed wrong."

"Good God, yes," I said. "They'd pretend he wasn't there."

"I hate the military so much that I'm ignorant of it."

"I wish I were. It's been shoved down my throat since I started Culver at thirteen. Oscar, Dick thinks I should come down there so that we could work the Army stuff out together."

"Oh, please do, Josh. Dorothy would love for you and Nedda to stay here. Come down this afternoon. I need you."

Packing my Dictaphone—which Oscar found as terrifying as a snake—I drove down with Nedda and brought Jim Awe to type.

Oscar and Dorothy owned a large working farm near Doylestown where Oscar raised prize Black Angus with the help of a Norwegian farmer who was also Oscar's masseur. Oscar was forced to raise cattle to keep his masseur happy.

Dorothy Hammerstein was not only warm and beautiful, but had a genius for decoration and for organizing an overflowing household.

I didn't plan to stay long. I would just get Oscar on the right track and dash back to New York to plan the production. But within a day I realized that Oscar was holding onto our talks like a man grappling up a cliff. We talked excitedly through an entire rough structure. Scenes bobbed up that neither of us had expected.

At first, my idea had been to use the tale "Fo' Dolla'," about the beautiful native girl, Liat, her lover, young Lieutenant Cable, and her repulsive mother, the foul-mouthed Bloody Mary. But Oscar had been caught by another story, "Our Heroine," in which a middle-aged, sophisticated French planter and a naïve American nurse fall in love. The part of the nurse was being written with Mary Martin in mind because of her huge success in *Annie*. When she finds out that the mother of his children was a Polynesian, she runs away from him, unable with her Little Rock background to accept the relationship. But her love eventually overpowers her prejudice and she returns to him and his family. (This story, incidentally, was so low key compared to the rest that it was eliminated in the paperback edition of Michener's stories, and readers who had seen the play wondered where we got the idea.)

Oscar's great contribution was to combine the two stories, making that of the nurse and the planter the major one. He then planned to use three other stories, the most important being the one about the coast watcher who hid in the hills and reported by radio movements of the Japanese fleet. Oscar had also asked James Michener for more comic material, and Jim wrote him a complete story of the GIs elaborate handling of laundry. Out of this we later got color for the character of Luther Billis.

When I arrived, he had written a lovely first scene which introduced Emile and Nellie, and the start of their love—the "Some Enchanted Evening" scene. He also had a couple of exciting pages somewhat later, on the meeting of Cable and Liat. For Nellie they had written the ecstatic song "I'm in Love With a Wonderful Guy" to be sung to her fellow nurses in an unwritten scene, but otherwise Oscar seemed to be—yes—a bit frightened.

He and I reviewed the sequence of scenes, and in two days we had it committed to memory. Just before I left he asked me to stay another day and help him through the difficult second scene on Bloody Mary's beach. I pulled out the Dictaphone and started acting all the roles into it. I was Billis, I was a Seabee, I was Lieutenant Cable. For me, military dialogue flowed easily. Oscar was amazed. When I got to Bloody Mary, suddenly he was talking and I was repeating his words into the mouthpiece. We were both so stimulated by each other that we kept on dictating into the night and through the next day. There was no more talk of my going back to New York. I just stayed.

Being Southern, I spontaneously spoke all of Nellie's lines in my Mansfield accent, and he was a very suave Emile de Becque.

The scenes were transcribed by our secretaries, Jim Awe and Shirley Potash, and we would proofread them for the next draft. Our wives collated the pages on the living room floor. After three-fourths of the first act, I realized that Oscar was throwing me lines for Emile de Becque, Bloody Mary, and sometimes for Captain Brackett, and I was doing all the rest.

We were going full out—when we came to a screeching halt. The last scene of the first act, Emile's party for Nellie, stopped us cold. We had imagined Emile would be entertaining his guests with erotic native dancers. We both felt we needed a divertissement here. The stage would be peopled with neighboring French planters and their wives. But when we started to write it, the whole tension vanished. Our hearts sank like plummeting lead.

Oscar suggested we go for a walk, and we stalked out the front door. We had not gone twenty paces when Oscar said, "Do you suppose it's those goddamned native dancers? Is that the blockage? What if we begin *after* the party, with the guests calling good-bye in French offstage?"

"That's right," said I, catching fire. "And then Emile pulls Nellie onstage by her wrists. They're both full of wine and he wants to get into bed with her this minute!"

"Exactly! They're high. They're passionate! They've been drinking all evening, and now they're sailing!"

We jogged back to the house, and took the stairs two at a time, waving casually to our dumbstruck wives in passing. In the study, I grabbed the Dictaphone and started rattling off "Bon soirs," and then described Emile pulling Nellie onstage to make love. After some wine-laced talk, Nellie and Emile break into a waltz, with Emile singing—Oscar's spontaneous lyrics:

> I'm in love, I'm in love and the girl that I love—
> She thinks I'm a wonderful guy!

Within a few minutes we had written what we were sure would be a high spot, and had done it in the same time it would take to play it onstage.

We worked hard every afternoon and evening, but I left Oscar alone in the mornings to chisel out the lyrics. We were both working against time.

At night with Nedda, in our room, she would ask, "Why are we still staying? Who's writing these scenes you're reading to us?"

When I described to her how Oscar and I worked, she'd say, "But you're writing again and you only signed a contract to direct. Oscar was to write it by himself."

"I know, but crazy as it may sound, he *can't* write this one. He doesn't understand the military or Little Rock. He needs me."

"Then you must tell him in the morning that you can't continue unless you're his *collaborator*. Don't get into another situation like Tom Heggen, for heaven's sake!"

"I don't think Oscar wants a collaborator."

"Who cares—he's *got* a collaborator—one *he asked for*. You don't like giving away your ideas any more than he does, do you? He's a grown man and a businessman, and so are you. Tell him tomorrow."

But the next morning I dreaded some kind of angry blowup which would destroy the whole undertaking, and so I didn't have the showdown I should have had then, and we continued to work ceaselessly, though Nedda never stopped telling me to state my attitude or quit writing.

Altogether, including the two days of planning, we took ten days to write the book for *South Pacific*.

Nedda and I drove, a bit shaken, back to New York. Oscar was to come within the next three days with more lyrics.

The intensity of this work was emotionally debilitating. After the writing of the description of Emile and Nellie clasping hands at the end, I had to leave the room because I was so moved. In my mind, I had just seen the first preview of *South Pacific* and I was astounded by its power. A single thought kept drumming through my mind: "It's going to win the Pulitzer Prize, and no one will ever know I wrote a word of it." In rehearsal I would be forced to say, "That's not what Mr. Hammerstein meant when he wrote that line."

At night, I found I couldn't sleep. Nedda called our doctor and explained my disturbance. He gave me a sleeping pill and some advice: "You've got to let this man know you're being torn apart. He's a human being—he's got to understand."

The next day before Oscar came, Dick Rodgers called. He said he had read the script on the train to Boston. His comment was, ". . . and I had a very pleasant trip."

"But did you like the script?"

He repeated, "I told you I had a very pleasant trip."

I wasn't in the mood for understatement, and especially from a man who had had no script whatsoever three weeks ago.

My lawyer was shocked at the intolerable situation. He wanted to talk to Oscar's lawyer, but I told him Oscar was my friend and I would handle it myself.

When our maid announced Oscar the next day, Nedda came over to me and kissed me, and I left the room.

Oscar was in our living room, reading the last pages of the newly typed script. He looked up at me. "What's the matter?"

I said, in a high, tight voice, "What do you mean, what's the matter?"

"You look strange. Are you all right?"

"I'm fine, fine." Then my head swirled. The rug before me seemed to split in two, while the floor below it yawned open, revealing a terrifying chasm fourteen stories deep. I could feel a great wind sucking me down into it, and then it all slowly closed in as I began. "Oscar, I think

I should get half credit for the book." The floor trembled a bit, but didn't open this time.

Oscar's face was immobile, but I thought he blushed slightly. After the briefest of pauses, he said, "I wish I'd said it first. I'm sorry you had to." Then he added, "Of course you must have credit. After all, you wrote it as much as I did. We'll work out the exact credits later."

I had a strong urge to run back and kiss Nedda, but I didn't. Oscar and I worked on a bit of polishing for the final draft, and Oscar left, saying he would be back the next day.

At once, I rushed back to Nedda and said, "He said *yes!*"

She shouted, "Let's open a bottle of champagne!" We had a merry, happy, wonderful evening.

The next day I walked on air—until Oscar appeared in the afternoon.

We sat down, facing each other. Looking painfully stern, he said, "In order to keep me from feeling that I'm being penalized by your demand, I will agree to the following arrangement. You may have equal credit with me for the book."

"That's wonderful, Oscar."

"That's not all. According to our contract, in the credits your name as director was to be in the same type size as mine and Dick's. But now Dick and I must have the top one hundred percent credit with the lead-in 'A Musical Play By Rodgers and Hammerstein.'"

"What?"

"*Your* name and *mine* as the book authors will be below that but with only sixty percent of the Rodgers and Hammerstein credit. And that's still not all. Your director credit must be *diminished* to sixty percent as well."

"Jesus, Oscar," I said, "that's a body blow."

"That's the only possible way we can go on. Of course, it goes without saying that you won't get anything whatsoever of the author's royalties."

"But," I said, in a shocked voice, "if you admit that I'm coauthor on the program, how can you deny it in the royalty distribution? A director's royalties *end* when the original company closes. An author's percentage goes on forever—foreign rights, amateur and stock rights, movie sale. It might mean a great deal to my family, to Nedda—to the children I hope to have."

"Josh," he said, and I could see he was really in pain, "Rodgers and Hammerstein cannot and *will not* share a copyright. It's part of their financial structure. Including you would weaken our position. My partners feel this strongly. It's impossible, Josh."

I couldn't face Nedda, back there in her blissful state.

I said to Oscar, "Oscar, why did you agree yesterday and then hit me so hard today?"

"Because I realized that the public, through previous announcements, was expecting me to write it alone. And so this was penalizing me. Now you're being penalized too."

At that moment, because I cared for him, I felt I could see deep into a suffering Oscar Hammerstein. Obviously, he was speaking lines he had been instructed to say—whether by Dick or their lawyer. I was not listening to a single man, but to a citizens' committee such as those during the French Revolution who decided who should lose their heads at the guillotine.

I also saw by Oscar's expression how hard he must have fought to secure for me as much as he did, and how equally hard it was for him to look me in the eye as he said what he had to say.

Oscar had had great success in his youth, first with Otto Harbach and then on his own with the great Kern on _Show Boat,_ and others. His talents had then fallen on barren ground for years. Show after show had failed until Dick Rodgers offered him _Oklahoma!_ Whereupon, overnight, he got the backing for _Carmen Jones,_ which was another fantastic success for him personally. He was at that time the top man in the theatre and it made him very nervous, so when Christmas came around he took an ad in _Variety_ to let the world know how he felt:

HOLIDAY GREETINGS
OSCAR HAMMERSTEIN 2nd
Author of

SUNNY RIVER	Six weeks—St. James Theatre, New York
VERY WARM FOR MAY	Seven weeks—Alvin Theatre, New York
THREE SISTERS	Seven weeks—Drury Lane, London
BALL AT THE SAVOY	Five weeks—Drury Lane, London
FREE FOR ALL	Three weeks—Manhattan Theatre, New York

I'VE DONE IT BEFORE AND
I CAN DO IT AGAIN

But he didn't do it again. In a few short years the names Rodgers and Hammerstein, with *Carousel* and the film *State Fair,* had become the strongest in the entertainment world. Oscar's new partner was brilliant, a near genius. I knew that Oscar had forced himself to accept second place to a younger and more successful man. He had to make adjustments, but he did so without complaint to avoid any friction with his new associate. Oscar was safe at last, and he didn't want to "rock the boat," or as we say even more vulgarly, "make waves."

I should have taken a strong, hard line, such as threatening to resign and then suing to stop production if a word of my dialogue was used, but deep in my innards *I wanted to do the show more than anything else in the world.* And I had the greatest respect for Oscar as a man, as a dramatist and as a human being. If Dorothy Hammerstein, whom I adored, could love him, then I could too. My feelings for Dick had suffered a sea change, but I still respected him. Therefore, I accepted the terms without conferring with Nedda or my own lawyer. But I made one last request.

"Suppose I switched a part of my director's royalties to the author's. It wouldn't cost the show any more, and then I would at least have some of the future earnings."

He looked pained again. "I'll ask our lawyers about it," he said, weighing each word. "But frankly, it doesn't sound feasible."

While the question of transferring royalties was being fought out in the snake pit by our lawyers, I decided to go ahead with casting. Nedda was most unhappy that I had agreed to such terms, and only acquiesced because I begged her to. She felt I could have forced them to share the copyright, and looking back I suppose I could have, since later, Lindsay and Crouse got them to share one for *The Sound of Music.*

Leland felt I had brought it on myself by letting them get control of the basic rights. Leland was torn between saying, "Josh, you were robbed," and "You deserve it, you bastard." But what he did say was, "You're at their mercy."

An enormous change had taken place in Dick Rodgers' life that affected our relationship. It came with his gigantic and worldwide success. He became, almost in front of our eyes, a monument. He was so sought after that he had to closet himself in an office and dictate letters daily in order to handle his business affairs and to fend off the many people who wanted to sap his talent. To me, his fun seemed gone—the fun he and I used to have.

And I tried to decide for myself, What is a Richard Rodgers?

It's a brilliant, talented, highly intelligent, theatrically sound, superbrain. It likes to work, it particularly likes to write music, which flows up plentifully from some underground spring. It plays the piano better than most composers. It's not given to smiling too much, and yet when it scowls I've found that does not indicate anything unpleasant; it is simply making a judgment, thinking things over, watching a private preview. It has a strong sense of discipline; it likes to be on time, to deliver work as promised. And when it works with an Oscar Hammerstein, that is accomplished frequently. But when it worked with a Larry Hart, well, that's when the scowl sets in. It pretends to hate business, and yet it is my theory that it is only really happy making contracts, haggling about royalties, salaries or theatre leases. I often believed it was a bit embarrassed about the ease of writing music, as though it were too easy, too soft a thing for a man to do. Therefore, it enjoyed being a hard-bitten businessman.

When I first knew Dick, he and I were cronies, pals, especially on the road when we were away from our families. We'd take out a couple of members of the cast and give them dinner, and have a warm, relaxed time of it until we were ready to rest up for tomorrow's rehearsal. Surely, Dick Rodgers did more for me, more to solidify my career in musical comedy, than any other person. He scowlingly (which means warmly) approved of me initially to direct my first musical, *I Married An Angel*. He liked my work on that in spite of the fact that I didn't. He insisted on having me for his next, *Higher and Higher*, and after I had had my well-publicized nervous breakdown, Dick was the first person to offer me another show, *By Jupiter*. After the war, he offered me *Annie Get Your Gun* while I was still overseas. And show after show till *South Pacific*.

So what happened? What made him change? Was it, as I suspected, stratospheric fame, the pedestal that the whole world put him on? Was it the money? Was it the business side of his life that erased the fun?

When he teamed up with Oscar Hammerstein there were all kinds of remarks that the big one is a nice guy but the little one is a son of a bitch. To me, Dick and Oscar were both tough as nails, and although Oscar was easier for me to get along with by that time because we somehow spoke the same language, Dick still had something for me that I could never shake off.

* * *

We went full steam into casting. The leads had been set months ago. Mary Martin was Nellie Forbush. She had agreed on hearing Oscar's first scene. Then Edwin Lester of the Los Angeles Civic Light Opera Company, who had just signed a two-year contract with Ezio Pinza, asked if we would take the contract over—providing Pinza was interested in playing our lead. We jumped at the chance of having such a great singing actor play Emile.

My old Princeton friend, Myron McCormick, was my first choice for Billis, and I cannot remember anyone else's being considered.

Only two roles seemed to give us trouble, Bloody Mary and Cable. But at an audition, Juanita Hall, a marvelous mulatto singer with an Oriental cast of features, took off her shoes and stockings and struck a squatting pose that said, "I am Bloody Mary and don't you dare cast anyone else!"

Young William Tabbert looked somewhat wrong for Cable until he started to sing, and then he looked absolutely right. But in talking to him I learned he was a "health nut" too. I told him that he had to lose about twenty pounds and firm up his body, which he promised to do before rehearsal.

Five days prior to rehearsal, I went to Bill Brown's Health Farm up near Garrison on the Hudson to get in physical shape for the big push. While I was there, back in New York rival lawyers were still sparring. The dickering that was going on would have chilled my blood and shriveled my soul had I known about it. As it was, my wife and agent handled it all and kept it from me out of fear that I would blow up and jeopardize the entire project.

I would learn of it all later, but as I drove home the day before rehearsals started, my mind was in a whirl with ideas for movement during songs, with wisps of dance, and particularly with the use of music under the dramatic pantomime for changes of thought a la Stanislavsky.

Dick Rodgers had hired Trude Rittman, a superb German-born composer, orchestrator and arranger, to work with me during the staging. This would be my first chance to have a true composer by my side during rehearsals, one who would create passages based on Dick's themes, to illuminate thoughts and feelings.

As my car approached New York it occurred to me that the operatic form I had first thought right for the Michener stories was being achieved.

* * *

At nine-thirty the next morning the bare stage of the Majestic Theatre began to fill with people.

The New York opening may be a musical's most exciting moment, but close to it is the first reading of the full score and book. Will it or won't it?

Bill Tabbert came over to me to show his new physique; he had lost two inches from his waist. Betta St. John, our Liat, was so beautiful she made everyone feel good just looking at her.

Mary Martin arrived at five to ten, and shortly afterward Pinza came in with his full coterie of accompanist, lawyer, arranger, wife and several others. Whispers had it he had been waiting in the alley until Mary showed up; the most important must arrive last.

Jo Mielziner showed the model of his settings, and we began to read.

The Spanish-American children, masquerading as Polynesian, Barbara Luna and Michael De Leon, sang "Dites-moi Pourquoi." Then Mary as Nellie and Ezio as Emile began speaking their offstage conversation. The thrill of hearing their voices together was enough for a start.

But the spell got a jolt when Pinza pantomimed a coffee cup and said, "Sooker?" Shades of the Black Pool oasis! I corrected him by saying softly, "Shh. Shoogar." With great effort, he said, "Sh-shoo-ker," and we continued.

Mary Martin sang "A Cockeyed Optimist" with her open charm, and quite soon the two of them began singing Dick Rodgers' insistent, marvelous tune, "Twin Soliloquies"—each using the same melody, but at a distance apart, with Oscar's words of tentative, doubting love. This was the moment when for me the show became great. But the song stopped too quickly; the music had to continue to strengthen the passionate, almost sexual, feeling. Trude provided the thrilling continuation later.

Soon Emile declared himself with "Some Enchanted Evening." When Pinza first sang the word "enchanted," it came out "enshonted" —but he worked hard, and before long his diction was both understandable and attractive. He was unique. His deep, sonorous voice, his massive muscular bulk, his magnetic eyes, brought back from the past the matinee idol.

Everyone loved him, especially Mary Martin. Unlike the usual star, she had no jealousy; she wanted Pinza to succeed. She knew that if the audience loved Pinza, they would know why Nellie Forbush did.

The second scene opened with the roughneck Seabees singing "Bloody Mary." Juanita Hall took off her shoes and squatted to read. "Hallo, GI! Grass skirt? Very saxy! Fo' dolla'? Send home Chicago. You like? You buy?"

McCormick treasured this part more than he did his Phi Beta Kappa key. He was a perfect opponent for the old girl.

When the men sang "There Is Nothin' Like a Dame," I imagined myself pacing back and forth in rhythm. I was getting excited.

Juanita Hall, with chilling concentration on Bill Tabbert's musculature, sang "Bali Ha'i." I looked at Oscar. How many peaks could a show have?

Yet they continued, song after song, each seeming more apt than the last because of a growing involvement with the story.

During lunch, Dick and Oscar seemed calm and so did Leland Hayward, who had entered that morning gray with nerves. But I was used to that Hayward apprehension.

I began the actual staging, placing the actors in approximate positions and asking them to go through sketchy moves. I threw together a rough draft of the first scene. Rather than perfect it then, I jumped right to the second, which was more complicated. I began blocking out "There Is Nothin' Like a Dame," and I started pacing as I imagined a caged animal would pace. The men followed me, restlessly pacing back and forth—killing time till the end of the war, till the chance of seeing women again. Then I asked Trude to repeat the song, and motioned one man to pace in one direction, another to go the other way, breaking the pattern constantly. Within fifteen or twenty minutes I had staged it. It didn't exactly fall into place, but it looked as if it had. It was an *acted* musical scene. I thought Stanislavsky would approve.

"There Is Nothin' Like a Dame" joined *Annie*'s "goon look" as one of the things most remembered about my work. The really hard work I did as director was never noticed—and never should be. My best direction was to give approval and encouragement. When an actor was on the right track I would say, "Keep it that way, that way you spontaneously did it. Except do it *again—exactly the same way,* so I know it is fixed in your memory." That's good direction in my book.

In two days the entire show was put roughly on its feet. Dick and Oscar were amazed and a bit frightened at how fast I had gone. I asked

Oscar for the second song he planned for Bloody Mary, the one which he called "Happy Talk."

Oscar said, "I decided to chuck it. I couldn't imagine how it could be staged, and I didn't want to give you any more problems."

I felt a surge of good-humored arrogance. "You write it, I'll stage it," I said.

The next morning, Oscar and Dick brought me the song, and as Dick played it the background rhythm for some reason made me think of two birds talking to each other. I imitated the rhythmic motion of their beaks with my thumbs and forefingers. Then I took the actors and Trude Rittman down to the piano in the theatre lounge. Betta St. John was a dancer and loved the finger gestures. While Bloody Mary sang to Cable about how happy life with Liat would be, Liat pantomimed to him a flower, and then at the word "dream" I had her rest her face in her two hands, palms front. We pantomimed the whole song in five or six minutes, and we showed it to Oscar and Dick. They were as delighted as we were.

Of course there were a few changes during rehearsal. Dick and Oscar had a late song for Pinza called "Now Is the Time," to be sung as he decides to go with Cable into enemy territory. But it seemed wrong. If Cable and Emile were going on a mission to save Allied lives, why didn't they get a goddamn move on instead of standing and singing, "Now is the time to act, no other time will do"? The song was quickly eliminated, but it had to be replaced just as quickly, because Pinza was frightened of anything new.

In an emergency meeting, the three of us decided it had to come well before the mission is even suggested. The mission should come *out* of the song, and of course the song must be a lament of losing Nellie. Dick asked for a title line that he could work on. One of us called out, "This nearly was mine."

"That's it," said Dick. "A big bass waltz." And he disappeared.

Within a day or two Dick and Oscar brought "This Nearly Was Mine." It was so beautiful that in staging it I just let Ezio stand there and sing. I feared that any fancy movement would detract from the effect of Oscar's heartfelt lines and Dick's rich, slow waltz. Pinza loved singing it.

Cable had no song to sing after he had made love to Liat in the hut. Oscar studied the scene again and again. He was fascinated by Liat's waiting for Cable's boat to come around the bend. One day they took me to the lobby and sang one they had just written. It began:

> My friend, my friend,
> Is coming around the bend.

I was so let down that I blurted out my first feelings. "That's awful! That's the worst song I ever heard. Good God, that's terrible!"

They looked at me in shock; no one had ever spoken to them like that before, I'm sure. I'll never forget Dick's stricken face. But they were professional enough to go back home and try again. A day later they turned up with another. It was a lilting schottische, the words of which began like this:

> Suddenly lucky,
> Suddenly our arms are lucky
> Suddenly lucky,
> Suddenly our lips have kissed.

When they finished, I was thinking so hard I didn't speak. Oscar said, "Well, have we passed the test this time, Teacher?"

"You're close," I said. "I love the tune, but isn't that song a bit lightweight for a hot, lusty boy to sing right after making love to a girl who will change his life?"

Dick rebelled. He announced uncharmingly that he was not going to go on writing till "this guy" agrees on a tune. He played a song they had dropped from *Allegro*. It was then called "My Wife." The melody was lovely, and I urged them to go ahead. Oscar spent two days writing new lyrics for it and it became the classic and powerful "Younger Than Springtime."

"Suddenly Lucky," too, had a reincarnation, for two years later when I heard Gertrude Lawrence sing "Getting to Know You" in *The King and I*, I knew where I had heard that tune before.

A week before rehearsals, Mary Martin had had her hair cut short like a boy's, and it bristled neatly from her head. One night she was struck by how quickly it dried after a shower. "Three minutes!" she told me. "Why not wash my hair onstage? It might be fun for the audience."

I said, "Remember, you suggested it. If all your hair falls out or breaks off . . ."

"I won't blame you," she said, "but ask Oscar anyway."

The moment I told him, he looked up and said, " 'I'm Gonna Wash That Man Right Outa My Hair!' It'll be a song." The two of us were looking for something to help her decide to break it off with Emile.

Dick had an instant tune for "Wash That Man." So, while she soaped her hair, Mary would sing in a jerry-built shower, copied from a snapshot one of our glider pilots made in Normandy. Then she would dance about flicking bubbles at the girls, wash and dry her hair as they sang, and finish with a flick of the towel. Surely the novelty of it would bring down the house. That took care of one of my beloved Mary's big numbers. I could breathe more easily.

We decided to do run-throughs without audiences every afternoon to develop a flow. The first was on the dark Belasco stage and it turned out to be almost the end of *South Pacific*.

After "I'm in Love With a Wonderful Guy," Mary had been re-hearsed to leap exultantly across the forestage and wanted to finish with a cartwheel. That day she leaped as usual, started her cartwheel, and halfway through dropped out of sight into the dark orchestra pit. There was a moment of horrified silence. I heard myself calling, "Mary, are you all right?" There was no sound. I found the strength somehow to stumble down to the orchestra pit.

Mary's body was crumpled over Trude Rittman, who was still at the piano. Mary had landed on Trude's shoulders, breaking her own fall but knocking Trude out. Trude came to quickly, severely shaken and in pain.

We had been within inches of terminal disaster. Instead of a cartwheel we substituted a good, safe high note.

We arrived in New Haven in great spirits, except that Pinza came with his platoon: accompanist, secretary, wife, lawyer and accountant. Rumors flew that he wanted to get out of the show, because he felt we had made Mary's role more important than his. That such a great per-former could doubt himself so much seems impossible. But the problem —if there was one—was settled for good on opening night in New Haven. Oh, there were many surprises that night!

The curtain rose modestly on the two children piping out "Dites-moi Pourquoi." Mary and Pinza entered immediately, a daring innovation of Oscar's, since generally stars come on late.

Mary's first song, "A Cockeyed Optimist," was aimed mostly to re-veal Nellie's character, and when she received only moderate applause

I was nervous, but Oscar said it was all we should expect. The "Twin Soliloquies" sequence was thrilling, provocative, as it had been at the run-throughs, and it led to Pinza's "Some Enchanted Evening." On his last soft, covered tone, the house burst into such applause that the scene couldn't go on. I watched Mary as she stood smiling up at Pinza, seeming as happy about it as he must have been. Obviously, both Nellie Forbush and Mary Martin loved that man.

And I loved her too, more than ever before. I loved her for her generosity of spirit, for her complete professionalism. I was even proud to have been born in Texas where she was born. I told myself, just wait till we get to her big songs. Pinza will have to cool his heels a bit for her.

The show went as we prayed it would, but it came to a strange halt at a point least expected. With real water, real soap and a real audience, Mary began "Wash That Man." We knew this would balance out Pinza's triumph. Sure as I was of it, I had still staged it with all the care and affection I could muster. Yet as she began to lather her hair, I sensed that something was wrong.

There was no concentration in the crowd. Mary and the nurses, flecked with soapsuds, came to a big finish, sure of applause. To my horror there was none. Not a handclap. I was sickened and ashamed. I had let dear Mary down, bumbled some way in the staging. Mary had followed my lead so trustingly, and here she was at a dead end.

There was worse to come.

The next major moment was Nellie's burst of joy as she proclaims to the world that she loves Emile. Dick and Oscar had written the incomparable "I'm in Love With a Wonderful Guy" not only to show Nellie's beautiful spirit but Mary Martin's free soul.

The verse was quite long and it built rhythmically as Nellie sang to the other nurses:

> I expect every one
> Of my crowd to make fun
> Of my proud protestations of faith in romance . . .
> Fearlessly I face you and argue your doubts away,
> Loudly I sing about flowers and spring!

That led to the chorus with the two lines Oscar wrote first when thinking of Mary in the part:

> I'm as corny as Kansas in August,
> I'm as normal as blueberry pie.

It was a moment so filled with celebration that I had taken a big chance and staged it as a mad clowning piece, using the word "corny" as the key. The nurses, catching her mood, did corny, happy, lowbrow jumps and falls and skips—a look-at-me-I'm-crazy moment. I tried to believe it would make up for "Wash That Man."

But again, I was wrong. The audience enjoyed the music and the lyrics, but the corny clowning was just cornball—or rather, embarrassing.

I saw Dick and Oscar's pained, stricken faces, but they were avoiding looking at me. I could imagine how poor Mary felt, and wondered about Pinza.

At the first curtain the applause was strong, but it didn't help my mood. In the lobby I looked for Nedda. She was with my lawyer, Morris Schrier. They had serious faces too, which I automatically interpreted as disappointment in the show. "It didn't go well, did it?" I said. They both said it went beautifully. "Then what is wrong?" I asked.

Nedda said, "Maury, please don't tell him now. You said you'd put it off until the show opened, and it's not over."

Anything that a lawyer says, to me spells doom, and this was no different.

"What is it?" I said, and Nedda suddenly left.

"Josh, it's about your contract."

"It's signed, isn't it?"

"Yes, but I want you to know that Mr. Cohen sent it over by messenger from the Reinheimer office the day before the first rehearsal—on the Sunday when you were on your way back from Bill Brown's. He's their lawyer and he said Rodgers and Hammerstein categorically refuse to let you transfer any of your director's royalties to author's royalties."

I said, "I expected that."

He said, "But there's something else, Josh. With the contract was a message from them saying that if the contract was not signed in two hours for you not to bother to come to rehearsal. They would get another director. Of course you were able to sign it close to the time so they didn't pursue that."

I didn't believe it. I still felt Dick and Oscar were my friends. They were incapable of such gangster threats. It must have been someone else's idea to bully me like that. I forced myself to believe in them.

Maury said, "Nedda didn't want me to tell you before because we knew it could affect your work in rehearsal."

For the moment I would try to avoid seeing Dick or Oscar. I needed time to think.

It was stupid of me to watch the second act, to try to concentrate. Over and over, I kept telling myself Dick and Oscar would not willfully stoop to such tactics, and if they had, what could I do? Go off and wail against a wall, or kick stones down some empty street? I surely couldn't leave the show. There was work to be done, and quickly. No matter what they felt about me, I had to go on, as though nothing unpleasant had happened between the envied authors of *South Pacific*.

To any normal person, the audience's final reception would cause joy. But that night, I was abnormal. I rushed to the hotel and into the elevator, where I met Mary's husband, Dick Halliday. He looked so gloomy I said, "Didn't it go terribly?"

"Terribly."

"We've really got to get to work."

"If work will help." He got off first and I continued up to my floor.

I told Nedda I wanted to be left alone in the bedroom to commiserate with myself. I didn't want any outsiders telling me how to feel.

She promised to keep people away while I sat and sulked in that dreary bedroom.

Soon there was a knock on the door and my sister Mary Lee came in. My sister, who, through inborn family fear, spotted the faults of everything I did, worried about me all of her life. Other occurrences she could take for granted or handle, but I was always a problem—her personal problem. Even as far back as the days when I was in Culver and she'd come back from vacations, I remember her panicked voice saying to me in the privacy of the front porch, "Josh, never, never go to bed with girls." And then, a year later, getting me to the same position on the same porch and saying, "Josh, never, never go to bed with boys."

I don't believe that Mary Lee ever enjoyed one of my shows, no matter how big a hit it was. She was just plain too nervous, too much a part of it, to know what she thought. It was as though she were taking some kind of school examination which she was fervently hoping to pass but felt was doomed to failure.

Still, I was hoping now that she would contradict me as I said, "It went dreadfully, didn't it?"

"Well, it was pretty bad."

"Oh, really!" I said. "But what about the audience? A lot of them seemed to like it."

"Not Mike Todd. I saw him walking up the aisle shaking his head slowly from side to side."

Just as Mary Lee said this, Nedda stuck a telegram under the door. I opened it. It said: "Josh, they'll never be able to top this one. Mike Todd." What timing!

An hour later, Dick Rodgers called. "I made Nedda let me get through to you. Josh, you don't seem to know we have a hit."

"No, I don't, Dick."

"We have, we have! Come on down to my room and I'll prove it to you."

Nedda and I went down, to hear our friends repeat all their enthusiasm. I drank a glass of champagne, but it tasted like barium. But anyway, Dick and Oscar obviously liked my work, no matter what threats they had made.

Next morning, to my surprise, Mary Martin seemed high and happy. I said, "I let you down. There was no applause on your two numbers."

"Maybe it was the way I did them," she said. "I'll get applause tonight. Don't worry."

Pinza, too, seemed to be in good shape. He was helping members of his entourage pile into taxis, heading back to New York.

The second night got a great response until Mary sang "Wash That Man," and again, she received the barest applause. I had watched carefully to see what was wrong, but I remained confused, and, as on the night before, "A Wonderful Guy" got very little too.

Molly Williams, Emlyn's wife, had come from New York to see it, and afterward I quizzed her about "Wash That Man." In her nice, chirping English voice, she said, "Oh, I thought it was marvelous when she washed her hair—terribly original. I really got quite excited, you know, and I was dying to talk to someone about it. But since I was alone, I just listened."

"Listened?"

"Yes, to what the other people were saying. They were wondering whether it would damage her hair, and what kind of soap she used—or was it soap?"

"Did you like the song she sang?"

"Song?"

"She sang it when she washed her hair."

"Oh, well, that explains it. I couldn't hear whether she was talking or singing. All I heard was people around me. It's terribly clever, you know, getting the audience to talk like that. Next time, I'll try to listen to the song."

I felt like an amateur. I had directed Mary to rub her head with water and soap just as she started singing the refrain "I'm gonna . . ." By the time she got "right outa my hair" there were the beginnings of suds. Obviously, she was trying to sing against a scene-stealer more powerful than a baby or an animal: soap!

The solution was simple. She sang the song first and *then* went into the shower and grabbed the soap. During the loud music that had been composed for the dance, Mary washed her hair and romped about, flinging soap and suds.

From then on, when they finished the number there was roaring approval. Mary was delighted, but not as much as I was. Half my Mary Martin headaches were over.

It was not until the second week in Boston that I guessed what might be wrong with "Wonderful Guy": it was the presence of the nurses that was killing the number. The song should be a soliloquy, with Mary's intimate feelings revealed. But the lyric was written to be sung to others. Casually, I said to Oscar, "Too bad the song can't be a soliloquy."

For a moment his face was expressionless. He was rethinking the scene. Then he said, "Of course. Good idea. I'll do it immediately." And he left the theatre.

Before the next performance Oscar had adjusted the lyric to eliminate "yous" and substitute "theys," and I restaged the scene with the girls exiting and Mary sitting on a box, down front, hugging the hat Emile had left and singing:

I'm in love with a wonderful guy.

After the first chorus, she did a small exuberant dance the two of us threw together in half a minute. Emile's hat was her dancing partner. Then she circled an upturned boat, one foot on the boat and the other on the floor, and afterward did a few awkward waltz clog steps on the boat. For the finish, she jammed the big panama hat over her eyes and sang the last note.

That night she tore the house apart. The ovation continued through the reentrance of the girls. From then on, the number was our highest peak. Oh, my God, we had solved both "Wash That Man" and "A

Wonderful Guy." As Dick Rodgers says, "Anybody can fix things with money. It's when things need brains that you have a little trouble."

Word had spread and *South Pacific* was a hit. It was a hit with the ticket buyers lined up at the box office, with the brokers who were already planning expensive vacations and new Cadillacs, and all the hundreds and perhaps thousands of people who are affected when Broadway has a new "big one."

We formed a company called South Pacific Enterprises to produce *South Pacific* scarves, dolls, perfume, underwear, sheets and pillowcases. We even had the audacity to hire the St. Regis Roof for our opening night party, a full-dress affair to which we invited all our friends plus the press.

Nedda and I chose to watch the New York opening—on April 7, 1949—from seats out front so that we could enjoy the audience. We knew we had clear sailing from the moment Mary Martin and Ezio Pinza started singing what we called the "Twin Soliloquies"—Dick's magical tune to Oscar's great concept.

The St. Regis Roof was a festival. There was extra excitement when Sam Zolotow, the theatrical-news editor and sleuth of *The New York Times*, came in with an armload of the next morning's *Times*. He called out, "It's a great notice. Nobody has to worry—it's a great notice."

I read it swiftly and, as one does, looked first for my name. To my horror it was not there. In giving credit for the authorship Brooks Atkinson had mentioned only Rodgers and Hammerstein. I was so angry I didn't care who heard what I said to Zolotow. "Why the hell did he leave my name out?"

"Oh, good God," he said. "I'll call him."

And it was lucky I protested, for the later editions carried a corrected line: "Rodgers and Hammerstein and Logan have given us . . ."

I knew then why people fight so hard to have their names in proper type. It's not just ego, or "the principle of the thing," it's possibly another job, or a better salary. It's reassurance. My name had been so minimized that I lived through years of having people praise *South Pacific* in my presence without knowing I had had anything to do with it.

That reached a painful peak when the 1950 Pulitzer Prize for Drama, which I had so coveted, was awarded to Rodgers and Hammerstein, but not to Joshua Logan. I was out of the country at the time, but Leo Friedman, the press agent for *Mister Roberts,* which was still playing, called the Pulitzer committee and asked them if the prize was for the songs alone.

"No, it's for the play. For the dialogue, the story."

Leo told them to read the program. They hadn't noticed my name in the small type. The award list had already been released, and although the committee telegraphed me an apology and sent me the certificate, and pointed out its error to the press, many papers didn't bother to print it.

I guess *South Pacific* was never going to behave exactly as I wanted it to. Even my mother got into the act. During dinner several nights later, she said, "You know something, Josh? You should *write.*" And when I said, "Mother, I just won the Pulitzer Prize for writing *South Pacific,*" she said, "Oh, *that.*"

South Pacific had added to my reputation as the nudity king of Broadway. The reputation started with *Mister Roberts,* when Leland came to me and said, "You've got to do something in this play to interest the women. After all, they're half our audience, you know."

In thinking about it, it struck me that what would appeal to women was the thought of the physical love they missed during the war, so when the crew takes its shirts off, a privilege given them by Roberts, I decided that women might prefer to see handsome, sculptured male torsos instead of the usual comic, flabby bodies in the corny service films.

But then I remembered something I had learned during my own part in the war—when I was doing a French civilian show. We had hired an act called The Brunos, a French "plastique" act, a combination of strength and male beauty. We had hired them in order to get as mistress of ceremonies the beautiful wife of the youngest Bruno.

I had been embarrassed by these almost totally nude men with small gold jockstraps displaying their Greek-frieze physiques in various muscular and artistic positions, and I had worried about my colonel's reaction when we showed the act to a thousand GIs, all male. But a thousand GIs thought The Brunos were great, and at the end of the act my applauding colonel was also slapping me on the back, saying, "Boy, that guy is built like a brick shithouse."

When I thought about it I realized it was identification. Each one of those GIs was saying to himself, "Wow, those guys have got great physiques. I used to look like that. They're men. They're one of us."

And from then on I used nudity whenever it was appropriate. The most fortunate use of it came with *South Pacific*. When we were working on the libretto, Oscar and I read aloud from Michener's book the last few pages of the first meeting of Cable and Liat. Young Cable comes into the hut and without even saying a word goes over and takes Liat in his arms, pulls her to him and kisses her. He gently pulls off her clothes and later there is "incarnadine proof" that she has never been made love to before.

This was a most erotic peak in Michener's book, but how could we duplicate it on the stage? We had to have a blackout for the act itself. But how could we tell the audience the moment the light came up that Liat and Cable had made sexual love? I solved it simply by suggesting that Cable take off *his* shirt. At the time, it seemed a shocking thing when I suggested it. Oscar said, "Well, you're nothing if not bold." But it turned out to be one of the most poetic and erotic moments in the play.

And again I discovered how much more stage nudity is noticed by the same sex than by the opposite sex. One of the toughest woman-chasing guys I know saw *South Pacific* on opening night and then saw it a year later. I expected him to complain about the loss of Pinza or a sloppier performance, but instead he said, "You ought to have those guys go to the gym and shape up—you know, the ones without any shirts on."

I said, "I'm a son of a bitch. Is that what you were looking at?"

He said, "No, but they used to look so great."

And a complete and parallel reaction came later when I had a nude girl, Nejla Ates, dance a belly dance in *Fanny*. It was only at the women's matinees that the house went wild. But my use of nudity compared to today's seems like an old lace Valentine.

Shortly after *South Pacific* opened, Lincoln Barnett, a *Life* magazine reporter and a former Princetonian, as well as a friend of Mary Lee's, asked to do an article on me for *Life*. He thought the story of a man who had had a serious nervous breakdown and then pulled himself together enough to keep on functioning in the theatre might be encouraging and moving for many readers. As that time, mental illness was such a verboten topic that many who needed help were afraid to seek it. It was hidden in the same closet as syphilis, TB, and homosexuality. His excellent article probably did more to make my name familiar to the public than the plays I had done.

But the article brought nationwide fame to someone else, too—Dr. Merrill Moore. For in it he appeared as a corpulent poetic saint, a New England Good Samaritan who picked up this ailing wreck and led him to mental salvation at the Pennsylvania Hospital.

As a new celebrity, Merrill Moore became to many readers not only a doctor but *the* mental doctor. The literate, the talented and the mighty lined up at his door or talked to him by phone. It is said that even the great Eugene O'Neill was sent to consult Merrill; Elliott Nugent quite openly talked about going to him. Reports came later to me that Merrill's first recommendation to a patient was that he should split with his wife, which quite often made the patient split with Merrill.

Since I was constantly being asked to come out of town in those days as an adviser or play doctor or what you will, I often found myself in Boston, and then Merrill was around, mostly to bask in the "incandescent discussions of working artists." I seldom consulted him, but I often took him to his favorite Greek restaurant. Later, as we talked in my hotel suite, when Merrill sat cross-legged at my feet like a blown-up child, I wondered if I was making a mistake allowing him to get so close to me and to my family. I didn't like his presuming he was in the theatre just because he had treated me. But when I'd even hint that, someone would say, "He's the man who saved you. You can never do enough for that man, Josh."

So continued his intricate, weblike involvement with us. He even presumed to make suggestions about my writing. It was then I found that I could not extricate myself from him. When I told him that I could no longer afford to keep him as my doctor, he asked, "Why don't you put me on your staff? I could be one of your publicity men. I'd be a business expense."

I was totally unprepared for the jolt I would get when I staged the second company of *South Pacific*. Naturally, the cast was physically different from the original. Janet Blair, beautiful and with a fine soprano voice, was a most charming Nellie. But she was terrified of being compared to Mary Martin. I had to assure her that I would give every element of her own personality a chance to be seen by the audiences so that they might soon stop comparing. Dick Eastham, who had understudied Pinza in New York, was more secure in the role of Emile.

Diosa Costello as Bloody Mary was the antithesis of Juanita Hall. Whereas Juanita had a face of Aztec stone, Diosa's was more like that of a frenetic witch doctor. She was terribly effective when she was allowed to move, so I let her move much more, instead of squatting still as Juanita did. Yet when she sang the songs "Bali Ha'i" and "Happy Talk" she was equally mesmerizing.

Certainly Ray Walston was a natural for Billis—an understated, sardonic and possibly wiser one than Myron McCormick's on Broadway, with his own prowling walk.

All four leads were in their way superb, and I was proud of my work until we showed it to our first audience. We simply put it full blown on the stage of the Majestic Theatre in New York on a Sunday, with the same sets, lighting and orchestra being used each night by the New York company, and we invited over sixteen hundred people to see it.

What I hadn't realized was that Dick and Oscar had evidently been so stunned by the hysterical success of the New York company that they believed *South Pacific* was only held together by the artists who played it, that it had no strength of its own. I, on the other hand, felt that it was a battleship, indestructible, especially since I had worked it out with all these new people.

At the end of the first act, with the sounds of the cheering audience still in my ears, I ran into the two of them backstage. They looked at me so angrily that I was startled. They went at me about what I had done to this beautiful play, how I had restaged it and ruined it.

I tried to explain to them that I had done what I thought was best, but nothing would make them believe that the company was a success. Fortunately, Leland came by and said he liked some of it better than the original and that it would make a million dollars.

Dick and Oscar still couldn't understand why I would let Diosa Costello move where Juanita Hall hadn't, and it finally developed into a series of seriocomic letters between Oscar and myself. In one of them he said to me, "You're a polo player. You should be allowed to ride your horse and swing your mallet wherever you want to, but second companies should be staged by croquet players—stage managers who can keep their feet on the ground." And I wrote back, "If it's staged by croquet players, it will be almost as exciting as croquet."

Finally, he resorted to something he'd heard about Gilbert and

Sullivan. He said Gilbert and Sullivan must be played exactly as it was originally staged, and it has been played exactly that way ever since 1875. My answer to that was a very carefully worded single, underlined, typewritten sentence which made him laugh: *"How would you know?"*

But in spite of the fact that the second company of *South Pacific* played for years to enormous houses and pleased every critic from here to San Francisco and back, they somehow never quite forgave me for restaging my own work; which suddenly, to them, had become almost holy.

I had been shaken to the marrow by this experience, and although I still have a letter from them offering me full coauthorship and direction of *The King and I*, a project I loved, I politely refused—a decision I will regret for the rest of my life.

But as it turned out, I wasn't out of it completely. During the writing of *The King and I*, Oscar suddenly sent for me, and I hurried to his office. He was shaking with emotion as he spoke. First, he made me read his lyrics to a new song for the show. He said he had started to write a song called "Tom," about the heroine's dead husband, and ended weeks later with a song called "Hello, Young Lovers." I was so moved by the beautiful emotion of the lyric that I figured that's why he asked me to come.

He said, "It's my best lyric, isn't it, Josh?"

I said, "Well, certainly I've never read anything better. But why do you seem so upset? You should be happy."

"I know I should, but I'm not," he said, with mounting emotion. "I finished it after digging away for three weeks. I thought it was my top work. I wanted someone to appreciate it. I sent it by special messenger to Dick and told the boy to wait for an answer, but he never came back. Then I waited for Dick to call me. I waited an hour. Then two hours. Then, to my horror, he didn't call that evening. He didn't call me the next day. It was hard to work while watching the bloody phone all day long. By that time I had broken out in a sweat. I began to think there was something wrong with the lyric. The third day I waited all day long, unable to work. A lost day. No call—nothing. I was determined not to call him. Besides, I was so frustrated my voice couldn't make a call. Finally, the fourth morning he called me, but it was a business call—Rodgers and Hammerstein office business—I don't know, something about a benefit someone wanted to do next March, or publishing some extra songbook, or allowing an amateur company to put on *Annie Get Your Gun,* or *Carousel* in concert form. I kept saying like an automaton, 'Yes, all right by me, yes, okay,' and Dick almost hung up—but just before he did he said, 'Oh, I got that lyric. It works fine.'"

And calm, contained Oscar Hammerstein stood there before me, broken to pieces. "You're the only person I could tell it to," he said. "You're the only person I know who would understand."

I tried to calm him by saying that Dick loves to understate things, and recalled to him how very coolly Dick had reacted to his first reading of our book of *South Pacific,* but nothing seemed to calm Oscar down. He started to pour out all the things he had kept bottled up for years, and then he stopped, abruptly stuck out his hand, saying, "Okay, that's it. You've helped me. Thanks."

I left the room as quickly as I could.

Meanwhile, my life was overflowing with activity.

Tom Heggen decided to take a large, old-fashioned apartment with Alan Campbell who was indulging in one of his rifts with Dorothy Parker. But Tom continued to spend a great deal of his time with us. He still had a key to our apartment, and sometimes we would find him asleep on our couch, waiting for us to come home. He had been extremely helpful to me when I asked him to read the script of *South Pacific,* asking him to be very strict with it from both a literary and military point of view. Tom was not too happy about this big musical as he felt excluded from it, and he picked up the script reluctantly. But his changes, though few, were accurate, and toughened some soft spots.

There was something tearing at Tom. After some drinks one night he told me he was unable to put down a word on paper. Every page he started ended in the wastebasket. When I asked him what he really wanted to do, he almost shouted, "I've gone through every feeling in the book about you. I've almost deified you and I've hated you. I've been grateful to you, then thought you should be grateful to me. I want to stop trying to top myself. What I really want to do is to *write another play with you.*"

I said, "Great, let's do one."

I had long felt there was a play in the true story of old Jim Kendrigan, a Havana football coach we had met in Cuba through the

McEvoys. He had become involved with some American mercenary pilots the Cuban rebels hired to invade Santo Domingo and divide it like a pie. It was Jim Kendrigan's job to keep the boys out of trouble, so he led them from one Havana bar and whorehouse to another.

The whole idea of these dislocated guys appealed to Tom. We even came up with a working title for it, *The Flying Tigers*. After a short trip to Havana, Tom said he wanted to visit his family in Minneapolis before starting work.

The phone was ringing. Nedda picked it up, and from the tense way she said, "Hello, Tom, what's the matter?" I felt my heart stop. She covered the phone with her hand and whispered to me, "He's on the twelfth floor of a hotel in Minneapolis. He's going to jump out of the window."

I got on the phone. He said he had read that a man he'd never met, Ross Lockridge, the young author of *Raintree County*, had killed himself that day, Tom felt Lockridge was like a twin brother. Everyone linked them. Each had had one big success. Tom was sure Ross had destroyed himself because he couldn't write anymore.

Nedda grabbed the phone and kept chatting for ten minutes or so. She urged him to go downstairs for a cup of coffee. We kept him on the phone for two hours. Only after he seemed to have gotten a grip on himself and promised us he would go to the lobby immediately would we hang up. The call had shaken us both and we tried unsuccessfully to contact Tom's brother-in-law. We didn't want to tell Tom's parents. A few days later, Tom arrived back in New York and began making notes on *The Flying Tigers*.

Tom's dependence on us had become so extreme that he seemed to do nothing without asking our opinion. We noticed he was taking barbiturates (bought in Cuba without prescription) two or three times a day, perhaps even more often. They seemed to relieve him somewhat of an inner ache.

One afternoon, Helen Hayes came up to our apartment for tea, and before she left someone asked her, "What are you going to do next, Helen?"

"I don't know. I have one secret ambition, and that is to do *The Cherry Orchard*. Of course, it would be a stretch for anyone to imagine dumpy me as a Russian beauty, but I'd like to try it anyway."

I remembered Stanislavsky's production in Moscow and how it had reminded me of plantation people from my childhood.

I immediately knew what I wanted to do, and with Helen. I would set *The Cherry Orchard* in the South, at the same period of Chekhov's play. Helen Hayes could play Ranevskaya as a romantic Southern woman—I remembered her mastery of the Southern accent as Norma in *Coquette*. The serfs would be freed slaves or children of slaves. But the orchard? What kind of bloom could remind my Southern heroine of the purity and immaculate innocence of her youth? The wisteria, of course, the wisteria I had watched all through my growing years, darkening our galleries and covering the roofs with pendant purple flowers. And I thought of the massive live oaks that lined the oyster shell driveways of the great houses farther south. I had seen trees which had been completely choked by the boa constrictor wisteria vines —and thus the oaks had become "wisteria" trees.

Before I broached the idea to Helen, I read all the translations of the superb play carefully. Some had poignance but never the lusty low comedy I remembered from the Moscow performance, and each was different. Constance Garnett had turned it into a sad, wistful, woe-is-me play and ignored the humor. Stark Young had come closest, but his still lacked the contrast I had seen.

I found a young Russian and asked him to translate the play with me verbatim, using only Chekhov's words and Chekhov's thoughts.

Meanwhile, Nedda and I were planning a trip through Spain in our Buick station wagon with Jo and Jean Mielziner. Just before we were to leave, Jim Awe told me, "I'm sorry, but I've taken a job in a production office and that's really what I want."

"You might have given me some warning. I could have got a replacement."

He said, "Don't worry. I've found a good replacement for you. His name is Joe Curtis."

"Is he honest?"

"He's from Concord, Massachusetts."

"Can he type?"

"Well, you'll have to take a chance on that. He was an Army court stenographer taking testimony from war criminals at Buchenwald and during the Battle of the Bulge."

"Does he know anything about the theatre?"

"He was company manager of *Anna Lucasta* for two years."

I searched desperately for other questions I should ask, and came up with, "Is he queer?"

Jim said, "I don't think so, but if you really want to know I'll make a pass at him and find out."

Joe Curtis, with his granite face, was almost forbidding looking on our first meeting. But clearly he was more than qualified, and I hired him. It was not until the letters he sent later to Spain that he began to reveal bits of his infinite warmth and understanding. He has been my assistant, secretary, editor, dialogue director, alter ego and friend ever since.

About a week before we sailed, Nedda and I came home and found Tom Heggen waiting with a book.

"To hell with *The Flying Tigers*," he said. "Here's a great book we can make into a play. I'm working on the rights."

"What is it?" I said.

"*The Brave Bulls* by Tom Lea."

I had only read the reviews, but I knew it had scenes in the bullring and on the farms where the bulls are bred. "How do we do the bullfights?" I asked.

"We'll figure out something—shadows or negative movies. Anyway, it's got hot dialogue and could make a smashing play. You go to your goddamned Spain. I give you permission. But concentrate on bullfights —take movies of them instead of your boring cathedrals."

It seemed ages since I had seen him so enthusiastic, so on fire. He talked as though his life depended on doing this play. I read the book overnight. It was surely a fine book. Perhaps rear projection could show the bullfights. Before we left, Tom insisted that we have a handshake agreement on dramatizing the book. We shook on it solemnly, and though he smiled, his skin flushed pink with emotion.

Our last words together were about the play, and, trying to keep me excited, he kept talking until we had to ease him gently into the elevator. As the sliding door closed, I glimpsed him standing there, looking suddenly abandoned. I wondered whether we shouldn't stay home after all and help him with the rights to the book—not to mention his laundry. Nedda and I talked it over for an hour or two. But we came to the conclusion that we had become crutches for him. He must be free to move, to write and to be Tom Heggen.

Six weeks later, after a bucolic trip through the stone cities of Old Castile and with one memorable stop for a picnic before the huge medieval castle of Coca (which I was to use many years later in my film, *Camelot*), we arrived at the Ritz Hotel in Madrid. There was a message for me to call Leland in New York. I called him from the lobby. His news was: "Josh, Tom Heggen just committed suicide!"

A moan escaped from me, and Nedda rushed to my side and put her ear to the receiver. Leland said Tom had been found drowned in eight or nine inches of water in his bathtub. "Couldn't it have been an accident?" I said. "Why was it so definitely pronounced suicide?" When I asked Leland if there had been an autopsy, he said, "Not yet."

We all knew Tom had bought hundreds of sleeping pills in Cuba, and I asked if an overdose had been involved.

"I don't know. They found lots of empty sleeping pill bottles in his medicine chest and razor blades in the tub."

"Had he cut his throat or wrists?"

"No. He was just dead, and I had to identify the body."

I was in such pain that I could not talk anymore. I hung up and we went to our room. Nedda and I sat holding each other for a long time in silence. Finally, she said, "We shouldn't have come."

"Of course we should," I said. "He didn't commit suicide, Nedda. Not this time. It was an accident. It had to be."

The idea of Tom's commiting suicide by drowning in a bathtub seemed physically impossible to me. How do you drown yourself in a bathtub? Lie in shallow water and push your head under with one hand? Perhaps if you accidentally fell asleep, possibly helped by sleeping pills, and caught water in your lungs. But how could a man slip down and drown without some spontaneous atavistic attempt to breathe? Who could hold himself underwater long enough to drown? Of course, with all those pills he might have become sluggish, but would he swallow lots of pills with a cool plan to lie in the bathtub and hope to drown? Ridiculous!

Still, the only important thing was that he was gone. Tom and his genius were gone from us forever.

Newspaper clippings of Tom's death arrived. There was more talk of empty sleeping pill bottles in the medicine closet. Nedda and I could have explained that: Tom never threw anything away, including wastepaper or empty shaving cream tubes, he just left the empty bottles on the shelf. And he dropped used razor blades down the bathtub drain to rust and flush away. Besides, would any man in the swift resolve of commiting suicide swallow pills and then put the bottles neatly back on the shelf before climbing into the tub to drown himself?

Unable to accept the lurid newspaper guesses, I wanted to go home and learn more. But the rest of the trip was all planned. Nothing I could do would bring Tom back, so we went wandering down to Seville, through Granada and back to Madrid, where Jo left us. Jean and Nedda and I headed north for Paris.

When I wasn't at the Flea Market I dictated my play, which I called *The Wisteria Trees*, in our little suite at the St. James and Albany Hotel where I had first stayed on my way to Russia.

One day, George Schlee asked me to have a drink with him. He wanted me to help persuade his close friend Greta Garbo to come out of retirement and do a motion picture. All I could say was, "Jesus! Yes!"

The day after he and Garbo had seen *South Pacific* she had sent me two beautiful red Venetian glass ashtrays because she couldn't find any of "Bloody Mary's shrunken heads." George felt that her enthusiasm for that show might be an inducement to work with its director. Also, George thought a Balzac story called "La Duchesse de Langeais" would be a good vehicle, and she, for the first time in years, found a story she liked.

Walter Wanger had promised to finance it and James Mason might star with her. The main thing was that I should meet Garbo again, and soon, so we could know each other better.

A secretive meeting was arranged in Vezelay, just an hour from Paris. Nedda and I drove there and wandered the streets on the lookout for a glamorous lady wearing a billowing dotted Swiss skirt and a big picture hat. I almost bumped into a gangling boy in very short pants, checkered shirt, Panama hat and sunglasses before I realized it was the fabulous Garbo herself, walking with Schlee. She was so lean and beautiful that it was hard to believe she was not the fourteen-year-old she looked.

Over aperitifs we talked for hours, about the Flea Market, about paintings and antiques, with only an occasional mention of "La Duchesse de Langeais." I promised to read the story as soon as possible, and told Garbo that it would be the highest honor to direct her.

That day, I never felt I was talking to a grown person. She had a child's laugh, and the things that amused her were childish things. Here was doomed Camille and noble Queen Christina and tragic Anna

Karenina suddenly transformed into Huck Finn. I defy anyone to make the person she is fit the women she has played on the screen.

I was on fire with the idea. If I hadn't started on the Helen Hayes project, I might have worked with a screenwriter and arrived at a script Garbo would have accepted. But I had to plead for more time, and later Wanger got into studio difficulties, and the whole project fell apart.

Schlee had worked hard and tactfully to make it happen, and I let him down with my delays. Of course Garbo has never returned, and perhaps she never really wanted to, but if only, if only . . .

Several weeks later we returned to New York and I started searching for the truth of Tom's death.

I studied the coroner's report which stated he had died of "submersion in fresh water in bathtub." But why had the coroner's report called it "probable suicide"? The newspapers called it suicide—without any "probable." People obviously wanted to believe he killed himself rather than the less dramatic but more likely accidental theory. Suicide makes a better story.

So, the legend prevails that Tom Heggen was so distressed by his inability to write a second novel that he took his own life. One theorist has written a book to prove that young American writers are often ruined by the Goddess of Success. Tom's life story was bent and his death slanted to prove the writer's theory.

Beyond its effect on Tom's family, I am not exactly sure why I was so troubled by whether Tom's death was an accident or self-planned. I certainly knew that earlier in Minneapolis he had threatened to jump from the window, though he did let us talk him out of it. I also knew that he took too many sleeping pills to calm his feelings of inadequacy.

That Tom was dead, that he was gone, was the terrible fact I had to face. I would never see him wrinkle his face or raise red blotches on his cheeks. We could never do _The Brave Bulls_. We could never take off into our wild, hilarious stratosphere of collaboration again. I would never again feel his sour disapproval of a small pompous mind. All about our rooms there were memories of him—photographs, letters, his notes in books, scraps of ideas. It was Tom who had given me, in spite of our one squabble about credit, the most satisfying, exhilarating, hilarious months of my life with _Mister Roberts_. I would never again laugh as loud as that. I would never again enjoy a bawdily poetic mind to equal his. I would never again care for another man as I did for Tom Heggen.

I don't know the deep hidden truth about him or his death. I do know there was a time when Tom tried to die. But I'm sure that the time he didn't try was when he did.

CHAPTER

16

The Wisteria Trees was so filled with memories of my background that I wondered if anyone else would even understand it. Everything depended on Helen Hayes and, since she was playing nearby, I invited her to Brookfield Center so that I could read the play to her. But Helen, though full of praise, gave not a smidgen of commitment.

So I decided to put the play on a back shelf for a while, and before long it was so deep in the files of my mind that I almost forgot it. This was helped by a most exciting offer from Robert Whitehead to do Carson McCullers' play of her own novel *The Member of the Wedding*, a Southern book I loved. I asked Bob Whitehead to prepare the contracts.

Then the next night I got a phone call with such terrible news I cannot remember who the caller was. Helen Hayes' daughter, the beautiful and talented Mary MacArthur, had just died of polio. I had directed her in her first play only a few months before.

Nedda and I rushed to Helen's house. Helen had always been small, but that night she was shriveled . . . shrunken . . . pitiful.

The day after the funeral, Charles MacArthur, Helen's husband, called and said, "Josh, you've got to save Helen. You must put on that play—and quick."

I had grown away from *The Wisteria Trees,* for my love for *The Member of the Wedding* was burning bright. But I said nothing of that to Charlie, just reminded him that Helen didn't seem to want to do it when I read it to her.

"Well, Helen doesn't talk much at first," he said, "but she believes the two of you could make something great out of it. She said so."

"Charlie, let me look the play over and see how I feel."

"Please, Josh, say you'll do it. Now."

"Charlie, I'll try—I'll certainly try."

Nedda, of course, was delighted, because she loved *The Wisteria Trees* and knew how much it would mean to my career to have written a play alone instead of being a perennial collaborator. She was sure Helen, once committed, would be great.

I hated to tell Bob Whitehead I couldn't do the McCullers play. And when he expressed his disappointment in his gentlemanly way, he made me even sorrier that I wasn't going to work with him.

Writing a play suggested to one by the immortal Chekhov was as tricky as walking on the wings of an airplane in flight. I knew I would be criticized. But if I had known what a violently confused reaction it was going to have, I wonder whether I would have ever undertaken it. He who tampers with a classic is apt to infuriate the self-elected authorities of the world.

But I tried. In about three weeks I completed a carefully revised manuscript.

With Leland, who wanted to coproduce, I urged Helen to tour the play first in the spring, then take a summer break and open in the fall in New York. Unfortunately for the production, Helen was in no mood to tour, and so though it was very late in the theatrical season for a dramatic play to succeed in New York, we went into rehearsal.

The cast included Walter Abel and Kent Smith, my old rival from University Players days.

The black actors who played the servants were outstanding: Ossie

Davis, Alonzo Bosan, Vinie Burrows and Reri Grist (the latter now an opera star).

Jo Mielziner's beautiful set had fan-shaped shutters that opened to reveal wisteria blossoms between white columns in the first act, green leaves in the second, and bare vines looking gnarled and twisted in the third.

Rehearsals were exciting. At the first run-through, with Helen in her little pullover, short skirt and flat heels, many were so moved that they were unable to speak. I began to believe that my play was better than I thought it could be.

I insisted on opening *The Wisteria Trees* at the McCarter Theatre in Princeton in the hope that a few of my former professors might still be around. Somehow I was hoping for my mother's sake that they might give me an honorary degree as they had Jimmy Stewart and Joe Ferrer. And I admit I was thrilled when the curtain went up in the theatre I had opened twenty-two years before as Sgt. Major Louis La Motte in the Triangle show *The Golden Dog* (telling bad jokes and disappearing for a moment when the stairway collapsed).

I made a few changes for Boston, eliminating as too gloomy the final moment when the ancient retainer Scott (Chekhov's Firs) is locked up accidentally in the deserted house—in effect buried alive. It seemed too darkly Russian to me. Besides, it was so cruel and heartless that it stole the show. I ended the play with the sound of the axes chopping down the trees.

In Boston we got some good notices, one superb, from Kevin Kelly, but there were a few reservations too, and I knew there was more to do. We postponed the New York opening and booked New Haven for one week and Philadelphia for two.

Sam Behrman told me, "It's good, except it's too close to Chekhov. Forget him and write your own play. Start from scratch."

It was a wise thing to say because the moment I took off on my own, just keeping the rudiments of the Russian plot, the scenes came to life.

At first, Helen, though determinedly cooperative, was a bit remote. I attributed that to her grief over Mary. Constant revisions also began to take their toll on her, and her task wasn't made any easier by having Charlie around pacing, worrying, listening to the audience. Once he even fainted on the lobby floor. This naturally upset her, and every time she worried, I worried.

The New Haven reception was much better, and a week later we went into rehearsal on the day we were to open in Philadelphia. I was surprised to find Helen uncommonly tense and sharp. She became particularly touchy when I suggested she make her first entrance at a slower pace, "in wonderment at invading the memories of her childhood room." I asked her not to dart about so quickly from one object to the other but if possible to move in awe of each remembered object. She looked as though I had asked her to do something obscene.

"Are you *sure* you want me to move *slower* on my entrance?" she said. "You're *sure?* Be awfully *sure.*"

"I'm sure, Helen. I really think it would be more effective."

"If I do that in a drawn-out manner, I will have to change my entire performance—my whole characterization."

I said, "No, you won't. I only meant for you to slow up just for that first short scene. The rest is wonderful."

"No, no, you said it. All these people heard you. I'll slow down when I come in and then I'll slow down for the rest of the play. I'll give the director what he wants."

She drove me to the point where I didn't know whether to say, "Please do it," or "Please don't do it." The best thing, I decided, was for me to keep quiet. Besides, I knew that it wasn't that which was upsetting her so. Her whole life had been dashed apart and her husband Charlie was himself so grief-stricken that he was unable to offer her support.

I had a bad premonition about that night.

Hoping not to upset her further, I didn't go backstage before the performance. The first scene played well, until Helen entered, but she moved in so slowly the audience must have thought she'd been drugged. Her drawled-out words seemed to be played at the wrong speed. It was like watching a faraway freeway accident, through a telescope. Leland and I stood at the back of the theatre, in cataleptic shock.

But Helen kept carrying out her baleful promise. The agonizing, sleepwalking slowness of her movements and speech lasted through the entire, now interminable, first act. After that, I shot backstage and said, "Helen, you win. Play it fast or slow, play it as you want to, and never allow me to make any suggestions to you again." Then I walked away.

Leland and I were so discouraged we decided to go back to New York at once. On the train Leland said, "I think we should close it, Josh. Take the loss. We can't bring in a performance like that. It's a public embarrassment to Helen and you. We'll go back tomorrow night and tell her. I'll bet she'll be relieved."

The next night, in Philadelphia, the house was full and the play seemed to be going well, but we were determined. At the curtain, we went to Helen's dressing room.

She did not give us a chance to say a word. In a bright, steady voice she said, "We must work, we must do everything possible to make this a good play. I will cooperate fully, listen to every suggestion. Let's all hold hands and say we're going to go ahead."

I took her hand, and so did Leland. For better or for worse, we had to go ahead.

Whatever the private hell Helen had been going through before, from then on she was the old Helen that I knew from *Happy Birthday* —prompt, eager, efficient, charming—and the cast, buoyed by her spirit, worked doubly hard for New York.

We opened at the Martin Beck Theatre on March 29, 1950, and though there was no question that it pleased the audience, I was still convinced the notices were bound to be difficult to take.

I had allowed my worryscope too much sway. Brooks Atkinson was not only favorable, he was lyrical. He wrote that this was better than *The Cherry Orchard*—and even I might have argued with him about that. John Chapman of the *News* was ecstatic about Helen's performance and the play, and the great John Mason Brown was most enthusiastic of all.

There were others, though, who insisted on pointing out how great the original was. Some, for instance, George Jean Nathan (like most "authorities" who never do their homework) kept blaming me for lines that were pure Chekhov and praising Chekhov lavishly for inventions of mine.

The play did sellout business and it looked as though we were going to pay off quickly. But as summertime came, Helen called Leland and me into her dressing room and said, "Let's close the play for the summer and open it again next fall, so we can *all* have a *nice* vacation." As Beatrice Lillie once remarked in a revue, "You could have knocked me over with a fender." After all that painful effort and all the expense and all her cheery promises of cooperation, to close it now and pretend we could reopen with the same momentum after three dark months— and to think I could have been doing *Member of the Wedding!*

Logan, Rodgers, and Hammerstein on *South Pacific*.
(JOHN SWOPE)

Ezio Pinza and Mary Martin in the final scene from *South Pacific*.
(JOHN SWOPE)

Helen Hayes and Walter Abel in *The Wisteria Trees*.
(VANDAMM STUDIO)

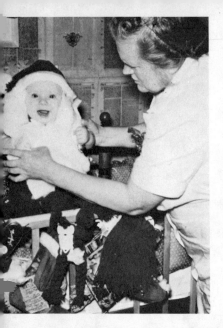

Above: Tom with Sue.

Left: Tom as Santa Claus.

Susan, Josh, Tom, Ann, Kathy, Nedda, and Johanna.

God help us, we closed the play the first of June, while it was doing strong business, and Helen took off for Ireland where she was photographed by *Life* magazine climbing across peat bogs. She returned refreshed for the fall run, but as the box office men predicted, the play never recovered.

Many years later, Helen told and wrote about her "odd, mad" behavior for years after Mary's death. She even said how grateful and guilty she felt toward me. I was touched, and regretted my bitterness when I saw her public attempt to apologize. I wanted to telegraph her and say, "Now *I'm* the one who should be having a breakfast of black coffee and humble pie."

There was nothing she ever did or ever could do that would keep me from loving her and thanking her for all she meant to me. She's one of the truly great people I ever worked with and she gave me far more pleasure than pain.

Nedda and I both wanted children, but there was no sign of one in the four years of our marriage. So, gradually, we stopped talking about a family until we moved to our large apartment and wonderful Finnish Aino came to work for us. Aino looked much like Mrs. Khrushchev, and she always spoke in a tone of high hysteria. When she was extremely happy, she sounded as if she were tearful. She could cook well, clean, sew, knit, crochet and tat, but her greatest accomplishment was her unbounding joy. On seeing the apartment, she wailed with approval. "Worry beeg, Meesta, Mees, planty room for babies. Mus' have babies queek to fill rooms!"

When I asked Nedda if she would be willing to adopt a baby, she said, "No, I'd be willing to adopt *two* children, but not one. My Ann was an only child, with no one to play with. And I always regretted it."

Fortunately, we knew a lawyer who could arrange for a private adoption of a child. He promised to try to find us one and then, when the time came, another. Aino immediately sat down and began to knit baby clothes.

Shortly after *The Wisteria Trees* opened, the lawyer told us a baby whose background was similar to ours was on its way and would be ready for adoption in a few months. Would we take the baby, no matter what sex? Of course we said yes.

My old friend, the English producer Binkie Beaumont, wanted to present *Mister Roberts* in London but only with a big name movie star.

We didn't have a name to offer until among the guests at a Theatre Guild cocktail party hosted by Armina Marshall and her husband, Lawrence Langner, we saw handsome and still young Tyrone Power. Nedda softly cooed in my ear, "Look at him! Wouldn't he be perfect for *Mister Roberts?*"

"Nedda, are you out of your mind? He gets a fortune for pictures. It would be impossible."

"Remember nearly missing Irving Berlin and *Annie,*" she said. "I'm not giving up like that. Ty used to come to my house when he was a child. I'm going to ask him."

She went over, and he said, "Yes." Furthermore, he was enthusiastic about the idea. He loved *Mister Roberts,* and it had been one of his lifelong ambitions to play in London, which his father had done years before.

Ty Power signed a contract to appear in *Roberts* for six months. For Pulver, we chose the former child star Jackie Cooper, who was now making a strong comeback; Russell Collins for Doc, and George Matthews for the captain.

Two days before we sailed for the London opening, our lawyer called to tell us it was a boy.

We stood at a huge plate-glass window and looked in at a sea of babies as the nurse picked one up in her arms. He was a wizened little thing with a face that seemed all nose, but we were close to tears and couldn't look at him enough. He was our son. And he would be safe in our absence with Aino and a practical nurse.

Without consulting each other, we had each thought of the same name for him: Tom—Thomas Heggen Logan.

We started rehearsals of *Mister Roberts* on the trip to London—using the squash court of the *Queen Elizabeth.* And the other passengers and crew provided an excited audience.

Right from the beginning, Ty Power had asked me, "Josh, please dig, will you?"

"What do you mean?"

"I've been in the movies so long that I've grown used to giving what they want—a 'Tyrone Power' performance. I'm a lot better than that, but no one ever pushes me anymore. You've got to whip me into being a great Mister Roberts. I know I can do it if you'll just dig."

I promised I would. And daily I learned more of what a powerful actor had been hidden behind those slick movie heroes, what a superb talent the public and the theatre had been missing.

Each evening we grew surer of our success. Of course, we hadn't yet seen the mammoth theatre into which we were booked. Binkie needed a large theatre to make back the costs of the production.

Jo Mielziner had been in London constructing a larger set to fill the yawning space of the Coliseum stage. He had added two decks to the original so that when it was lit, it looked like a battleship. We had to add about fifty extras so that decks would be used. All this made the show seem like an extravaganza.

It wasn't Mielziner's fault, it was something Binkie believed in. There was nothing we could do to remedy matters but to dim the lights on the upper decks. But it was totally impossible to scale that set down to the appropriate size.

So, although the performance was at the highest level, we got very mixed reviews. Ty had a huge voice and he was at his very best, but he and the play were simply swallowed up by that cavernous place and so was the rest of the cast. Furthermore, the reviewers obviously didn't "get" *Mister Roberts*. Ordinary seamen in the British Navy were more disciplined than ours, and so the childish pranks our sailors used to fill their boring days did not strike the English as funny, only as tawdry and rebellious.

Nedda and I guessed that *Mister Roberts* would run in London for the length of Tyrone Power's contract: six months.

We packed up to go back home and see our son. The morning of our departure a present arrived from Ty Power: a pair of very rare eighteenth-century Battersea enameled candlesticks. They were as distinguished, handsome and gracious as the man who sent them.

We returned to the most perfect child imaginable. Gone was the funny, wrinkled face with the dominating nose. He smiled at once, and that day he laughed so much that he kept unseating himself and sliding over onto his side—and that made him laugh more. He's the only baby I ever met with a belly laugh.

Nedda had had a child before, but Tom was my first. My new joys were bathing him, playing with him, talking to him and eliciting that laugh.

That Christmas, Miss Alice Witt, who was Tom's nurse by then, kept us out of the nursery for an hour, then summoned us. On a little red chair in his crib sat five-month-old Tom, dressed as Santa Claus, in red suit and cap, with a white beard of absorbent cotton. As if he had been waiting for us, he rang a large bell when we came in and burst into howls of laughter. It was the most exciting Christmas Nedda and I had ever had.

Alice Witt allowed Tom to do things we never imagined were possible for a baby of that age: to crawl around the room, for instance, and even down several precipitous steps. We watched in terror, but she assured us this would help him develop the proper muscles and a sense of distance and balance.

It was clear that, with our enlarged family, the house in Brookfield Center was too small. Also, we needed something closer to New York. We found just what we wanted on Old Long Ridge Road, near Stamford: a beautifully restored farmhouse, dating back to the seventeenth century.

In the grounds were two ponds, surrounded by enormous willow trees; one pond could be turned into a swimming pool. There was also a commodious greenhouse, and a four-car garage built like an early carriage house, with a second-story six-room apartment for the gardener. Since little Tom had a niece, Ann's baby daughter Kathy, we called our house, "The Large House of Uncle Thomas."

By this time Hank Fonda was touring the country with a company of *Mister Roberts* that would be seen eventually in Los Angeles—which meant by the motion picture colony. Because of the importance of that opening I flew to San Francisco the week before to see that the play was in good enough shape to have its full impact. I was shocked at how bland it had become. Fonda, of course, was impeccable. But the cast around him was more understated than he was. They were all under his spell. They were all Mister Roberts. They seemed smug and almost pompous to me, instead of ebullient. I rehearsed and tried to bring back the wild comedy, and I was so intent on improving the play that I didn't realize I was upsetting Fonda.

The night before it opened in Los Angeles I called him to say I was sorry that time had run out before I could finish my work. He said, "Thank God for that."

I was amazed. "Didn't you want me to bring it back to its original spirit?"

"No," he said. "I don't feel it's *my* play anymore."

"No, you son of a bitch, but it's mine!"

Leland told me that the next day Hank stormed into his room in Los Angeles and said, "If that goddamned Logan directs the picture, I won't play in it."

I was furious, as it had always been agreed that I should do the picture. But I knew I couldn't have given in—not if I wanted to preserve the energy, the freshness that the play could have. When an actor controls a play, it has a terminal illness. I couldn't give in to a star facing the panic of change. Not even at the risk of a temporary loss of friendship.

Rodgers and Hammerstein asked me to stage *South Pacific* in London. I was to arrive ten days before the opening, for, to save money and stage, Dick's favorite assistant, Jerry Whyte, would do the preliminary block-in directing based on my original.

Once again, no sooner were all the arrangements made than our lawyer called to tell us of a newly born child. Nedda would have her wish, a sister for Tom.

The infant girl was driven to our apartment at River House two days after the call. My sister Mary Lee received her from an intermediary and carried her up to Nedda on a pillow.

She had a little intense face, very much like Tom's, but with a smaller nose. We named her Susan after my mother and Harrigan for Nedda's father.

When I reached the Drury Lane to see my first rehearsals of the London company of *South Pacific,* I really expected to see a finished product. Dick Rodgers had raved about the work of Jerry Whyte, who had always been jokingly referred to as "Dick's hatchet man," and I was sure he would try and do the best possible job.

What I found reminded me of the "croquet game" that Oscar had suggested in our battle of letters. Every move on the stage was within a millimeter of the move that was made by the New York company, and every reading was a tape recording played at the right speed. It was perfect—and at the same time perfectly awful.

But most of all I couldn't believe my eyes and ears at the performance of Mary Martin, who to me could do no wrong. She was still charming, pretty, vivacious, but too *carefully* so. She was strident and mechanical. She lacked her greatest gift—spontaneity. Wilbur Evans as

De Becque had an excellent voice and was extremely attractive, but he needed confidence badly. And Muriel Smith, who had dazzled me as the original Carmen Jones, certainly had all the equipment to play the lusty old Bloody Mary, but she was confused and therefore bland. Even the acerbic, wise, amusing Ray Walston was a pale photograph of himself as Billis. It was Ray who told me that Oscar had tried to help direct Peter Grant, the young man who played Cable, but had given up.

Rodgers and Hammerstein were not around much as they spent most of their days before the opening at press conferences. I was so puzzled, I didn't know what to do. Yet I knew that if the show went on this way it surely would crash.

The biggest blow to my morale came when I went over to talk to Mary Martin and saw her shrink from me. I had just opened my mouth to speak when she said, "I don't want any changes, Josh," and when I answered, "Who told you I was going to put in any changes? Dick? Oscar? Jerry Whyte? Did they call me a polo player?" she just repeated it: "I don't want any changes, Josh," and her lips were trembling. Someone had given her the idea that I wanted to change all of my original direction, which was far from true.

I decided my best course was to avoid saying anything to Mary, and to work on the rest of the cast. Without moving a person one inch to the right or the left I tried to pump energy and excitement into the performance, starting with Muriel Smith, who began to blossom.

Then, studying the Drury Lane, I saw that Wilbur Evans was in an upstage pocket while singing his first song, "Some Enchanted Evening": he was hard to see and hear. So I decided to face Mary Martin and ask her permission to move him downstage the way I had done it in the second company. I pointed out that if that song failed, the whole show would suffer. Besides, I said, all she had to do was listen to him. But it meant that Mary would have to turn her face, as she had not done with Pinza, in order to be seen by the audience. She was unnerved by the idea, yet when Wilbur showed joyful enthusiasm at moving downstage, she agreed. We brought in a small stool and got the whole number moved down at least eight feet closer to the audience. That move downstage was the only change I made in that production.

But the reserved and careful Mary Martin I was directing now at the Drury Lane was still not the Mary Martin I had directed in 1949.

The night before we opened I talked to Dick Halliday about his wife, and he said that she really was terribly worried. "Not only does she have to get used to all these new people, but don't you see, the last time she appeared in London—at the Drury Lane—was in Noel Coward's *Pacific 1860*, and it was not a success. And Noel complained about her. She's determined to show them tomorrow night, and terrified that she won't be good enough. But don't talk to her, Josh. If you have the slightest criticism she'll lose her nerve."

I had a feeling that I should leave the theatre. I had done my job. I'd done the best I could under the circumstances, and I was ready to leave the stage door, knowing I was defeated and wishing that I had never come. I stopped as I remembered the shocking time years ago when Anita Loos and Helen Hayes and I were in 21 with Noel Coward soon after *Pacific 1860*.

"She's not very good, you know. She hasn't much talent," Coward had said.

I was so bowled over I couldn't look at Helen, and later when he left the three of us agreed that if Mary Martin was not good, the trouble lay with *Pacific 1860*.

Of course! That must be a large part of the mood that Mary was in. She was to face Noel Coward again on opening night, and also the London public that had seen her fail. And at the same time she was trying to adjust to all the myriad changes that come from playing a show with new people in every other role.

All stars who have had long runs have trouble adjusting to new faces, new readings, to say nothing of new chemistry. It pulls the plank from under them and they feel they're falling. It's one of the most painful and dangerous things in our theatre. As I had learned even so recently from Henry Fonda, any star, any person who has to carry a show on his or her shoulders, has built a protective covering. The covering for Mary had been smashed: how could anyone be expected to play the part of lusty, happy, healthy Nellie Forbush while quaking with fear?

I turned and walked into Mary's room, pushing myself past Dick.

When Mary saw me, her face turned white. "Now, Josh, really, I don't think I can listen to any more—"

"Mary," I said, "you are the greatest Nellie Forbush that ever lived. You created her, but now you've got her covered up with a veil. She can't quite be seen. She's draped in panic, in doubt. But it's a very thin disguise she's hiding behind. Mary, just let Nellie burst through it. I've doubted this way and I know how you feel. Listen to me, honey.

William Blake helped me get over it once with four short lines of verse. Mary, look me in the eyes and let me tell you what he said."

I felt I had at least caught her attention and I spoke the words quietly to her:

> "He who Doubts from what he sees
> Will ne'er Believe, do what you Please.
> If the Sun and Moon should doubt,
> They'd immediately Go out."

She looked at me for a long time and then came close, putting her arms over both my shoulders and placing her cheek against mine. Then she whispered in my ear, "Thank you, Josh. Let's rehearse."

"Now?"

"Right now. Here in the dressing room. I want to go through every song for you—and William Blake."

She sat at her dressing room table and sang "Wonderful Guy" in her original unrestrained, quietly jubilant way. I didn't have to comment. She could see by my eyes how I approved. Richard was looking at the ceiling, hoping to conceal the fact that his face was flushed with excitement.

Mary did all the songs, closing her eyes for a second before each one of them.

All I said was, "Nellie Forbush is back with us, folks. Back with us! Back with us!"

When the three of us left the stage door, it was pouring. Mary's chauffeur had an open umbrella, as their car was about half a block away. When we passed the front of the Drury Lane, we saw an endless line of people there in the downpour, many on stools, some with newspapers held over their heads, some with umbrellas, but most just getting drenched. The chauffeur told Mary that they were going to wait there all night, till the box office opened and gallery tickets went on sale.

Mary called over to them, "Thank you for coming so early, but we're not ready with the show yet."

They laughed, and one of them shouted back, "Sing us a song, Mary."

"All right," she said, and in a loud, clear, happy voice she sang "I'm in Love With a Wonderful Guy," and at the end she slipped her arm through mine and squeezed it. The crowd cheered, and I was just plain overcome. They kept yelling, and she kept on singing until she'd done every one of her numbers in the show, and the crowd kept on shouting and cheering. In pouring rain, she threw them kisses, and we went off to the car.

Mary was ecstatic, joyous, free. I thought again how powerful art is, the art of words. I might have talked to her for hours and not been able to do what William Blake had done with a few rhymed thoughts. He had taken a near disaster for all of us and turned it into a triumphant life peak.

Nedda and I had decided to make the trip to London the beginning of a trip around the world. With young children to bring up, there might not be another convenient time. So, three weeks later we were in a small hotel in Benares, India, when we got a cablegram from Nedda's daughter Ann, saying, "It's Johanna Lockwood Lester." Nedda had another granddaughter, who was partly named for me.

The next morning, we got up at five o'clock and went down to the nearby Ganges. As we were paddling along the greasy, pea-soup river, we watched the high wall of earth which had been worn and fashioned into many levels and steps. It was swarming with poor, near-naked figures of all ages, most of them very thin. Many stepped into the green water and scooped up handfuls of it which they poured back over their faces in worship of the holy Ganges. On higher levels, richer families cooked meals or gave alms to ragged beggars with broken or maimed bodies.

Close by us, a young woman held a tiny baby and washed its face with river water. She opened the baby's mouth and with a bit of the Ganges she massaged its gums with her finger. Eight feet away, the corpse of a dead camel floated by that baby.

It was then I noticed the man—a man whose memory will remain with me always. He was extremely thin and wore a small bit of frayed cheesecloth which scarcely covered his loins. His ageless face was universal. The startling thing about him was *his* gaze as he looked at *me*. It was clear he was wondering what I was, where I had come from, what I ate, what I thought about and what Gods I prayed to.

We wondered about each other for several moments. It occurred to me that if I was as far removed from him as he was from me, and yet we were both trying to live in the same world, we simply must know more about each other or we were both doomed. I thought, I'm in the theatre. I must do a story that would help us know the East, and vice versa. And I determined to find one.

Marshall, my kid brother, was in charge of the United States Information Service library in Mandalay. It could be reached only by the daily cargo plane that carried vegetables from Rangoon. We took that smelly trip and enjoyed seeing him again, and driving about in his jeep, and being in the beautiful green, green country dotted with hundreds of statues of Buddha.

I began buying native papier-mâche toys to bring back to the children. By the time I reached Japan I had a lurid collection of Burmese, Siamese and Indonesian toys.

Japan was spectacular. It completely bewitched me, and Nedda as well. Very few examples of Japanese theatrical art had been seen in the United States at that time. The wild, screaming Kabuki theatre, the sober, overly refined Noh theatre, the all-girl opera companies, the huge, agile Bunraku puppets (their masked puppeteers in black leotards)—so much opulence, melodrama and excitement.

James Michener was in Tokyo. We met him and his wife at the Press Club, discussed our enthusiasm for the Japanese theatre, and I urged him to write a stage or screen story about American GIs and their contact with Japanese culture, with emphasis on the Japanese theatre. Whether I convinced him that night or whether he had had the idea long before or got it independently later, he eventually wrote such a story.

CHAPTER

The story of *Wish You Were Here*. How can I put it: rags to riches, sow's ear to silk purse, also-ran to Derby winner. It was one of the most major minor miracles in modern theatre history. And with all the cliff-hanging suspense of *The Perils of Pauline*.

I had known Harold Rome for years. The man with the stern face and the laughing eyes. His *Call Me Mister* was and is a passion of mine. Arthur Kober, famous author of *Bella*, was a rounded, cultivated, warm and enthusiastic man with a twinkling smile. The two of them knew the Catskill syndrome thoroughly. It was Arthur's play *Having Wonderful Time* that was being musicalized, the story of one of the Jewish summer resorts to which young city girls—stenographers and switchboard operators—go for two weeks' vacation, hoping to find a mate. It featured a young girl, her elderly fiancé and her new-found romance with a law student waiter.

The story was so funny, the small talk so full of pretentious locutions, the search for a mate so naïve, so apparent, that I began to find myself intrigued. And hearing Harold's funny-touching songs won me completely.

They asked me to collaborate as well as direct, but I was worried about how we would attract the public. There was no part for a star. All of the cast were twenty-year-olds, and in those days there were few stars that young. Still, youth and beauty could be "merchandized"—we could make it a kind of Catskill Ziegfeld show. I pictured girls parading in scant bathing suits in front of grinning boys around a—yes, why not?—swimming pool. A real one dug into the stage floor of the theatre. It would be a spectacular setting for comic dives, a Catskill Aquacade, with lovely Jewish Loreleis in clinging wet bathing suits.

Harold and Arthur were fascinated by the idea of the pool. So was Leland. He became an instant coproducer. Jo Mielziner said it would work, but it would have to be permanently installed, meaning we couldn't have a pre-Broadway tour. But Herman Bernstein, our manager, was so excited by the pool that he said he would sell preview benefits to Jewish charities for three weeks before we opened and for two weeks after, to give us some kind of financial backlog.

Arthur and I followed the play closely in writing the book.

In a mammoth casting call for seventeen-to-twenty-year-olds we found some charming, handsome and talented young people: Phyllis Newman, eighteen; Florence Henderson, seventeen; Tom Tryon, just out of Yale; Jack Cassidy, Sheila Bond, John Perkins, Sidney Armus. And on and on.

Our script and Harold's score were almost finished, except that Harold was still trying to write a title song. I was so determined to get a hit record to help publicize the show that I kept sending the poor guy back to the piano. Twenty-three tries later he stole a melody from himself. A second act song, "Who Could Eat Now?" fitted the title phrase, so suddenly it was:

> They're not making the skies as blue this year,
> Wish you were here . . .

It was exciting, but I still didn't feel it had a climax—an emotionally satisfying ending. "Please, Harold, one more try—get an ending with sex." He went out, and came back smiling. He sang:

> They're not shining the stars as bright.
> They've stolen the *joy* from the *night* . . .

The previews were confounded confusion. The pool was the most beautiful set I had ever seen, and the cast equally beautiful and young with resounding voices. But many things did not work in the script, especially the main plot. One actress had to be changed, and we got darkly luscious Patricia Marand (I turned to Dick Rodgers for a gorgeous girl who could sing and wear a bathing suit, and he sent Pat).

There are no secrets on Broadway. Rumors of our plight and opinions of how to fix it hopped from the Forty-fifth Street Imperial to Forty-eighth, and zigzagged back to Forty-third, flew around the Astor Hotel and found food and rest in every restaurant and bar.

Nedda was eating an early supper at Frankie and Johnnie's steak house during one of these frantic days, when the waiter serving soup said, "Have you got rid of that leading man yet?"

She was surprised but decided she ought to listen to any opinion which might help me. "Which one?" she asked. "The comic leading man or the romantic one?"

"Don't ask me, lady, but you'd better get rid of him," he said, and was off.

Not having out-of-town notices to guide me, I invited several people I respected to see the show. Elliot Norton came down from Boston. He said it was beautiful to look at but the story didn't hold his attention. "I'm interested in that old man. Why is he such a minor role? He should come back."

Dorothy and Herb Fields saw it and agreed, but added that the leading girl was never in enough trouble to create suspense. "She blithely gives the old man back his engagement ring the moment the play starts, and she's free. What kind of trouble is that? She should be too afraid of that old bastard to break off. He should be able to lord it over her, bully her. It would give a threat to the story, suspense which is lacking."

I asked Leland for another week to work, but he was so disgusted with the whole venture he said, "Let's open the damned thing and take the loss." Leland was Lewis Carroll's Duchess regarding flops. "Off with their heads" was his motto.

June 25, 1952 arrived, the hottest and steamiest day in New York's history. The theatre had no air conditioning so we left the doors to the alleyways open and turned on roaring fans. The near-naked cast was actually sweating, and so was the audience. There was only one cool and one successful scene, the swimming pool. I remember thinking of it as a vast Impressionist painting in the middle of a city dump. The evening was a crying flop. There was no chance. No chance at all.

Nedda and I gave a drooping party at our apartment for the cast (with rented fans and blowers), and when the notices started coming in, the party melted completely away.

The next day, at a business conference, Leland begged me to close the show. I couldn't even listen. We had two weeks of sold-out audiences and as many afternoons to rehearse changes. I am always stimulated by challenge, even enjoy it; it makes me feel braver, more daring than I really am. I remember the doctor at the Pennsylvania Hospital who said to me, "You thrive in disturbed conditions."

My belief in all those kids who were hanging onto this play and us for their start in the theatre, my belief in inventive Harold and these accurate and tuneful songs, and in Arthur with his extraordinary insight into Jewish charm and vernacular, my regard for Jo's fantastically lush production—all of it, all of them, must be saved. I refused point-blank to close it.

Leland said, "Well, I'm not going to stick around for the death rattle. How long can a flop last? Nancy and I are off to tour the blue Aegean on Alexander Korda's yacht."

I said, "The only blue water I'm interested in is in that hole in the floor of the Imperial stage."

My urge to rescue the show now approached controlled mania. But as for fixing it, I didn't even know where to start.

I decided to sit in the audience that second night and pretend to myself that I was a paying customer seeing it fresh. I planned to react to what I liked or didn't like and remember everything without notes. What had the critics hated so much? Wasn't there *something* savable about it?

The curtain hadn't been up five minutes when I got an unpleasant reaction from something that I hadn't noticed before (mostly because it was such an integral part of Arthur Kober's original play). When Teddy gave back her engagement ring to old Herman Fabricant who had driven her up to camp, the sympathy of the audience left our leading lady and traveled off with the rejected old man. I felt the same way. It was as obvious as a sudden change in the weather. My God, Dorothy Fields and Norton were right! Fabricant must be made into a heavy, and poor Teddy must fear him and, better yet, be in absolute terror of her mother who dotes on the old man's money. Yes, that's much better! We'll have Teddy come to Camp Karefree because of the pressures at home which are driving her to the verge of a nervous breakdown. She has been bursting into tears too often when she should be happy. Her marriage to the old man is only a month away. Herman would leave her now *not* because she sends him away, but because he wants her "to stop all your crying and get in good shape for the wedding."

Of course! That would help. We must *care* for Teddy. Not feel she's aloof. Why didn't I see it before? She's our heroine. She's our story. I began writing more scenes in my head.

We had opened last night, a Thursday night. This was Friday. There would be two shows the next day. The cast would be occupied. If I could get Arthur to help, we could rewrite tomorrow, Sunday and Monday. I could give the new scenes to the cast Monday night and we could maybe get it in Tuesday night, six nights after the opening. It would be a rush but speed's what we needed.

Oscar Hammerstein had told me that he once figured out the arithmetic of "word of mouth," that theatrical phrase we all use so vaguely. For every person who sees a show, Oscar estimated that twenty people heard about it, whether it was good or bad—family, relatives, business associates, barbers, lawyers, and so forth. If it's *bad,* that person keeps twenty people away; if it's *good,* the talk could *sell* twenty tickets. So, if a thousand people see a good performance, twenty thousand others might want to see it.

If I could really improve it by the sixth performance I still had ten sold-out benefit audiences who just might leave the theatre recommending the show. I hurried home and called Kober. He had crawled into a hole somewhere near Long Beach and was incommunicado. Harold's voice sounded weak, but he gave me permission to cut any songs I had to. I rattled through the changes I had in mind, but he could listen with only half an ear. I could tell that he too had lost hope, which only made me feel another surge of mad determination.

Nedda and I drove to the country that night, with me practicing dialogue into her ear the whole way. She couldn't quite keep up with my racing thoughts, but she was dear enough to pretend to.

The next day, I dictated six or seven new scenes and made musical and dialogue cuts necessitated by the plot change. Joe Curtis had volunteered to come out and type. The next morning, Sunday, Nedda and I drove up to Paul Osborn's near Newtown, Connecticut. I read him the scenes and he helped edit them a bit. After an optimistic supper with Paul and Millicent, I started the hour drive back to our house in Stamford.

Over the car radio we heard Barry Gray, the radio commentator, who had invested in our show, welcoming members of the cast to his restaurant interview program. To my surprise, he introduced Leland with the jolly remark, "I guess 'our' show got clobbered, huh?"

I was excited. With these fifty-four new pages, and Leland there on the radio giving the play some publicity, we were on our way.

But what was Leland saying? "We haven't got a chance, Barry. When those fellas are against you, there's no use fighting 'em."

"Right," said Barry cheerily. "How long will you keep it going?"

"We have a couple of weeks of sold-out benefit houses, but after that, well, I'd guess we might run a week or so. As for myself, I'm off to Greece on a boat. This has been very tough on me. I'm sorry you lost your money, Barry, but that's show business."

Nedda and I didn't dare say anything for fear of my driving into a ditch.

Monday morning, I read the new pages to Harold and Arthur, but didn't wait for their reaction. The important thing was to get this new material in. How else could we sell tickets? We couldn't take an ad quoting the reviews; there was nothing good to quote. And our publicity people told us the columnists wouldn't print items about the show. Our only hope was to make people like it and tell others.

After the Monday night performance, our fifth, I read the cast the new pages. They felt it was better than the original and worth a try; at least it lifted their spirits. Then I handed out copies and told them it would all go in the next night, and to be at rehearsal the next day at one o'clock with as much memorized as possible. They were more than slightly thunderstruck.

At one the next afternoon, we ran through the new scenes as many times as we could. I said, "No matter what happens tonight, don't panic or run offstage. If you forget, you'll be prompted. Now get some coffee, grit your teeth and spit on your hands. We're gonna do it."

That night, a play from another world, a nether world, was seen on Broadway. Marshall Jamison, my assistant, stood in the pit beside Jay Blackton, the conductor, and read each line of the new scenes out loud like a Neapolitan opera prompter while the pale-faced actor concerned listened and repeated it in only a slightly louder voice. The show plugged jerkily along, and why the audience remained seated through it I will never know. There was no laughter; that would have spoiled the stunned mood. The fact that the play did seem to us better than it was on the previous night had to be the height of wishful thinking. There just couldn't have been any word of mouth that night; the audience was struck speechless.

The cast needed no prompting on the Wednesday matinee, and by the evening performance there was even a lumpy marshmallow smoothness.

The ninth performance, Thursday night, we really began to see a new show. If any word of mouth were going to start, it would start that performance. We rehearsed every day, and Harold wrote two new songs and soon laughs were rolling.

The third week had no previous advance sale and no benefits sold, so the audiences were sparse, but there were enough people to gauge the reaction.

The gross for that sparse third week was twenty-five thousand dollars, slightly less than half of a sold-out week, but I was impressed that we had had that many customers for a play that had been almost spat upon. Some poor bastard must be telling some other poor bastard to see it, or all the seats would be empty. But I'm sure the cast saw only the sparse houses and felt we were failing.

At the next Monday rehearsal I pulled all the eloquence I could muster. The despair was suffocating. We did rehearse a bit, but in the middle of it I got so low myself that I let them all go home—and I drove off to Stamford.

That night, after playing listlessly with the children, Nedda and I ate in silence. About ten o'clock, I decided to face the worst. I called the box office to check on what we had taken in that evening.

"Mr. Logan," the treasurer said, "funny thing happened. We went up two hundred dollars tonight over last Monday night. I wouldn't count on anything, but it's better than two hundred down."

When I told Nedda, she perked up. "Two hundred dollars! A few people talked, didn't they?" Then she added, "Oh, my God! Isn't it awful! We've got to wait twenty-four hours to find out what tomorrow night's gross is! With horse racing, we only waited half an hour."

I didn't go to rehearsal the next day, as they were going over new songs, but I did send a message for the cast that the box office had picked up a bit.

That night I called the box office again. We had gone up four hundred dollars over last Tuesday! On Wednesday matinee, up a thousand dollars; Wednesday night, up two thousand dollars. We woke the babies up and danced around the room to make them laugh. And son of a bitch! On Thursday night, it *sold out!* And we sold out with standing room for two years!

Soon, Eddie Fisher had a record of our title song on "The Hit Parade." The words "Wish You Were Here" were repeated exactly twenty times in each chorus, so when it was broadcast twenty times a day the title of our play got to be almost unforgettable.

Our company became a happy family: trips were made daily through the lobby to count the people in line, apartments were leased, cars were bought and several members of the cast dared to have babies. When a dream comes true, you soon forget that it was once only a dream.

David Merrick had acquired the rights to the French films *Marius, Fanny* and *Cesar,* a trilogy about life on the Marseilles waterfront by Marcel Pagnol. Merrick, a St. Louis lawyer, had had a few jobs in the theatre and wanted to be a producer. He asked if I would see the movies, in the hope I might be interested in the project. I didn't quite see the first film, *Marius,* as a musical, but Nedda and I found *Fanny* moving and hilarious, often at the same time. It was a great, almost classic, love story, and so beautifully done that I could scarcely imagine its being done that well again. Still, I called David Merrick and said, "I'm on fire to work on it. If you can wait for me, I'll do it with you. I have two commitments to finish first."

We agreed that we would offer it to Hammerstein and Rodgers, who were put on earth to do the score, and I hoped Oscar would do the book with me.

Knowing I had this magnificent project ahead of me, I went ahead with my other plans.

While I was preparing *Wish You Were Here,* William Inge had called me. The author of *Come Back, Little Sheba* was offering me his new play, *Front Porch.* He told me, "I think there's something sunny about your work, and I'd like to have some sun on this play."

There was tenderness, beauty, comedy and theatrically effective scenes in what Inge gave me, but the new play sprawled so that it was hard to comprehend. It was about an athletic young drifter and brag-gart, Hal Carter, who arrives in a small Midwestern town in search of a former college buddy. And it was about Rosemary, a ridiculous, touch-ing, awkward schoolteacher, who saw in Howard, a bachelor store-owner, her last hope for marriage. And it contained a scene which struck me as one of the most beautiful and revealing in American theatre, the scene in which Rosemary got down on her knees and begged Howard to marry her. There was a romance between the mus-cle-flashing Hal and the most beautiful girl in town, Madge, and their scenes together were filled with a hint of sexuality that for its time was daring. I immediately saw what a fine play this material would make if Bill would organize it properly.

I called Lawrence Langner, head of the Theatre Guild, which was producing the play, and said I would do the play if Bill would work with me on it.

Bill had taken a house in Old Greenwich and so could drive over to my Stamford house easily for meetings. At one of these sessions Bill suggested that Hal and Madge should never touch each other until they dance together. I urged him to write it that way. I also insisted he try to rewrite, putting all the action in a single set—the backyards of two adjacent houses—instead of his original sprawling six sets.

The major difficulty with the play was Bill's last act, which consisted of complete frustration for everyone. He even turned the beautiful Madge into the "town pump," an ending which, I was convinced, would leave the audience as unhappy as it did me. Yet each time I asked Bill to develop a more conclusive ending, he went away, worked hard and came back with the same one, only drearier. He was afraid of being slick, of pandering to the public with a "happy ending," so he kept writing this endlessly slow dimout. Everything was negative: Hal left Madge; Madge's rich suitor, Alan, left town; Howard left Rosemary; and Madge, besmirched, walked back to the dime store with local boys catcalling. It was such an attenuated rosary of disap-pointments that I had a feeling the audience might go to sleep. There had to be some kind of finish in the same language as the rest of the play.

He went off to try again.

About this time Norman Krasna offered me his latest play, *Kind Sir,* with the explanation that it probably couldn't be cast, because the only actors right for it would be Alfred Lunt and Lynn Fontanne.

I read it in one evening, and I was amazed again at the way Norman could take a small misunderstanding, a white lie, and turn it into a full-length, funny and even romantic play. A distinguished man, to keep out of the matrimonial trap, tells any woman *before he gets involved with her* that he is already married. It did not have the GI humor and lustiness of *John Loves Mary,* but it was brilliantly constructed and had the glamour and delightful aura of drawing-room comedy that had been missing from the theatre for years.

I sent it to Leland and he liked it too. I told him I had insisted with the Guild that he and I coproduce the Inge play with them, and that he and I would produce *Kind Sir* together, and that whatever the next production was, he was in on that too.

He thanked me, said "Great," but with no enthusiasm, and went off to Long Island where he and Nancy had bought a house. A week or so later, I received a note from him: "Josh, please forgive me, but may I bow out of all three of those projects? I just don't feel like producing for a while."

I was hurt, naturally, after all our ups and downs together, and wondered if I had done something to offend him. And then I said, "What the hell." I was a big boy now. I might just be able to go ahead without him.

Although Leland had always pretended to be tough, he was perhaps the warmest friend I ever had. I counted on his taste and advice even when sometimes it seemed erratic. If there is such a word in the American language as "class," Leland not only invented it, he lived it better than anyone else in our profession. I was always proud that he had grown to like me as much as he did and became the godfather of our son.

Before we began casting, the Guild and I persuaded Bill Inge to change the title from *Front Porch* to *Picnic,* for it was a town Labor Day picnic that motivated much of the action of the play, and it had an ironic quality when applied to the story—which in its present form was no picnic.

Theresa Helburn of the Guild had retired, so I worked mostly with Lawrence Langner and his charming and straight-talking wife, Armina Marshall. They helped Bill and me during casting. Langner's judgment was quick and accurate. But more than that, his enthusiasm was enough to lift us all through any problems.

Without Lawrence Langner there could have been no *Picnic*. I was so discouraged with the first draft that I gave it up. Lawrence gave nothing up. He held on to any play of quality with the teeth of a terrier. He "worried" a play into shape. One day he called me and said, "I've been working with Inge until we have two good acts and one last impossible act with so many negative scenes that I can hardly read it. But I think if we go into rehearsal, Bill will see how bad it is and give us something else. He's promised me he'll try. Will you come back in and take a chance?"

Langner's zeal got to me. I said, "Yes." It was then I knew what had held the great Theatre Guild together all those years.

The part of Hal required an uninhibited actor who could brag, pose, disguise his shabby background with golden stories and then collapse. Ralph Meeker, who had played Mannion in *Mister Roberts,* had the attractive qualities the role needed as well as the emotional range. After he read for us several times, we all agreed he was perfect.

I saw Madge as the girl on the Art Nouveau candy box—romantic, moody, sensuous and yet fundamentally innocent, even gullible. Bill Inge had said finding the right actress would be no easy task. But I knew there was a man who could solve any girl problem. I called Dick Rodgers. "Dick, I've got girl trouble again," and I explained the kind of girl we needed.

There was a pause that I recognized as Dick stepping into his private thinking chamber.

"Janice Rule. I'll send her over this afternoon." And sure enough, that afternoon "Madge" walked in.

Janice's beauty was and is extraordinary in this day and age. With her high cheekbones, long auburn hair, transparent skin and enormous eyes, she was better than Art Nouveau. She was pre-Raphaelite.

For Millie, Madge's teen-age, tomboy sister, who was bright but yearned for love, an unknown actress in her twenties begged to be allowed to read for me in costume, sure that I would think her too mature if I just interviewed her.

I was intrigued. A young boy-girl appeared onstage in blue jeans, a man's shirt with its tails hanging out and a little Confederate corporal's cap. Her face was scrubbed shiny, and she spoke with a slight impediment as if she were wearing braces. She electrified us all. There was our Millie, with all her various emotional and comic shadings. And that was the beginning on the New York stage of one of our greatest actresses, Kim Stanley.

The role of the hearty yet haunted schoolteacher, Rosemary, required still another bravura performance. An unknown actress came onstage to read, and the impossible happened again. This odd, roughhewn woman with a strong Middle Western accent made it clear that she was at heart a tender, yearning human being. It was Eileen Heckart, and our cast gained even further stature.

For Madge's mother, Flo, a woman whose husband had deserted her, I chose an actress from *The Wisteria Trees* who still had enough glamour to suggest that Madge's mother was once as beautiful as Madge—Peggy Conklin.

We needed a Norman Rockwell type for Howard, Rosemary's dedicated bachelor, and a good actor whose career had been a string of bad luck read for us with embarrassing accuracy—Arthur O'Connell.

None of us, though, was really clear about the character of Alan, Madge's suitor and Hal's college chum. So we closed our eyes and cast the part as though we were pinning the tail on the donkey. At least he was old enough to be Hal's senior class friend and tall enough to go out with Madge.

For the bit part, Joker, a young filling station attendant who made a one-line pass at Madge, there applied a handsome young man who had left the Yale Drama School and was selling encyclopedias to support his wife and three children. He got the part of Joker and he also became Hal's understudy. His name was Paul Newman.

The understudy we chose for Madge and Millie was talented enough to play either one of them. Her name was Joanne Woodward.

I asked Nedda to come to the first reading of the play so she could see the marvelous cast.

In the reading the play jumped to life immediately, except for that ephemeral last scene. At least by that time Langner and I had prevailed upon Bill to eliminate Howard's desertion of Rosemary.

But what Bill hadn't taken into account was how dynamic Hal and Madge's relationship was to an audience. I felt it would seem artificial, indeed inartistic, to separate these two people. Lawrence felt the author would be criticized for straining to get an unhappy, Chekhovian inconclusiveness, unsuited to the play he had written up to then.

After the reading, Bill came home for lunch with Nedda and me, and asked Nedda bluntly what she thought of the play.

She answered just as bluntly, "I loved it with all my heart, every minute of it, until the end, and then I just hated it. I hated the way those two were separated after having my hopes encouraged. I was disappointed and frustrated."

"But we can't just have a 'corny' happy ending."

I jumped in with, "It wouldn't be corny or happy. If Madge left with Hal, a worthless braggart with no money and no real job, it would ultimately be a disaster. Oh, they'd have a bit of sex all right, but no security and not the decent life she and her mother had dreamed of. She'd obviously end up where her mother is, deserted by her man, saddled with brats and destitute. It would be grim history repeating itself. Is that happy? Is that corny?"

I could see Bill suddenly flush and stand up. He said, "What if Madge appeared at the door with a suitcase, wearing a flowery chiffon dress, tall six-inch heels, and a picture hat? She says, 'Mom, I'm going to Tulsa.' Her mother groans and begs her to stay, holding her, pleading with her, but Madge cannot be deterred. She pulls away from Flo—breaks the umbilical cord—and walks slowly and inevitably toward the bus station—while her mother collapses sobbing on the steps."

Nedda and I were touched by the strong feeling he had created. He said he'd write it immediately, and left.

After lunch, I announced to the cast, Armina and Lawrence what Bill had outlined, and everybody cheered. Everybody said they had found the original ending as flat as I had.

Our celebration was premature however. Bill Inge did not appear the next day, and when he didn't appear on the third day, I knew he was backtracking.

On the fourth day he came and handed me a new third act. It was virtually the same one I had seen before, only much, much longer and more turgid. Hal was thrown out of town a little more slowly this time, and Madge still walked back to work at the dime store, to an extra page of catcalls from the local boys. I was so discouraged I almost gave up.

I didn't dare show it to the cast. It would destroy their morale. I just asked the stage manager to take over the rehearsal while I went out into the lobby with Bill. I told him with passion how they had been looking forward to a less depressing ending. This one would kill their spirit. "Bill, please, just write the one you outlined. If it isn't good we won't use it. We already have this version. Let's at least *see* another one."

He was very angry. *"All right,* I'll write it," he said. "But *I want you to know I don't approve."* He turned sharply from me and left.

The next morning he brought a last scene, exactly as he had outlined it to Nedda and me. The cast leaped on it like ravenous animals. Without question, it struck the right note. It was satisfying, yet with a hint of the implied tragedy that ran through the play.

After a week of rehearsal, it was clear that the actor who played Alan was wrong. Since Paul Newman was so good in his bit, I asked Bill if we couldn't reverse the ages of Hal and Alan, making Alan a freshman who hero-worshiped an upperclass Hal at college.

Bill liked Newman so much that he rewrote the part quite quickly, and we made the switch. For a while it seemed all our problems were over.

I asked Marshall Jamison to find a record with a rhythmic tune for Hal and Madge to dance to. He eventually came up with an arrangement of "Moonglow" that seemed ideal. It was a "play along record" for student soloists to practice with, a disc of only rhythm and harmony with the melody left out. Against the insistent rhythm, the slow jitterbug dance that Meeker and Rule did made the moment a memorable erotic experience.

Because I had a cast of true artists, I tried to give them complete freedom in rehearsal. I remained an observer, an editor. I told them to sit and stand when they felt like it. Then if anything seemed confused or wrong, I might throw out a hint. In a word, they'd act and I'd handle traffic.

With actors reared in the old school, this would not have been possible. But with this gifted cast, I knew the play would gain from their instinctive gestures and readings. Because of my permissiveness I became, at least during our rehearsal period, the most popular director ever.

Bill Inge came in and out like a shadow at twilight. If he was unhappy, we didn't know it. Nor did we really know it when he was happy. He watched the rehearsals with the face of an impassive, blue-eyed Buddha.

Our pre-Broadway tour began in Columbus, Ohio. The cast gave an exciting performance at the Columbus opening, but there was some-

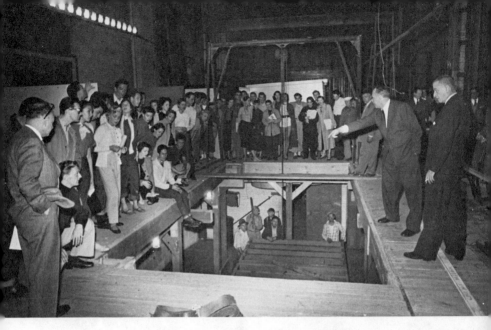

Digging the swimming pool for *Wish You Were Here*.
(LENT BY THE MUSEUM OF THE CITY OF NEW YORK)

The swimming pool in action. (LENT BY THE MUSEUM OF THE CITY OF NEW YORK)

The set of *Picnic*. Ralph Meeker holding forth to, on left, Kim Stanley, Paul Newman, Eileen Heckart, Arthur O'Connell, and Peggy Conklin, while Janice Rule listens from stair railing and Ruth McDevitt from right stoop.

(ALLAN GRANT, TIME LIFE PICTURE AGENCY © TIME INC.)

Picnic.
Ralph Meeker and
Janice Rule.
(ZINN ARTHUR)

Wedding for Rosemary. Left to right: Ruth McDevitt,
Reta Shaw, Arthur O'Connell, Eileen Heckart, Kim Stanley,
Elizabeth Wilson. (ZINN ARTHUR)

Charles Boyer and Mary Martin in *Kind Sir*.

Josh waiting to make
personal appearance on
the Ed Sullivan Show
done in his honor.
(ZINN ARTHUR)

hero. _We_, the creators, think this _slob's_ heroic!! They don't realize that _we see_ those unattractive things about him as clearly as they do. To them, a true hero wouldn't brag, wouldn't lie, wouldn't show off, wouldn't be a bit sweaty at times—but _they_ think _we_ don't feel that way. They think we believe everything he does is _attractive_. And that all fits with what David Merrick said.

I called Bill Inge and told him what I had discovered.

"Josh, if you can think of anything to do, do it. Write it down and I'll okay it. In the meantime, just put it in, if you feel it will help." He obviously thought it was a disaster.

Lawrence and I decided the most reliable character to put across our attitude toward Hal was Alan. All the ladies adored Paul Newman. Here are the lines we put in, although they were changed later for publication:

FLO: But a fraternity! Don't these boys have more . . . breeding?

ALAN: Maybe, but fraternities like to pledge big athletes— But I know what you're thinking, Mrs. Owens.

LO: How did the other boys feel about him?

LAN: They didn't like him, Mrs. Owens. When he came around, every man on that campus seemed to bristle. When I first met him I couldn't stand the way he bragged and swaggered and posed all over the place, and then I found out that Hal's really a nice guy, believe it or not.

We checked it with Bill Inge by phone. He changed a word or two we put it in. From that night on, the play was a hit. The audience w exactly where we stood on the subject of Hal and where they d.

e opened in Boston to out-and-out enthusiastic reviews and packed ences. Tennessee Williams hugged me and shouted that he loved here remained only small bits to perfect.

anting further reassurance on the artistic integrity of the ending ad, I met Elliot Norton and let him read Bill's previous ending, lid the same with the visiting English critic, Kenneth Tynan. and Norton both felt as we did and so did Williams. "His first is depressing without even being tragic," said Elliot.

opened _Picnic_ in New York, February 19, 1953, to rapt atten- emendous laughter, suspense, tears, "ohs" and "ahs," silence and

thing about the play that was wrong, something intangible that clo
the reaction. Why hadn't we sensed this before? It takes an audien
make cataracts drop away.

The next morning, the reviews were divided. One man talked
poetic beauty of the play, another was offended by certain lines
tions, particularly those of Hal. Bill Inge's face was puffy and
white. He could scarcely talk when I asked him how he felt.
tered a bit and went to his room, and on from there to New Y
out seeing anyone. He never saw another performance until
tour ended.

Back in Columbus, I looked for a catalytic agent for those
tious elements of the play. We had three more towns bef
New York.

We expected a warmer reception in St. Louis, Bill Inge's
but the reviewers flaunted the play to mock its author, wh
newspaper theatre critic there. The attack was so violen
subscribers canceled tickets, and it looked as though *Picni*
dle away before it ever reached New York. One night,
less than a hundred seats sold, Leland and Nancy Hayw;
it, and I felt I couldn't bear to face their condescension
ingly enough, they felt that whatever was wrong coul
they urged me not to give up.

In Cleveland, I found white-faced, black-moustache
in the lobby. He told me that since we were going to
Fanny he wanted to become familiar with the way I
was welcome. "You just stick around, and if you o
solve this play I'll reward you some way—maybe with

The Cleveland reviews, with the exception of W
called *Picnic* one of the finest American plays, wei
ones we had gotten in St. Louis.

I asked Merrick the reason for this dichotomy
sure," he said, "but it has got to have something t
character. Every time he comes on, I bristle. I o
swaggers, brags and poses all over the place." I li
still puzzled.

That night, two men came up the aisle talkin
only two very vehemently spoken words: *"Some*

Hero! I felt as though I were in a comic
bulb had turned on in my head. Hero? *Th*

even a sexual hush in the audience when Madge and Hal danced the slow jitterbug. The play I almost gave up was to be my biggest dramatic success.

Yet, when the play was published, Bill wanted to print his original ending. I warned him that would hurt his chance for the Pulitzer and the Critics' prizes, which were pending, so he reluctantly stuck to our playing script.

But, strange as it seems, over the next fifteen years, to fill in some of the gaps caused by his failures, he rewrote the last act of *Picnic* hundreds of times, and twenty years later got a different version produced under the title *Summer Brave*, which was later brought with unfortunate results to Broadway.

To me, it is one of the saddest moves in a pitiful life. It's as though he killed his favorite child just before killing himself (which he finally did). Perhaps he can be excused—though I can never excuse him—nor, I'm sure, could Maxwell Anderson—for going back to his original ending with Madge walking to the dime store—a Madge who has just had a public affair and is now, it seems, "fair game." To leave his leading lady a lesser person than she started out to be is to me unforgivable.

But almost more important, whatever possessed Bill in those painful years of failure to destroy the greatest scene he ever wrote—the scene in which Rosemary gets down on her knees to beg Howard to marry her? In *Summer Brave*, Howard *agrees to marry her* early in this scene, and thus the agony of her rejection is no longer there.

Ego plays strange tricks, and the burden of gratitude even stranger ones. Bill was able to accept my single set concept for the play in place of his diffused settings. He incorporated into his script the lines we all put together to describe our onstage attitude toward Hal. All of this became part of the printed William Inge script. He also accepted the wonderful notices from all quarters, the two years of sold-out houses in New York and on the road, and the royalties with which he bought, among other things, a Modigliani. He accepted graciously as sole author the Critics' Award and the Pulitzer Prize, the huge movie sale and the worldwide success of the movie itself, and yet he would not give up until he had announced—with his finger pointed at me—how foolish the world was to like this golden play.

Bill is dead now. His lonely life is over. I cared for him in the years before as much as he would allow anyone to care. I helped bring him his biggest success, but no one was allowed to bring him what he lacked most and must surely have wanted more than he could say—love and someone to love.

How could my bloody worryscope push its ugly snout up through that vast expanse of 1953 success and find a single thing worth pestering me about? But it did.

Nothing could pull me out of my downward swoop. Here I was loaded with hits: at the very next theatre to *Picnic*, *Wish You Were Here* was selling out; *South Pacific* was playing to capacity audiences both in New York and London; and there was a fine road company of *Mister Roberts* with Tod Andrews which was breaking records everywhere. Why, then, did I persist in feeling that there were dark clouds coming up over my horizon?

Rodgers and Hammerstein brought a ray of sunshine through my gloomy clouds by being truly impressed by the French movie, *Fanny*. Oscar particularly wanted to settle the contract agreements quickly.

The gloom came back in a rush, however, when they insisted that the credits begin "Rodgers and Hammerstein present FANNY," with no other producer mentioned. Although this production would be Merrick's chance to establish his name, he agreed to that condition, asking only that below the title there be another line saying "In association with David Merrick." The Rodgers and Hammerstein lawyers sent back a message, "No. Forget the whole thing."

Merrick had spent years and taken many trips to France, clearing the rights to the trilogy, had personally persuaded Pagnol and paid him thirty thousand dollars; also, he had lined up enough backers to finance the production. Certainly he deserved some credit as producer. I put his case before Oscar with all the eloquence I could muster.

Oscar told me he had never wanted to do any show more than this one, but that Dick was adamant. Rodgers and Hammerstein could never be persuaded to share credit with an unknown. Oscar sounded so unhappy that I didn't press the point any further.

Years later, just before he died, Oscar said to me, "We should have done *Fanny*. To hell with the billing. We should have done *Fanny*."

In spite of everything in our business dealings, Oscar was one of the best friends I ever had and, I suppose, in our profession, along with Irving Berlin, the most talented, the man with the greatest range. Our differences were violent but stimulating. Losing him and Dick on *Fanny*, however, was another Rodgers and Hammerstein body blow.

I staggered about, cursing my fate. I wouldn't have Dick's peerless melodies, and I wouldn't have Oscar's warm, human lyrics. Dick had been my friend since he first took a chance on me on *I Married An Angel*. Although our differences had grown more heated at times than mine with other people, I still had a respect for his judgment on every aspect of the theatre that I have never quite had for anyone else.

Theatre people are generally considered by others to be a special breed. Theatre people can fight each other like wild beasts in a jungle, like shrill, keening housewives, and strangely enough at the same time love each other with a devotion that lasts a lifetime. I feel that way about Rodgers, Hank Fonda, David Merrick, Mary Martin, Helen Hayes, Paul Osborn, Harold Rome, and on and on—all of them. I would do anything for them and I'm sure they would do anything for me, no matter what we have said or what we are going to say in the future.

Merrick, who has since become America's most famous producer excepting perhaps Ziegfeld, has been called everything from "The Undertaker" to "The Abominable Showman." Yet he was from the moment I met him, calm, brilliant and extremely realistic. He had always known that Dick and Oscar would want to shut him out, and had thought of alternatives to keep me interested. He came up with some exciting suggestions.

Number one was the distinguished playwright, S. N. Behrman, to collaborate with me on the book. Although I knew Sam fairly well, I wasn't sure he would be willing to collaborate with anyone. However, when we showed him the picture he soared as high as I had, and soon we were a soaring team. We decided first to translate all three French plays (which had preceded the movies), hoping to capture the Marseilles flavor and also to become completely familiar with the salty characters. It was going to be a trip across quicksand as there was so much argot. Those translating sessions are among my dizziest and highest memories. We played with words and phrases in swooping exchanges of wild ideas. If I never finished the play, I would be rewarded enough just by meeting daily with Sam, the only man I ever knew who could charm birds off trees.

We still had the problem of finding a strong enough lyricist and composer to make the project work, and my first tentative suggestion was Harold Rome, whom I had grown to respect during *Wish You Were Here*. Sam was hesitant—until I sat him down and sang him the entire scores of *Wish You Were Here* and *Call Me Mister*. He was enchanted, or pretended to be in order to shut me up.

David Merrick wanted Alan Jay Lerner and Burton Lane, but at the moment they weren't available, so Sam and I urged him to accept Harold. We approached Harold, who agreed to give it a try.

In the middle of all this, in June 1953, Princeton made me a Master of Arts (honoris causa) and I made a speech to the senior class. Mother was there and was guardedly pleased.

I had to start thinking about the cast for Norman Krasna's *Kind Sir*. We hit on the idea of Joan Crawford; she had not played on the stage before, but we had heard she was looking for a vehicle.

She thought the play delightful to read, and I asked her if she would play in it.

She said, "First, I want to read at least two acts from the stage, so you can see if I project properly."

Norman and I excitedly arranged a reading, and Joan Crawford read two acts for us, and thrillingly. Then she read the third act. It was as though she had been on the stage always.

We were so delighted and relieved that we said, "You are wonderful. We loved you. Let's sign the contract."

But she said, "Oh, no, never. I just wanted to know whether or not I could do it, for my own satisfaction. I could never play a long run on the stage. I'd be bored to death. But thank you for letting me make the experiment."

This was a new experience for us—planned frustration. Norman left me to hate the world by myself while he went back to California. Then fearing I might lose faith in the project, he called me two days later with the news that Charles Boyer had read it and was willing to play the man, if we could find the right leading lady.

"In that case," I said, "I'm going to fly to London and ask Mary Martin, who is finishing *Pacific* in two weeks."

Nedda and I took off almost immediately, for not only did I want to talk to Mary about *Kind Sir*, but also I wanted to tell her more about *Fanny*, which we had once discussed. In fact, if I had had enough scripts available, I would have signed her up for the rest of my life.

CHAPTER

After a year's run, *South Pacific* was still filling that beautiful Drury Lane in London, and the English audiences were as much in love with Mary Martin as I was.

Mary and Dick greeted us warmly and took us to their apartment for supper. She seemed to enjoy my reading of *Kind Sir,* and asked for time to think it over. The thought of playing opposite Charles Boyer delighted her, and she seemed to like the possibility of *Fanny*'s coming afterward.

Flying back, though, I had the terrible feeling that she would do neither of them, and that we wouldn't hear from her ever again. None of this doubt did I dare mention to Nedda, for I knew what she'd say.

Sam Behrman, Harold Rome and I, pushing like hell, finished a rough draft of the first act of *Fanny* and had sketched out the second, when Mary Martin came home. By now she had become enthusiastic about *Kind Sir,* and when we screened the movie *Fanny* for her, she, like all of us, fell in love with it.

Norman, though, was pressing me for an answer to give Boyer, so I told Mary that since Boyer was available now, we should take advantage of it and do *Kind Sir* right away. It would be an opportunity to show the world how good she could be in a straight play—and besides would give us a chance to finish *Fanny* at a normal pace.

She agreed, and I decided that although my name would be listed as producer, my silent coproducers would be Mary, Boyer and Krasna, who would be sharing everything equally. Jo Mielziner would do the sets and the legendary Mainbocher, the costumes.

I wanted an all-star cast, and I got one: Meissen-made Dorothy Stickney to play Mary's older sister, and my old pal Frank Conroy (Mr. Brink) for her husband. To play Mary's close friend and companion, Margalo Gillmore, and Margalo's real-life husband Robert Ross as her stage husband.

Things were going too well. What could go wrong?

When I said we would open in New Orleans, everyone thought I was going out of my mind (and I probably was), but I convinced myself it was a brilliant stroke. I wanted to be far away while we made changes, and I also knew that opening in such an unusual place would collect us some national publicity. Deep down, I had a childish motive. I wanted to show off a bit to Louisiana, and have all my aunts, uncles and cousins read about me in their local newspapers. There was also the pleasure of playing in a city with great restaurants.

The whole venture so excited me that I found myself unable to sleep.

When rehearsals got underway, I found that I was not behaving as usual. After I had staged a scene for the first time, I let Marshall Jamison take over so that I could take a walk to cool off. That happened several times. Then I noticed that our butler, Monsen, was often in the back of the theatre, and each time I went up the aisle to ask him what he wanted, he offered me a sleeping pill, with the explanation that it was on the prescription of Dr. Merrill Moore, who had flown in at Nedda's request. And I didn't even remember that I had seen him! I gulped the pills down, several times a day, thinking of Tom Heggen, and wondering if it wasn't dangerous to take so many, but they did calm me a bit and I kept on directing.

* * *

One night during the first days of rehearsal, Nedda and I were at dinner at Sardi's when Jim Michener came over to my table. He told me a new novel of his was being offered for sale by telegram to the movies, at the end of the week. "Josh," he said, "the telegram is being sent out next Friday. Maybe you'd like to accept its terms. I'd love you to do it. It's called *Sayonara*—the Japanese word for 'good-bye.' There are two intertwined love stories, one that ends in a double suicide and the other in a parting. It's about the GIs from Korea and the Japanese girls they meet on leave in Japan. The girl in the main love story is an actress in the Takarazuka all-girl opera company."

It was the same background Jim had talked about a year before in Tokyo. Jim went on to tell me that Rodgers and Hammerstein had already turned it down, which was all he needed to tell me to set my adrenalin working. I almost leaped at it. I promised I'd do it as a musical, probably with Irving Berlin doing the score and Paul Osborn the book, and after that I'd make a movie of it. All I wanted to know from Jim was what I had to pay to secure the rights.

Jim told me it would be offered on a sliding scale which could obligate me to pay two hundred and fifty thousand dollars.

I said, ignoring Nedda's worried look, "I accept! I'll write you a check right now!"

"Josh, first you've got to read it—I'll send you the galleys tomorrow—and then talk to your lawyer. But we can't make any move until you receive the offering telegram."

My head was whirling with excitement and with trying to keep my plans straight, and more than that, with sudden exhaustion. On the way home, Nedda held my hand tight. Again, I didn't sleep. I thought about *Sayonara* instead of *Kind Sir*.

The next day I contacted Ben Aslan, a partner of my lawyer Bill Fitelson who was out of town, and also broached the project to Irving Berlin and Paul Osborn. David Merrick agreed to produce it with me, sight unseen, and two nights later the two of us and Nedda drove down to Jim's house in Pennsylvania to meet with Jim and his agent, Helen Strauss of William Morris. By that time, I had read the novel and knew it was a beauty. I was stubbornly sure of the public's interest in a story of soldiers in Korea, and I knew firsthand how fascinating and beautiful the Japanese theatre would be on the stage and on the screen—sure enough to risk two hundred and fifty thousand of my own money.

Osborn and Berlin read the novel quickly and concurred. So I drafted the acceptance of the telegram offer with Ben Aslan. We accepted all terms, but I stubbornly insisted on adding a sentence. Although Ben warned me that legally I should deal only with the terms mentioned and add nothing else, I added that I would guarantee to produce it beforehand as a show. I was certain that was what Michener wanted, or else why should he seek me out and not a movie man?

The original telegram had stated that in case there was more than one acceptance, the author had the right to choose the purchaser.

The next day I learned that Michener had chosen me; I owned the rights to *Sayonara*. My jubilation was only slightly mixed with a bit of fear that, if for some reason the picture was never made, or if it failed, I'd lose all the money I had in the world.

During all these demanding negotiations, I kept directing *Kind Sir*.

At night I was on the phone frequently with Mary or her husband and with Boyer. Although they were charming, I had the feeling they were disturbed. I grew more and more agitated and excited. I tried to convince Nedda that my overwrought state was healthy. All my wishes were coming true. *Kind Sir* looked fresh and glamorous, *Fanny* was going to be a masterpiece, and *Sayonara* was going to be the most beautiful picture ever made.

But things were not going to be as easy as all that.

Two days after I had sent the telegram, Bill Fitelson flew back from his vacation on Cape Cod. He and Ben told me that I was being sued, jointly, by Metro-Goldwyn-Mayer, Twentieth Century-Fox, and William Goetz Productions, all of whom had accepted Michener's telegram offer exactly as stated, with no frills.

They claimed that my added inducement had made my bid invalid and Michener's acceptance of it illegal. I was dumbfounded.

"Michener made the choice," I said, "of his own free will."

"That has nothing to do with it," said Fitelson. "Unless you work something out with them, they can keep you from making the movie. What we've got to do is prepare ourselves for a nasty lawsuit with endless appeals."

"But it *can't* be dragged out! It must be filmed now, while the Korean War is on, while the troops are flying to Japan on furloughs. Besides, someone could easily steal the idea of a Japanese-American love story and that would kill this one."

"There's nothing we can do about that, Josh," said Bill. "You're going to be called for a pretrial examination. We've got to fight them, and it will take a very long time."

After that, I had to force myself to go to *Kind Sir* rehearsals, and whip myself to concentrate.

Still, I found I had extraordinary energy. Although I wasn't aware of it, I exhausted everyone who tried to keep up with me. Again I was directing—as I had directed *Charley's Aunt*—quickly, efficiently and with seemingly effective ideas. The whole cast took on my excitement, and if they suspected I was in a strange state, they never showed it to me.

Certainly Norman Krasna was delighted, and he was the one I most had to please.

The time came for New Orleans, and Nedda thought the trip to Louisiana would calm me. Three-year-old Tom and his nurse came with us and two-year-old Sue stayed with Aino in New York.

New Orleans welcomed us as if we were royalty. On entering the city I saw an electric sign reading, "Welcome Kind Sir, starring Mary Martin and Charles Boyer, and directed by Louisiana's own Josh Logan."

But the real thrill for me was seeing David Merrick appear in my hotel room doorway carrying an elaborately dressed antique French automaton—a blackamoor fashioned years ago in France; when wound up, he actually smoked a hookah and blew smoke rings from his lips. I collected such antique toys but had only found them in France. The sober-faced Merrick, who boasted a heart of stone, had flown here, scoured the smartest shops for an appropriate gift and brought it to me himself.

The city was so in awe of *Kind Sir* and its stars that I was afraid the opening night audience could not relax enough to enjoy the play. I insisted, against strong protests from everyone, on appearing in front of the curtain before the play started. Once out there, I told the audience that this was a wild comedy: "Please don't take it seriously. Have some fun." Most everyone thought my speech unnecessary, and in truth it was. Nothing could make the audience feel at ease: they were in shock at seeing live celebrities.

But all the national magazines did cover our opening, and I was happy to lead the reporters and photographers all over the city for local color. At this point, Merrill arrived from New York. He seemed determined to separate Nedda and me, although he denied it. He told her to go home. She went, but anxious about my state, asked her daughter, Ann Lester, to come down and keep me in sight.

During that week there were jaunts with reporters I hazily remember —to marble blocked cemeteries, to Avery Island (home of Tabasco) and trips into Cajun country, to the great Louisiana mansion Oak Allée.

Subconsciously, I began to feel I became too enthusiastic in conversation. Also, my explosive temper seemed to flare up until I was often on the brink of a battle. Ann was able to pull me away in the nick of time.

My day was so full with the press and New Orleans that I spent almost no time rehearsing. I gave a few notes and listened to what Norman Krasna said about the performance.

One morning, Merrill walked into my hotel room.

"Hello, Mr. Micawber," I said.

"Josh, I'd sho' like to see somethin' of the country 'round here. I've never seen Louisiana. Since the show is goin' so well, I take it the cast could use a little vacation from you so they can polish their performances by themselves. Why don't you and I go for a short trip?"

"Let's go, Docaroo!! Anywhere but a hospital."

We hired a limousine, and Merrill had his five bags put in the trunk. I carried a small suitcase with a few changes of underwear and pajamas, but before I stepped into the car, I growled at Merrill, "You're not going to lock me up, are you, Doctor?"

"I swear to you and to heaven, Josh, you'll never go to a mental hospital while you ah in my care. Come on, less go."

We drove along the coast to Biloxi, where I could show Merrill where I had vacationed when I was a child. I had taken a camera along with me and I often stopped the car to take a picture of things that reminded me of my childhood.

At an antique store, I grew so excited at the old relics that I began buying everything I liked—a brass inlaid Pleyel piano, two brass chandeliers with rose glass shades, an ornate cabinet with raised brass designs. I knew this buying was strong proof of manic elation, but I couldn't stop myself—and Merrill never tried to stop me. Of course he couldn't have, even if he had tried. I put all else aside. I couldn't even remember how long *Kind Sir* was to play in New Orleans or where it was to go after that. Oh, yes—St. Louis.

There would be moments of honest panic when I would plead with Merrill, "What am I to do? I don't want to go into a hospital!"

"Just rest. Stay away from the play. They're all professionals—they can handle themselves. Don't worry."

It was in a hotel in Mobile, Alabama, that I discovered Merrill packing his suitcases.

"Where are you going?" I asked.

"Josh, my poor mother is dying of cancer, and I've got to go to Nashville to see her. You'll be all right. The driver is reliable and he'll get you back to New Orleans. Nedda will come down if you need her."

The truth, which I wasn't to learn for a long time, was that Merrill couldn't wait to get away from me, as I had exhausted him. He'd been having a lovely time gossiping around the cast. But being with me had become work.

I was panicked at being left alone—the trip hadn't been *my* idea. What the hell was I doing there?

After he left, I wondered where I should go next. Merrill had warned me to stay away from the play, but there was really nowhere else to go. I figured the show was in St. Louis, so I went to the airport and flew there.

After checking into a hotel, I headed for the theatre and arrived during the first intermission. I saw Norman Krasna in the lobby talking with Groucho Marx, an old friend of his. The two of them looked at me in shock as I approached them. I asked them how the show was going.

"Fine," said Norman. "It's got very good notices. You'll be very happy."

I told Norman that I would go backstage after the performance, and he, in the kindest possible way, hinted that it wasn't necessary. From the cautious, overly solicitous way he spoke, I realized that more people knew I was ill than I thought—and there began the creeping fear that they were all conspiring to have me captured and hospitalized once again. My skin flushed with the embarrassment of panic. All the horror of being hunted was coming back. Soon the doctors would begin to close in on me. I must escape immediately before I was recognized by the others. I pretended to Norman and Groucho that I was going to step outside for a breath of air, and I hailed a taxi. The driver was a friendly looking young man, and when he asked me where I was going, I said, "I'm not sure. Just head north."

He gave me a worried glance. "Are you all right?"

"I'm fine. Listen, could you stop someplace where I could buy some white wine?"

"Sure," he said affably, and he took me to a liquor store where I bought four or five bottles. Back in the car, I asked him to keep heading north. God knows why.

We talked, and I learned that he was a twin and that his brother had two children and a very nice wife and he generally spent his day off with them. I told him I would like to meet them sometime.

I noticed that we were approaching a drugstore, and I asked him to pull over. Having left my suitcase at the hotel, I needed a toothbrush, razor and shaving cream. As soon as I got them, I went back to the cab. By this time the driver was relaxed and acted as if it was fun to drive a nut who had no destination.

Since it was late, I asked him to find a motel where I could spend the night, and to pick me up the next morning so we could visit his brother's family.

His brother's house was on the outskirts of St. Louis. My new friend's identical twin brother welcomed us without hesitation, and his thin young wife was clearly lovely in spite of the spotted, formless housedress she wore.

They took us out to the tiny backyard, where two toddlers were playing. There was a little sandbox and a few rusty toys—and we sat and spent the day talking about my life and theirs and anything that occurred to us, and of course drinking wine.

They were such innocent, generous, kind people that I soon felt very much at ease. I knew as long as I was in trouble they would care for me, and I wanted to repay them somehow. I wrote down their names and addresses, gave them mine, and we promised we would write to each other. For years after I sent the children and their parents and uncle presents and a check at Christmas, and they sent me two bottles of white wine.

The day with them had managed to allay my panic, and I went back to the hotel and sat more peaceful but wondering what to do.

Although I have no clear memory of the next few days, I have been told that I made many telephone calls and eventually showed up at rehearsal in Cleveland. Norman told me that I started directing and that I was not only lucid but filled with inventive ideas. He would never admit I was odd or strange.

Nedda, meantime, infuriated by Merrill, had found her own doctor, the famous Lawrence Kubie. He was strong enough to take over the case and call me directly in Cleveland. I was longing for help and this authoritative man made so much sense that I agreed to to to Philadelphia and sign in again at my old alma mater, the Pennsylvania Hospital. Joe Curtis and Ann Connolly Lester flew there with me. In Philadelphia, after talking for a few minutes to the admissions doctor, I announced—to general horror—that I had changed my mind. I wanted to take everyone for a great meal at Bookbinder's.

Joe Curtis and Ann went with me, and my mother, whom I had called, came down from New York. The talk at the table was that I should go back to the hospital, and again I felt a return of that terror: the whole world was converging on me. I insisted on calling this dinner "the last supper." Just before dessert, I said, "Excuse me. I have to go to the bathroom."

I walked through the main room of the restaurant and out an exit into the street. I took a taxi headed for the railroad station and boarded a train for Washington. I felt I wanted to go south.

Oh, my God, I thought. Where could I go where people would be gentle, where they would care for me and not force me to live behind bars?

Mansfield was the only place left for me. Silly little Mansfield and it was still there.

> Mansfield is a lazy town,
>   And melancholy too.
> It has a sort of haze about it
>   Made of smoke and honeydew.
> I can't remember everything that
>   Happened to me there.
> But I remember that I loved it,
>   Loved to breathe its air!

Where did all that verse come from? Oh, yes, I wrote it all those years ago in the Pennsylvania Hospital! Those first few days of my illness I decided to write an epic saga about my childhood. How did it go from there?

> It's full of little cousins still,
>   And uncles too—and people;
> Not to mention Granddaddy
>   And the college with its steeple—

But Granddaddy was gone now. Only Will, Uncle Will, was still there. He's the nicest man in the world and he's got a big house. He'll surely let me stay, hide me, for a while at least—or would he? Would the doctors let him? No, I'd better not see Will. But I just *had* to see Mansfield—walk around the streets after dark when I'd be safe from detection. Just to be in Mansfield for a while would make me feel better. It would cool my eyes and calm my head and settle my raging gut.

On the nonstop plane from Washington to Dallas I settled back in my seat and felt clear-minded for the first time since Bookbinder's. I was safe from the prying world, at least for a while. I felt my scalp relax and my face muscles almost form a smile. Just thinking of silly old Mansfield was a balm, a sedative . . .

> And the college with its steeple—
> Or was that called a belfry?
> I never could make up my mind.
> It seems to me there was a bell
> That had a gracious sound and kind.

When the plane from Dallas to Shreveport took off, I huddled in a back seat with a newspaper to cover my face, for I was getting close to people who might know me. As we landed, less than an hour later, I wondered if this airport was old Barksdale Field transformed. Was this where Colonel Noble, my stepfather, conducted his doomed experiments for his cotton-dusting business? We had all thought it so promising, and Mother had invested her money and ours before it collapsed. Poor Father, how did he live through the failure and the guilt?

Oh, my God, suppose somebody here working in the airport remembers Colonel Noble or Mother and recognizes me? I must be careful. Oh, my God, I'm all right—that was twenty years ago. And yet, that's not really so long . . .

In Shreveport I walked as quickly as I could without exciting curiosity to the rent-a-car people and showed them my license and identifications. I hated giving my real name but I had to. I got a convertible coupé and the directions to an obscure motel not too close to town. Driving to it, my heart leaped a bit. I would be in Mansfield within an hour.

I registered at the motel, left my raincoat with a camera in the pocket and a few odds and ends in the room, and came out and headed the car for Mansfield.

How odd! I had just traveled from Texas to Mansfield again, just as I must have done when my mother and father moved from Texarkana, before Mary Lee was born. We didn't live on Polk Street then; that came later. Our first home was a big two-story house in South Mansfield, near one of my father's businesses, the Logan Lumber Company that burned wood in an eternal fire with wood scraps from the mill. And next door was the white frame hotel that Daddy named for me, The Hotel Joshua, which he built for his staff and for visiting salesmen. There was a wide field across from our house there with an old broken-down bit of fence in the middle. Somewhere you could climb it and hide yourself in a mass of yellow jasmine, almost as sweet to smell as Cape jasmine or chinaberry flowers. But that was all gone by now—the hotel crumbled away, the house, even the lumber company, and the eternal fire was out.

I drove up old Polk Street and pulled over to a stop directly across from Granddaddy's house. The green wisteria leaves almost covered the fact that the paint was peeling and the white flakes of it that remained were stained with dirty rain marks. There was still a bit of the scroll-cut gingerbread banister showing, and I imagined that above and over the roof was where you once could see the steeple, the belfry, of Mansfield Female College.

From my little bedroom window, I heard those young girl sopranos, their scales, their arpeggios, every morning of my childhood life, but looking now from the car I knew that even if I got out and went around the house, through the garden and the lot, to see the college close, it would be painful, for the college was no longer there.

Only the bottom floor was left; the grand upper stories had been torn down and reroofed to make a house for Mansfield's most successful undertaker. My God, he'd buried the college. Everything was dead—everything . . .

I walked down the street a bit to the far end of the yard so as to keep from being observed, and crept through some strange new bushes and vines until I came upon Jolly Den, our little playhouse that Granddaddy had built for us. It was still standing exactly as it was—weathered, of course, and rickety from the years. The paint had gone long ago, but the porch was there still, and the little steps, and even one of our small chairs, all frazzled and blotched. When I stuck my head through the door, I could see a few bits of the old wallpaper. To

think I once used to be able to walk into it standing erect; now I was
bent double.

I thought I heard a sound, and stood up quickly, banging my head
against the ceiling. Then almost crawling out onto the little porch, I
could see the old fig tree was gone, but the pecan tree was standing tall,
the tree that I had climbed as Phoebus, the rising sun, and from the top
of which I had fallen. I didn't dare go near the old but still beautiful
house, though it seemed deserted.

> Now, in our house, including me,
>   There was my sister, Mary Lee,
> Aged one or so—and Amy Lane,
>   Who once had been my father's nurse
> But now was queen of three;
>   I.e., my mother, me and Mary Lee.

The old cemetery down the road would be safe. There wasn't likely
to be anybody there to watch me. As I walked down deserted Cemetery
Lane, which was quite close by, I passed two little weather-beaten,
shacklike houses. I went over and looked at one of them closely. I had
once known it well.

Since before I could remember, it had been Amy Lane's house,
where she slept and provided for her daughter and son and also where
she left them early in the morning to take care of the three of us.

> All three respected Amy Lane!
>   She had a way of saying things
> And meaning them. While laughing
>   With a toothless cackle.
> Making orders crackle!
>   And when we had the pip
> She'd use her velvet whip.

And now, Amy Lane was gone—long gone—and Carrie, her beautiful
daughter, had married and moved away, and Amy's son was very successful someplace in Louisiana, or had been. I felt extraordinarily
peaceful: just thinking of Amy Lane had calmed my palpitations and
made me feel freshly washed, an innocent.

> Amy Lane was black—or gray—
>   Or brown—and sometimes purple.
> Her skin was leather-like and soft—
>   Quite fascinating to the eyes,

> And aromatic to the nose
>   Of those who loved her true
> And listened to her too . . . !

Once in the cemetery, my feet seemed to take me without hesitation to my father's grave. There, under masses of honeysuckle which I had to push away, I read his name: Joshua Lockwood Logan II. It was a huge, shiny granite stone. In the blink of an eye, the honeysuckle vanished, and so did the tombstone and all the grass and in their place there was a yawning rectangular hole, dug deep down. Close by was a huge mound of freshly dug clay, slick with wet, rank to smell. Over it, in some attempt to cover its ugliness, was some cheesecloth piled with flowers, but I couldn't smell the flowers for the clay.

There were undertaker chairs lined up six or eight in a row behind each other, and I was sitting on one, at the end of the first row, dangling my legs with Granddaddy next to me holding onto my arm to keep me from falling off. It was my father's funeral, and I was almost three, so I was allowed to go while Mother felt she had to stay at home with Mary Lee, who was a tiny baby.

I don't remember much about the funeral, except that it was long and talky and the folding chair was hard. I kept moving my legs, trying to make my seat feel better.

It had to be my very first memory. But why was it fading? If it was important enough to show itself, then why couldn't I hold on to it?

Funny, but I swore I could hear something coming from my father's tombstone. A muffled voice, but what was it trying to say? But this was ridiculous! I couldn't hear anything; I was just tired, or maybe—yes—sick. Dear God, had he been sick too? My kind of sick—mad sick—crazy sick? No one in my family had ever been like that. Never! We were spotless! My father died of pneumonia in Chicago. He died of pneumonia in Chicago.

I leaned against the honeysuckle and tried to pull myself together. I felt shaken, faint.

> Mansfield is all tangled up
>   In honeysuckle vine
> Deep in a mossy vat
>   Of pork-shank brine,
> Wrapped in Spanish moss
>   Sticky with *cuite*

> And sweet-gum drip!
>   Don't cross Polk Street!
> Don't risk the trip.
>   Mud's too thick and there's quicksand.

"What am I going to do now?" I asked out loud. But there was no one to answer. I looked about at the graves around me—my Logan grandfather's, and over my left shoulder, Grandmother and Granddaddy Nabors'—and beyond them all those unknown Civil War soldiers from the Battle of Mansfield, with no inscriptions on their tombstones, because nobody knew who they were, or because the years had wiped out their names. If they could only wipe out mine.

Maybe, since I'm so close, I really should go see Will. He's the gentlest man I know. Oh, no, he'll have to be honest if a doctor calls him, or Nedda. I mustn't tell Will anything. Or anyone else.

I was so tired I wanted to sink to my knees, roll over on the grass near my father's grave, and just lie there. But the only thing to do now was go back to limbo, to that nameless motel, and try to get a night's sleep, then not forget to pay for my room so I wouldn't be traced, and take off for—take off for nowhere—just follow my nose. Or like Charlie Chaplin, disappear into the sunset with a funny walk.

Back at the Shreveport motel, before going to my room, I decided to pay my bill. I was very uneasy; I knew I shouldn't sleep a full night there. It would give the doctors twelve more hours to trace me. I'd leave now. Yes, this minute. Should I even take time to pick up my coat, camera and toilet articles? Yes, I must do that—they would be proof I'd been there. I'd better rush. I'd better . . .

I ran stumbling up the steps to the second floor and unlocked my room. The motel bed looked inviting, but I didn't dare lie down on it for a second. I might fall asleep. I snapped up my things, banged the door shut, leaving the key in the lock, plunged down the stairs, got into my car and started to drive away.

A second before I moved onto the road, another car drove into the gate and blocked my way. Two men got out and ambled over to me.

My flight was over, for I knew immediately that whoever they were, they were looking for me. They were dressed in street clothes and their car had no special insignia, but they had to be police. Braving it out, I asked them, "Are you looking for Joshua Logan?"

They were youngish, pleasant-looking men. In a soft Southern tone,

one of them said, "That's right, Mr. Logan. Would you like to take a little ride with us?"

"Sure," I said, trying quickly to give myself a moment to think. "But what do I do with this rented car?"

He answered, "We'll take care of all that." Now I knew they meant business. I better withhold any resistance till an opportunity presented itself. "You just step right in here."

I got in the back seat and one of them sat with me while the other drove. I didn't ask them where they were going. Besides, I didn't want to know. All I really knew was that they were trying to be pleasant companions. They told me stories about themselves and what life was like in Louisiana today. Our conversation touched every subject but me.

Like that wonderful Tennessee Williams play I read, in Cuba, the one I wanted to do with all my heart. What was the last line Blanche du Bois said to the man who was taking her away? "Whoever you are, I've always depended on the kindness of strangers."

The trip was long, and it wasn't for several hours that I realized we were headed for New Orleans. I was sure I was being taken to a hospital, but when we got there we parked in front of the city jail, and they escorted me in.

One of them spoke to the desk sergeant, who nodded and then I was led by an officer down a corridor to the "tank," a large, humid room smelling of sweat and lined with double bunks with lumpy, naked mattresses. The only vacant one was assigned to me.

When I turned to ask why I was there and what was going to happen to me, I found that the officer had left. The others in the cell, most of them unshaven, red-eyed, smoking cigarettes with trembling hands, watched me with no curiosity whatsoever.

How could a free man be locked up in a jail without someone telling him why he was there? Who arranged this? Then I realized I'd never asked! Maybe they would have told me if I'd asked. And maybe the reason I didn't ask was because I figured this was where I belonged.

All that was left to do was climb into my sheetless bunk.

It wasn't until the next morning that I was led out to a front room and saw Merrill Moore. He was waiting for me. I had not seen or heard from him since he had left me in Mobile.

My first question was, "What happened to your mother?"

"She's still very ill, Josh, but so are you. And I'm afraid you've got to go with me and get well—the way you did before, in a hospital."

There was no point in my saying anything.

What I didn't know was that he had been ordered to do this by the doctor who had called me in Cleveland, the one Nedda had put on my case, Dr. Lawrence Kubie, the dean of psychiatrists and psychoanalysts. Kubie found Merrill's behavior toward me so casual that he told Merrill to hospitalize me and then go into treatment himself.

This was to be the last time I ever saw Merrill. He died a few years afterward, and I learned from friends and patients that he had been sick for a long time before that. Certainly Merrill was an original and obeyed his own rules, but I doubt had he been more orthodox if I would ever have listened to him when I was in that manic state in Boston; because his behavior was so close to mine in his wild flights of imagination, he was able to save my life.

Merrill took me to the St. Vincent de Paul Hospital where he introduced me to Dr. Bick, who was going to be in charge of my case.

It was a Catholic hospital, where all the nurses were Sisters of Mercy, with wide, fluttering white bonnets, and I felt as if I were looking at an Italian movie laid in a convent. I imagined Granddaddy watching me. What was a nice Methodist boy like me doing in this papist place? I followed the doctor past locked, barred rooms, and through the apertures I could see bits of padding on some of the walls. My room was sparsely furnished and antiseptic.

Before that, on the way to the hospital, Merrill had told me about my family. Nedda, he said, was so upset that she was seeking medical care, but more remarkable than the facts he told me was the terms he couched them in. He spoke of her as if she were a nuisance, a complainer, a joke of a person and tried to get me to laugh about her condition. I longed for him to stop talking and leave me alone with my more normal inmates. He did.

Here I was in a mental institution once again, and once again with no idea when or if I would ever get out. But there must be some hope—I had gotten out before and my life had continued. But would that happen the next time? Would there be a next time? Would the rest of my life be an endless going in and out of asylums? And I was really baffled about how it all had happened. Supposedly, I had been under the care of a competent doctor ever since my first breakdown. Why then, had I become sick again? Hadn't he realized this was coming?

That night I decided it was ridiculous to stay in this hospital, and I planned to get out as soon as I could—with the doctor's permission or without it. I began watching for a chance to escape. I thought the best way to get out was simply to wait until the door to the ward was open and then walk right out.

I looked up and it *was* open! I knew I had to move quickly. Someone had brought a package in, and left the door open while he or she dropped it off. Without waiting, I walked out of the ward, then down a flight of steps and along a hall until I passed the entrance. No one seemed to be watching me, so I continued on and out into the street.

Not far away was a cement platform with a small group of people waiting for a streetcar to town. I joined them, hoping the streetcar would arrive quickly, but nothing was in sight. I waited and waited, and I watched. I thought, I'll have to start walking. I'll have to get lost somewhere, or they'll come after me.

Finally, I saw the lights of the streetcar approaching far down the street—but, at the same time, I noticed two huge men, led by a nun, come out of the hospital. The nun was pointing at me.

They walked quickly to me and I stood transfixed with fear. Both of the men grabbed me and said, "All right, let's go."

I heard the nun cry out, "Grab him hard! Drag him back!" in a nasty, snarling voice. Her tone infuriated me and I struck out at her, trying to knock her hat off. If I could have made her fall I would have felt very happy, but she was too quick for that. In spite of the huge headdress she wore, she was as agile as a boxer, and hissed like an angry swan.

I tried to fight back, but they lifted me off the ground easily and carried me several yards. Then I gave up and walked obediently back into the hospital.

I was not put into the room I had been in before, but into another whose walls, floor and ceiling were fully padded, a room with iron bars on the doorway. The iron door clanked shut behind me, and I sat on the padded floor as there was no furniture.

My fury had exhausted me and I fell into a numb sleep. The next morning, the doctor appeared, along with two male nurses who were rolling in a large metal cabinet which was covered in dials and electrical outlets.

"Don't do that to me!" I cried out. "That's electric shock, isn't it?"

"Don't worry. It will be good for you. You'll like it," said the doctor.

"But, uh, my family won't allow me to have electric shock. My mother said it would dull my talent."

"Your wife has given me permission to do anything I feel is right for you, and I feel this is. Now, relax and lie down. Please cooperate."

As the two male nurses approached, I lay back. Salve was put on my temples and then a steel headpiece was clamped on my head. Electric connections were adhered to my chest and wrists.

Maybe it will kill me and maybe that's good. Oh, God, let it kill me, but fast, please.

The doctor said, "Now be very calm."

I could only think to ask, "Will it hurt?"

"Not a bit," he said. "Just be calm."

I could see his hand move to pull the switch, but I never saw him complete the action. In a fraction of a second, I was in total oblivion, having felt nothing. When I woke up, the room was empty. I had been placed on a bed, and I felt quite refreshed. In fact, I felt better than I had in months and months.

All the anxiety that had been pressing about inside my brain had disappeared. I was no longer angry with the poor nun, or the people who had dragged me back in the hospital. All I wanted to do was lie there and enjoy this cool peace that was flowing through me. If this was electric shock, then I wished I had had it years ago.

Nedda told me later that she had begged Merrill to give me three or four electric shock treatments over weekends during *Kind Sir* rehearsals. It might have been enough, it might have saved the whole venture. But Merrill had said he was in charge of my case, preferred his own authority and sleeping pills.

The day after, I was moved to a larger, less confined room, because my belligerence had vanished, Nedda told me.

One day, while I was in the lounge of the ward, a nun sat near me on the same settee and began to read a magazine. I looked over and saw a full-page color illustration of an improbably beautiful Japanese girl lying back on a mat, while over her, looking ready for action, was a handsome American pilot.

Intrigued, I slid slightly closer to her to see better. Just as I suspected, it was the initial installment of James Michener's new novel, *Sayonara.*

The very name so delighted me that I let out a happy gasp, and the sister looked over at me, somewhat offended. I pointed to the magazine and said, "I own the movie rights to that story, you know."

"No, I didn't know—but I'm very happy for you," she said, with that overly sweet voice that nuns use to mean, "Who are you kidding, Mac?"

I searched out another copy of the magazine and cut out the picture and the title, and pasted them on the wall of my room. They made me feel closer to the outside world—although they also made me know how far away I was from *Sayonara.*

After scarcely three weeks, during which I had six benign electric shock treatments, the doctor told me I was well, and that I had been granted permission to see my wife, who was waiting for me in a private room. If, after seeing me, she agreed I was well, I could go home to New York with her. The final decision was hers.

I found Nedda sitting in a room, her face strained and serious.

We held onto each other for a long moment, since kisses seemed too lightweight for such a time. I talked to her calmly about my days in the hospital. She told me little things about the children, and said then, "The doctor wants me to make the decision about whether you should come home now."

After a pause, I asked carefully, "What are you going to tell him?"

She said, "I want *you* to tell *me* what to say. I want you to tell me if you are well. If you say you are, then we'll go home."

I told her that my greatest wish was to return with her and that I was well.

Dr. Kubie had suggested that I stay at our Stamford, Connecticut, house with a male nurse for some weeks of quiet rest until I was ready to return to work. There I would have the children near me and I could putter in the greenhouse and garden. My favorite male nurse, Milton Cooke, who had been with me during my recuperation in 1940, agreed to come up from Philadelphia and stay with me for a while. Together, Cooky and I went for long walks and talked, and often Joe Curtis would come up from New York with my correspondence and we would answer letters for a few hours.

Because of our love for flowers, Nedda and I had provided the back-

ing for a flower shop which was run for us by a talented designer of
flower arrangements, Pleasance Mundy. Pleasance brought out a tiny
Christmas tree as an example of the things she was preparing for the
busy Christmas season which was coming soon. Her miniature trees
were perfectly decorated, except that they needed tiny wrapped pack-
ages to complete the illusion. As a form of occupational therapy, Cooky
and I wrapped cubes of sugar, midget matchboxes, anything small, with
tissue paper and tied a wisp of colored string around each one. It was
not quite as difficult as engraving The Lord's Prayer on the head of a
pin, but it was as near as I will ever get. I made hundreds of them, and
I found it as much an escape as making string mats and hooking rugs, as
Cooky and I had done all those years ago.

Gradually, I became aware of the maelstrom my illness had caused.
While I had been in the midst of my nightmare, Nedda had been having hers. She was convinced that Merrill Moore had resisted having me
enter a mental hospital because he was loath to let the world know that
he had failed with me after thirteen years in his care.

It was then that I learned the facts of my capture. After my disap-
pearance in Philadelphia, everyone was frantic with worry. The first
sign of me came when I called Joe Curtis at his apartment, a call I do
not remember. Joe kept me on the phone as long as he could, while he
sent a friend to trace the call. All the operator could tell him was that it
was coming from Louisiana, but that was clue enough to guess precisely
where in Louisiana I might be.

The police took over from there.

Merrill still resisted putting me in a hospital, and that was when
Nedda appealed to Kubie.

I was still anxious about what my friends, my co-workers, not to
mention the public, thought of me now. What had been said about me
during my absence? How much had been printed in the columns?
How much damage to my life had all the gossip done?

Milton Cooke kept assuring me that there was nothing to worry
about. All people really cared about was that I was back, and I was
well. It was much more important that for the time being I should
drift. So I kept on at my painstaking task of wrapping sugar cubes, or
playing with the children, and taking long walks with Cooky—and for
the first time in years, resisting making telephone calls. To be truthful,
it wasn't hard to stay away from the phone, for I was afraid of what I
might hear.

Kind Sir had opened to a million-dollar advance—the largest ever for a nonmusical play—but the reviews had been poor. My great idea of pairing Mary Martin and Charles Boyer in a light romantic comedy had backfired. The public came to see a combination of *South Pacific*, *Algiers* and *Mayerling*. With their appetites set for a juicy steak dinner, they had been served fish. Exquisitely prepared fish, but nevertheless not steak. And the shock to the taste buds caused not only disappointment but anger.

I knew *Kind Sir* was a good play. It had all of the craftsmanship of the best Pinero farce—plus the charm and elegance of something by Lonsdale or Maugham.

No movie company bid for the rights, so when, years later, Norman Krasna offered to buy them himself for ten thousand dollars, a ridiculously low figure, everyone involved with the show—Mary, Charles and myself—accepted Norman's offer.

What we didn't know was that Norman had already secured Cary Grant and Ingrid Bergman to star in the movie, and later he and the director Stanley Donen filmed it under the new title, *Indiscreet*. It received enthusiastic notices as a piece of writing from discriminating movie critics all over the world.

I went to see the film, expecting to find an entirely new story—but other than a few changes in location, which required a few added lines, it was *Kind Sir* verbatim. To me, Norman Krasna's writing and my taste were more than vindicated. Had I been well, it would have been another story.

The difference between my position now and what it was after my first breakdown in 1940 was that then I had been an unknown outside of the relatively small theatre world. But now, thanks to that *Life* magazine article and, later, Ed Sullivan's TV program on me, I had become a near celebrity.

The Sullivan program was meant to be a tribute to my shows—Ed gathered casts from all over the country for it, and Jimmy Stewart made a special film of Triangle days—but I was determined not to brag and to turn it instead into a plea for mental health by telling the story of my own nervous breakdown. Ed was terrified of CBS's reaction. It was in the days when mental illness and such was verboten on television. But he took a chance with me. I spoke, and then Ed asked me to list the shows I had done since my breakdown. I scarcely got past *This Is the*

Army, Annie Get Your Gun, Mister Roberts and *South Pacific* when the audience broke into cheers and yells.

My mental illness had been discussed in front of sixteen million viewers, and I was subject to greater scrutiny now than ever.

Since I had not heard from David Merrick, Sam Behrman or Harold Rome, I assumed that the whole *Fanny* project had gone into eclipse—or at least my involvement with it had. Certainly the latter would be understandable—a huge project like that shouldn't be placed in the hands of someone just out of a mental hospital. Therefore, I made no attempt to contact them.

After several weeks, Milton Cooke said, "You don't need me anymore. You're just holding on to a prop. You're all right. Why don't you let me go back to Philadelphia?"

He was right. He'd been a fine companion and I would miss him, but I knew I had to let him go.

Nedda's Dr. Kubie approved of this, and asked me to come in town to see him and discuss finding a doctor for myself. He did not feel it was right to treat the husband of a patient.

When I was in his office, this sober-faced but very wise man went very quickly over my mental and emotional history, and he pointed out something about me: I wanted a father so badly that I always unconsciously turned the attractive older men I worked with into my father, and then when they unknowingly behaved unfatherly I grew angry and frustrated because they did not live up to my standard. Not knowing the subconscious position I had given them, they did not behave as permissive fathers but as the ordinary businessmen they were, and grew angry back with me—which maddened me even further.

It seemed to make sense: Oscar . . . Dick . . . Leland . . . Sam Behrman . . . Ezio Pinza . . . Dwight . . . Richard Bennett—all of them likely father figures. I had not realized this tendency of mine, but it explained a lot, and as I left Dr. Kubie he gave me the address of another doctor he thought would be helpful to me in studying myself.

I made a date, and soon found myself in front of still a new face, that of Dr. Burness Moore, who had studied my case history carefully. It was a bit disturbing that his last name was the same as Merrill's, but I forced myself to put it out of my mind.

In discussing my childhood I heard myself saying, almost as if by rote, "My father died of pneumonia in a hospital in Chicago when I was three years old."

After a slight pause, Dr. Moore said quietly, "Your father cut his throat with a pocket knife in a health sanitorium in Chicago. I think it's about time you knew that, Mr. Logan."

I was so astounded that I asked him to repeat the statement three or four times, and then demanded to know how he could know facts I had never heard of in my life. My blood was pumping back and forth through my head while he told me of the doctors who had passed it on until it reached him. It had been originated by a Mansfield neighbor of my mother's now living in New York. She came to Dr. Crawley the moment I had my first breakdown and said, "These are the facts. Will they help?"

I couldn't wait to leave Dr. Moore's office and took a taxi to my apartment, where I rushed to call my Uncle Will in Louisiana.

"Yes, Josh," said Will, "it's true."

"But," I said, "they always told me he died of pneumonia."

"He did die of pneumonia. It was the blood from his throat that went into his lungs."

"But why didn't anyone tell me? Why didn't my mother tell me?"

"She never wanted you to know, Josh. I can't tell you why, except I imagine she thought it would be too painful for you."

"It's not painful, Will, it's a relief, because at last I know the truth. The boil has been lanced and the sore is clean. In fact, I'm feeling better than I have in a very long time. Now I know my father, and for the first time in my life. I feel close to him for the first time. He must have been very much like me."

"He was," said Will. "Very much. And I hope you won't tell your mother you know."

"Of course not, and—thanks, Will." And I hung up.

For a day or two I wandered about the house, pulling yellow leaves off geraniums and skimming the willow leaves off the pool. The children were still too young to talk to, so I played with them a bit in the yard, and in between games we stared at each other, smiling.

Nedda was very discreet. Her father had meant so much to her that she felt a special closeness to me at this time.

And then suddenly I felt an unquenchable thirst for work. I went to the telephone and called a few of my friends and associates—Marshall Jamison; Bob Linden, the wonderful stage manager of *Kind Sir*; and

Alan Anderson, Max's son, who was in charge of *Picnic.* I told them how well I felt and to give my love to the various members of the casts.

The news I was well must have spread quickly, because David Merrick called to say, "I hear you're all right now. We've been waiting for that. Isn't it time for you to go back to work with Sam and Harold on *Fanny?*"

"David, are you sure you want me to go on with this? You were in New Orleans. You know what I was like."

"You were sick. But you're well now, and I hereby order you back to work. Besides, Sam needs you, and so do I."

Merrick was nothing if not a realistic man, and there was no reason for me to believe he was not telling me the truth.

But when he hung up, all the nagging doubts and niggling fears I had felt before rushed back—and even doubled. The son of a bitch was doing it to make me feel better. But was it the milk of human kindness or the milk of human magnesia? David's too tough to be a Good Samaritan. Why should a cold-blooded, owlish lawyer from St. Louis decide to take a chance with his career on me?

"He needs you," said Nedda. "*You're* the one that made it a project for him. You surely know he collected a foolproof dossier on you before he first offered it to you. His offer is sincere as steel—he means it. And I'm not going to listen to your appeals for sympathy, and I'm not going to give you any. Just call him up and say you're going to see Sam, then call up your beloved Sam Behrman and go ahead with your life."

I wanted to believe everything she said, but I couldn't. I couldn't rid myself of the decaying Dorian Gray picture the public and the theatrical world must have painted by now of poor broken down Josh Logan. I was only forty-five years old, but I felt exhausted by this last experience, hollowed out, as though I were a live fish disemboweled.

That night, at supper with Nedda and the children, I tried to tell a few weak jokes, which got weak laughs, and went to bed with the most worthless magazine I could find. After a few seconds, I dropped it to my lap and stared into space.

Nedda, by my side, was pretending to read a book, but I knew that out of the corner of her eye she was watching me.

"I can't do it, Nedda," I said. "I can't go through with *Fanny,* and I'm not sure I can go through with anything else. I just haven't got the zest. I'm not sure that I could ever be effective again in the theatre. I've run out of juice."

Nedda shut her book, leaned over to the sofa beyond the bed, grabbed the needlepoint pillow Mary Martin had made for me in London, and said, "Here is one of your prescriptions, Doctor. Why not try it on yourself?"

I knew what was on the pillow but I looked at it anyway to quiet Nedda. On one side Mary had stitched a pastoral scene with a setting sun and a rising moon. On the other side, done lovingly in petit point, the words I did not want to read:

> He who Doubts from what he sees
> Will ne'er Believe, do what you Please.
> If the Sun and Moon should doubt,
> They'd immediately Go out.

"And they've gone out completely, Nedda. My sun has and my moon too. If you want to know where I am, I'm on the other side of that moon, the permanently black side, and for Christ's sweet sake don't let anyone send messages to me to 'Buck up, Josh!'"

At that moment the fateful telephone rang. The goddamned *deus ex machina*. In my state of mind, it was as though I had planned it to happen at the proper time, as if I had rung the bell myself. I answered.

"Hello? Joshua Logan?" It was a woman's voice. "Mr. Harry Cohn is calling."

"Harry Who?" I asked.

Her voice became sharp. "Mr. Harry Cohn, president of Columbia Pictures. Hold on, please."

"Hello—Josh Logan?"

"Yes, Mr. Cohn."

"Harry to you, Josh. You know I bought *Picnic*—you and the Guild sold it to me."

"That's right, Mr. Cohn."

"Well, I've got a good screenplay. Dan Taradash wrote it, and he and I wonder if you'd direct it."

"You mean you want me to direct the picture?" I said, controlling my voice.

"That's right. Bill Holden's agreed to play the lead. I've got a girl under contract who'd be great for Madge, Kim Novak. Are you available?"

Available. Had I ever been more available? And yet, why was he calling? Didn't he know about me?

"Mr. Cohn, did you know I've been sick for the past few weeks . . . ?"

"That's right, and now you're okay. Is that correct?"

"Yes, I am—I think."

I could feel Nedda's eyes burning the back of my neck.

"I mean, I am fine. No *think* about it. How soon would you want to start shooting? I have to do a musical first. *Fanny* for David Merrick."

"That's O.K. Bill Holden's not free for a year."

I put my hand over the mouthpiece of the telephone. "It's Harry Cohn. He wants me to direct the film *Picnic*."

"Of course he does," Nedda said. "You know *Picnic* better than anybody. You're an authority on *Picnic*. You're *the* authority. He'd be lucky to have you."

"Would you let me make it in Kansas?" I said to Mr. Cohn. "In the flat part where all those grain elevators are?"

"You can make it any fucking place you want to—as long as you turn out a great picture that makes millions for Columbia."

My head filled with visions of scenes on Kansas picnic grounds—a beauty-queen ceremony, with Madge being crowned in a fake-ermine cloak. Could Roz Russell be persuaded to play the schoolteacher? My God, I'm beginning to feel better!

"Logan? Josh?" It was Harry Cohn calling me back to attention.

"I was just thinking about it, Harry . . ."

He said, "Well, don't think about it—*do* it! Confidentially, Taradash wants to direct it himself, but he'd step aside for you. Besides, I don't *want him* to direct it—I *want you* to direct it."

Harry Cohn was an even tougher man than David Merrick, and he was risking more than David Merrick—say three or four million dollars more. And on me.

Recalled to life—recalled to life—recalled to life. My God, it was better than *A Tale of Two Cities*. I was Doctor Manette coming out of the darkness of the Bastille, blinking my rheumy eyes at the sunlight. Charles Dickens had been writing me all along.

"Harry?" I said.

"Yes?"

"Have your lawyers, or whoever, get in touch with my lawyers tomorrow. I'll be happy to direct *Picnic*—and thanks for wanting me."

I hung up and leaned my head on Nedda's soft white shoulder. I could only imagine the future. I couldn't see through its curtain, nor could I see the whole new career I would have. I could not even see the day that the scientists were going to discover a simple white clay called lithium carbonate which would eliminate my manic-depressive days forever.

But anyway, as always, the future is another story.

CHRONOLOGY

Josh Logan's role as
director, producer, and/or writer
is in italics above each title.

Director and coproducer
TO SEE OURSELVES, a play by E. M. Delafield
Produced by Jack Del Bondio and Joshua Logan
Ethel Barrymore Theatre, April 30, 1935
Cast: Patricia Collinge, Reginald Mason, Earle Larimore

Director
HELL FREEZES OVER, a play by John Patrick
Produced by George Kondolf
Ritz Theatre, December 28, 1935
Cast: Louis Calhern, John Litel, Myron McCormick

Dialogue director
THE GARDEN OF ALLAH, a David O. Selznick film
Directed by Richard Boleslawski
Released November 19, 1936
Cast: Marlene Dietrich, Charles Boyer, Basil Rathbone, C. Aubrey Smith,
Tilly Losch, Joseph Schildkraut, John Carradine

Dialogue director and second unit director
HISTORY IS MADE AT NIGHT, a Walter Wanger film

Directed by Frank Borzage
Released March 28, 1937
Cast: Charles Boyer, Jean Arthur, Leo Carrillo, Colin Clive

Codirector with Arthur Ripley
I MET MY LOVE AGAIN, a Walter Wanger film
Released January 14, 1938
Cast: Joan Bennett, Henry Fonda, Louise Platte, Dame May Whitty,
Alan Marshall, Tim Holt, Dorothy Stickney

Director
ON BORROWED TIME, a play by Paul Osborn
Produced by Dwight Deere Wiman
Longacre Theatre, February 3, 1938
Cast: Dudley Digges, Frank Conroy, Peter Holden, Dorothy Stickney

Director
I MARRIED AN ANGEL, a play by Richard Rodgers and Lorenz Hart.
Music by Richard Rodgers; lyrics by Lorenz Hart
Produced by Dwight Deere Wiman
Shubert Theatre, May 11, 1938
Cast: Dennis King, Vera Zorina, Vivienne Segal, Walter Slezak,
Audrey Christie, Charles Walters

Director
KNICKERBOCKER HOLIDAY, a play by Maxwell Anderson. Music by
Kurt Weill
Produced by the Playwrights' Company
Ethel Barrymore Theatre, October 19, 1938
Cast: Walter Huston, Ray Middleton, Richard Kollmar, Jeanne Madden

Director
STARS IN YOUR EYES, a play by J. P. McEvoy. Music by
Arthur Schwartz; lyrics by Dorothy Fields
Produced by Dwight Deere Wiman
Majestic Theatre, February 9, 1939
Cast: Ethel Merman, Jimmy Durante, Mildred Natwick, Richard Carlson,
Tamara Toumanova, Dan Dailey, Jr., Alicia Alonso, Nora Kaye,
Maria Karnilova, Jerome Robbins

Director
MORNING'S AT SEVEN, a play by Paul Osborn
Produced by Dwight Deere Wiman
Longacre Theatre, November 30, 1939
Cast: Jean Adair, Dorothy Gish, Russell Collins, John Alexander,
Enid Markey, Effie Shannon

Director of sketches
TWO FOR THE SHOW, a revue by Nancy Hamilton. Music by
  Morgan Lewis
Produced by Gertrude Macy and Stanley Gilkey
Artistic director, John Murray Anderson
Booth Theatre, February 8, 1940
Cast: Eve Arden, Brenda Forbes, Betty Hutton, Keenan Wynn, Alfred Drake

Director and coauthor
HIGHER AND HIGHER, a play by Gladys Hurlbut and Joshua Logan.
  Music by Richard Rodgers; lyrics by Lorenz Hart
Produced by Dwight Deere Wiman
Shubert Theatre, April 4, 1940
Cast: Jack Haley, Shirley Ross, Marta Eggerth, Leif Erickson,
  June Allyson, Vera-Ellen

Director
CHARLEY'S AUNT, a play by Brandon Thomas
Produced by Day Tuttle and Richard Skinner
Cort Theatre, October 17, 1940
Cast: Jose Ferrer, Nedda Harrigan, Arthur Margetson, Mary Mason,
  Katherine Wiman, Phyllis Avery

Director
BY JUPITER, a play by Richard Rodgers and Lorenz Hart. Music by
  Richard Rodgers; lyrics by Lorenz Hart
Produced by Dwight Deere Wiman and Richard Rodgers
Shubert Theatre, June 3, 1942
Cast: Ray Bolger, Benay Venuta, Constance Moore, Bertha Belmore,
  Vera-Ellen, Nanette Fabray

Additional direction
THIS IS THE ARMY, a musical revue by Irving Berlin
Produced for benefit of Army Emergency Relief Fund
Broadway Theatre, July 4, 1942
Cast: Irving Berlin, Ezra Stone, Gary Merrill, Burl Ives, Julie Oshins,
  Hank Henry

Director
ANNIE GET YOUR GUN, a play by Herbert and Dorothy Fields.
  Songs by Irving Berlin
Produced by Richard Rodgers and Oscar Hammerstein 2nd
Imperial Theatre, May 16, 1946
Cast: Ethel Merman, Ray Middleton, Harry Bellaver

Director
HAPPY BIRTHDAY, a play by Anita Loos

Produced by Richard Rodgers and Oscar Hammerstein 2nd
Broadhurst Theatre, October 31, 1946
Cast: Helen Hayes, Louis Jean Heydt, Enid Markey

Director and coproducer
JOHN LOVES MARY, a play by Norman Krasna
Produced by Richard Rodgers, Oscar Hammerstein 2nd and Joshua Logan
Booth Theatre, February 4, 1947
Cast: Nina Foch, William Prince, Tom Ewell, Loring Smith,
   Pamela Gordon, Max Showalter, Ann Mason

Director and coauthor
MISTER ROBERTS, a play by Thomas Heggen and Joshua Logan
Produced by Leland Hayward [and Joshua Logan]
Alvin Theatre, February 18, 1948
Cast: Henry Fonda, David Wayne, Robert Keith, William Harrigan,
   Ralph Meeker, Steven Hill, Jocelyn Brando, Marshall Jamison,
   Harvey Lembeck, Murray Hamilton, Brian Keith

Director, coauthor and coproducer
SOUTH PACIFIC, a play by Oscar Hammerstein 2nd and Joshua Logan.
   Music by Richard Rodgers; lyrics by Oscar Hammerstein 2nd
Produced by Richard Rodgers, Oscar Hammerstein 2nd, Leland Hayward
   and Joshua Logan
Majestic Theatre, April 7, 1949
Cast: Mary Martin, Ezio Pinza, Myron McCormick, Juanita Hall,
   William Tabbert, Betta St. John

Director, author and coproducer
THE WISTERIA TREES, a play by Joshua Logan
Produced by Leland Hayward and Joshua Logan
Martin Beck Theatre, March 29, 1950
Cast: Helen Hayes, Kent Smith, Walter Abel, Peggy Conklin,
   Douglas Watson, Ossie Davis, Bethel Leslie, Vinie Burrows,
   Alonzo Bosan, Reri Grist

Director, coauthor and coproducer
WISH YOU WERE HERE, a play by Arthur Kober and Joshua Logan.
   Songs by Harold Rome
Produced by Leland Hayward and Joshua Logan
Imperial Theatre, June 25, 1952
Cast: Patricia Marand, Jack Cassidy, Sheila Bond, Paul Valentine,
   Sidney Armus, John Perkins, Larry Blyden, Florence Henderson,
   Tom Tryon, Phyllis Newman, Frank Aletter

Director and coproducer
PICNIC, a play by William Inge

Produced by the Theatre Guild and Joshua Logan
Music Box Theatre, February 19, 1953
Cast: Ralph Meeker, Janice Rule, Kim Stanley, Paul Newman,
 Peggy Conklin, Eileen Heckart, Arthur O'Connell, Reta Shaw,
 Elizabeth Wilson, Ruth McDevitt, Joanne Woodward

Director and producer
KIND SIR, a play by Norman Krasna
Alvin Theatre, November 4, 1953
Cast: Mary Martin, Charles Boyer, Dorothy Stickney, Frank Conroy,
 Margalo Gillmore, Robert Ross

Director, coauthor and coproducer
FANNY, a play by S. N. Behrman and Joshua Logan. Songs by
 Harold Rome
Produced by David Merrick and Joshua Logan
Majestic Theatre, November 4, 1954
Cast: Ezio Pinza, Walter Slezak, Florence Henderson, William Tabbert

Director
PICNIC, a Columbia Pictures film. Screenplay by Daniel Taradash
Released February 16, 1956
Cast: William Holden, Kim Novak, Rosalind Russell, Arthur O'Connell,
 Cliff Robertson, Betty Field, Susan Strasberg

Director and producer
MIDDLE OF THE NIGHT, a play by Paddy Chayefsky
ANTA Theatre, February 8, 1956
Cast: Edward G. Robinson, Gena Rowlands, Anne Jackson, Martin Balsam,
 June Walker

Director
BUS STOP, a 20th Century-Fox film. Screenplay by George Axelrod
Released August 31, 1956
Cast: Marilyn Monroe, Don Murray, Arthur O'Connell, Hope Lange,
 Betty Field, Eileen Heckart, Robert Bray

Director
SAYONARA, a Warner Brothers film. Screenplay by Paul Osborn
Produced by William Goetz
Released December 5, 1957
Cast: Marlon Brando, Miiko Taka, Red Buttons, Ricardo Montalban,
 Myoshi Umeki, James Garner

Director
SOUTH PACIFIC, a Magna—20th Century-Fox film. Screenplay by
 Paul Osborn

Released March 19, 1958
Cast: Mitzi Gaynor, Rossano Brazzi, John Kerr, France Nuyen,
Ray Walston, Juanita Hall

Director
BLUE DENIM, a play by James Leo Herlihy and William Noble
Produced by Barbara Wolferman and James Hammerstein
Playhouse Theatre, February 27, 1958
Cast: Chester Morris, June Walker, Carol Lynley, Burt Brinckerhoff,
Warren Berlinger, Pat Stanley

Director and coproducer
THE WORLD OF SUZIE WONG, a play by Paul Osborn
Produced by David Merrick, Seven Arts Productions and Joshua Logan
Broadhurst Theatre, October 14, 1958
Cast: France Nuyen, William Shatner, Sarah Marshall, Ron Randell

Director and producer
TALL STORY, a Warner Brothers film
Released April 6, 1960
Cast: Jane Fonda, Anthony Perkins, Anne Jackson, Marc Connelly,
Ray Walston, Tom Laughlin

Director
THERE WAS A LITTLE GIRL, a play by Daniel Taradash
Produced by Robert Fryer and Lawrence Carr
Cort Theatre, February 29, 1960
Cast: Jane Fonda, Dean Jones, Joey Heatherton, Sean Garrison,
Gary Lockwood

Director and producer
FANNY, a Warner Brothers film. Screenplay by Julius J. Epstein
Released July 6, 1961
Cast: Leslie Caron, Charles Boyer, Maurice Chevalier, Horst Buchholz,
Lionel Jeffries

Director
ALL AMERICAN, a play. Book by Mel Brooks, music by Charles Strouse,
lyrics by Lee Adams
Produced by Edward Padula and L. Slade Brown
Winter Garden Theatre, March 19, 1962
Cast: Ray Bolger, Eileen Herlie, Anita Gillette, Ron Husmann,
Fritz Weaver

Director
MR. PRESIDENT, a play. Book by Howard Lindsay and Russel Crouse.
Songs by Irving Berlin

Produced by Leland Hayward
St. James Theatre, October 20, 1962
Cast: Robert Ryan, Nanette Fabray, Anita Gillette

Director
TIGER TIGER BURNING BRIGHT, a play by Peter S. Feibleman
Produced by Oliver Smith and Roger L. Stevens, in association with
  Lyn Austin and Victor Samrock
Booth Theatre, December 22, 1962
Cast: Alvin Ailey, Claudia McNeil, Diana Sands, Cicely Tyson,
  Robert Hooks

Director and producer
ENSIGN PULVER, a Warner Brothers film. Screenplay by
  Peter S. Feibleman and Joshua Logan
Released July 31, 1964
Cast: Walter Matthau, Burl Ives, Robert Walker, Jr., Jack Nicolson,
  Larry Hagman, Peter Marshall

Director
READY WHEN YOU ARE, C.B.!, a play by Susan Slade
Produced by David Black
Brooks Atkinson Theatre, December 7, 1964
Cast: Julie Harris, Estelle Parsons, Lou Antonio

Director
CAMELOT, a Warner Brothers film. Screenplay by Alan J. Lerner
Released October 25, 1967
Cast: Richard Harris, Vanessa Redgrave, Franco Nero, David Hemmings,
  Lionel Jeffries, Pierre Olof

Director
PAINT YOUR WAGON, a Paramount Picture film. Screenplay by
  Paddy Chayevsky. Music by Frederick Loewe and André Previn; lyrics
  by Alan Jay Lerner
Released October 15, 1969
Cast: Lee Marvin, Clint Eastwood, Jean Seberg, Ray Walston

Director
LOOK TO THE LILIES, a play by Leonard Spigelgass. Music by
  Jule Styne; lyrics by Sammy Cahn
Produced by Edgar Lansbury, Max J. Brown, Richard Lewine and
  Ralph Nelson
Lunt-Fontanne Theatre, March 29, 1970
Cast: Shirley Booth, Al Freeman, Jr., Taina Elg

Director, coauthor and coproducer
MISS MOFFAT, a play by Emlyn Williams and Joshua Logan. Music by
   Albert Hague; lyrics by Emlyn Williams
Produced by Eugene V. Wolsk, Joshua Logan and Slade Brown
Shubert Theatre, Philadelphia, October 7, 1974
Cast: Bette Davis, Dorian Harewood, Dody Goodman, Avon Long,
   Nell Carter

Director, author, lyricist
RIP VAN WINKLE, a play by Joshua Logan. Music by Trude Rittman
Produced by Ralph Allen
Kennedy Center, January 26, 1976
Cast: Anthony Quayle, Annie McGreevey, Michael Petro, Deborah Fezelle

INDEX